Alban Berg

For Ernest

Constantin Floros

Alban Berg

Music as Autobiography

Translated by Ernest Bernhardt-Kabisch

Bibliographic Information published by the Deutsche Nationalbibliothek
The Deutsche Nationalbibliothek lists this publication in the Deutsche Nationalbibliografie; detailed bibliographic data is available in the internet at http://dnb.d-nb.de.

Cover image: Alban Berg

Revised and expanded version of the German original edition:
"Alban Berg. Musik als Autobiographie" by Constantin Floros.
© by Breitkopf & Härtel, Wiesbaden, Germany.

Library of Congress Cataloging-in-Publication Data
Floros, Constantin, author.
 [Alban Berg. English]
 Alban Berg : music as autobiography / Constantin Floros ; translated by Ernest Bernhardt-Kabisch. -- First edition.
     pages cm
 "Revised and expanded version of the German original edition: "Alban Berg. Musik als Autobiographie" by Constantin Floros. Wiesbaden, Germany : Breitkopf & Härtel, c1992.
 Includes bibliographical references and index.
 ISBN 978-3-631-64597-0 (alk. paper)
 1. Berg, Alban, 1885-1935. 2. Composers--Austria--Biography. 3. Second Viennese school (Group of composers) 4. Berg, Alban, 1885-1935--Criticism and interpretation. I. Bernhardt-Kabisch, Ernest, 1934- translator. II. Title.
 ML410.B47F513 2014
 780.92--dc23
 [B]
                    2013039321

ISBN 978-3-631-64597-0 (Print)
E-ISBN 978-3-653-04684-7 (E-Book)
DOI 10.3726/ 978-3-653-04684-7
© for the English edition: Peter Lang GmbH
© for all other languages: Breitkopf & Härtel KG, Wiesbaden
Internationaler Verlag der Wissenschaften
Frankfurt am Main 2014
All rights reserved.
PL Academic Research is an Imprint of Peter Lang GmbH.

Peter Lang – Frankfurt am Main · Bern · Bruxelles · New York ·
Oxford · Warszawa · Wien

All parts of this publication are protected by copyright. Any utilisation outside the strict limits of the copyright law, without the permission of the publisher, is forbidden and liable to prosecution. This applies in particular to reproductions, translations, microfilming, and storage and processing in electronic retrieval systems.

www.peterlang.com

Table of Contents

Foreword 1

1   Part One: Personality Aspects 3

1.1   Principles 3
1.2   Creativity 5
1.3   Asthma 10
1.4   The "Godforsaken" City 17
1.5   Composing in the Country 24
1.6   The Insidiousness of Success 27
1.7   Humanity 29
1.8   Longing for Happiness or Deliverance through Art 32
1.9   Fidelity 35
1.10 From Goethe to Wedekind 37
1.11 Irony and Skepticism 45
1.12 Image of Woman 48
1.13 Love of Nature 51
1.14 Religiosity 55
1.15 Faith, Love and Hope 58
1.16 Commitment to Radical Modernism and German Music 61

2   Part Two: Theoretical Presuppositions 65

2.1   Questions Regarding the Psychology of Creation 65
2.1.1 Inspiration as Gift from On High 65
2.1.2 Experience as Condition of Creation 67
2.2   Inward and Outward Nature 69
2.3   From Overt to Covert Program Music 72
2.3.1 Schönberg and Program Music 72
2.3.2 Berg and Program Music 76
2.4   Fate and Superstition 78
2.5   Numerology 81
2.5.1 Preliminaries 81
2.5.2 Schönberg's Number: The Ominous 13 82
2.5.3 Berg's Number: The Fateful 23 84
2.5.4 Berg and Numbers 86
2.6   Tone Ciphers 88
2.7   Magic Music 93
2.7.1 *Doctor Faustus* as Point of Departure 93
2.7.2 Mirror Magic 94
2.7.3 Magic Squares 98
2.8   Symmetry and Palindrome 100
2.8.1 The Idea of the Retrograde in Schönberg 100

2.8.2 Parallelisms and Mirror-Symmetric Structures in Berg 102
2.9 Tonality, Atonality and Dodecaphony: Transvaluation of All Values 106
2.9.1 The Atonal Cosmos as Counter-Universe 106
2.9.2 Embracing Complexity 108
2.9.3 Berg's Specialty: Tonal Elements in Dodecaphony 110
2.9.4 Transvaluation of the Tritone 112
2.9.5 The Tonal as Symbolizing the Abnormal and Trivial 114

3 Part Three: Life and Work 117

3.1 Helene and Alban: "The Story of a Great Love" 117
3.2 The String Quartet for Helene 127
3.2.1 The Autobiographical Background 127
3.2.2 Genesis of the Work: From Tonality to Free Atonality 129
3.2.3 Tectonics 133
3.2.4 Semantics: Echoes of Schönberg's *George Lieder* and Wagnerian Motifs 138
3.3 March of an Asthmatic: The Third of the Orchesterstücke op. 6 142
3.3.1 Genesis and Autobiographic Occasion 142
3.3.2 Musico-Semantic Hints 145
3.4 *Wozzeck* as a Message for Humanity 151
3.4.1 An "Opera of Social Compassion"? 151
3.4.2 The Characterization of Three Figures in the Opera:
 the Captain, the Doctor, and Wozzeck 153
3.4.3 The "Epilogue" to the Opera as "Author's Confession" 154
3.4.4 Excursus: The Epilogue as "Invention on a Key" 158
3.4.5 *Wozzeck* as a Parable 159
3.4.6 Some Thoughts about Music between the Two World Wars 161
3.5 Berg, Schönberg and Webern: Profiles of a Friendship 163
3.6 The Chamber Concerto:
 Homage to Schönberg, Mathilde and the Schönberg Circle 167
3.6.1 Genesis of the Work 168
3.6.2 Three's a Charm 170
3.6.3 Tectonics and Number Symbolism: The Numbers Three and Five 171
3.6.4 Thema scherzoso con variationi: "Freundschaft." – The Schönberg Circle 174
3.6.5 Adagio – Mathilde 177
3.6.6 Introduzione: "Thunderstorm" – Grief at Mathilde's Death 186
3.6.7 Rondo Ritmico: the World as a Kaleidoscope 189
3.7 From Helene to Hanna:
 The Two Versions of the Storm Lied *Schließe mir die Augen beide* 195
3.7.1 Genesis 195
3.7.2 Dodekaphonics: Fritz Heinrich Klein's All-Interval Row and the *Mutterakkord* ... 198
3.7.3 Comparison of the Two Versions 202
3.8 String Quartet for Hanna: the *Lyric Suite* 204
3.8.1 The State of Reseach 204
3.8.2 Autobiographic Background: Sources and Documents 206
3.8.3 Genesis and Overall Conception 209

3.8.4 Berg's Analysis of the *Lyric Suite* 214
3.8.5 Allegro gioviale (giocoso): "Clinking of Cups" 218
3.8.6 Andante amoroso: Hanna with her Children and with Alban 222
3.8.7 Allegro misterioso: The Confession...227
3.8.8 Adagio appassionato: Ardor, Passion, Explosion and Transfiguration 237
3.8.9 Presto delirando: Terror and Torment after the Parting...........................242
3.9 Largo desolato: Sleep and Death – *Liebestod* 251
3.10 Aspects of *Lulu* 261
3.10.1 Berg's Reading of Wedekind's *Lulu* Tragedy 261
3.10.2 Lulu's Rise and Fall..265
3.10.3 Characterization of Persons, Passions and Ideas......................................269
3.10.4 Musical Shaping..273
3.10.5 Parallel Situations and their Musical Treatment.......................................278
3.10.6 Lulu's Bond with Dr. Schön...281
3.10.7 The Catastrophe Rhythm and the Fatal Five 284
3.10.8 Persecution Mania...286
3.10.9 Alwa = Alban?...288
3.10.10 Music in Slow Motion 290
3.10.11 From the Spoken to the Sung Word 292
3.11 The Violin Concerto: Requiem for Manon and Berg's "Farewell" to the World..294
3.11.1 The Biographical Background: Manon Gropius and Alma Mahler 294
3.11.2 A "Birthday Homage" for Alma: Willi Reich's Hermeneutic "Paraphrase"......296
3.11.3 In Berg's Workshop..299
3.11.4 Reconciliation of Opposites: Dodecaphony and Tonal Thinking..............304
3.11.5 Andante and Allegretto: Visions of a Winsome Girl 307
3.11.6 Allegro and Adagio: Death and Transcendence 318

Afterword: Berg – a Janus Face...329

4   Appendix 331

4.1   Unpublished Aphorisms of the Young Berg...331
4.2   Abbreviations 333
4.3   Notes..333
4.4   Selected Bibliography 363
4.5   Index of names 383

Photograph 1: Alban Berg

(with kind permission of the Alban Berg Foundation Vienna)

Foreword

The central point of this book is the realization that the creative work of Alban Berg, which in recent years has moved to the forefront of scholarly interest, is largely rooted in autobiography, so that therefore one can gain access to the music by studying the "inner biography" of its creator. Accordingly, the first of the three parts of this volume outlines a character portrait of this great composer. His music proves increasingly an image of his emotional and intellectual constitution. Part two considers the conditions relevant to a deeper understanding of Berg and of the Second Viennese School generally: questions of the psychology of creation, of art theory, of aesthetics, philosophy and weltanschauung, the concept of a magical music, the diverse artistic means by which Berg semanticizes his music, and the relations between tonality, atonality and dodecaphony. In part three, then, Berg's key works will be analyzed and semantically deciphered in terms of his "inner biography."

My study is based not only on the sources in print but also on the rich unpublished material: on the as yet unpublished correspondence between Berg, Schönberg and Webern (comprising some 3000 pages of typescript), and on Berg's many notes (such as his collection of quotes), drafts of letters, personal copies of books and music autographs (sketches, particellos and clean copies), largely preserved in the Music Collection of the Austrian National Library. I have also repeatedly been able to view and study Berg's library in his Viennese apartment in Trauttmannsdorffgasse 27, Hietzing, now the seat of the Alban Berg Foundation.

A passionate love of the music of Arnold Schönberg and Alban Berg has been with me since my youth, when it was awakened by Hans Swarowsky and Gottfried Kassowitz, my teachers in conducting at the Viennese Academy of Music from 1951 to 1953.

My initial interest was above all in Berg's and Schönberg's compositional techniques. I sought to track down the secret of their music's expressive power. My first lecture courses as a young adjunct instructor (*privatdozent*) at the University of Hamburg fifty years ago (1961-62) dealt with Schönberg and Berg. Early in 1975, my treatise on the esoteric program of the *Lyric Suite* appeared – until then no one had talked about any covert programs in Bergs music. In 1979, I began to study Berg's sketches to nearly all of his works systematically. In 1985, I received a lasting impression from the magnificent Berg exhibition in the sumptuous grand hall of the Austrian National Library at the Josefsplatz. Between then and 1992, I mostly worked on this book, published in that year in its original German version.

The book would not have been possible without the constant help and support of several institutions and individuals. My thanks go above all to the Music Collection of the Austrian National Library and their director, Hofrat Dr. Günter Brosche, the Alban Berg Foundation and its president, Professor Gottfried von Einem, and the Music Collection of the Viennese Municipal and State Library and its director, Dr. Ernst Hilmar. They gave me permission to study, excerpt and copy valuable "Bergiana" and put microfilms at my disposal.

The German edition of this study was published in Wiesbaden by Breitkopf & Härtel in 1992. In the same year, the Austrian National Library acquired the now famous annotated score of the Lyric Suite, as well as Berg's secret letters to his "distant beloved" Hanna Fuchs, which I published in an annotated and commentated edition in 2001. In 2008, that edition appeared in English at Indiana University Press, Bloomington, under the title *Alban Berg and Hanna Fuchs. The Story of a Love in Letters*, translated by Professor Dr. Ernest Bernhardt-Kabisch, the translator also of the present text. The latter contains some fresh research results – inter alia about the biography of Hanna Fuchs and the „Carinthian Song" – and has profited from numerous questions put to me by Professor Bernhardt during the translation process. My most heartfelt thanks go to him. I also owe a debt of gratitude to Professor Dr. Altug Ünlü for his formatting of the book, and to Michael Rücker and Thomas Papsdorf of the Peter Lang International Publishing House for harmonious collaboration.

Hamburg, February 2013

Constantin Floros

1 Part One: Personality Aspects

> "Man's mind is his fate." Herodotus
>
> "A man's life is his character." Goethe, *Italian Journey*, Frascoli, October 2, 1787 (Quotation Collection No. 705)

1.1 Principles

> "That is the rebus of Berg's music. One could hardly characterize it more simply and accurately than by saying that it resembled himself." Theodor W. Adorno.[1]

The prominent sociologist, philosopher and aesthetician Theodor W. Adorno did not think much of the Romantic notion of a unity of life and art, biography and creative work. He was skeptical of the view that experience was an indispensable precondition of artistic creation, asserting, on the contrary, a belief that the subjective conditions of the genesis of works of art, that is to say, everything personal and biographical, were irrelevant. In Adorno's philosophy, the composer as a private person is of no interest whatever. Adorno saw in him merely the producing "instrument" – a "subordinate executive organ."[2]

These reflections – evidently inspired by Hegel's *Phenomenology of the Spirit* – crop up both in Adorno's book on Mahler of 1960 and in that on Berg of 1968. A familiarity with them is needed if one wants to understand many a formulation of Adorno's that otherwise will seem strange. Of Mahler's symphonies, for example, he remarked that "their process toward externalization, toward totality" was little bound to the "private person," which rather made itself an instrument for its [the totality's] production."[3] And of Alban Berg, whose pupil in composition he became in 1925, he wrote in a similar vein: "In the eleven years during which I knew him I always sensed more or less clearly that the empirical person wasn't quite involved, wasn't quite in the game," "His own person he treated at once cautiously and indifferently, like the musical instrument he was to himself."

If one remembers that Adorno's special domain was dialectics, one will understand why nevertheless the personality of the artist played a significant role in his aesthetics. Thus his entire book on the composer circles about the thesis that Berg's music ("at once excessive and frail") was Berg's "mirror image." Adorno thought he could see certain traits of Berg's personality reflected in his music. Berg's enormous sensitivity, his desire for happiness, his hedonism and his pessimism, the sternness of his convictions – all this, according to Adorno, gave Berg's music its characteristic stamp. To illustrate with some quotes: "If Mahler once said about the landscape around Lake Attersee that he had wholly composed it away, Berg, in so many respects Mahler's heir, could have said the same of his inner landscape." "The specific sadness in his music is probably the negative of his desire for happiness, disillusion, a lament of the fact that the world did not answer to the utopian expectations his nature harbored." "Something voluptuous, luxuriating, that is inseparable from his music and his orchestra also colored his desire for happiness."[4]

The long and the short of these observations is that, despite Adorno's reservations, the personality of the artist cannot be separated from his creative work. This is true especially of Arnold Schönberg, Alban Berg and Anton Webern, who, like the contemporary Expressionist poets and painters, had a strong need for expression and self-expression. Whether or not one adopts Adorno's principles, it is certain that inquiring into Berg's personality can contribute significantly to a deeper understanding of his music.

An inquiry of this kind must depend primarily on Berg's written utterances, especially his correspondence with his wife and with his friends Arnold Schönberg and Anton Webern. These letters afford profound insights into Berg's psyche, his way of thinking, his views about art, as well as his "inner" biography. Additional information can be derived from reminiscences and testimonies by persons who were close to him or at least knew him. Of special interest here, besides the comments of Helene Berg, are the reminiscences of the publisher Hans W. Heinsheimer, the writer Elias Canetti, and the musicologist Willi Reich, who had been a pupil of Berg's, as well as those of Theodor W. Adorno, published originally in February of 1936 in the journal *23*.[5]

The author not being a trained psychologist or psychoanalyst, rigorous psychological methods will not be applied in this book.[6] The goal of his investigation will be attained if, based on the sources, he succeeds in drawing an authentic personality profile of Alban Berg.

1.2 Creativity

> "We have an obligation to write." Webern to Berg, August 18, 1917

> "Think of nothing but your work. That is what matters most." Webern to Berg, September 19, 1921

> "I have never been one of the fast workers." Berg to Webern, July 26, 1920

Hans W. Heinsheimer, to whom we owe some solid character sketches of Berg, observed of him that there was a hardly another composer whose fame rests on so small a number of works. Berg's reputation, he felt, depended on his two operas, *Wozzeck* and *Lulu*, on the Violin Concerto and the Lyric Suite. Beyond that, there was little, viewed objectively, that had really succeeded in gaining a broader audience.[7]

These remarks are apt. Berg's oeuvre is undeniably smaller than that of Schönberg, and it is true that he produced very slowly and that he was aware of this peculiarity. After *Wozzeck*, which is marked opus 7, he stopped numbering his works because he was ashamed of their small number.

Several reasons can be cited for this slow production tempo: the asthma from which he suffered ever since his fifteenth year, and which at times rendered him unable to work; his extraordinarily deliberate mode of composing (conceiving, sketching, executing); the psychological inhibitions he had to overcome in working; personal and family-related difficulties that beset him; and, finally, the many "occupations" that kept him from composing. These included, inter alia, his many musicological publications, essays, analyses, guides (his collected writings add up to a sizable volume[8]); the piano scores he produced for works of Schubert and Franz Schreker;[9] the voluminous and time-consuming correspondence he conducted with extreme conscientiousness; and, last but not least, the lessons he regularly gave. All in all, Berg was more industrious than appears; often, even, he did not feel up to his heavy work load.

Berg began to compose around 1901 – amateurishly, as he wrote to Schönberg nearly thirty years later. By the time he became Schönberg's pupil, probably in October of 1904, he had already written more than thirty songs.[10] During his long apprenticeship (from 1904 to 1911), he produced, besides several unpublished compositions, also the first published ones: the Piano Sonata op. 1 (1907/08), the Four Songs for Solo Voice and Piano op. 2 (1909/10), and the String Quartet op. 3 (1910). The first years after his marriage to Helene Nahowski (on May 3, 1911) were not particularly productive. In 1912, the Orchestra Songs op. 4, after picture postcard texts by Peter Altenberg, were written, in 1913 he composed the Four Pieces for Clarinet and Piano op- 5, and in 1914 he worked on the Three Orchestra Pieces op. 6.

In the years 1913 to 1915, Schönberg on several occasions made it clear to Berg that he was not satisfied with his productivity and his lifestyle. He thought he observed a "reduction," an "artistic diminishment," spoke of a lack of "self-discipline," criticized Berg's compositions, reproached him with "poor time management," urged him, among other things, to write short, merely informative and matter-of-fact letters, and admonished him to complete any work he had undertaken at all costs and not let himself be distracted by anything. Berg, who at that time was in an unimaginably close dependency relation to Schönberg, (one feels tempted to speak of downright minority), took these criticisms to heart and resolved to improve in every way. He outlined "a program of a lifestyle" according to which "all hitherto partly unconscious, partly inescapable deficiencies are to be rectified."[11] At times, of course, he felt deeply wounded by Schönberg's criticism and could not hide his resentment.

In the long time span between 1917 and 1925, Berg completed only two works: *Wozzeck* and the Chamber Concerto. Until about 1923, he was hardly known as a composer, outside of a small circle of friends, colleagues and initiates. He had strong doubts whether he would manage to have a successful career as a composer. He therefore decided to devote himself to writing *about* music alongside his compositional work. He seems for some time to have regarded music journalism as a means of securing a living.

For this reason he accepted the offer from Universal Editions to become a contributor to the *Musikblätter des Anbruch* (Music Leaves of the Dawning).[12] In early 1920, he wrote a brief guide to Schönberg's symphonic poem *Pelleas und Melisande*, and in the spring of 1920, the polemic essay against Hans Pfitzner. On January 15, 1920, he told Schönberg: "Besides composing, I would rather do nothing but produce guides, analyses, essays about you and your work and make excerpts of your compositions." In 1921, he worked intensively on a book about Schönberg, in which he hoped to do greater justice to the admired art of his teacher than Ego Wellesz had done in his book.[13] He even considered writing a similar book about Alexander von Zemlinsky.[14] These plans did not come to fruition, however, because composing was more important to Berg after all – because he felt he had to come up with a new musical work. To his teacher Schönberg, he confessed on July 9, 1920: "After an almost year-long pause, I have a feeling – I might almost call it a 'sense of duty' – to compose something. Since 1914, I have not produced a finished composition. First there were the five summers of war with their infrequent furloughs. 1919 [was] the first substantial summer, and now these six, seven weeks, which, if I had not, as I said, torn myself away, [I] would certainly fritter away in Vienna." And on February 12, 1921, he wrote again to Schönberg: "You are quite right: I have to compose again. Even for reasons of my continued livelihood, I have to get another work done, and thus even relinquishing a source of income such as I would obtain from a book about Zemlinsky, and which I could certainly use, is not carelessness, no mere irresponsible yielding to my compositional inclinations."

Not only Schönberg, but Webern, too, admonished Berg time and again not to neglect his compositional work. Webern, who was highly dissatisfied with his activities as a theater *kapellmeister* because it did not leave him enough time for composing, believed he had found in creativity the meaning of life and sought to convince his friend of the same. On August 18, 1917, he told Berg of a plan of Schönberg's to establish an artist colony in the country ("in clean air, in direct contact with nature"), in which Schönberg, Webern and Berg would be engaged in creative work. In many of Webern's letters, the thought recurs of creativity as a task for life, a duty and a mission. "That we others should do nothing but dwell in ourselves in order to produce one decent work after another": these words of Goethe, addressed to Schiller, had impressed Webern deeply;[15] he made them his own. He liked to compare human existence to that of a tree, which does nothing "but blossoming and bearing fruit: after all, that is what we are in the world for."[16] And on May 3, 1930, he confessed to Berg: "We really should speak of nothing but of our works and what is connected with them. That, after all, is the most important thing. Isn't what the three of us achieve, and of course Kraus, the only reliable thing in our time? I believe that is the one thing that will last, and therefore also that we have a lofty mission."

In 1923, Berg was able to register his first successes as a composer. Around this time he probably abandoned the idea of music journalism as a profession. In 1924 he nevertheless wrote the weighty and voluminous treatise *Warum ist Schönbergs Musik so schwer verständlich?* (Why is Schönberg's Music so Difficult to Comprehend?), and even in the next several years he repeatedly came forward with articles, essays, texts, lectures and interviews. He commented on current issues in music production and musical life and elucidated some of his own works. Ever since the successful premiere of *Wozzeck* in Berlin in December 14 of 1925, however, his passion was exclusively one of composition. The editorial jobs he had to do from time to time became a

7

burden. On August 10, 1927, he wrote to Webern: "I have a great deal to do here – all things that are connected with the Universal Edition, a ridiculous amount of professional correspondence; but all things that leave not the least feeling of satisfaction when they are done. By contrast: what euphoria after one successful measure – not to speak of the feeling after a happily completed movement – let alone after the final double bar."

Schönberg alluded to the "psychological inhibitions" Berg had to overcome in composing. We can learn more about that from the correspondence. Like many other creative people, Berg had repeated doubts about his creative talent and the quality of his productions, especially as a young man. Above all, Schönberg's criticisms were apt to make him unsure. To quote some instances from the letters: in early August of 1912, Berg completed the piano score of the third and fourth movement (*Litany* and *Transport*) of Schönberg's second String quartet op. 10 and sent it to the Universal Edition. On August 5, he wrote to Webern; "I hope it [the piano score] is all right; as after every completed work, I have doubts about its quality." In June of 1913, Berg visited his teacher Schönberg in Berlin. On June 14, he thanked him for the "reproach" he had received from him (!) and added: "for my doubts about myself are always so big that the least criticism on your uinquely authoritative part nearly robs me of all hope." This letter demonstrates especially vividly how hard Berg could be hit by the criticism of his teacher. His self-confidence seems to have been severely shaken during his work on the *Three Orchestra Pieces* of 1914, as the following passage from a letter of July 20, 1914, to Schönberg reveals: "Otherwise my time of late has been spent working on the Orchestra Pieces, whose fate, of course, perpetually disquiets me. After all, I must ever ask myself whether what I am expressing – over whose measures I often sit brooding for days – is really better than the things I did last. And how am I to judge that? I hate the latter, so that I was already about to destroy them altogether, and about the former I have as yet no judgment because I am still in the middle of them."

Berg's self-confidence will certainly have become much stronger after the successful reception of *Wozzeck* on many European stages. Erich Alban Berg, the composer's nephew, related numerous anecdotes and repeated many of his uncle's statements that make it apparent that after 1921 Berg became increasingly aware of his artistic importance.[17] But even in his late years Berg had occasional doubts of his creative potential. On May 18, 1930, he congratulated Schönberg on the completion of his film music *Begleitmusik zu einer Lichtspielszene* op. 34, reported his intention of dedicating himself altogether to the composition of *Lulu*, and added: "I hope I can still compose; these long pauses always generate agonizing doubts in me."

Berg regarded the creative act as so lofty, and composing itself as so arduous a matter, that beginning a new work always caused him great anxiety, as is proven by several passages in his letters. On September 18, 1925, at a time when he was making plans to compose the Storm poem *Schließe mir die Augen beide* and the *Lyrical Suite*, he wrote to Webern: "And now, may I succeed with the most difficult of all leaps – the one into beginning a composition!" And in a letter to Schönberg of April 26, 1928, he similarly commented on his intention to set Gerhart Hauptmann's glass works fairytale *UndPippa Tanzt* (Pippa Dances): "We already think a lot about going to the country, and I therefore of the new work, with all the fright that I have of every new work."

While there are many "external" and "internal" reasons that can be cited for Berg's relatively slender oeuvre and his low production tempo, the main cause is no doubt the extraordinarily deliberate manner of his working. As the often very extensive extant sketches show, he always approached his work with great caution. He tried out all the various solutions of a given compositional problem he had posed for himself, considered every possibility, made calculation about the extent and the proportions of the movements, sketched out themes, motifs and rhythmic events, scrutinized every detail and left nothing to chance. Ever since the *Lyrical Suite*, he used complicated tables and twelve-tone series, which he analyzed exhaustively. His entire oeuvre is characterized by a constructivist, quasi scientific quality – more precisely, a peculiar synthesis of spontaneity and calculation.

In April of 1930, Franz Schreker sent Berg an inquiry whether he would accept a teaching post for composition at the Berlin Academy of Music.[18] This honorable offer touched Berg in his "innermost being."[19] In his thorough and cautious way, he weighed all the pros and cons of the call, but then, in a letter to Schreker dated May 8, declined with thanks. For reasons he cited the "uncommonly slow mode" of his "musical production" and the desire to bring to a conclusion the "hardly begun work" on his *Lulu*.

1.3 Asthma

> "But I am writing this while hardly able to breathe." Berg to Webern, September 17, 1926
>
> "I believe more and more that there are no diseases except mental ones." Berg to Schönberg, July 9, 1928
>
> "You are probably right in asserting that there are only 'mental illnesses': as long as I am working (composing), I am well; as soon as I am prevented, I get acid reflux, etc." Webern to Berg, September 28, 1929

Judging from Berg's accounts in letters to Schönberg and Webern, his health must have been extremely fragile. Very often he lamented that he did not feel well, that he was unable to recuperate "in spite of the utmost care,"[20] or that he was ill. Frequently he complained of asthma attacks, weak nerves, "upsets," physical and nervous collapses, as well as stomach troubles and jaundice. Under the circumstances, it was no wonder that he was often unable to work. Rarely only did he report to his friends that his state of health had improved or – even more rarely – that he felt well.

Berg suffered his first severe asthma attack on July 23, 1900, when he was fifteen-and-a-half years old.[21] From that day, to which he ascribed a fatal significance, to the time of his death, he was plagued by this condition; there were only a few years during which he was spared. The attacks were at times so severe that he thought he would die. Thus a letter to Schönberg dated August 113, 1917, reads: "The first week I still suffered from the after-effects of my years of captivity: asthma attacks of a degree of severity that I once actually thought I would not survive the night." (By "captivity" Berg meant his military service during the War, which he regarded as a form of slavery.) In a letter to Webern of June 16, 1922, one can read: "At night, frequently asthma, sitting on the edge of my bed. I am out of sorts in other ways as well. I am in every respect incapable of work, fritter away my time. Can't even concentrate on a decent book." And again to Webern on September 17, 1926:

On top of all this work, I was ill recently, a severe catarrh, and therefore decided – when the opportunity arose – to quickly come up here [to Trahütten in Styria], hoping I would recover and be able to work again more quickly. Something that unfortunately proved to be illusory: the irritation of the respiratory tract for the time being has occasioned an especially strong asthma, so that I can't even think of working.

The military service during the war-years of 1915 to 1918 took a lot out of Berg. In early October, he was sent to a reserve officer training school in

Bruck on the Leitha River, to be trained as an officer. Naturally he was not adequate to the physical and mental demands of the training program, and he suffered a complete collapse. On November 6, he was transferred to a military hospital. From the examination report he sent to his wife we can gather, among other things, that he had suffered from the asthma since his childhood and that there was no prospect of a cure (ABB 298). The military attest issued on November 15 is no less instructive. It reads:

> Bronchial asthma with pulmonary dilation and chronic bronchitis as a resultant condition, the edges of the lungs extend up to a hand's breadth and more beneath the angulus scapulae. Dense alveolar rattle across the entire lung, apices somewhat muted, the sound of the breath there rough; heart very small (cf. x-ray). Patient complains of typical bronchial asthma attacks with great difficulty in breathing and substantial sputum during the attack; also trouble breathing and heart palpitations from even minor physical strain.[22]

The result of this examination was that he was placed before the super-arbitration commission and declared fit for relief service.

Berg worried greatly about his asthma. He consulted several physicians, let himself be treated by them and gradually learned to trace his ailment to diverse factors: certain climatic conditions, pollen allergy, nervous-psychic stresses and "deeper, spiritual" reasons,"[23] which, however, he did not divulge. Let us try to survey them.

During the night of September 5/6, 1909, Berg wrote to Helene Nahowski from Venice that the air there was good for his "sensitive respiratory organs" and that at least he knew now that he had no incurable disease but that he was "only a victim of the lethal climatic conditions of the Austrian Alpine lands (ABB 129). In 1912, he went to see a head physician in Vienna, who diagnosed "a nervous overexcitement as hypersensitivity of the mucous membranes."[24] The nasal membranes, the medico thought, were irritated by airborne pollen, which resulted in sneezing, congestion and even hay fever. The doctor advised Berg to avoid meadows and woods. This diagnosis must have appeared plausible to Berg, as he could not explain to himself why he never suffered from asthma in Vienna, but had some symptoms of it in Hietzing and "immediately severe attacks" in the country. It must also have become clear to him why the asthma attacks plagued him mostly during the summer months. A new treatment based on the most recent researches (inhaling of atropine, adrenalin, etc.), as he wrote his teacher on May 6, 1913, did not bring any major relief – let alone curing the condition.

In September of 1920, Berg had to undergo treatment at the Park Sanatorium in Hüttendorf-Hacking. After his discharge there, he suffered a relapse and had to be treated at the sanatorium again. A blood test, as he told Schönberg in a letter of October 28, definitely pointed to bronchial, and only secondarily to nervous, asthma. "But none of the physicians really know much about treating this disease." He now wanted to try lactic-acid calcium, which he was to take daily for several months. Besides, he had started on an atropine regimen, which was supposed to "be very effective and guarantee long-term relief from asthma."

The treatment seems to have helped for a sustained period. In July of 1923, however, he was again plagued by asthma. In a postcard to Schönberg, he discoursed about the causes of the renewed illness and concluded: "Although I just did not want to admit it to myself, and still don't, the many trips and finally the complicated move here [to Trahütten in Styria] have been rather too hard on my 'nerves.' Add to that the colossal climate contrast. The weather altogether! My worries about Helene's state of health, who of late has had to suffer a lot again. And the nervousness before beginning a new work."[25]

Four years later, at most – in Trahütten, where he spent the summer months – Berg suffered from asthma again. "The transition to the country, always perilous for me," he wrote to Webern on July 21, 1927, "was downright catastrophic this tine." The asthmatic troubles, he explained, were this time accompanied by digestive disorders. Several factors had helped to set off the illness: nervous breakdown, the strains of the last season, the many premieres of *Wozzeck*, the trips "with their inevitable agitations," and "the purely personal experiences" of the last six months (the death of Berg's mother and Helene's thyroid operation).

Severe asthma also impeded Berg's ability to work in the summer of 1928. "It was, of course, to be expected," he told Schönberg on July 9, "that barely arrived up here [in Trahütten] I would have trouble breathing. But this time it is particularly protracted. My sensitivity to extreme changes is evidently becoming more pronounced with the passing years." All this, he continued, had to do with his "delicateness." Though in "psychic things" he thought he had mastery over it, could even repress it in such a way "that one might get an impression of thick-skinnedness, even mental banality," he was unable to get control of it "in physical respects." His body refused to tolerate the great contrasts between city and country air, mountain and lowland climate and also revolted against "the Middle European imposition to accept differences in temperature of 40 or more centigrades in the time span of a few months without any reaction." These confessions are followed by two sentences that make clear that Berg was aware of the deeper psychological-spiritual causes of his sufferings: "But perhaps the whole thing is more pathological than organic in nature! As you know, I believe more and more that there are no diseases other than mental ones."

To this conclusion Schönberg had come already in 1911. He, who himself suffered from asthma and shortnss of breath, and also knew a lot about hypochondria, [26] had certainly by this time realized that the causes of Berg's malaises were psychological and spiritual and even went so far as to think that his asthma was due to autosuggestion. With all due respect for his teacher, Berg was unable to accept this view and wrote to him in the summer of 1911: "Add to that that my asthma has not gotten any better and torments me every night, notwithstanding your attempt to make me think that the whole thing, as you said, is due solely to autosuggestion."

Yet Berg had long since realized himself that his fragile health, his fits and slips were ultimately due "to a weakness of the spirit," a spirit "that 'wants to' but 'cannot'."[27] "Perhaps the whole matter," he disclosed to his teacher also in the summer of 1911, "is a consequence of my highly affected nerves. Or is the latter not rather the consequence of those mental-spiritual defeats?" Those were, he added, irresolvable questions, and all of neurology and psychopathology were nothing but matters of convenience: "science, too, seeks for comfort wherever things might get uncomfortable."

This is a good time to speak about Berg's troubled relation to psychoanalysis. Influenced by Karl Kraus, he had numerous reservations about it. He came into close contact with it at the latest in 1913, when his friend Anton Webern became ill and let himself be treated by a psychoanalyst. The story of this illness and its therapy affords profound insights into Webern's psyche and at the same time throws light on Berg's attitude toward psychoanalysis, so that it deserves to be told.

Webern had, as already indicated, a strong, downright idiosyncratic animus against his activities at the theater, which he regarded as his undoing, mainly because they kept him from his compositional work, in which he saw the meaning of his life. Whenever, during the winter of 1912-1913, he was supposed to conduct at the opera theater in Stettin, he regularly fell ill.[28] He suffered from depression, steady worsening nervous conditions, fever, and sleeplessness and in early August of 1913 had to consult two Viennese physicians. After one of them, the neurologist Dr. Groß, was unable to diagnose the least trace of an organic disease, both doctors urgently advised Webern to undergo psychotherapy.[29]

13

On August 4, 1913, Webern turned to Alfred Adler, at the time the most prominent psychoanalyst in Vienna along with Sigmund Freud.[30] Adler had originally collaborated with Freud, but then fell out with him and founded his own school and journal of *Individualpsychologie*. Central to his theoretical edifice are the striving for power and the inferiority complex.[31]

Adler thought he could cure Webern if he could see him every day for a month,[32] and declared that according to the maxims of the psychotherapeutic method Webern would be nearly cured the moment one had found the cause of the morbid condition by means of "analysis" – "the basis or cause would turn out to be something trivial"[33] (läppisch). After three sessions, Adler could already disclose to his patient that his condition was "self-generated," that he had created his illness within himself as a kind of escape from the "knocks" and "battles" of "life."[34] Webern, on the other hand, was initially convinced that his fits and pains were imposed by fate. They had been "imposed" on him in order to "keep" him time and again from matters he was not supposed to pursue, not because they were bad but because they did not befit him.

To understand this somewhat peculiar notion better, one needs to know that Webern was originally thoroughly antipathetic to Adler's treatment and explanations: he thought them too easy, "cheap," even "superficial," Believing, as he did, in a higher meaning of things, in a higher providence and the mysticism of a Strindberg and Swedenborg, he interpreted his malaise as a sign, an admonition to give up composing!

The reports about Webern's illness had greatly shaken Berg and forced him to wrestle with psychoanalysis. As yet he had no firm opinion about it. In a letter to Schönberg of August 9, 1913, he expressed his sympathy with Webern and asked his teacher: "Do you think having a psychoanalyst makes sense? What can he know if he is not by chance an absolute genius?" And to Webern himself he wrote on the same day: "And I can't even tell you if I believe in such a treatment as that by a psychoanalyst. Sometimes it seems to me as though there might be something to things like psychoanalysis after all – more, at any rate, than mere error, let alone fraud, I am thinking above all of Freud and – as disagreeable as it may perhaps seem to you – Steckel, the Freudian disciple known to me from the feuilleton in the daily paper. But whether these doctors have ever really cured any severe neurological diseases, I do not know."

Meanwhile Adler was having success with his therapeutic efforts. Already on September 29, 1913, Webern was able joyfully to report to his teacher: "I am almost completely well. I am now fully convinced of the importance and validity of Dr. Adler's method. If I now get any of my fits again, I will right away ask myself: what does that mean again, to what is that a reaction. And I hardly need an answer: the question, the taking notice already suffices to resubmerge the fits completely thereby."

This letter is important also because in it Webern sought to explain the basic difference between Freud's approach and Adler's method. Whereas Freud generalized and reduced everything to sexuality and the Oedipus complex in particular, Webern thought, Adler treated every case quite individually: "With Adler, every case is the first of its kind." Important here is also Weber's note that Karl Kraus's assaults on psychoanalysis referred not to Adler but to Freud and his adherents (especially Wittels). Kraus was particularly annoyed, according to Webern, by a treatise that had been sent to him, in which Goethe's "Sorcerer's Apprentice" is "regarded as the representation of one hopelessly addicted to masturbation!"

In spite of the good news of Webern's recovery, however, Berg did not abandon his reservations about psychoanalysis. In a letter to Schönberg of October 3, 1913, he thought that "perhaps this entire treatment of the psychoanalyst is not the right one. Although, on the other hand, much of what Webern reports about it is very persuasive and attractive. But then again that seems very different from what Kraus attacks."

Photograph 2: Berg at an early age

(with kind permission of the Alban Berg Foundation Vienna)

Both for Webern and for Berg, Schönberg was for many years teacher, confidant and supreme authority all in one. They confided to him their personal worries and emotional anxieties and asked for his advice. Schönberg, a good

15

judge of human nature from observing himself, thought a great deal about the nature of his favorite pupils and tried again and again to help them also in their personal lives. Berg he seems to have regarded as extremely sensitive, delicate, gentle and overly "soft." In a very instructive letter addressed to Berg, dated May 17, 1915, he appealed to Berg's manliness, sought to rouse his aggressiveness and belligerence, and wrote: "You are furious because I wrote to you that you had been dreaming! But I would like to make you even a lot angrier – so angry that you will jump up one day and knock a skillet about my noggin (or someone else's, I'm not anxious for it)! [...] So, please: wake up! I'll say it again: nowadays it is more necessary than ever to be a man. Remember that in a few months you may have to wield a bayonet!" The letter, which also tells us a lot about Schönberg's character, also contains the sentences: "What you need is the kind of work where you have to scrap. You should look for a job like that! Look: battle has never stopped for me, and thus I am always awake. Naturally, as I have to be prepared for the night attacks of all the obscurantists" (Dunkelmänner).

To return to Berg's asthma: he was firmly convinced that "deeper, spiritual" causes were responsible for it. On September 20, 1929, he reported to Webern about asthmatic relapses and their causes: "Yes besides the undoubtedly real reasons of climatic contrasts, probably also deeper, spiritual ones (you know my axiom: there are only mental diseases!). Insofar as I can see through them, I fight them successfully. But there is always an unresolved remainder." So he was only partly conscious of the deeper causes of his malaise.

Modern medicine defines bronchial asthma as a psychosomatic disease, in which psychic processes carry the same weight as somatic ones. According to Arthur Jores and Margit von Kerékjártó, a merely somatically oriented therapy cannot bring about a real cure of the disease. Only the psychotherapeutic one, combined with a breath and relaxation therapy, can produce a lasting success. All asthmatics, the authors contend, are anxious individuals, who suffer from a profound existential anxiety. They cannot properly deal with their aggressions, are wanting in contact and the ability to give of themselves. They lack a quality that is indispensable for coping with the world: a "basic trust in the world, but also the trust in, and affirmation of, the self." Most asthmatics are, "covertly or overtly," severely depressive. Their basic frame of mind is that of "subterranean anxiety and a constant state of feeling threatened."[35] There is no doubt that several of these symptoms also apply to Berg.

1.4 The "Godforsaken" City

"Vienna will always be Vienna. That is the most dreadful of all threats." Karl Kraus

"It's so sad that people in Vienna are so nasty." Webern to Schönberg, May 4, 1911

"It recently occurred to me: the reproaches justly made these days against Vienna, and against Austria generally, have probably always been justified, even in the days that might still pass muster, and yet Germany's culture has always emanated from there." Webern to Berg, August 30, 1912.

"That's Vienna in all its meanness…" Berg to Schönberg, August 9, 1913

"In other ways, too, I dread Vienna and everything connected with it." Berg to Gottfried Kassowitz, 1916[36]

"And I have to summon all my powers of concentration for my work, so as not to abruptly break off this summer sojourn (especially given the filthy weather), in order to be in Vienna as well, where that otherwise so godforsaken city is now, well, not godforsaken." Berg to Schönberg, July 13, 1926

"Then Vienna can drown again in its muck, which rains down incessantly from the sky." Berg to Schönberg, January 10, 1927

"Particulars in person next week, when, horrors, I shall set foot on Viennese ground again." Berg to H. Watznauer, 1928[37]

"In the evening, supper with Lehár music (Philharmonics, Tauber, enough to make you puke! – oh, that Vienna!!!)" Berg to Helene, March 8, 1934 (ABB 640)

"Real artists, however, have never been understood in Vienna." Egon Friedell[38]

"Elsewhere, people make room for genius. Here they smooth his way out of the country." Paul Stefan[39]

In his obituary on Berg, Heinrich Jalowetz registered great amazement about the deceased's close link to his homeland and his rootedness in his native soil. His life, Jalowetz thought, had been outwardly uneventful:

> He was the only one in our circle who never left the soil of his native city; indeed, from the day he took home his bride, he lived and

worked in the same small, quiet apartment in a secluded lane in the suburbs, which always seemed to hide its entrance from the visitor.⁴⁰

Speaking more exactly, if one excludes the summer vacations, Berg did indeed live most of his life in his native city of Vienna. Soon after his marriage, Helene and he occupied the apartment at 27 Trauttmannsdorff-Gasse in Hietzing, where he remained until his death. But it is, of course, an exaggeration to say that he never left the precincts of his hometown, since from 1920 on he had gone on numerous trips abroad. Yet in contrast to Schönberg and Webern, he never took a job in another city – in spite of his many complaints, he remained in Vienna, despite his feelings of discomfort there. He evidently harbored a kind of hate-love for his birthplace: it is safe to speak of a Vienna trauma. He sometimes dreamed of emigrating to Spain or Corsica,⁴¹ Vienna was at times hateful to him,⁴² yet he could never resolve to live and work in another city, another environment. In an undated letter to Webern he wrote:

> You also must not think that if I complain about Vienna I do it because it is fashionable nowadays to rail at Vienna. When I complain, and especially only to you, I always know that I would be even more uncomfortable in another city and would certainly yearn to be back in Vienna. Only at the moment the concept of a metropolis is such a ghastly one to me that I would grumble about every large city where I am staying.

He loved life in the country. In a letter of September 10, 1913, to Schönberg, he set forth his ideas about a life-style that would please him. His "home," he thought, would have to be in nature, not in the so-called "cultural centers." Proximity to such a one would be desirable, but it would have to be a real cultural center, like Berlin, not "such a pseudo-metropolis" as Vienna was. What repelled him about large cities was their "millions of disagreeable people, houses, streets, etc." After his return from Berlin in 1925, Vienna seemed like a "sea of stone" to him.⁴³ One is reminded of Expressionist urban poetry (e.g., Julius Hart, Detlev von Liliencron, Georg Heym), in which sea metaphors play a prominent role.⁴⁴

There were, to be sure, special reasons for Berg's dislike of Vienna, that "museum of coffee houses": he could not feel at home in a city in which his revered teacher Schönberg did not receive the deserved recognition.⁴⁵ The conditions prevailing in the city's cultural life, the taste of the conservative public, the institutions of the musical life, the dominant music criticism – all of this could only make him feel uncomfortable and arouse his displeasure.

But the key sore point of his Vienna trauma was the painful experience that the Schönberg School was denied recognition in the acknowledged music center of Vienna. He was persuaded that the music cultivated by the Schönberg circle was the only one that was adequate to is time, yet he found time and again that the circle was anathema in Vienna.

It is no exaggeration to say that of all the composers working during the first half of the 20th century, Arnold Schönberg was the one most vehemently attacked. No one else encountered such spiteful hostility, no one else had to undergo so many humiliations. Many in Vienna, we learn from his early friend David Josef Bach, regarded him as a lunatic and a humbug.[46] The Viennese music theorist Emil Petschnig had the audacity to call him a "psychopath."[47] Above all his atonal and dodecaphonic works encountered fierce resistance.

Schönberg never obtained a permanent position in Vienna. He was at times in extreme financial straits. Among the most shocking documents of his biography is an attachment to his tax return for 1913, in which he petitions for a lower classification, since, owing to an insufficient income, he was compelled to incur debts, which he had to repay in the following years.[48] Berg and other friends initiated a relief action to subsidize him financially and boost his morale.[49]

It exasperated Berg that the Viennese had not made it possible for an artist of Schönberg's stature to devote himself to his creative work free of financial worries. He was angry about the calumnies against Schönberg, the hostility he met with, as well as about the Viennese press which at times reported Schönberg's successes in Berlin as failures, and he spoke of "baseness."[50] Depressed about the conditions in Vienna and full of bitterness, he wrote to Webern: "With every performance we only harm Schönberg instead of helping him."[51]

The cramped conditions under which Schönberg lived in Vienna, and, above all, the nearly unanimous rejection of his music forced him to look for a commensurate sphere of activity outside of Austria. Having stayed in Berlin already from 1901 to 1903 thanks to a teaching position at the Stern Conservatory, he considered moving to Berlin once again in 1911. As he wrote to Berg: "I must finally get away from Vienna. As you know, I have always wanted to. It is impossible here. My works suffer, and I have no chance of a livelihood in Vienna."[52]

In June of 1912, he received a call as a master teacher for composition at the Vienna Music Academy. In declining the offer in a letter to the president of the Academy, Karl Wiener, of June 29, 1912, he cited as his chief reason his dislike of Vienna and declared bluntly: "For the time being I cannot yet live in

Vienna. I have not yet gotten over what was done to me there, I am not yet reconciled."[53]

A major reason for his decision to move to Berlin was the prospect, held out by Max Reinhardt, of a performance of his dramas *Erwartung* (Expectation) and *Die glückliche Hand* (The Right Knack). That plan came to nothing. But in Vienna, and elsewhere, too, these works did not get performed until late. The *Erwartung* was not premiered until 1924, fifteen years after its genesis (in Prague, under Alexander von Zemlinsky), `and for the Viennese premiere of the *Glückliche Hand*, completed in 1913, Schönberg had to wait for eleven years.

Not that he was completely unsuccessful as a composer in Vienna. Some of his works were received favorably, such as the important chorus *Friede auf Erden* (Peace on Earth) and the piano pieces op. 11 and 19.[54] Above all, the premiere of the *Gurrelieder* on February 23, 1913, in the Great Hall of the Music Society (*Musikverein*) enjoyed a brilliant success – for a change, even the press was full of praise.[55] Weightier, however, were the frequent failures and the scandals provoked by his concerts – most of them financed by Adolf Loos.[56] A spectacular scandal followed the premiere of the Second String Quartet op. 10 on December 21, 1908.[57] But that was exceeded by the unparalleled scandal scenes into which the concert of the Academic Association for Literature and Music on March 13, 1913, in the Great Hall of the Music Society, degenerated. The program of this concert, which has gone down in music history, included, the *Six Pieces for Orchestra* op. 4 by Webern, Zemlinsky's *Maeterlinck Songs*, Schönberg's first *Chamber Symphony* op. 9, two of the *Altenberg Lieder* by Alban Berg and Mahler's *Kindertotenlieder*.[58] The concert had to be broken off after the *Altenberg Lieder*: a tumult broke out, crowned by the notorious face-slapping scene between the physician Victor Albert and Erhard Buschbeck, subsequently dramaturge at the Burg Theater.[59]

This scandal-shrouded concert had consequences. It very likely reinforced Schönberg's decision to create a forum for the New Music in Vienna and thus to contribute to the reformation of the conservative Viennese music life. The *Verein für musikalische Privataufführungen* (Society for Private Musical Performances) founded by him, in any case, served the aim of "providing a regular home for the fosterage of contemporary music in Vienna [and] of keeping the public continuously informed about the changing status of musical production."[60] He called for exemplary performances so as to effectively obviate the "difficulties and hindrances against which the New Music has ever had to struggle." And in order to preclude those notorious scandal scenes from the start, he stipulated that the performances should be in every respect non-public. Only members had initially access to the society's concerts, and "all expressions of applause, disapproval and appreciation" were to be excluded from the performances. Berg, who initially contributed a great deal to the work of the society, composed the first prospectus of the society, dated February 16, 1919, and elaborated on Schönberg's ideas by saying: "The performances must be withdrawn from the corrupting influence of the public, that is to say, they must not be oriented toward competition and must be independent of approval and disapproval."[61]

The activities of this legendary society are a piece of music history. In the 117 concerts that had been given by the end of 1921, numerous works of composers were performed who represented the avant-garde of the time. Of Berg's compositions, the following were presented there: the Piano Sonata op. 1, the Four Songs op. 2, the String Quartet op. 3, the Four Pieces for Clarinet op. 5 and the *Reigen* (Round Dance) – the second of the Pieces for Orchestra op. 6 – in an adaptation for two pianos *à huit mains*.[62] It is especially noteworthy in this connection that after the fracas of 1913, Berg's works were not performed for a long time in public concerts in Vienna. The Chamber Concert was inaugurated, on March 11, 1927, in Berlin under Hermann Scherchen, and, as is well known, the premiere of *Wozzeck* likewise took place in Berlin (on December 14, 1925).

Only four years after this premiere, and after *Wozzeck* had already been staged in Prague, in Leningrad and in several German cities, the work was finally performed at the Vienna State Opera on March 30, 1030, under the baton of Clemens Krauss. The reception of the work was mixed. Ferdinand Scherber reported in the *Signale* that Berg's music was received partly with "hymns of enthusiasm" and partly with "execrations," and thought that the opera had become "a matter of musical, and even of a political, partisanship."[63] For all that, *Wozzeck* was given seven times in Vienna in 1930, four times in 1931 and three times in 1932.[64] Berg himself, to be sure, was not satisfied with the reception of the work by the public or by the critics. In a letter to Clemens Krauss, probably from the year 1932, he complained about the prospect of the opera's being dropped from the repertory and ascribed it to the special constellation in Vienna's musical life, the power of the Church and the power of the press. Vienna's musical life, he thought, was subject to dictatorial influences, "which emanate, on the one hand, from Archbishop Piffl and, on the other, from Dr. Korngold" (referring to the Viennese music critic Julius Korngold[65]). And he regretted that this situation remained opaque to most people:

> But very few see through that, and nothing thus keeps the bulk of Vienna's music public from being of the opinion in a case like that of *Wozzeck* that the opera, if it had not exactly fallen through in Vienna, was nevertheless to be regarded as finished, since it did not manage to earn even a dozen performances.[66]

In the same letter he deplored the fact that the Viennese press had not taken the "smallest notice" of the New York premiere of *Wozzeck* (in November of 1931[67]).

Berg's aversion to Vienna was directed against the authorities of the city's cultural and musical life, against Franz Schalk, under whom the Vienna Opera experienced a heyday between 1918 and 1929, against the Philharmonic Orchestra and against the Viennese music critics. On September 3, 1931, Franz Schalk died, and musical Vienna commemorated him in diverse ceremonies. In a letter to Schönberg of December 10, 1931, Berg commented on "Vienna's so-called artistic life" and the "ghastlinesses of the countless Schalk commemoration ceremonies," in which he "took part only in the form of properly caustic written refusals."

He likewise had little good to say about the Vienna Philharmonics. He thanked the musicians who had made the Viennese premiere of *Wozzeck* possible with the words: "What it means to me, who have been working in Vienna as a creative musician for a quarter of a century, to be played for the first time in my 45 years by the 'Philharmonics,' and then right away with such a carefully prepared, evening-filling work";[68] but later utterances make clear that he never stopped resenting them because they did not generally play the works of Schönberg and Webern, or his own. In a letter to Schönberg of November 30, 1913, Webern, too, vented his anger because the Philharmonics had played a symphony by Wolfgang Erich Korngold, telling his teacher: "But for the Philharmonics to play *that*! The dogs, who never played a note of yours, who never voluntarily played Mahler! Who overlook every good, mature production! Let them play it by all means, but the other things, too."

Berg was particularly exasperated about the Viennese music criticism, which feuded against the works of Schönberg and atonal music generally. Furious about the polemical reporting, he mounted a counterattack in 1920 with the essay "Wiener Musikkritik" (Viennese Music Criticism), in which he took critical issue with two newspaper articles by Julius Korngold and Dr. Elsa Bienenfeld. He censured the carelessness with which both handled "musical things" and charged them in so many words with inability and impotence. However, he blamed the strong influence of the reviews on public opinion above all on the "lack of musical education of the public in general" and on the "naïve faith and respect with which the newspaper reader *still* accepts everything that is served up to him in his gazette" (Schr. 182). Berg's altercation with the two reviewers is so inexorable, the diction of the essay so acidic, and the arguments presented so forceful that one can see why both Emil Hertzka and Schönberg advised against publication.[69]

"Renowned in the world, a leper in Vienna" is how Elias Canetti characterized Berg's relation to his native city.[70] The aperçu may seem captious, but it contains a kernel of truth. From the Berlin premiere of *Wozzeck* on, at the latest, interest in Berg's music began to spread abroad. Numerous of his works were performed in the United States and in many European countries. But his music encountered little resonance in Austria, which embittered him greatly and frequently prompted sarcastic remarks. Undoubtedly he had numerous resentments against Vienna. Thus he wrote to Helene on March 9, 1934, that he would permit a concert performance of *Lulu* in Vienna only after the planned premiere in Berlin. He added sarcastically: "In the friendly foreign countries (USA, England, Holland, Belgium, France, Czechoslovakia) concert performances can begin right away. The hostile foreign country (Austria) can wait!" And he added the following jingle (perhaps with apologies to Friedrich Hollaender and the "Blue Angel") (ABB 641):

Mein Apparat ist ja so ganz	My radio is altogether
Aufs Ausland eingestellt,	Tuned to lands abroad
Denn das ist meine Welt	That alone is my world
Und nicht Wien!	And not Vienna!

1.5 Composing in the Country

"For creative work, and its success, it takes being happy and profound solitude." Schumann to Clara Wieck in 1838[71]

"I am nowhere happier than where there is no talk of any of this – in the country. But it is hard for me to be a country dweller in the big city!" Berg to Webern, n.d.

"We are well, and we wistfully await the end of the lovely days in the country, when we have to return to the dreadful city." Berg to Schönberg, August 2, 1913

"I am so happy that I finally have [the song] – that I can enjoy it here in this pure nature remote from all city muck."

"Nowhere, however, do I find more of the concentration necessary for getting to know a work of art than here – far away from all the petty influences and distractions of the city." Berg to Schönberg, July 27, 1915

"Nevertheless I don't get around to composing here, it doesn't work in Vienna, which is why I want to get to the country as soon as possible." Berg to Schönberg, March 13, 1927

"I'd love to be there for it! But I have to get to work, hence off to the country." Berg to Schönberg, May 16, 1927

Berg disliked Vienna also because he was unable to compose in the city. He could not find the time, the peace and quiet, the leisure and the concentration there for what meant the most to him: his creative labor. So he fled to the country in order to be able to compose – to the nature that inspired him. He had repeatedly discussed this situation with Webern, who in this respect was different, that is to say, more disciplined, and Webern advised him, on October 26, 1928, to arrange his winters in such a way that he would have time to compose – apparently without success. Most of Berg's works were to all appearances conceived and sketched during the summer sojourns in the country. He used the long months of the winter for the compositional elaboration. In this respect he can be compared to Johannes Brahms and Gustav Mahler, who were likewise "summer composers."

In his letters, Berg complains time and again about the many meaningless occupations that "rob" one of three-fourths of one's time in "city-living" and that distracted him from composing. He felt worn out by his many obligations, thought he lacked all leisure. Periodically he was indeed heavily occupied with writing about music, which took much of his time. Especially

24

after Schönberg's move to Berlin in 1925, he also had a great many pupils to teach. In addition, there were visits from friends, diverse meetings to attend, and keeping up with a very lively and voluminous correspondence, whose extent one will be able to gauge only once one delves into his papers.

The contrast between the hateful city existence and the idyllic, creative life in the country is the subject of many letters.

Berg often enthused about nature, which, he thought, unlocked to him the creative realm, the world of music. On September 132, 1910, he wrote to Schönberg from Trahütten:

> And I have no longing for Vienna, even though operas and concerts are performed daily there, for I can assure you, dear Herr Schönberg, that here in the country I am more deeply immersed in music than at the Vienna Opera or the hall of the Music Society.

And Webern he told on August 10, 1927:

> You will by now [...] be so enmeshed in country life that you can't even imagine this professional city life any longer. The difference is really so enormous that I have to say – about myself at least – that one is downright two different people: in all one's utterances and desires and living habits. This goes so far with me that in the one situation I can hardly understand the other. And now I am stuck again so completely in the midst of this miserable city life that the sun and air of Trahütten, and places there that keep rising up in my thoughts again and again, seem as if from a fairytale.

Webern incidentally felt much like Berg: he, too, dreamed of a creative life in the country. On August 17, 1917, he wrote:

> My dream: a beautiful house in the country, next to Schönberg, and then work. In pure air, in the most immediate contact with nature. But that will happen. Schönberg is promoting the founding of a colony. You'll be along. – I can't exist in the city.[72]

Webern's heart's desire came true: early in June of 1918, he moved to Mödling (58 Neusiedlerstraße), into a dwelling that was only a five minutes' walk from Schönberg's home.[73]

Berg was used to the country and country life from his youth. His first summer domicile was the Berghof, an estate at Lake Ossiach in Carinthia, which his father Conrad had purchased in 1894.[74] Here the young Berg would spend his summer months, and here his first compositions originated. He seems to have felt happy there, for even after the sale of the estate in the spring of 1920[75] he often stayed there as a summer guest. On September 13,

25

1926, he told Schönberg that he had spent between fifteen and twenty summers at the Berghof.

After their marriage in 1911, Berg and Helene frequently stayed at the country house of the Nahowskis in Trahütten in Styria. Here, for example, the twelve-tone lied "Schließe mir die Augen beide" and the *Lyric Suite* came into being.

In 1932, Berg acquired the Forest House in Auen near Velden at Lake Wörth in Carinthia at an auction. There he felt especially happy, there he could be very productive, and there he worked at the *Lulu* and at the Violin Concerto. He once remarked that at the Forest House he had composed more in two years than during the ten years before. Louis Krasner, who visited him there in the spring of 1935, pointed out to him that Brahms had composed his Violin Concerto on the other side of the lake.

Nature was for Berg synonymous with the primordial, the pure and unspoiled. In a way, the country offered him protection from the city, which to him was something of a menace. As soon as he set out for the country, he felt liberated from daily cares and irksome duties.

In the country he was able to work intensively and concentratedly. Two passages in his letters provide us with information about his way of working. To Webern he wrote on June 22, 1931 from the Berghof:

> I am living here as I always do in the country: up early, work the entire forenoon, toward noon to the baths, after dinner ½ hour of rest, then work again (mostly making clean copy, or perhaps correspondence!), then to the car to drive between 30 and 120 kilometers. To bed around 9:30 or 10.

And to Schönberg he reported on August 26, 1932, also from the Berghof:

> Back in Trahütten when I wrote Wozzeck and the Lyric Suite, I really worked all day. In the morning at the piano, in the afternoon during long walks. Well! I hope to find such concentration here, too, once the 'season' is past and my family affairs have quieted down as well.

1.6 The Insidiousness of Success

"To please many is bad." Friedrich Schiller. Inscription on Gustav Klimt's painting *Nuda Veritas* (1899)

"Only the mediocre is really 'popular' everywhere." Richard Specht, *Gustav Mahler* (Quotation Collection No. 654)

"To be popular one has to be a mediocrity." Oscar Wilde, *The Picture of Dorian Gray*, ch. XVII (Quotation Collection, No. 955

"General popularity must not disconcert us." Webern to Schönberg, November 24, 1913

"Art is not meant for everybody. For if it were meant for everybody, it would not be art." Arnold Schönberg

"I am conscious of the fact that a complete understanding of my works cannot be expected for several decades. The minds of musicians and listeners have to mature before they can comprehend my music. I know that and have personally renounced present success, and I know that – success or no – it is my historical duty to write what my destiny orders me to write." Schönberg to K. Aram, November 15, 1947[76]

The nineteenth century regarded the artist – the true artist – as a kind of prophet, who foretells and anticipates future developments as in a flash of lightning. His contemporaries, it was thought, cannot comprehend the genuine artist because he is far ahead of his time. The composers of the Second Viennese School were also imbued with this conviction. They firmly believed that genuinely new art would be understood and appreciated only by future generations. As a prime historical example of this they referred to the fate of Beethoven's music – a theme that Theodor Loos picked up in order to reduce to absurdity the lament about the audacity and incomprehensibility of avant-garde music. According to Loos, contemporaries of Beethoven took offense at his compositions and thought he was writing such "dreadful dissonances" because he had "diseased ears." Yet a century later people listened rapturously to the works of the "sick, mad musician."[77]

All his life, Schönberg was occupied with the questions what art is, for whom the artist creates, and why some composers are successful and others not. He had reached the conclusion that genuine art and popularity were essentially irreconcilable and that a true artist could make no concessions to fashion and the market.[78] New, true art was to him a matter for the initiated. He regarded popularity as a dubious symptom and distrusted those of his fellow composers who were successful. Alban Berg seems to have adopted his teacher's ideas early on: late in July of 1907, he wrote to a female friend of his youth to America:

> For what with all the stuff that is being composed together now, and is also praised by both press and public, taste is only too easily corrupted. The really good attains recognition only late – and if it happens early it is usually only a matter of fashion. The masses have now arrived at Wagner, that's now their meat!!"[79]

Until his 38th year, Berg achieved little recognition as a composer. Apart from student recitals at Schönberg's, or the concerts of the *Society for Private Musical Performances*, his works were rarely played in public. In an attempt to become better known, he felt obligated to print and publish several of his compositions at personal expense. He realized that that was not a very good starting situation, and he begged Webern not to mention it to anybody, "since the multitude immediately devalues anything that is self-published."[80] In a like vein he told his pupil Gottfried Kassowitz that his opuses 3 and 5 (the String Quartet and the Four Pieces for Clarinet) were self-published, and added: "Naturally the so-called broad public need not know that this is done at my expense, since the like would immediately discredit the composer and the compositions."[81] Even the piano score of the *Wozzeck* of December 1922 was still self-published; Alma Maria Mahler had borne a part of the costs.

The year 1923 marked a turn in Berg's artistic life, inasmuch as it brought him recognition and the first real successes. In the course of the "Austria Week" of a Berlin music festival, Webern performed the first two of the *Three Pieces for Orchestra* op. 6 – "*Präludium* and *Reigen* – for the first time with great success, and during the International Music Festival in Salzburg, the Havemann Quartet, on August 2, turned Berg's opus 3 into a success that was nothing short of sensational. In reference to that, Webern wrote to Berg on August 23, 1923: "I have the certain feeling that performance of your works will now go up very rapidly, that you are approaching a good time!" On June 24, 1924, Berg was awarded the City of Vienna's Artist Prize.[82]

Shortly before that, on June 16, 1924, Hermann Scherchen had conducted the *Fragments from Wozzeck* at the All-German Music Festival in Frankfurt am Main. After the tumultuous applause from the audience, Erich Alban Berg relates, Berg wandered alone through the streets of Frankfurt, tormented by doubts as to the honesty of his composition, "since the broad public had liked it so much."[83]

Theodor W. Adorno has a similar report about the Berlin premiere of *Wozzeck* in December of 1925: that he had stayed with Berg until deep into the night "in order to literally console him about his success." "That a work, even one conceived like Wozzeck's visions in the field; one that could stand up to Berg's own criteria, could please an official audience was inconceivable to him and seemed an argument against the opera."[84]

It would be absurd to think that Berg was not happy about the successes of his works; but they were somehow uncanny to him. As we learn from Adorno,[85] whereas Schönberg envied Berg his successes, Berg envied Schönberg his failures. After Berg's death, Schönberg wrote a letter to Webern, in which he also broods about Berg's success as a composer and attributes it to "several genial traits" in Berg's "makeup":

> Now another one of us has gone, of us who were only three to begin with, and now the two of us have to bear this artistic isolation all alone. And what is the saddest thing: the one of us who met with success, who could at least have enjoyed that, to whom, had he lived, this bitterness would not have fallen to the extent that it would have spoiled every bit of joy in the performance of his works and in his impact, as is the case with the two of us! Certainly, he, too, had to suffer from the general pressure weighing down on us, from the hatred that pursues us. Even so, thanks to some genial traits in his makeup, people believed him, and he could have relished it.

1.7 Humanity

> "For to transmute bitterness and outrage into wistfulness and pity – that is the task of life we have to solve if we do not want to end in despair." Baroness von Heyking, *Briefe die ihn nicht erreichten*, letter no. 27 (Berlin, 1900) (Quotation Collection, no. 523)

> "Our pitiful present, hypocritical in life, has to scrape together the lost humanities in art." Karl Kraus (Quotation Collection, no. 750)

> "Philanthropic people lose all sense of humanity. It is their distinguishing characteristic." Oscar Wilde, *The Picture of Dorian Gray*, Ch. III (Quotation Collection, no. 949)

Many of those who knew Berg personally, or were closely associated with him, concurred in testifying to his love of humanity. The publisher Hans W. Heinsheimer called him one of "the few truly great men" he had encountered and "by far the most humane, the least arrogant, the most modest, most pleasant, friendliest" of them all.[86] Elias Canetti spoke of Berg's love of human beings, "which was so strong that he could resist it only by his penchant for satire."[87] Willi Reich averred already during Berg's lifetime that "sincerity and benevolence toward friends and fellow strivers, coolly objective disapprobation and good-natured distancing of the malevolent" were the outer marks of Berg's "pure humanity."[88] Readers of the *Berliner Morgenpost* learned on December 11, 1925, that, at the risk of his own life, Berg had at the last minute succeeded in rescuing a person from the rails of the Friedrichstadt subway – only seconds before the train roared past the spot.[89]

Berg was a confirmed pacifist, who loathed the horrors of war. The letters to his friends and to his wife make clear that the war years 1914 to 1918 took their toll of him as well. Especially the time of his military service was excruciating to him. One can readily understand that the sensitive, delicately strung Berg was unable to cope with the rigors of military life. On August 16, 1915, he reported for duty, was trained and detailed for guard duty, which worsened his already unsettled state of health. Since he kept collapsing, he was, on January 26, 1916, declared fit only for ancillary service as a scribe."[90] He was posted to the personnel assembly point at the Bisamberg, then to the Mustering Commission in Vienna and finally to the War Ministry. On June 24, 1918, he wrote to Schönberg that "as a result of the years of drudgery" he was "completely downtrodden and degraded to the point of self-contempt."

The events of the war, the crudeness and brutality confronting him everywhere, the loss of friends – all this shocked and agitated him. Many of his letters from that time document his deeply felt humanity.

In great dismay he reported to Schönberg about a stratagem he had heard about and that was praised as "capital." Germans, or Austrians, had thought up the following:

> In order to lure the Russians from their trenches, a bell would be rung by means of a string, which the night before had been suspended from a tree that stood near the Russian trenches. The heads of the Russians appearing thereupon – some 25 of them – proved easy targets for the deadly bullets. And even if it was curiosity – but perhaps with one or the other it was a momentary forgetting of the situation brought about by the sound of the bell reminding them of past times and dear places – then what is being called "capital" here is in fact dreadful beyond measure.[91]

He could not face the thought that in war one had to kill fellow human beings. Like Karl Kraus he thought it infamous that "human should kill human."[92] The letter to Schönberg just cited continues:

And as self-evident as it had been to me until then that the enemy had to be annihilated – and that can after all be done in no other way than by individuals annihilating one or more individuals – at that moment it suddenly came to me that a short time ago it might have been possible for me to have to draw a bead on human beings, actual human beings – and that – if I had not been declared unfit at the mustering – my mind would certainly have sunk under this necessity of having to kill human beings."

With great sadness, he mourned the victims of the war, the fate so many of his friends, pupils and comrades had met with. Thus he wrote to Schönberg on August 13, 1917:

In other ways, too, I cannot find, nor can I compel, the peace I need for work. Thus I learned a few days ago that one of my pupils, who had given me much joy by his great gift for light music and by his great attachment, has died in his twentieth year of the after-effects of a pneumonia he contracted on the battlefield and then as a flight-lieutenant during flights across the Alps. (He is the second this year; a third pupil has been in Russian captivity for more than a year; a fourth (Adam) with his legs wounded and frozen and probably ruined for life.) –"

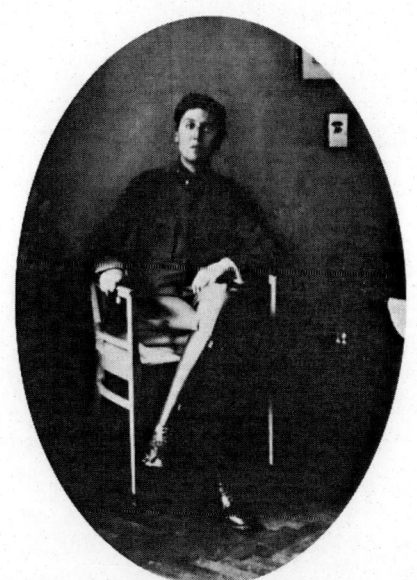

Photograph 3: private in the infantry (1915)

(with kind permission of the Alban Berg Foundation Vienna)

Theodor W. Adorno held that Berg's humanity also colored his music. "No music of our time," he wrote in 1968, was as humane as his." *Wozzeck* he regarded as "the prime model of a music of real humanism."[93] Ernst Bloch had commented similarly in 1935 (33 years earlier). "As for Berg's *Wozzeck*," he wrote, "the object of his music is neither the automatic severity of a particular fate nor the sublime one of a cathedral, but the poor, suffering human being, the abyss of the unsheltered weather within and without him."[94]

1.8 Longing for Happiness or Deliverance through Art

> "An intention for man to be 'happy' is not included in the plan of 'creation'." Sigmund Freud, *Das Unbehagen in der Kultur*

> "The longing for happiness is stilled in poetry." Gustav Klimt, Beethoven Fries (1912), detail of picture III

One can certainly say of Berg that he was very well read and well versed in literature. He had a subtle feeling for language, a highly developed literary sense, and was deft in turning a phrase. It is therefore all the more astounding that he had difficulties in school (he had to repeat both the tenth and the eleventh grade) and felt unsure, of all things, in the subject of German. To avoid mishaps he asked his friend Paul Hohenberg in 1904 – the year of his passing the *matura* (graduating examination) – to help him with the writing of his essays. One of the topics set was "What are the aims of humanity?"[95] Berg had thought a great deal about the content and structure of the essay but asked Hohenberg to suggest some specific examples, "references" and quotations. Of the two parts of the essay, the first was to treat of the individual aims ("the pursuit of happiness," "self-development"), the second of the general weal of mankind (with reference also to family, state and nation). At this time, Berg was of the opinion that human beings sought their fortune in the following areas: wealth, honor, pleasure, power, peace of mind and freedom.

Berg's quotation collection[96] includes many observations about happiness – a subject he thought much about. A 64-page letter of October 18, 1906, to Hermann Watznauer about Ibsen's *Doll House* (*Nora*) seems to suggest that the twenty-one-year-old longed above all for love and fame. He writes:

> Perhaps one day women will act like Nora, perhaps one day the cry of longing hitherto dying away unheard will come true: "I hope when I step out into the great big world, I meet a noble, magnificent maiden, who beckons to me, who shows me the way to fame!"[97]

In his 1936 obituary about Berg, Hector Rottweiler spoke of Berg's measureless and hopeless "longing for happiness."[98] In 1968, he noted: "He was, as his letters to his wife drastically testify, by no means the ascetic artist that by the sternness of his mentality he yet also was."[99] Berg was indeed not ill-disposed toward hedonism. – if one takes that to be the doctrine that man's greatest happiness is his capacity for pleasure. He fully appreciated good food, a good bottle of wine, a warm bath.[100] Helene worried at times that he was apt to partake too freely of alcohol.[101] He had a strong fascination for pictures with an erotic aura. He adored Correggio's *Jupiter and Io* – a painting that in his youth hung over his nightstand.[102] Among diverse notes for *Lulu*, there was an issue of the journal *Die Kunst* from the year 1912 with a representation of Franz von Stuck's painting *Inferno*, which may have stimulated him.[103]

On August 20, 1910, he wrote to Helene that he suffered much from the loss of "Lebensgenuß," enjoyment of life – "as otherwise there is not one pleasure of life on earth that would not be accessible or comprehensible to me" (ABB 177).

Berg was strongly taken by a performance of Frank Wedekind's *Büchse der Pandora* (Pandora's Box) on May 29, 1905, at Vienna's Trianon Theater. He added the following passage from Act III to his quotation collection: "Let him who can feel secure in his bourgeois status vis-à-vis these blooming, swelling lips, these big innocent child's eyes, this rosy-white abundant body throw the first stone at us." Wedekind, sensuality, sexual liberation, the hypocritical morality of a crumbling bourgeois society – these were topics that greatly interested him at the time. In a letter to his American friend Frida Semler of November 18, 1907, he hailed Strindberg and Wedekind as "great psychologists" and called sensuality "an immense force implanted within us" – the "pivot of all being and thinking."[104]

Berg's thirst for happiness had more than one facet, however. Thus defeatism and resignation are the reverse side of his hedonism. Already in the quotation collection, hedonist sentiments (*On the Enjoyment of Life*, no. 428) are prominently balanced by quietist ones like the following: *Of Reaching Happiness* (no. 159): "No, it is a vain illusion to try to win happiness by struggle. Only in peace - in peace with oneself and the world can happiness be found." *Of True Happiness* (no. 160): "There is only one kind of happiness: the happiness of repose. To know that the coming day will rise with the same sun that sank yesterday. To desire nothing, to fear nothing." (Both quotations are taken from a book entitled *Gottesfriede* [God's Peace] by Peter Nausen.). The collection also included aperçus about happiness by Shakespeare and Nietzsche. Berg evidently regarded it as something of a mirage – "the mind's fair 'tomorrow' that never comes."

The bitter experiences Berg underwent during the war years and the collapse of many illusions seem to have altered his outlook on life: a pessimistic mood is implicit in many places in his letters. Defeatism and resignation, incidentally, also characterize the overall mood of many of Webern's letters. On July 14, 1920, he wrote to Berg: "What I have learned above all during the last years: resignation, resignation. And this outlook I also find pretty much in all the great ones – though I also believe in what Strindberg says: 'suffer everything, except humiliation'." Whereupon Berg replied on July 26:

> Everything you say – about the manifestation of our friendship during these last 2 years, about nature here and in the mountains generally, about my essay on Pfitzner and about your final perception as to 're-signation' – is wonderful and true. I have come to a similar conclusion in the course of time, one largely congruent with yours: "re-nunciation." I have become quite a virtuoso in that, from the gratification of all bodily desires up to that of the spiritual, emotional ones.

In his treatise *Das Unbehagen in der Kultur* (*Civilization and Its Discontents*), Sigmund Freud proposes the thesis that happiness, in the moderate sense in which it can be acknowledged as possible, is a problem of the "individual libido economy," and discusses the "interesting case" that "happiness in life is sought primarily in the enjoyment of beauty."[105] This formula seems to fit the passionate artist Berg. If he knew Gustav Klimt's Beethoven Fries, he will have identified with the picture bearing the subtitle "The longing for happiness is stilled in poetry." He found his fulfillment in artistic creation, which in a way offered him a substitute for what was denied to him in life.

We spoke at the outset of Adorno's attempt to find correspondences beween certain traits of Berg's personality and his music. We may recall his obsevation: "Something voluptuous, luxuriating, that is inseparable from his music and his orchestra also colored his desire for happiness."[106] Nobody will deny that the element of sensual sound is strongly developed in Berg's music. In this respect it differs substantially and fundamentally from that of Webern.[107]

1.9 Fidelity

"Fidelity is the striving of a noble soul to become equal to something greater than itself. Continuous attachment and love makes the servant equal to his master, who otherwise is entitled to regard him only as a paid slave." Goethe, *Wilhelm Meister*, Book IV, Cap. 2 (Quotation Collection, no. 860. See nos. 477, 630 and 638 for additional aphorisms about fidelity)

"Oh, you know only too well how unchangeable my faith and love is." Berg to Helene, July 29, 1909 (ABB 98)

"My chief character trait is fidelity (in a previous incarnation I must have been a *dog*, and may I become one again – in a later one, that is, start from scratch again! – and perish of the distemper if I sin against fidelity). Fidelity not only to *you*, but to *myself*, to *Schönberg* (who really does not make it easy for a person) – and to Trahütten, too. And as to the latter: now, while outside the green-brown landscapes fly past, I have twinges of conscience that in these days of artistic battle, of ambition, of hunger for fame, of chasing after money, I am nearly forgetting the sacred Trahütten. (But once the bustle is past, nothing will keep me from a month-long stay up there!) So: with such a conservative bent, how could I not but *be, and forever remain, all the more faithful to you, my precious darling!!* Believe me, as I believe it of you." Berg to Helene (ABB 540)

Berg wrote the letter to his wife from which the last quotations above are taken on November 11, 1925, on the train to Prague, close to half a year after his fateful stay in Prague with the family of the industrialist Herbert Robettin – a stay that had plunged him into a profound emotional crisis. Helene Berg, from whom her husband's passion for Hanna Fuchs-Robettin had not remained hidden, was naturally alarmed, since Berg would again be staying with the Robettins during his renewed sojourn in Prague. In this letter, Berg now seeks to dispel her misgivings and to reassure her. Even so, the sincerity and honesty of his protestations are not to be questioned. Although he had fallen passionately in love with Hanna Fuchs-Robettin, he was greatly attached to his wife and really could not live without her.[108]

Fidelity clearly meant much to Berg. He did not exaggerate in saying that he was faithful to himself, to music and to Schönberg. He was faithful to his principles, his aims, and above all his creative work, even though until 1923 he had really been unsuccessful as a composer. And he was faithful to Schönberg, although as a Schönberg pupil he was looked at askance by many and even calumniated.

Schönberg himself knew how to appreciate his pupil's attachment. In an essay written in 1949 – long after Berg's death – he emphasizes fidelity as Berg's chief character trait, saying: "He always stood faithfully by me and kept his loyalty to me throughout his brief life." *Wozzeck*, he noted, had been one of the greatest operatic successes "because Berg, the diffident young man, was yet a strong personality, who remained true to his ideas, just as he remained true to me when he was to be almost violently forced to break off his studies with me." And Schönberg concludes this belated obit with the aperçu: "It is the mark of a great personality to elevate the belief in one's ideas to the level of one's destiny."[109]

Adorno, too, spoke emphatically of Berg's fidelity. He tells that as a farewell for a long period of time, Berg had written Alberich's dream entreaty to his son Hagen in Wagner's *Götterdämmerung*, "Sei treu!" on a postcard to him. Berg, he says, had been true, had kept faith, like no other – faith even where he knew of the profoundest estrangement – and where would he not have to have known about estrangement?"[110]

Fidelity is related to conservation, constancy, persistence. Can one deduce certain peculiarities of Berg's music from this "chief character trait" of fidelity? His "conservative bent," as he put it, might explain to a certain extent why, despite the boldness of his music, his relation to the tradition is closer, more ardent, than in Schönberg or Webern. He wrote new music without altogether abandoning the link to the tradition, without burning all the bridges behind him.

In his analysis of the *Seven Early Songs*, Adorno tried to characterize Berg's relation to the "subjective-romantic" tradition by means of the formula "Treue zum Schein," fidelity to semblance or appearance[111] – an attempt that is not wholly convincing. Far more apt (and, moreover, more dialectically balanced) is his aperçu: "With faithful insistence, Berg, one of the boldest musical inaugurators of the twentieth century, yet preserved the postulates of the nineteenth, conserved the unbroken even after the break."[112]

1.10 From Goethe to Wedekind

"Why does our heart pound at names like Strindberg, Oscar Wilde, Gerhart Hauptmann and even Wedekind, Altenberg, Karl Hauer, Weininger, Wittels, Karl Kraus and Hermann Bahr – if we do not have within us the same striving and desire to transmute the ideals they fixed with their pens into real, tangible life??!!" Berg to Helene, August 15, 1907 (ABB 16)

"I know what Strindberg means to you, or better, I have an inkling, seek to apprehend it." Webern to Berg, May 29, 1912

"Persuaded by Strindberg, I cannot think otherwise than that I am being punished." Webern to Schönberg, October 2, 1912

"Do you know what makes life bearable to me? That I can occasionally imagine it as just a semi-reality, a bad dream inflicted upon us as a punishment." August Strindberg, *Legenden*, pp. 333f. (marked by Berg)

"In matters of art, I confess that I do not hate excess; moderation has never seemed the mark of a vigorous artistic nature to me." Baudelaire, "Wagner et *Tannhäuser* in Paris," *Oeuvres complètes*, ed. Claude Pichois (Paris, 1976), 2:807 (marked by Berg and related to Schönberg)

"But it has always been in the nature of our intellectual development that a man who takes a decisive step forward in any intellectual territory will be hauled before the judge for violating just that territory." Frank Wedekind, Foreword to *Die Büchse der Pandora*, p. 8 (marked by Berg)

"Have there ever been people who were made happy by love? And what is their happiness other than that they sleep better and can forget everything?" Frank Wedekind, *Die Büchse der Pandora*, p. 92 (marked by Berg)

To understand the work of any major composer of the 20th century, one needs to ask about his intellectual horizon. Berg was one of the most educated musicians of the century. The more one delves into his correspondence and surveys his library,[113] the more one marvels at the breadth of his reading. He had a close relationship with both literature and pictorial art – before he started to compose, he wanted to be a poet – and associated with many well-known artists. Not only musical but also literary themes are frequent subjects of his letters, many of which are in turn of a high literary quality.

In his obituary on Berg, Soma Morgenstern tried to sketch Berg's intellectual world, in which, in his view, five prominent personalities of Viennese Modernism occupy places of honor: Gustav Mahler, Arnold Schönberg, Karl Kraus, Adolf Loos and Peter Altenberg, whom Morgenstern invoked as Berg's "lode-stars." [114] Certainly these five artists were of special importance for his development. Berg profoundly venerated Mahler, idolized Schönberg, regarded Karl Kraus as an authority (portraits of these three artists hung and still hang in his Hietzing apartment on Trauttmansdorffgasse) and associated intimately with Adolf Loos and Peter Altenberg.

Susanne Rode has published a voluminous monograph on Berg's relation to Karl Kraus, which is based on numerous documents and contains much that is revealing.[115] As no less a witness than Elias Canetti testifies,[116] Karl Kraus enjoyed tremendous authority in early 20th-centuiry Vienna as a sharp-tongued, greatly feared critic of language and society. Berg was a passionate reader of Kraus's *Die Fackel* (The Torch) – in a letter to Helene he called it a "marvel of deepest wisdom and loftiest humor" (ABB 193) – attended Kraus's lectures whenever he could manage it, admired his histrionic talent and inimitable style of delivery, and came to his defense on the occasion when Kraus was attacked for having championed Jacques Offenbach.[117] There can be no question that the influence Kraus exerted on Berg's intellectual world was a major one and that Kraus's social criticism powerfully impressed the young Berg. Numerous poets and writers, however, had a fixed place in Berg's literary pantheon.

A first insight into Berg's intellectual world is afforded by his repeatedly cited quotation collection, which he kept from May 1903 to the end of 1907, entitling it *Von der Selbsterkenntnis*, "Of Self-knowledge." The collection consists of 11 booklets and an index volume and contains no fewer than 1161 quotes and aphorisms from 233 authors,[118] among whom the most frequently cited are Goethe, Henrik Ibsen, Karl Kraus, August Strindberg, Arthur Schnitzler, Oscar Wilde, Friedrich Nietzsche, Peter Altenberg and Frank Wedekind. The thematic spectrum of the excerpts and the wealth of the anthology are astonishing. A detailed study of it reveals it as a mirror of the subjects that greatly interested both Berg and his contemporaries and that were hotly debated at the time. Thus one will find in this anthology observations about the nature, destiny and peculiarities of human beings, about the relation between, and psychology of, the sexes (especially female psychology), about the then much-discussed topics of women's emancipation and the problems of marriage, reflections about love, about the nature of artists, about questions of morality and especially also sexuality, and, last not least, aphorisms about society and the press. In addition, Berg included also some passages from his letters and aphorisms of his own (listed in the index volume under the rubric "my own products"), which are first published here in Appendix I.

In analyzing Berg's intellectual ambience, one has the start from the "Viennese Modernism," the literature, art and music of the turn of the century in Vienna – a culture that was basically a melting-pot of the most diverse influences. There were numerous coincident trends: Naturalism, Beyond Naturalism, Decadence, Symbolism, Impressionism, Art Nouveau, Fin de Siècle, Expressionism.[119] It would be hard to reduce these many directions to a single common denominator: clearly there were different factions and fractions.

Hermann Bahr read the era in terms of the reaction to, and more precisely a surmounting of, Naturalism. But he had some trouble in defining the concept of Decadence. Naturalism, he thought, was a simplistic idea. It sought to explain human beings in terms of their environment, "as the result of the conditions surrounding them and determining their nature." The Decadents, by contrast, all had in common "the strong urge away from the shallow and crude Naturalism to the depth of refined ideals."[120] Bahr isolated three earmarks of Decadence: the "dedication to the nervous," the "love of the artificial from which every trace of nature is erased," and "a febrile addiction to the Mystical."[121]

But while Bahr championed the movement, Karl Kraus professed to hate the "phony, trumped-up Decadence, which everlastingly flirts with itself."[122] He brought no less a charge against Bahr than that of having prompted young people "to write un-German."[123] It is certain, at any rate, that the "Viennese Modernism" can not be subsumed under the concept of Decadence, since it also strongly accentuated forms of cultural, linguistic and social criticism. Among the writers by whom one sought to orientate oneself were Baudelaire, Oscar Wilde, Henrik Ibsen, August Strindberg, Frank Wedekind, Otto Weininger and, not least, Friedrich Nietzsche – all of them authors whom Berg engaged intensively and critically.

In the *Doll House* letter to Hermann Watznauer already cited, Berg disclosed that many of the books he had read had elicited, even brought about, his "Nature worship, for which he thanked and venerated them ("from Goethe down to Altenberg"). He added that he owed his image of women, his critical attitude to the press and much besides "for the most part" to his reading of Goethe, Ibsen, Wilde, Kraus and Weininger. The remark suggests that around

39

1906 these five authors were the fixed stars in Berg's intellectual heavens (Weininger's famous *Geschlecht und Charakter* (*Sex and Character*) had appeared in 1903 and caused a sensation). Not that Berg – in every respect a critical spirit – identified in everything with the authors he read: he had his own opinions and was skeptical of all philosophic systems and grey theories, "even if they were by Weininger."

Henrik Ibsen was a model figure for Berg at least until 1906. In contrast to Mahler, who had a rather detached attitude toward the Norwegian dramatist,[124] Berg was a great fan of his "master dramas"[125] and regarded him as one of his "living ideals." As a "youngster" he wrote a "whole mining drama"[126] under the influence of Ibsen. His veneration for Ibsen is documented in the quotation collection, in which no fewer than 23 of Ibsen's dramas are represented, and in the letter about the *Doll House*, a play that fascinated the Berg family: family members even harbored the thought of committing its roles to memory and performing the play, though that plan did not come to fruition.[127]

From roughly the autumn of 1907, however, August Strindberg began to occupy the place in Berg's intellectual world held until then by Ibsen. The more Berg turned to Strindberg, the more his interest in Ibsen waned, and it would be no exaggeration to say that Strindberg remained for many years his favorite author. He debated about Strindberg with Helene and with friends and read his plays, novels and stories with great enthusiasm. Strindberg is a recurrent subject in Berg's correspondence with Webern during the years 1911 to 1916. It would not be going too far to call Berg a regular Strindberg expert. He was familiar with the editions of Strindberg's writings, kept track of new publications, and was eager to acquaint himself with works he did not yet know. He owned the 32-volume collected German edition of Strindberg's works (in the translation of Emil Schering), as well as diverse single volumes, including the "chamber plays," a volume of seven one-act plays, one containing the *Inferno* and the *Legends* (dated 11-17-1910 by him); and *To Damascus* (dated 12-4-1912). These four volumes contain numerous underlinings, marginal markings and comments in Berg's or Helene's hand, from which it is clear that Berg at times identified with specific characters in Strindberg's plays.[128] Berg also knew the posthumously edited works of Strindberg, which he must have esteemed highly, since he made a present to Webern of them.[129]

Berg's admiration for Strindberg was truly limitless. His comments about him were invariably exuberant. In a letter to Helene of July 25, 1909, he lauded the "gigantic greatness of a Strindberg" (ABB 89), thought that Strindberg was one of the greatest, most surpassing phenomena of the time (ibid.,), and emphasized that the Swedish author, unlike a Knut Hamsun, had achieved "significant things in all areas" and "from youth into old age" was continuing to create and coming up with fresh surprises (ABB 90). At this time, Berg already had an exceptional command of Strindberg's productions: he knew the autobiographical writings, the five novels of the present, the historical dramas, the eleven one-act plays, studio plays and the dramas *Dance of Death* and *The Father*.

Two years later, Berg read Strindberg's "Three Modern Stories," deeming "The Roofing Ceremony" to be fabulous.[130] The year after, he was carried away by the plays *At a Higher Court* and *Crimes and Crimes*. In a letter to Webern of July 1912, he called them "unprecedented works, especially the first one of unearthly greatness." He was thrilled to read that Strindberg had planned to include music in both plays. He was so enchanted with Strindberg that for some time he thought of setting these chamber plays as an opera.[131] Schönberg, too, had once considered asking Strindberg for a "text."[132]

Webern was likewise a fanatical admirer of Strindberg. He immersed himself in Strindberg's works – on May 10, 1914, he wrote to Schönberg that he was then reading *To Damascus* again and read Strindberg "generally all the time" – engaged them time and again, and attended performances at every opportunity.[133] In his letters to Berg and Schönberg, he repeatedly brought up the subject of Strindberg, told them of his impressions in reading him. Since his Strindberg reception is of significance also for Berg's, we should take a somewhat closer look at it.

Webern clearly had a strong affinity to Strindberg's intellectual world. He was impressed not only by Strindberg's representation of the existential predicament and of the problems of marriage, but also by the religious or mystical side of his art. He praised the "faith in a good outcome" in the *Jahresfestspiele*.[134] *To Damascus* seemed "the highest reality, nothing but ghosts" to him.[135] He pondered Strindberg's conviction that God himself had given laws to humanity,[136] and regarded Strindberg's maxim of having "one foot here, the other 'there'" as the "chief" commandment: "Work but also pray." Only thus life was at all bearable.

Generally, Strindberg's idea that life was merely a semi-reality, a bad dream "imposed on us as a punishment," seems to have impressed both Berg and Webern. Berg marked this sentence in his copy of the *Legends*, and Webern firmly believed that adversities humans had to contend with, and pains of all kinds, were "imposed" as penalties. In such pains he thought he recognized the meaning, the "That" of the Swedenborg-Strindbergian formula "Do not do That."¹³⁷

There can be no doubt that Strindberg was a favorite author of both Berg and Webern. In comparing Strindberg with other authors, they always preferred him. Thus Webern remarked about Strindberg's *Historical Miniatures* he could not help but say that "when Strindberg speaks about servants, one feels infinitely elevated, and when Maeterlinck speaks of eternity, really not at all."¹³⁸ Ibsen, too, came off badly in any comparison with Strindberg. Thus the symbolism in *Peer Gynt* seemed unclear and confusing to Webern, whereas Strindberg's figures could say "the simplest things and reveal something unheard-of."¹³⁹

Berg and Webern were a good deal younger than Mahler, so that their intellectual world differed considerably from that of Mahler, whom they deeply revered. An episode reported by both Paul Stefan¹⁴⁰ and Richard Specht¹⁴¹ is characteristic of this difference. After his second return from America in 1909, Mahler had urged Schönberg's pupils at a social gathering to read Dostoevsky, his favorite author, which, he said, was more important than counterpoint. Whereupon Webern replied ("in his pleasant boyish manner"): "Please, we have Strindberg." Berg, who was probably present at this conversation, marked the passage in his copy of Specht's Mahler book.

Specht, to be sure, was wrong in thinking Mahler had noticed that the young musicians to whom he was talking did not know a single line of Dostoevsky. Berg, at least, was a passionate Dostoevsky devotee; his library contains numerous Dostoevsky volumes. He knew both *The Brothers Karamazov* and *The Demons*, besides other works. In a letter to Helene, he praised, besides the depth of thought and the powerful conception, also the "grandiose content" of the *Brothers Karamazov* (ABB 249). The numerous markings and underlinings in his personal copy¹⁴² indicate that he was deeply impressed by Dostoevsky's reflections on the relation of masters and servants, on prayer, on love and the contact with other worlds, on faith and on hell and hellfire.

Berg's intellectual horizon, as we have noted, was wide. His extensive library, now in the possession of the Alban Berg Foundation, conveys a vivid impression of the enormous scope of his reading. Numerous authors had a lasting influence on his intellectual world. In what follows we will focus on three additional ones, who were also important for his creative work: Charles Baudelaire, Peter Altenberg and Frank Wedekind.

Baudelaire has been called the poet of "modernity." According to Hugo Friedrich, he paced off in is own self all of the phases that are forced upon us by modernity: anxiety, hopelessness, the collapse in the face of a fervently wished ideality that ever recedes into nothingness.[143] His lyricism and his prose (the notorious cycle of poems *Les Fleurs do Mal* had appeared in 1857) were extensively noticed by Viennese Modernism.[144] Hermann Bahr regarded him as one of the chief representatives of the Decadence and called his poems a paradigm of synaesthetic art. [145]

Berg discovered Baudelaire for himself in August of 1910. Until then he had known nothing of him but his name and had not read anything by him. In 1910, he read Baudelaire's *Little Poems in Prose* with great fascination and wrote an enthusiastic letter about them to Helene (ABB 184f.). He greatly liked the book, he wrote, and had found in it "many beautiful, previously entertained thoughts": what he had thought about the love of Nature for years he discovered again in this fifty-year-old book. He would like to call Baudelaire the "singer of clouds and the sea."

Berg clearly identified with Baudelaire at this point in time. The *Petits poèmes en prose* seem to have piqued his curiosity about this French author, prompting him to acquire the five-volume German edition of Baudelaire's works by Max Bruns. He also owned a German edition of Baudelaire's *Intimate Journals, Pictures and Drawings*,[146] and the *Flowers of Evil* in Stefan George's German translation.[147] Numerous markings and underlinings in these volumes document that he was especially interested in Baudelaire's views about women, love and art. No doubt he likewise read Bruns's introduction to Baudelaire's essay "Richard Wagner and *Tannhäuser* in Paris" with great interest. How highly he esteemed Baudelaire one can also gather from the fact that for Christmas of 1911 he presented Webern with a Baudelaire volume.[148]

Between 1925 and 1929, Berg's hitherto primarily passive occupation with Baudelaire took on the traits of a productive reception. The momentous events of the year 1925, the profound crisis into which his feelings for Hanna Fuchs-Robettin had plunged him, and the knowledge of the hopelessness of his love rendered him especially receptive to Baudelaire's peculiar moods and ideas. At this time he seems to have immersed himself into reading the *Flowers of Evil*. The bleakness of many of the poems, the palliation of chaos must have strongly spoken to him. Thus he was not content merely to subtend the sonnet "De Profundis Clamavi" from Baudelaire's poetic cycle to the Finale of the *Lyric Suite* (*Largo desolato*), but he also associated the fifth movement (*Presto delirando*) with Baudelaire's Autumn sonnet. And judging from Berg's frame of mind after the affair with Hanna Fuchs, it seems logical that the concert aria *Der Wein* is likewise based on three poems from *Fleurs du Mal*.[149]

43

Berg was personally acquainted not only with Karl Kraus and Adolf Loos, but also with Peter Altenberg (1859-1919), a writer who for a while had been passionately in love with Helene Nahowski and later adored Berg's sister Smaragda Eger. Altenberg has entered into literary history as the "Socrates of the coffeehouse," as "genius of the trivial" (Franz Kafka), and, above all, as a master of the prose sketch. Nearly all of his sketches have an autobiographical dimension: his life was reflected in his writings.[150] Karl Kraus highly esteemed him, despite the impressionistic subjectivity of his sketches, calling him a "true poet." Altenberg himself characterized his texts by saying: "Are my little things then poems?! Not at all. They are extracts. Extracts of life. The life of the soul, and of the serendipitous day, evaporated to two or three pages...."[151] Berg quite possibly valued Altenberg's texts not least for their very subjectivity and their psychological subtlety.

In any case, he set this willful writer a monument with his *Orchestra Songs after Picture Postcard Texts* by Peter Altenberg, op. 4. The five lieder capture the peculiar atmosphere of the texts; Berg searches out their every prompting and nuance. But he also counterpoints the impressionism of the texts with strict constructive bonds.[152] There are a number of partly hidden thematic connections between the five songs, and the theme of the concluding passacaglia is already concealed in the prelude to the first song.

The third song of the cycle, "Über die Grenzen des All" (On the Limits of Space), representing the axial center, deserves to be accentuated because it expresses the uneasiness of people around 1900 about the new discoveries in physics and depth psychology and the existential threats they implied. Berg's setting of this lied has become famous, not only for its twelve-tone chord at the beginning and again at the end to symbolize the universe, but also because of its toneless recital of the portentous words "plötzlich ist alles aus," "suddenly all is over." The middle portion of the lied is dominated by a sixth interval, which is first sounded at the end of the A part and now attains constructive importance.

Finally, one of the most recent writers to fascinate Berg, and into whom he immersed himself, was Frank Wedekind (1864-1918). The German author is already represented with fourteen quotations in the quotation collection.[153] In the letter to Frida Semler of November 18, 1907, Berg lauded him as the "apostle of sensuality" and called him another "great psychologist" along with Strindberg – "a judge of human nature in the fullest sense of the word." Posterity, he added, would have to decide whether he was also a great poet – he himself thought so.[154]

Berg's intellectual world is characterized by a remarkable breadth. Goethe and Wedekind stake out its extent. Its center, however, is not in Romantic literature and poetry, but the accent is clearly on "modernity." Berg had a predilection for contemporary authors, occupied himself mainly with current topics, and in many respects took progressive positions – that is to say, he was very open to new ideas and sided with them.

Particularly instructive in this connection is a study of the texts that the composers of the Second Viennese School preferred to set to music. Jan Maegaard, who devoted an insightful inquiry to this topic,[155] found that, besides a few classics like Goethe, Rückert and Lenau , Schönberg, Webern and Berg until 1907 often set modern poets and preferably contemporary ones. Thus Berg, until 1907, composed also poems by Paul Hohenheim and Frida Semler, who were friends of his. The modernist tendency and the preference of contemporary poets seem to have continued for some time after 1907 as well. Thereafter, however, the paths of the three composers started to diverge. While Schönberg began frequently to write his own texts and Webern exhibited a notable predilection for folk poetry and texts by Goethe and by Hildegard Jone, Berg, in his two operas, turned to older texts, albeit still highly topical ones. The problems dealt with in Büchner's *Woyzeck* and Wedekind's *Lulu* tragedy had lost none of their relevance in the 'twenties and 'thirties.

1.11 Irony and Skepticism

> "As for Shaw's sarcasm – his irony and derision of man and world – that was modern 10 years ago! Today, every salesman, every servant girl is sarcastic!" Berg to Frida Semler in 1907[156]

> "The border between seriousness and irony was fluid." Adorno about Berg[157]

If one can believe the reports of his pupils and friends, Berg developed a tendency toward black humor in his last years. According to Adorno, he occasionally amused himself during joint walks around Schönbrunn by "thinking up obituaries the Vienna newspapers would one day hold in readiness for him."[158] Long before his death he must therefore have had intimations of mortality. No less suggestive is an incident related by Willi Reich. When Berg was stricken by furunculosis and blood poisoning, and had to be given a blood transfusion on December 19, 1935, he personally thanked the blood donor – a "young, simple Viennese" – and, after the latter had left, said to Reich with an "indescribable" expression: "If only I don't turn into an operetta composer now!"[159]

Clearly, humor, black humor (Adorno spoke of "desperate humor"), irony satire, even sarcasm were nothing alien to him. His nature seemed to be marked by a peculiar mixture of amiability and profound skepticism. The latter, however has to be viewed against the background of his time.

Skepticism was a prime characteristic of Viennese Modernism. In 1892, the essayist Marie Herzfeld sought to conceive the *fin de siècle* as an era of decadence, of "wearied souls" and of, well, skepticism. The skeptic, she thought, wants to savor himself and the world solely as a dilettante, as he was unable to cope with reality, having smashed his God, rendered Nature lifeless, doubted every enthusiasm away, and "punctured [all] illusions."[160]

Not only skepticism was a trait of the turn of the century, however, but frequently also satire rising to the point of sarcasm. The satiric spirit was a tradition in Vienna ever since Johann Nestroy. Karl Kraus, who invoked Nestroy, was a mordant satirist[161] and probably influenced Berg as such. Satiric aphorisms, paradoxes and sarcastic aperçus by Bernard Shaw and Oscar Wilde were *en vogue*. It was fashionable to shine especially by corroding analysis.

The critical spirit of his time strongly appealed to Berg. Many of the aperçus he excerpted for his quotation collection (QC), are critical in tenor, criticize nearly everything: human nature, love, women, the prevailing morals, the institutions of state and society. Their tendency is to extenuate nothing, to idealize nothing, but to put the finger on every weakness. The spirit of skepticism and criticism is strongly represented in the collection. To convey a concrete impression, I will cite examples from two thematic areas.

One subject is human feebleness, vanity and insufficiency:

"All human beings – have grey souls …

all like to put on a bit of rouge." Maxim Gorky, *Night Asylum*, Act III, (QC 336)

"Whenever I had been among humans, I was less human on my way home." Seneca, *Epistola* 7, (QC 345)

"Who well can say, an ancient proverb holds,

From this well surely I will never drink!

It is the time decides, Lord – and one's thirst." Grillparzer, *Ein Bruderzwist in Habsburg*, Act V, (QC 404)

"Willfulness is the energy of stupidity." Saying, (QC 662)

"Man is the most conceited of animals, the poet is the most conceited of men." Heine, (QC 692)

"Verily, a polluted stream is man. One has to be an ocean to receive a polluted stream without becoming unclean." Nietzsche, *Zarathustra*. "Zarathustra's Prologue" (QC 721)

"Man is something that must be overcome." Ibid. "Of the Joys and Passions" (QC 722)

"But it is with man as it is with a tree. The more he aspires to height and light, the more do his roots strive earthward, downward, into the dark, - the deep, - into evil." Ibid. "Of the Tree on the Mountainside" (QC 723)

"I assure you, there are moments when one expects to see all of one's inner being collapse – the more self-conquest a man takes upon himself, the more easily he will break down."

Frank Wedekind, *Lulu*, Pt. I, *Erdgeist*, IV, 8 (QC 836)

"A fellow who is not a little vain, Should on the spot go hang himself." Goethe, *Faust*, Faust's Study (QC 983)

"The greatest joy, almost the only one that can still be savored in old age, is schadenfreude." Josef Unger, *Bunte Betrachtungen und Bemerkungen* (Motley Reflections and Observations) (QC 1023)

"A neat and tidy person should change his views at least once in a lifetime." Wilhelm von Scholz, *Aphorismen* (QC 2003)

"To be an educate person means to be able to display one's little knowledge cleverly and cleverly conceal it." Ibid. (QC 2004)

The other topic is the fragility of marriage:

"There are marriages, where two people can bear to sit at table with a ghost between them – to have a ghost between them on their bed at night, and still to go on living together for twenty years or more." Gabriele Reuter, *Ellen von der Weiden* (QC 596)

"Isn't marriage a splendid invention! You can do whatever you want to, and parents and siblings come to congratulate you on top of that." August Strindberg, *Marriage Stories* (QC 647)

"And better yet wedlock-breaking than wedlock-bending, wedlock-pretending! – Thus spoke a woman to me: 'Indeed I broke my marriage vow, but first my marriage broke – me!'" Nietzsche, *Thus Spoke Zarathustra* "Of Old and New Tables" (no. 24) (QC 740)

Some of Berg's own aphorisms included in the quotation collection strike one as downright cynical, e.g., "Hours of weakness are readily followed by days of weakness" (No. 50). I am not aware of similarly cynical remarks from his later years. Adorno was certainly right in noting that Berg virtually ignored the cynical dimension of Wedekind's *Lulu* tragedy.¹⁶²

1.12 Image of Woman

"Women may have considerable talents, but no genius." Arthur Schopenhauer, *The World as Will and Idea*, vol. II, ch. 31 (Quotation Collection, no. 798)

"No woman is a genius. Women are a decorative sex. They never have anything to say, but they say it charmingly. Women represent the triumph of matter over mind." Oscar Wilde, *The Picture of Dorian Gray* (Quotation Collection, no. 950)

"A woman cannot be herself in our present society, an exclusively male society, with laws written by men, and with prosecutors and judges who judge female conduct from the point of view of men." Henrik Ibsen, *Notes on Present-day Tragedy*, 10-19-1878

"I do not maintain that woman is evil, immoral; I maintain on the contrary that she is incapable of being evil; she is merely amoral, mean." Otto Weininger, *Sex and Character*

"Folly, you rule the world, and your seat is a beauteous female mouth." Heinrich von Kleist, *Michael Kohlhaas* (Quotation Collection, no. 661)

"Women want to look attractive dressed and attract looks undressing." Karl Kraus, *Abfälle* (Refuse) (F. 202) (Quotation Collection, no. 823)

"Strindberg's truth: the world order is threatened by the female. Strindberg's error: the world order is threatened by woman. It is a mark of confusion, when an erring person speaks the truth." Karl Kraus, (*Nachruf auf Strindberg* (Obituary on Strindberg)

"There are two kinds of women: those that are stupid and those that think they are clever." Alban Berg (Quotation Collection, no. 964)

The relations of the sexes and the emancipation of women were controversial questions much debated during Berg's youth. Feminism was on the march and found an eloquent champion in Henrik Ibsen. His play *The Doll House* (*Nora*) tells the story of a wife and mother who, with a heavy heart, leaves her husband, her children and her home to go her own way.[163] Gerhart Hauptmann's Anna Mahr (*Einsame Menschen*) and Frank Wedekind's Francesca likewise presented images of female emancipation. August Strindberg and Otto Weininger, on the other hand assumed postures against emancipation. According to Annegret Stopczyk, Weininger, in his notorious book *Sex and Character*, reduced women to the "medium of all badness."[164] His attitude toward the women's movement culminates in the bold-printed sentence: "The ultimate opponent of women's emancipation is woman."[165] Ernst Bloch justly called Weininger's book the "most vehement misogyny known to history."[166]

To all appearances, Berg's view of women was rather conservative. He did not think much of the women's movement, he did not like emancipated and politically active women – the suffragettes – and he disliked the Countess Geschwitz in *Lulu* partly because of her claim to be a champion of women's rights.[167] His ideal was the natural, faithful, soulful, and loving woman, the "woman without book learning," as he told Hermann Watznauer in the *Doll's House* letter. Several of the quotations included in his collection suggest the conclusion that he regarded fidelity as a prime virtue in women as well as in men. Thus he noted down the quote "The instinct of woman is fidelity" from the *Goldmensch* by Mór Jókai (no. 477) as well as his own maxim (no. 630): "Woman, be faithful! Your solar mission to warm, to shine!" Sentences like the following also provide a hint as to how he envisioned the roles of the sexes: "Men have one love – the world! Women have one world – love" (no. 635) and "Love is the content of a woman's life. But the eternal ideas, overall progress, care for the general welfare are, and were until now, the content of a man's life." (no. 470)

Among the types of women he did not like were obviously those that behave like men, those that had lost their natural grace and ability to love. In the quotation collection, Maxim Gorky's aperçu, "What has been read in books suits a woman as ill as the master's suit does his lackey" (no. 890) and Richard Wagner's "A political man is repulsive, but a political woman is ghastly" provide a counterpoint to Berg's own ideal of a "woman without book learning."

Besides idealizing statements about women, the quotation collection also includes numerous critical ones, Speaking disdainfully, or at any rate critically, about women seems to have been popular in many masculine circles around 1900. To quote some of these voices:

"Beautiful women die twice." Fontenelle (QC 392)

"As for women who are already fallen one can only sink along with them, especially if one is mad enough to want to raise them up to one's own level." Alexandre Dumas, *The Clemenceau Case* I. 3 (QC 384)

"Women, like minors, live by their expectations." Oscar Wilde (QC 586)

"Whether sinful or pure in morals? /Better straight away bury them all! /I'll divide them into those that are fallen /And those that were given no chance to fall." Karl Kraus (QC 753)

"If a cognoscente in women falls in love, he is like a physician getting infected at a sick bed: martyrs of their profession." Karl Kraus, *Abfälle* (Refuse) (QC 754)

"One thing is to be borne in mind: some women are speculators in virtue." Arthur Schnitzler, *Freiwild* (Fair Game), Act I (QC 805)

"For even women will at times forgive, If one forgets one's respect with grace." Goethe, Paralipomena to *Faust* (QC 984)

The criticism of many of the apothegms cited is directed above all against the moral pretenses regarding women. At a time in which the satirical spirit was so particularly active, it was inevitable that Goethe's both mystical and idealizing representation of the "Eternal-Feminine" in the concluding verses of *Faust II* ("Das Ewig-Weibliche zieht uns hinan," "The Eternal-Feminine draws us on high") would become a target of irony and derision. Berg's quotation collection contains a veritable anthology of parodistic paraphrases of Goethe's celebrated lines:

"Das Ewig-Weibliche zieht uns an" ("attracts us" or "dresses us") Ibsen, *Peer Gynt* IV.6 (QC 114)

"Das Ewig Weibliche zieht uns hinab" ("drags us down") Nietzsche (QC 116)

"Das irdisch Weibliche	The earthly feminine
Ist unser Grab,	Is our tomb,
Das ewig Leibliche	The eternal bodily
Zieht uns hinab"	Drags us down.

Arno Holz, *Die Blechschmiede* (The Tin Smithy) (QC 380)

"Das Ewig-Weibliche zieht uns auf" ("pulls our leg") Frida Semler (QC 455)

"'The eternal feminine draws us on high,' it is said somewhere… Very nice and very noble… But there is also another feminine, which is just as eternal and which drags us down …Drags us down so far that finally we do not know if there is still a puddle anywhere that we haven't taken the measure of … Some get away because their genius wears high boots, but many a one goes down as a mudlark." Hermann Sudermann, *Es war (The Undying Past)* (QC 467)

To these partly sarcastic paraphrases, Berg adds his own, which seems to top all the others in cynicism. It goes (no. 117): "Das Ewig-Weibliche zieht uns aus" ("strips us bare").

1.13 Love of Nature

"Nature is so god-filled. Daily I swear to myself that I will spend the end of my days in the country, after my life's beginning had sadly condemned me to the city."

"Oh! All that is beautiful – Nature and Art – is ever new, each day is new, and only the philistine always sees the same thing." Berg to Helene, November 18, 1912 (ABB 233f.)

"And then your Nature enthusiasm. You write of the many valleys stretching toward the Choralpe." Webern to Berg, August 30, 1912

"… and live altogether for my work and for my joy in Nature – the Nature that you love so much as well." Berg to Webern, August 19, 1918

"…because the last few days in Gastein I wholly lived for Nature. I even was – marvel, my dear friend – on the Gamskarkogel, 2465 meters – splendid beyond description; yet I will describe it to you." Berg to Webern, June 1, 1922

The antithesis of Nature and Culture, of Creation and the Human World is a subject that preoccupied many thinkers and artists at least since the 19th century. Franz Liszt made it a central theme in his symphonic poem of 1850, *Ce qu'on entend sur la montagne*. The subject was of special importance also for Berg, who loved nature and art above all things and saw in nature a symbol of the original, unspoiled and profound, as opposed it to the quotidian and to the social institutions, in which he found much to criticize.

Key thoughts about his conception of nature are found in his letter to Hermann Watznauer of October 16, 1906, the noted letter about Ibsen's *Doll's House*. In it, Berg professes to venerate Nature fanatically and to regard her in many respects as his "school mistress." Nature offered him, he adds, something "more imperishable than all the philosophic systems and grey theories." Nature and the human spirit seem opposites to him.[168] Particularly telling in this letter, however, is Berg's enumeration of what he regards as the "natural in everything": "woman without book learning – judgment without law codes – hatred of the innovation most inimical to nature: 'the newspaper'."

These formulations help us to grasp both his understanding of nature and his criticism of the social system. As shown above, he pleaded for "natural" women and took sides against female emancipation; he attacked a judicial system whose judgments in his opinion often contravened the natural feeling of justice; and he warred all his life – no doubt strongly influenced by Karl Kraus[169] – against journalism and the press.

The events of World War One gave him ample occasion to brood about the polar relation of Nature and humanity. He was pained by the crass discrepancy between the peace, the purity and tenderness of nature, on the one hand, and the "horror" and the "infinite misery" of the time, on the other. In a letter to Schönberg of December 14, 1914, he lamented the "frightfully wretched things" of the war and their "indispensable but nauseating concomitant phenomenon," the "newspaper." He confessed that he would much rather dwell "deep inside of nature, or more precisely high up in mountains secluded from the world" and return to that world only long after peace had been concluded. The news that a cruiser had fought until the end, "whereupon the entire crew with their admiral had perished," had shocked him deeply.

Berg's reflections on Nature in the *Doll's House* letter do not always seem consistent. Thus he proclaims, on the one hand, to regard Nature "in many respects as teacher," though with some exceptions, for example in music. On the other hand, he confesses to belonging to the category of human beings "who proceed in the retrograde way to the knowledge of Nature." And he goes so far as to assert: "These [people] find, for example, that ever since painters started to paint the soil purple, and distant mountains blue, nature had actually – become like that." One can better understand these rather peculiar views if one takes into account that when Berg wrote this letter he was evidently under the spell of Otto Weininger. The latter's arguments about the relation of Nature and Art culminate in the paradoxical sentence: "Art thus creates Nature, and not Nature Art."[170] His premise is the axiom that the Nature "the artist calls his eternal teacher" is merely the self-produced "norm of his own creation," "not in conceptual concentration but in perceptual infinity." Thus mathematical theorems were "realized music," not the other way around, "mathematics itself the representation of music conformed from the realm of freedom to the realm of necessity, and hence the imperative of all musicians a mathematical one." These sentences of Weininger's seem to have impressed the young Berg.

In a hitherto unpublished letter draft, Helene Berg reports about Berg's mode of living: "The summer months were given exclusively to his compositional work. He lived then altogether withdrawn in the Koralp region or at one of the Carinthian lakes, in profoundest community with nature, specifically the mountain world." Berg's letters document that he was indeed intensely attached to nature and receptive to natural beauty. He loved both the Austrian Alps and the lakes, and although he regarded the beauty of nature as beyond description, he yet could not resist the temptation to give literary expression to his enthusiasm for landscapes.

In a letter to Helene of November 17, 1912, he enthused about the "stone-grey" Lake Ossiach and the unbelievably beautiful winter landscape (ABB 231). The appearance of the lake enchanted him even more the following day:

> You know my predilections for dreary landscape moods [he wrote to Helene]. The lake is black, turbulent, it is to me like the low, low new sounds of *Pierrot lunaire*, which always billow so and are so full of a need for utterance. I always hear them when I see the lake. (ABB 233f.)

The remark seems to suggest that Berg was in some way synaesthetically endowed.

The summer of 1919 he spent again on the Berghof. He was fascinated by the appearance of the "fresh green." On June 2, he wrote to Webern: "I always have to think of you, whose semi-home this region also is. The Karawanken covered with snow, the pomp of flowers, the overflowing wealth of nature." But he was thrilled also with Styria, especially with Trahütten. In a letter to Schönberg of September 2, 1923, he confessed to be captivated "as ever" by the beauty of the country, and he specified what had impressed him so deeply: for one thing the unique panorama (the view toward the north and east extended to more than 50 miles), and for another, the variegated appearances of the sky, which presented a plethora of images: a "gigantic black wall of clouds," thunderstorms with lightning, a rainbow, the setting sun as well as wafts of mist. Rays of the setting sun reminded him of pictures by El Greco.

But as much as Berg was taken with the lakes and enthused about Trahütten, his most passionate love was for the Austrian mountains. He yearned for the mountain world, and he ascended into the mountains as often as he could. He corresponded about it with Webern, who was an enthusiastic alpinist as well.

Together with him he went on mountain tours, which he reminisced about later.¹⁷¹ On May 20, 1924, he invited Webern on a "cozy mountain tour" with him. In the summer of 1925, Berg was on the Koralpe. For two years, he told Webern in detail on September 29, he had not been on any mountain, and he had suddenly given in to a year-long wish. The tour had been a very strenuous one – "That one day brought me nine hours of solid marching, mostly in severe cold, and not very good trails, time after time down and up again; nowhere any opportunity to rest under a roof" – but he had again gathered many impressions "for life."

Berg's mountain fervor was at times so intense that he wondered if the profound nature impressions were distracting from his work. On July 23, 1931, he told Webern: "The day before yesterday I was at the Glockner House, and the impression was so overwhelming that I was altogether unable to work! I tell you, I have never before experienced anything so magnificent! Such a day, such clearness, yet all the mountains covered with snow. I cannot describe it to anyone, and only you will understand it without that."¹⁷²

Parenthetically one should note here that Webern ascribed a deep religious and spiritual significance to nature. It was his unshakable belief that there were significant correspondences between Nature and the "intellectual" realm. He spoke of this repeatedly in his letters to Berg. On July 14, 1920, he wrote: "The effect that something in nature has on me I apprehend intellectually." Though the meaning of the flora seemed inscrutable to him, he thought he sensed "an unheard-of idea" behind it. And he confessed that all his life he had been struggling to "reproduce musically" what he sensed there: a major part of his musical production could be traced back to that.¹⁷³

Soma Morgenstern wrote in his obituary of Berg: "He had the profoundest connection to Nature. She rarely beamed winsomely upon him. Espying her abysses, hearkening to her demons, he did not transfigure her." The accuracy of this characterization of Berg's nature experience is confirmed if one recalls that in his art, too, Berg displayed an unmistakable penchant for sinister moods in nature. One need only think of the Field scene (I.2) and the Pond scene (III.4) in *Wozzeck*.

1.14 Religiosity

"Religion has whoever seeks something higher in Being than life can give or take." Jean Paul (Quotation Collection, no. 178)

"Faith is not the beginning but the end of all knowledge." Goethe (Quotation Collection, no. 182)

"Believe me, the word 'accident' is blasphemy. Nothing under the sun is accidental." Lessing, *Emilia Galotti* (Quotation Collection, no. 195)

"For man proposes, but God disposes, and man does not have control over his actions." Thomas à Kempis, *The Imitation of Christ* (Quotation Collection, no. 342)

"If one is at home in the mountains, he may study philosophy or natural history for years and have done with the old God – but if he once again feels the foehn and hears an avalanche breaking through the wood, his heart will tremble in his breast, and he will think of God and of dying." Hermann Hesse, *Peter Camenzind* (Quotation Collection, no. 546)

"Religion is not belief, dear Miss, religion is exegesis!!" "Im Garten" from *Revolutionär* (Quotation Collection, no. 625)

"Clericalism is the creed that the other is not religious." (Quotation Collection, no. 752)

"Religion is not to be despised just because there are hypocrites." William Thackeray, *Samuel Titmarsh* (Quotation Collection, no. 927)

"Is it not our eternal aspiration, from the human to bring ourselves to safety in the divine." Berg to Helene, August 4, 1910 (ABB 175)

"Therefore stay 'aloft,' it's always open up there." Webern to Berg, September 26, 1926

Opinions are divided about Berg's religiosity. Hans Ferdinand Redlich rightly pointed out that as the son of Catholic parents Berg grew up in a Catholic home (his father had started a trade in devotional articles, which his mother continued after the father's death), and he spoke of a naturally acquired "Catholic component" in Berg's mental world, from which he derived Berg's increasing mysticism over the years, his fondness for Balzac's Seraphita, for Swedenborg and for the Catholic ceremonies.174 Adorno, on the contrary, thought: "It was in keeping with his pessimism that he did not reveal any positive religious tendencies, despite the unmistakable Catholic character of his nature – though that might have changed by the time he wrote the Violin Concerto."175 Erich Alban Berg, again, asserted that his uncle was not at all bigoted or pious, but nevertheless a believer. "His greeting was never an empty phrase, I have never heard anything other than 'Grüß Di Gott' and 'Grüß Sie Gott' from him."176

Which of these views approximates the truth? If, to begin with, we look at the Quotation Collection, the numerous aperçus cited above suggest that Berg was vitally interested in religious questions and especially in the sources of religiosity. The passage from Hermann Hesse, for example (no. 546) might remind one of Romain Rolland's sense of a special feeling within himself, which, as he wrote to Sigmund Freud, never left him, which he found confirmed by many others and could presume in millions of people: "a feeling he wanted to call the sense of 'eternity,' a feeling of something boundless, unlimited, quasi 'Oceanic'."177

A number of utterances of Berg's indicate that he sensed this "oceanic" feeling – the ur-source of the religious – in himself. We gain insight into this, to begin with, from his correspondence with Webern, who was deeply religious, who frequently counseled him, encouraged him, and at times took on the role of a mentor. Webern not infrequently professed that trust in God, "resignation to the will of God," and the faith in a good end were especially important to him.178 Among the troubles of life, faith was a quieting agent for him. Nature, and especially the mountain region, opened a religious perspective to him. Sojourns in the mountains were a heart's necessity to, and had a cleansing effect on, him, He felt them to be a purification from all the dross, an elevation above all the lowlands, of existence.

For this reason, Webern also admonished Berg time and again to go into the mountains. The "up, up" became as it were a categorical imperative. In a letter of July 19, 1912, we read:

> Go up higher. Where the air gets thin, you will altogether lose your asthma. For a cure, as a health treatment, you should for once spend many weeks as high up as possible. I am convinced that would help. You yourself say, after all, that you always feel better at Trahütten. So then up up! That is the only thing that befits a human being. Inwardly and outwardly up, up!"

He knew from experience, he writes in the same letter, "that everything, but really everything that still flourishes in higher places is better than the same thing down below." And in another letter he remarked of the mountain regions that they were "endowed with the grace" of God: "People there are every bit as filthy or not as elsewhere: but for all that it is still the worthiest whereabouts to be 'up above'."179

Webern speaks about his immense yearning for the "up above" also in another letter to Berg, dated July 12, 1912, which is especially instructive also because Webern there refers to Mahler and the symbolism of the cowbells in his symphonies. Weber enthuses about the virtues of the mountain climate, about the mountain flowers, and also about the victuals there, and goes on:

> Everything that is needed for a noble human thriving is up there. Where should human beings be then? Up there. Up there, how does that sound to us? Is it not more than a mere symbol? "The wanderer on the highest heights," who no longer hears anything except the cattle bells as the only remaining sound from this earth. That is what Mahler once said to the orchestra as they were rehearsing the Seventh Symphony.

Evidently Webern here cites a remark of Mahler's reported by Edgar Istel, according to which the bells in the Seventh Symphony characterize a "dying earthly sound" still audible to one who stands "on the highest peak in the face of eternity."180

Webern's letter must have left a deep impression on Berg. With great exuberance he replied a few days later:

> My longing for an ideal airplane [...] is no hankering after technical accomplishments, with which there is certainly no getting at the art of flying, but my yearning for the "up above." Just imagine: to be able to fly above the highest mountains, where not a sound of the earth reaches one any more – not even the cowbells – marvelous, marvelous.

That this passage has a religious connotation is proven by a letter of Berg's to Helene that was very probably written in 1923 or later.181 It is the letter in which Berg subtly interprets the opening movement of Mahler's Ninth Symphony. Here he associates the Beyond explicitly with the very thin air over the mountains and with airless space (ether).

In sum, there can be no doubt that, like Schönberg and Webern, Berg was deeply religious. He deemed life a "gift of God"182 and believed in Divine Omnipotence at least from time to time. In a letter to Schönberg of January 18, 1815, he wrote about a severe earthquake that had afflicted Italy:

> Here God has for once demonstrated how without any human contribution – within 10 seconds – he can dictate a 'list of casualties'

57

of which even the nations that have been warring for months cannot have any conception.

Berg's already quoted remarks about the Viennese Archbishop Piffle, who is said to have exerted an enormous influence on the musical life of Vienna, indicate that he was not always well-disposed toward ecclesiastical potentates. That skepticism, however, does not detract from his religiosity. An irreligious artist could not have composed the Bible scene in *Wozzeck* or the concluding chorale of the Violin Concerto as soul-stirringly as he did.

1.15 Faith, Love and Hope

> "But faith is higher than love, for in it resides free will!"
> Alban Berg, Autumn Letters 1903 (Quotation Collection, no. 213)

On August 8, 1909, Berg attended a performance of *Parsifal* in Bayreuth. Deeply moved, he wrote to Helene the very same evening that the work had made a "gigantic, vivifying and shattering impression" on him. It would be a "vain undertaking" to want to write such a music (ABB 107f.) A few days later, he criticized, also in a letter to Helene, the Bayreuth ballyhoo ("an empty delusion"), but praised *Parsifal* as a "singular wonder-work" and Wagner as the "greatest German" (ABB 112-114). The impression Berg gained from this *Parsifal* performance is likely to have been lasting. A caricature by Frau Elke Miethke-Juttenegg in the guest book of the "Berghof" depicts him at the grand piano facing a piano score of *Parsifal*, while a Schönberg volume lies next to him on the piano stool[183] – a patent allusion to Berg's temporarily having preferred Wagner's *Parsifal* to Schönberg's music.

Central to the text of the "consecrational stage festival play," we know, are the three Christian virtues of Faith, Hope and Charity or Love. Already in his treatise *Religion and Art*, Wagner confessed that he would want their sequence to be changed to "Love, Faith and Hope."[184] Love in the Christian sense was the highest dictate to him. Consequently he stated the idea of the Prelude to Act I to be the triad of "Love – Faith – Hope," explaining that the first theme symbolized Love, the second theme Faith (that is to say, the "Promise of redemption through Faith"), and closing his programmatic elucidation with the sentence: "Once more we hear the Promise, and – hope!"[185]

Since that performance of *Parsifal*, at the latest, and after an intensive study of its score, Berg seems to have devoted much thought to the three Christian virtues. One cannot say that he was interested in their theological implications. Rather, he sought to gain clarification of his own (often difficult) personal situation, often formulated a personal creed, and in doing so adduced the ancient Pauline virtues, but secularized them entirely. What was close to his heart and moved him in his inmost soul, his love for Helene and for Schönberg, his passion for music and for his work, and in addition his worries about the future – all this he often connected with the venerable triad of theological concepts, which he defined in very personal terms. He used them repeatedly in order to verbalize psychological issues, to articulate his will, his feelings and his desires. In several letters he talks of his faith, his love and his hope.

Thus in the summer (July or August) of 1910, Berg tells his beloved Helene in a letter about three "happy" dreams that had made him blissful. (ABB 173f.). He dreamed, he wrote, that his publisher had informed him that the entire edition of his two works (i.e., the edition of his Piano Sonata op. 1 and that of his Four Songs op. 2) was out of print, necessitating a second printing. Then he dreamed of having "a long, exciting, highly interesting conversation" with Karl Kraus. But it was the third dream that moved him the most. "At last, at last we had each other. – You were with me in my room at the Berghof, and we celebrated the holiest, grandest thousand-and-first bridal night!!" And with little hesitation, he interpreted the three dreams tersely and succinctly as follows: "*Faith* in myself and my vocation. *Hope* for a better, best life here below (through intercourse with the noblest and holiest). My *Love* for you."

For some time after his wedding (on May 3, 1911), Berg lived in a state of euphoria. He thought he could share everything with his wife. On November 20, 1911, while traveling to Munich, he wrote to her that his admiration for Nature proved his fidelity to her, and that the same was true of his enthusiasm "for our music" and his fanatical devotion "to our faith, our love and our hope for everything truly sacred and everlasting" (ABB 218).

Despair and hope seem to have been the poles of his frame of mind during the war years. Especially revealing here is a letter to Schönberg dated January 18, 1915, which at the same time shows his extraordinary attachment to his teacher. Here we read among other things:

> I now have the certain feeling that everything that at present shocks, torments and worries us and has been doing so for a long time (I mean not just the war generally but also personal things) will shortly end well and that an entirely new age will commence.

And somewhat later he writes:

> The hope for a better time, which, after all, would consist only in my being able to live near you again, which in turn would only be possible

if you were to come to Vienna – this hope (which, as I said, never left me entirely) just barely held me up in such times of despair.

Some months before the end of the War, Berg's thoughts revolved around Helene, Schönberg and himself. On June 13, 1918, he wrote his wife in especially telling words about his *love* of her, his *faith* in Schönberg and his *hope* for himself (ABB 353):

> My golden girl! I must write you about three things: your letter, my dress rehearsal yesterday (the ninth) – and my petition. Odd: you, the friend, myself! Or: Love, Faith, Hope – (for when I think of myself, I ask not what is but what will be! I can agree with myself only in reference to the future: that is, in hope). But even odder: a fourth thing does not exist for me. Besides this world, the world of the composer friend as the representative of music and my own (one is egotistic to that extent anyway), no world exists for me. That the fourth one, the family, does not exist I may perhaps still have an opportunity to prove to you in this letter!

In 1933, compelled by the political developments, Schönberg immigrated to the United States via Paris. To cheer him and to celebrate his 60th birthday on September 13, 1934, his Viennese pupils and friends readied a festschrift, which came out in time at Universal Editions.[186] Berg's contribution consisted in an artful poem, in which he dedicated the as yet not quite finished opera *Lulu* to his revered teacher and friend. The triptych of faith, hope and love, appearing as an acrostic, provides the frame of the poem, which represents one more document of Berg's belief in Schönberg and of his love for him, and which at the same time expresses the hope that the German and Austrian homeland, which in 1934 misjudged its great son, would celebrate him as a master by 1974 at the latest.

Berg had a penchant for hidden connections and correspondences and for numerology. It must have seemed significant to him that the autumn of 1934 was the thirtieth anniversary of his having become Schönberg's pupil (in October of 1904). Accordingly, the triad plays a major role in the construction of the poem. Berg thanks Schönberg – the master and friend – for the present of his friendship and tuition he had given him for three decades (a time span "that attained eternal values through you"), and reminds Schönberg that he had dedicated his chamber concerto for his 40th birthday. No less interestingly, Berg triply incorporates, and varies, the literary motif of the Faith-Love-Hope triad in the poem. To realize the poem's explosive nature, to be sure, one has to take its ominous historical context into account.

1.16 Commitment to Radical Modernism and German Music

> "The kindest, most conciliatory person in life, Berg in art loved the combative, the severe, the uncompromising, the inexorable." Soma Morgenstern

> "The public, in fact, uses the country's classics as a means of holding up progress in the arts." Oscar Wilde (Quotation Collection, no. 549)

> "For the middle road is the only one tat does not lead to Rome." Arnold Schönberg, Foreword to the *Three Satires* op. 28 (1925)

To grasp the psychological situation in which Schönberg, Webern and Berg found themselves even before World War One and especially in the 'twenties and 'thirties, one has to keep in mind that they occupied a position of extreme, radical modernity within contemporary musical production. They formed the avant-garde, literally the vanguard, of the New Music, and therefore also were the target of violent attacks. No wonder they felt unrecognized and isolated, outside the trend. They closely followed the productions of their fellow composers in Austria, Germany and other European countries and, comparing them with their own artistic endeavors, felt superior. They were firmly convinced that the future belonged to twelve-tone composition. Nearly all Schönberg pupils regarded their teacher as the master who had secured the "German hegemony in music."[187] Berg wrote on July 13, 1926, that he was convinced one would be able to compose in future only after his method, "when all the other tootling of the I.G.f.N.M. (i.A.) (forgive the crude joke) will long since have sunk into oblivion."[188]

An immersion into the correspondence between Schönberg, Berg and Webern makes clear that they were at least periodically impelled by a sense of mission. They could not boast of any striking successes with the public, but they consoled themselves with the thought that the highly demanding music they cultivated was ahead of its time and would be fully understood and appreciated only by the next generation, or the one after that. It was in these terms that Berg interpreted the rather curious fact that Schönberg dedicated his Wind Quintet op. 26 to a clueless child, his little grandson "Bubi Arnold."[189] Berg, who had a feel for analogous situations, pointed out that as late as 1847 – twenty years after Beethoven's death – it was still possible to write derisively about the Ninth Symphony (a work he esteemed very highly[190]). The lesson he derived from that was that it was always hard for truly demanding music to establish itself, and he resigned himself by saying that in view of these conditions one had no choice but "flight from such contemporaneity into as distant a future s possible."

Considering how lofty the demands were that Schönberg, Berg and Webern made on themselves, and how unique the artistic direction they had embarked upon was, it is understandable that they would at times speak rather critically about their fellow composers. In early August of 1922, Webern attended a music festival in Salzburg. Greatly disappointed, he wrote to Berg on August 12: "The entire festival was one failure – miserable. It is indescribable what one had to endure in terms of hideousness, inability, dilettantism."

In the following year Berg visited the same festival in Salzburg. On August 19, 1923, he reported to Webern about the concerts he had heard. He spoke sardonically about several composers and their "Janissary music or pitiful psalmody" and made no secret of the fact that these experiences had strengthened his conviction that the Schönberg School was superior to all others. The entire passage is replete with interesting and telling details:

> On the whole the entire chamber music festival came off quite serenely – except for the compositions from abroad, which were rather meager. Even Milhaud, Bliss or Honegger, etc. are feeble and unpleasant, let alone the others: Janisssary music or pitiful psalmody the only modes of expression of these people – a style, by the way, that also rubs off on the German music. By the end of the festival I was unable to listen any longer to this kind of humor (false basses) and this gelatinous, melody-less muddling-on.
>
> But as unpleasant as all that was, it had one good effect: how it raised my self-esteem. How reassured we can be! What masters we are by comparison! Incidentally, there were also encouraging things: e.g. Krenek! And interesting ones: Walton, an Englishman, Busoni, Bartók, and agreeable ones: Ravel, Casella, Kodaly. –

The criticism of Milhaud that is quietly announced here soon evolved into a decided rejection. In a letter to Webern of August 11, 1924, Berg takes the field against the "A- and Poly-tonalists," spoke of "Milhaud's Indian music" (*Indianermusik*), and sarcastically proposed to call the composers of the Group of Six the "Six Indians" "as distinguished from the Sioux" (which he very likely pronounced Seeooks).

The long since latent tensions between the Second Viennese School and the other representatives of musical modernism became considerably more acute in early September of 1925. Schönberg participated in the Venice Music Festival and seems to have called down the wrath of many of his colleagues there. He made the mistake of answering the provocative question of Edward Dent, the British president of the International Society for New Music, whether he thought he was the only true composer at this festival, in the affirmative. On September 22, he told Webern in Mödling about the "debacle" of modern music: "including Stravinsky, of whom he said he had his hair done in a pigtail ["hat sich einen Bubizopf schneiden lassen"]; he 'bachels' (Bach imitation)."[191] Even then he seems to have conceived the idea for his *Three Satires* op 28, which were completed by the end of 1925, were published in 1926 with Universal Editions, and earned him nothing but enmity.

Photograph 4: the mature artist

(with kind permission of the Alban Berg Foundation Vienna)

In the second of the *Three Satires* ("Vielseitigkeit" [Versatility]), he vehemently attacks Stravinsky, whom he calls "Modernsky," reproaching him with musical infantilism ("Well, whom do we have here that's drumming away so? My, if it isn't little Modernsky") and accusing him of trying to sound like "Papa" Bach. The texts of the other two satires ("At the Crossroads" and "The New Classicism") likewise do not lack for plainspokenness. Even then Schönberg prefaced the whole with a polemical Foreword, in which he announced that he wanted to hit four groups of his composing colleagues in particular: first, the representatives of moderate modernity ("pseudotonalists" and others "who merely nibble at dissonances to make themselves seem modern"); secondly, the classicists in the widest sense of the word (those "who pretend to go 'back to …'"), thirdly the folklorists; and fourthly, all those "…ists" in whom he could only see "mannerists."

The *Three Satires* can be understood only as a reckoning with each and every direction of the period's musical modernism.¹⁹² Schönberg was evidently unshakable in his belief that his road of twelve-tone composition was the only one that led to Rome. He was radical in his advance and not prepared to make any compromises: tolerance toward other directions was not something he could be credited with. (The refusal to make concessions was regarded as a virtue by the Viennese School.) He was particularly opposed to the "New Classicism" then in fashion, heaping nothing but scorn on it in his little cantata op. 28, no. 3. Anton Webern put it far more detachedly in a letter to Hildegard Jone of August 6, 1928, saying that "today's" classicism copied the style "without knowing anything about its meaning."¹⁹³ In this context it seems important to note that the Berg pupil Theodor W. Adorno advocates the rigorous standpoint of the Second Viennese School in nearly all of his publications dealing with the New Music. His great polemical essay "Strawinsky und die Restauration¹⁹⁴ is all but unthinkable without Schönberg's satires of 1925. Infantilism, for example, is a point also of Adorno's Stravinsky critique.

Photograph 5: Alban Berg

(with kind permission of the Alban Berg Foundation Vienna)

2 Part Two: Theoretical Presuppositions

2.1 Questions Regarding the Psychology of Creation

2.1.1 Inspiration as Gift from On High

> "What is usually called invention, that is, a real idea, is, so to speak, a gift from on high, inspiration, i.e., it is not my doing." Johannes Brahms[195]

> "One does not compose, one gets composed." Gustav Mahler[196]

> "The artist's creative activity is instinctive. Consciousness has little influence on it. He feels as if what he does is being dictated to him." Arnold Schönberg[197]

The question as to the relative weighting between life and creation, and specifically the question as to the priorities the artist himself sets down in his life's plan, opens central perspectives for a deeper understanding of the psychology of the creative individual. Theodor W. Adorno made some statements about this question that bear thinking about.

> In the eleven years in which I knew him [he writes about his teacher Berg] I always sensed more or less clearly that as an empirical person he was not quite with it, did not fully play along; at times that came through in moments of mental absence, which exactly tallied with the expressionless expression in his eyes. He was not identical with himself in the way that is idolized by the existential ideal, but had something oddly unassailable, even something indifferent, spectator-like, such as Kierkegaard, merely from his Puritanism, has decried it about the aesthetic. Passion itself became, while he yielded to it, material for the work of art.

And a few lines later:

> Berg's empirical existence was subject to the primacy of production; he honed himself as its instrument, and the sum total of his worldly wisdom boiled down to creating conditions that would permit him to wrest the oeuvre from his physical weaknesses and psychological resistances.[198]

These observations tell us that Berg was at bottom totally absorbed by his creative work, without being always conscious of it. He subordinated his "empirical existence" to his "production." Of special importance here is the statement that he made himself the "instrument" of his production. "The personal self," Adorno says elsewhere, "he treated at once carefully and indifferently, like the musical instrument that he was to himself."[199] Adorno made similar observations about Mahler. In his widely read book of 1960, he protested against the notion that Mahler had compositionally expressed his "inner personal problems" in his music, and held instead that, "in their advance toward externalization" [*Entäußerung*], his symphonies were very little tied to a "private person," "which in reality made itself the instrument for their production."[200] And elsewhere he went so far as to assert, rather oddly, that the composer reduced himself to becoming a "subordinate executive organ" once the objective logic of the work of art had been set in motion.[201]

The notion that art is of divine origin, and that the true artist does not belong to himself but serves the Genius, goes back to antiquity. Already among the ancients, inspired artistic creation was regarded as a gift from above, the gift of the Muse, the guardian divinity of the rhapsodist. Medieval manuscripts touchingly depict Pope Gregory the Great receiving the inspiration for the liturgical chants that bear his name: the Holy Spirit, in the form of a dove, whispers them into his ear.[202] The 16th century, the age of humanism, revered the concept of the *ingenium*, and the 19th century carried on a regular cult about the concept of genius.

Louise Duchesneau has carefully studied the role of inspiration in the process of musical creation and isolated three variants: inspiration from "above," from "within" and from "without" – that is to say, a metaphysical-religious source, a psychological-physiological one, and a sociological-cultural one. In particular, she showed that the idea of an inspiration from "above" runs like a red thread through nearly the entire length of the European history of ideas, a common bond, as it were, between the religious faith of Hildegard von Bingen and the aesthetic conceptions of Johannes Brahms, Hans Pfitzner and Karlheinz Stockhausen.[203] In conversations with Arthur M. Abell, Brahms thus referred to "superconsciousness" as the force from which all really great composers derived their inspiration.[204] Hans Pfitzner, who defined the unconscious as that "which composes in me,"[205] also thought that the genuine work of art emerged from "metaphysical depths" and sometimes came about even against the will of the artist.[206] And Karlheinz Stockhausen emphatically confessed a cosmic inspiration.

The idea that the true artist does not belong to himself but was led by the instinct of production was also by no means foreign to Richard Wagner. On September 23, 1859, he wrote to Mathilde Wesendonck from Paris:

> In the face of real life I confidently let myself be guided by my instinct: something is being willed with me that is higher than the

merit of my personality. This knowledge is so inherent in me that I often smilingly forbear asking whether I want or don't want. The odd genius whom I serve for the rest of this life is in charge, and he wills that I complete what only I can bring about.[207]

Schönberg, too, was quite familiar with the notion that the artist, in Adorno's words, becomes an "executive organ" to a higher power. In his Prague address on Gustav Mahler of 1912, he said about the latter's Ninth Symphony: "His Ninth is very remarkable. The author here hardly speaks as a subject. It almost appears as if for this work there was another, hidden author, who merely used Mahler as his mouth-piece."[208] In his last years, Schönberg, too, felt like the mouth-piece of a divine power.[209]

2.1.2 Experience as Condition of Creation

> "Mahler said that only from suffering and most arduous inner experience has a work of his ever sprung." Natalie Bauer-Lechner, Summer 1893[210]

> "My music is 'lived,' and how are those to relate to it who do *not* 'live,' and whom not a breath of the whirlwinds of our great era ever reaches." Mahler to Oskar Bie, April 3, 1895[211]

> "The human being is what he experiences; the artist experiences only what he is." Arnold Schönberg[212]

> "If what I write is not what I have experienced, my life will someday perhaps be directed by my compositions, which would then be sheer prophecies." Berg to Schönberg, April 10, 1914

During the 19th and early 20th century, several views regarding the sources of artistic inspiration coexisted. Besides the notion of inspiration as a gift from above, a widely shared view was that the artist creates from "inner experience" – a conception that appears to go back in part to Goethe and to the Romantics. Many composers, among them Wagner, Mahler, Bartók, Schönberg, Webern and Berg, were firmly convinced that there was a close connection between life and art and that experience was the indispensable precondition – even a *condicio sine qua non* – of artistic creation.

Thus Mahler confessed on diverse occasions that many of his symphonies were conceived autobiographically. His most "personal" works include the *Songs of a Wayfarer*, the *Kindertotenlieder*, and the first two symphonies, as well as the Sixth, the socalled "Tragic," the *Song of Earth* and the unfinished Tenth Symphony.[213]

67

Composers who adhere to the experiential theory are opposed to formalism and the aesthetics of artistic autonomy. For them the work of art is far more than a mere artifact. Thus Béla Bartók wrote in a letter of 1909:

> I firmly believe and declare that all true art reveals itself through the impressions from the external world absorbed by us – under the influence of our *experiences*. Whoever paints a landscape picture solely in order to paint a landscape, whoever composes a symphony only in order to compose a symphony, is at best nothing but a skilled artisan. I cannot conceive of artistic products otherwise than as expressions of the artist's boundless rapture, despair, sorrow, anger, vengeance, derision, sarcasm...[214]

Arnold Schönberg proclaimed all his life that the artist's greatest striving was to express himself.[215] He was a decided opponent of the views of art as mere craft. His essay "Probleme des Kunstunterrichts" (Problems in the Teaching of Art) begins with the (untranslatable) credo: "Ich glaube: Kunst kommt nicht von Können , sondern von Müssen"[216] – art is not a matter of craft but of compulsion, not of what one *can*, but what one *must*, do – thus hitting on a fundamental distinction between the craft of the artisan and the "need to express" of the artist, and postulating that what needed to be nurtured was the striving for "veracity." From all this it seems to follow that he regarded experience as a condition of artistic creation. On April 13, 1912, he wrote to Berg that he was reading Richard Wagner's *Mein Leben* with great interest. He had, he noted, expected insights into the "inner experiences" that "destined [Wagner] to his works," and regretted that Wagner, "evidently on purpose," spoke almost exclusively of "external experiences."

Webern, too, at least for a while, swore by experience as the decisive inspirational source. On July 12, 1912, he put the question to Berg "Tell me, what makes you compose?" and went on to confess: "With me it's like this: an experience keeps haunting me until it turns into music, with a definite connection to the experience, often down to details. And it turns into music quite often." And in the same letter he reveals to Berg that, except for his violin, and a few of his latest orchestra pieces, all his compositions from the *Passacaglia* on had been related to his mother, who had died six years earlier. A few days later, on July 17, 1912, he confirms these statements in another letter to Berg. Here we read: "I also want to tell you that the grief about my mother keeps growing in me. Almost all of my compositions grew out of my thinking of her." And he added: "What I want to express is always the same. I offer it up to her as a sacrifice. Mother love is the highest; the love of the mother."

After what has been said, it would come as a surprise if Berg had not likewise been an adherent of the "experiential theory." He, too, who gave much thought to basic questions of the creative process in art, regarded experience as the decisive creative impulse. He reflected about the distance between the experience and the point "where it assumes musical form," and he was likewise aware that many experiences do not take on artistic shape at all. He also knew that, "sadly," often it stopped with a "lifeless form, into which life is never breathed" (ABB 252).

Berg firmly believed that experience was primary and had to precede creation, but, following Mahler, he also considered the possibility of a dialectical inversion of the relationship. That will be discussed in detail in our analysis of the March from the *Three Orchestra Pieces*.

2.2 Inward and Outward Nature

> "At the lowest level, art is simple imitation of nature. […] At its highest level, art is exclusively concerned with the reproduction of inward nature." Schönberg[217]

> "With the artist, the outward is not only determined but also created by the inward, as in every other kind of creation, all the way up to the cosmic one." Wassily Kandinsky[218]

> "Everything I have written bears a certain inner resemblance to me." Schönberg to Berg, August 5, 1930[219]

> "If Mahler once said about the landscape around Lake Attersee that he composed it all up, Berg, in so many respects Mahler's heir, could have said the same of his inward nature." Adorno about Berg[220]

The question about the relation between art and nature – a central subject of art theory and aesthetics – is, as we know, answered variously. Whereas Aristotle, the originator of the concept of mimesis, taught in his *Poetics* that art was simply the imitation of nature, there already existed the opposite conception of art as an image of the Platonic ideas, as the product of the artist's imagination, his visions and dreams.[221] A third, mediating view, widely shared in modern theory, is that art is an *idealized* imitation of nature.

In discussing the theory of imitation in relation to music, one must not fail to differentiate between *outward* and *inward* nature. For music, if understood exclusively as the art of sound, can imitate outward nature only to a very limited extent.

In his *Harmonielehre* (*Theory of Harmony*) of 1911, Schönberg categorically opposed the conception of art as "simple imitation of nature." Art, he thought, could be understood as such only at its lowest level. At its highest level, art was exclusively concerned with the reproduction of *inward nature*. Thus defined, it represented "not merely the objects and occasions that make an impression, but above all these impressions themselves." He also pointed out that at every level of art "the imitation of the model, of the impression or the complex of impressions," was "only of relative exactness."[222] When he formulated these sentences, Schönberg said in the Foreword to his *George Lieder* op. 15, he "broke through all the barriers of a past aesthetics."

Interestingly enough, Wassily Kandinsky voiced similar ideas at the same time. His path-breaking book *Das Geistige in der Kunst* (*Concerning the Spiritual in Art*), which appeared late in 1911 (with a publication date of 1912), is the manifesto of a new aesthetics, which moves away from the imitation of "outward nature," tending instead "toward the non-natural, the abstract, and toward inward nature." In his effort to point out new directions for the pictorial arts, Kandinsky orientated himself on music. In music he saw the one art that was "outwardly altogether emancipated from nature" and therefore did not have to "borrow outward forms for its language from somewhere"; and he thought that

> An artist who does not regard even artistic imitation of natural phenomena as his aim, but is a creator who wants to, and must, express his inner world, observes with envy how such aims are naturally and easily attainable in what is today the most immaterial art, namely music.

Kandinsky came to know Schönberg and some of his works in 1911 and wrote about them full of enthusiasm: "Schönberg's music introduces us to a new realm, where the musical experiences are not acoustic but purely spiritual ones. Here is where the 'music of the future' begins."[223]

He was also quite taken with Schönberg's pictures, some of which he knew. On November 16, 1911, he wrote to him that he thought he recognized two separate roots in these pictures: on the one had, a "pure" realism, ("i.e. things as they are and *as such* sound *inwardly*") – a" fantasy" he was especially fond of – and secondly, "dematerialize [sic], romantic-mystical sound" – a principle by which he also painted himself.[224] At Alban Berg's request, Kandinsky also wrote an article about Schönberg's pictures, which appeared in 1912 in the festschrift for Schönberg, and in which he expands on these ideas. "Schönberg's pictures," Kandinsky stated at the beginning of the essay, "are of two kinds: Some are people and landscapes painted directly from nature;

others intuitively felt heads, which he calls 'visions'." "The two kinds," he goes on, "differ outwardly; inwardly they originate from the same soul, which sometimes is set to vibrating by external nature, at other times by the inner one."[225]

As one can see, the differentiation between *outward* and *inward nature* was evidently a leading idea of Schönberg's as well as of Kandinsky's around 1911 – an idea that very likely also impressed Berg profoundly. There can be no doubt that Berg's views about the relation between music and nature resembled those of his teacher Schönberg. Already in the *Doll House* letter of October 18, 1906, he made it clear that he did not regard nature – one should say *outward* nature – as music's teacher or "school mistress." There were things, he explained there, that could not be gauged with the yardstick of nature – "things sprung from the human spirit, towering high above the material world – things that perhaps are real only in our longings." Among these, he thought, was music and "some poetic works that are written from a yearning heart."[226]

The relation of art to nature seems to have been ardently discussed in the Schönberg circle in the years 1911 and 1912. Webern, too, thought about it. He was very skeptical about the mimetic theory and insisted on the autonomy of the work of art, which, he thought, did not imitate even the heartbeat. On July 12, 1912, he wrote to Berg:

> The "reality" of the work of art is not a symbol, an imitation neither of outward nor of inward nature. It does not imitate the pulsation of the heart. It is something unique: it has its own pulse. Otherwise everything would be imitation in relation to one thing. Yes, perhaps it is so. That one thing is God. Except that the word imitation does not quite fit here.

2.3 From Overt to Covert Program Music
2.3.1 Schönberg and Program Music

"Music is wonderful in that one can say everything in such a way that the cognoscenti understand it all, and yet one has not given away one's secrets, those one does not confess even to oneself. But titles do give away. Besides: what had to be said, the music has said." Arnold Schönberg, diary entry, January 27, 1912[227]

"Music can imitate man as he is inwardly, and in that sense program music is possible." Arnold Schönberg, ca. 1917[228]

"I am not against what you call 'program music'. [...] If a composer is able to describe a skyscraper, a sunrise or springtime in the country – that is all right. The occasion and source for that are insignificant. What is important is always the result." Arnold Schönberg in November of 1933 (in his first American radio broadcast) (GS I, 302)

Schönberg's first three published works are vocal music – lieder for voice and piano after poems by diverse poets. His next two compositions belong unambiguously to the genre of explicit program music. The string sextet *Verklärte Nacht* (*Transfigured Night*) op. 4 is based on Richard Dehmel's poem of the same title, which is reprinted in the score, and the symphonic poem *Pelleas and Melisande* op. 5, composed in 1902/1903 at a suggestion of Richard Strauss, follows the drama by Maurice Maeterlinck. Schönberg's subsequent instrumental works – the two string quartets op. 7 and op. 10, the first chamber symphony op. 9, the Three Piano Pieces op. 11 and others – seem to be *absolute* music, as they have no programmatic titles: to the uninitiated they give the impression that Schönberg has turned away from program music. In 1921 – Schönberg was then working on the dodecaphonic piano suite op. 25 – his friend David Josef Bach declared: "Never is there a poetic, philosophic, literary, pictorial theme or a covert program to his music"[229] – a declaration that in no way corresponds to the facts, nay, is downright false. The appearances are misleading: the more one studies Schönberg's music, the clearer it becomes that the venerable concept of *absolute* music is not applicable to it and that Schönberg had a very close affinity to program music and to "lived" music generally.

In 1984, the American musicologist Walter B. Bailey usefully compiled all those of Schönberg's works that exhibit, in neutral terms, "programmatic elements."[230] The results of this compilation are striking. We learn, to begin with, that prior to 1900 Schönberg started work on three programmatic works, which remained fragments: the sextet for strings "Toter Winkel" (Shielded ["Dead"] Angle) after Gustav Falke, the symphonic poem "Hans im Glück" (Hans in Luck) after the Brothers Grimm story of the same title, and the symphonic work "Frühlings Tod" (Death of Spring) after Nikolaus Lenau. In 1905, two years after completing the symphonic poem *Pelleas und Melisande*, he composed a further programmatic work for oboe, clarinet, violin and piano, which also remained a fragment: "Ein Stelldichein" (A Rendezvous), after a poem of the same title from Richard Dehmel's volume *Weib und Welt* (Woman and World).

In the years 1914 and 1915, moreover, Schönberg worked intensively at a spaciously designed programmatic symphony for soloists, mixed chorus and large orchestra, to be based on poems by Dehmel (from *Schöne wilde Welt* [Beautiful Wild World] of 1913) and Rabindranath Tagore (from *Gitanjali* of 1814), plus biblical verses and a text of his own entitled "Totentanz der Prinzipien" (Principles' Dance of Death). The first movement of this incomplete work was intended to be purely instrumental. The subject of the symphony, which invites comparison with Mahler's Second and Eighth, was a representation of various stages along the Path of Enlightenment. In 1937, finally, i.e., 23 years later, Schönberg sketched out yet another programmatic symphony ("Symphony in Four Movements"), whose philosophic program apparently had to do with Schönberg's turn toward Judaism.

Comments by Schönberg himself, reports by his pupils and entries in his sketches, moreover, go to prove that another seven of his completed and printed works are based on secret programs. The works in question include the first three string quartets op. 7, op. 10 and op. 30, the Five Pieces for Orchestra op. 16, the Suite op. 29, the Piano Concerto op. 42[231] and the Trio for Strings op. 45.

Why, one asks, did Schönberg keep the programs of these works a secret? Why did he conceal his evidently close relation to program music? An answer to this question has to take a number of things into account.

To begin with, one has to consider that several of his works are emphatically autobiographic – based on secret programs that for personal reasons could not be disclosed. This is true above all of the first two string quartets. The first of these, in D minor op. 7, has a secret autobiographic program that was not discovered until 1986.[232] If one can give credence to it, Schönberg, in 1904 or 1905, left his first wife Mathilde for another woman, but eventually returned to Mathilde. Several years later, the reverse of the situation occurred:

in the summer of 1908, Mathilde left her husband and their two children and moved in with the painter Richard Gerstl, whom she loved. Schönberg entertained thoughts of suicide and made a will. Against this background, the second string quartet, op. 10, with its famous quotation "Oh du lieber Augustin, alles ist hin" (everything's gone), is to be viewed.[233] It is thus understandable why Schönberg much later, in a conversation with his pupil Dika Newlin, spoke of the program of the first string quartet as of a "very definite, but private" one.[234]

The Suite op. 29, written in the years 1924 to 1926 and dedicated to Gertrude Schönberg, likewise has a "private" program, namely the story of the composer's love for his second wife, whom he married in 1924. In the sketches to the work, she is referred to once as Fräulein Kolisch (Fl. Ksch waltz) and another time as Frau Arnold Schönberg (Fr AS Adagio); and surely the choice of the folksong "Ännchen von Tharau" as the theme of the variations movement is also no mere happenstance.

Autobiographic in concept, finally, is also the String Trio op. 45 of 1946, which describes Schönberg's experiences after his heart attack.[235] Schönberg told Thomas Mann, his neighbor during their Californian exile, about the experiences "he had secreted in the composition."[236]

Then also we have to keep in mind that, around 1910, Schönberg conceived art and music, as we have shown, as the reproduction of "inward nature." His chief endeavor was to give musical expression to his psychic life. Even in 1928, a time in which an anti-romantic outlook was in vogue, he defined Expressionism as the "art of representing inner processes" in his Breslau (Wroclaw) lecture "Die glückliche Hand" (The Right Knack).[237] It would not be amiss to describe many of his instrumental works from the atonal period – such as the Three Pieces for Piano op. 11, the five Pieces for Orchestra op. 16, the Six Little Pieces for Piano op. 19 and the Sound Track for a Motion Picture Scene op. 34 – as psychograms. Theodor W. Adorno surely hit on something true, when he observed: "The first of the atonal works are minutes in the sense of psychoanalytic dream transcripts."[238]

Thirdly and lastly, we should note that after the conception of the chamber piece *Ein Stelldichein* in 1905, Schönberg took permanent leave of all "literary" program music. After this date, he did not compose any instrumental works based exclusively on a literary model. It evidently went against his grain to borrow his programs from existing literature. In accordance with his maxim that the true artist must express himself, he constructed his own programs, freely inventing them. Very instructive in this respect is his essay of 1911 about Franz Liszt, a musician whom he revered and called a "prophet." Liszt, he wrote, realized correctly that what mattered in art was less the skill, the artfulness, the play with the material, than what stood behind it, that is, "the personality, the genuine artistic being, which draws from unmediated intuition." But Schönberg criticized that Liszt furnished "second-hand poetry" instead of "exclusively letting his own form of intuition, the poet within himself, be immediately expressed in music." Liszt, he thought, had "smothered" the poet within himself by "letting other poets interfere too much with him."[239] Schönberg was anxious not to make the same mistake. In the program symphony projected in 1914/15 he did resort to passages from the Bible and to poems by Dehmel and Tagore. But by their unique combination and the addition of texts of his own he shaped something altogether new, which he was able to call his own. In this he followed the example of Gustav Mahler, who in his Eighth Symphony had managed to fuse, musically and spiritually, two such heterogeneous texts as the Latin Pentecostal hymn *Veni creator spiritus* and the concluding scene of Goethe's *Faust II*.

After the symphonic poem *Pelleas und Melisande*, Schönberg carefully refrained from attaching poetic or programmatic titles to his works and even to individual pieces. Instructive in this respect is the rather complicated genetic history of the titles of the *Five Pieces for Orchestra* op. 16, which the Leipzig publisher C. F. Peters agreed to publish in 1912.[240] Henri Hinrichsen, the owner of the house, having suggested that the work be given a synoptic main title, Schönberg initially balked at the idea but then changed his mind and decided to attach titles to the individual pieces, which, however, would not "give away" anything, "as they are partly obscure and partly saying something technical." On Jnuary 28, 1912, he entrusted the titles he came up with to his diary as follows: "I. *Presentiments* (everybody has them), II. *Past* (everybody has it, too), III. *Chordal Colorations* (technical) IV. *Peripety* (should be general enough), V. *The obligatory* (perhaps better the 'finished' or the 'infinite') *Recitativo*."

Schönberg had reasons to shy away from titles. Program music, viewed at the end of the 19th century as the one area in which musical progress was still possible, was very popular with the public at the beginning of the 20th but had fallen into disrepute among many of the professionals.[241] A number of composers, who had become smitten with the idea of *absolute music*, saw in program music an heirloom of Romanticism, which they wanted to overcome by any means available as a hopelessly antiquated genre. Schönberg's thinking was anchored in the expressive aesthetics of the 19th century – he had little use for the notion of *absolute* music. Yet as the leading figure of musical modernism, he did not want to be labeled a Romantic and thus avoided everything that could make it appear as though he pined for the aesthetic postulates of Romanticism.

However, the wide diffusion of slogans like Neoclassicism, Neobaroque, Folklorism and others after The First World War, and the hostility he increasingly experienced, compelled him in 1925 (after the experiences at the Music Festival in Venice) to proceed to a counteroffensive. In the last of the *Three Satires* op. 28, he made fun of those of his fellow composers who were selling themselves to the *new classicism*, jeering: "I won't stay Romantic, I hate the Romantic; tomorrow already I'll write purest Ántique!" Three years later he more discreetly mocked those colleagues who thought "that the age of Romanticism lasted until November 1918 and that everything written until then was long since antiquated."[242]

There can no longer be any doubt that a large part of Schönberg's instrumental work is designed as program music, albeit one *sui generis*, one that frequently bears autobiographical traits and is based on secret programs, which the composer in a number of cases hinted at in conversation, but which he did not wish to disclose officially, according to the maxim that he wanted to keep his secrets to himself, and guided by the conviction that those "in the know" would understand it all anyhow – an overly optimistic expectation. A major task of future Schönberg research will be to analyze the works structurally and semantically and to investigate their genesis, so as thereby to bring to light the composer's often encrypted intentions. The view that secret programs do not pertain to the "aesthetic matter" is questionable,[243] as is the view that Schönberg's music should be seen as autonomous music, that is, as pure "form and structure."[244]

2.3.2 Berg and Program Music

Program music has always been vulnerable to arbitrary interpretation and crass misunderstanding. This liability has led many composers to be rather reserved about explicating their works hermeneutically. Even Richard Strauss, who had raised program music to an apex, repeatedly refused to furnish his tone poems with detailed programmatic explanations.[245] In 1907 the editors of the journal *Der Morgen* asked him to provide a kind of program for the first issue, which was to be devoted to music. Strauss responded by writing the article "Gibt es für die Musik eine Fortschrittspartei?"[246] (Is there a Progressive Party in Music?), which, however, contained the following statement:

> I generally dislike programs. To one, they promise too much; another they influence too strongly; a third claims to be hampered too severely in the exercise of his own imagination by programs; a fourth prefers not to think anything except to rethink what someone else has thought for him; a fifth grouses his way through with another excuse – in short: programs are inopportune.

It should be emphasized that these remarks do not by any means constitute a plea against program music as such, only a distancing from explicit programs.

Berg probably read Strauss' article shortly after the appearance of the issue (on June 14, 1907) and included the quoted passage in his quotation collection, where it has the number 1085. At this time he had begun to compose his Piano Sonata op. 1, which he would complete the following year.

The question of program music was a theme, as we have seen, that at the beginning of the 20th century greatly occupied Schönberg. He may well have discussed it frequently with his pupils. Berg, in any case, basically shared his teacher's attitude toward program music. In the famous "Open Letter" addressed to Schönberg on February 9, 1925, he hinted that he sympathized with program music – a genre looked at askance at the time – and spoke of a "Romantic" propensity.[247] The decisive fact is that all of his mature instrumental works – the String Quartet op. 3, the Pieces for Clarinet op. 5, the Three Pieces for Orchestra op. 6, the Chamber Concerto, the *Lyric Suite*, and the Violin Concerto – are based on programs he concealed, disguised, or merely hinted at because they were too personal, too "private."

The truth is: Berg was incapable of composing without a "program." He needed an extra-musical stimulus. With him, personal experience was the indispensable condition of the creative process: the autobiographic reference was all-important for composing. Despite their technical complexity, his instrumental works are thus "lived" music. Most of his vocal compositions, too, are in a larger sense autobiographic: the Four Songs op. 2, the Altenberg Songs op. 4, *Wozzeck* and the concert aria *Der Wein* (Wine); even in *Lulu*, one can detect autobiographic elements. So that one can summarize by saying: Berg's entire oeuvre can be placed under the rubric "Music as Autobiography."

2.4 Fate and Superstition

> "Man does not do everything by himself. He also plays into the hands of fate." Anzengruber, *Der Schandfleck* (Quotation Collection, No. 433)

> "Fate is a state of mind. Everyone's will forges his own." Schönberg, *Die Jakobsleiter*[248]

> "I feel that in not too long a time fate will bring us back into lasting and physical proximity; will it be better then?---" Berg to Webern, July 20, 1920

> "I have already learned this much: all resolution is irrelevant, what has to come will come." Webern to Berg, August 23, 1920

> "So-called superstition rests on a much greater depth and delicacy than unbelief." Goethe[249]

> "Superstition is largely the expectation of calamity" Freud, *Zur Psychopathologie des Alltagslebens*[250]

> "I am getting more and more superstitious." Berg to Helene, July 13, 1914 (ABB 258)

Theodor W. Adorno's *Philosophie der Neuen Musik* contains some suggestive statements about the connection between twelve-tone technique and astrology as well as superstition. In his view, the numbers game of the twelve-tone technique and the compulsion it exerts put one in mind of astrology. Altogether, the rationale of dodecanism, like astrology, gambling and the interpretation of signs, approximated the superstitious belief in such powers as "seem to determine existence without being themselves existent." For this reason, the belief in fate was always apt to attach to constellations: "those of the stars and then those of numbers."

Adorno defines fate as "dominion reduced to pure abstraction" and maintains that fate is inseparable from the sway of nature. The concept of fate seemed to have been modeled on the experience of domination, "arising from the predominance of nature over the human being." The fact that fate unfolds of necessity – "blow after blow" – he explains by noting that man's every step "is prescribed to him by the old predominance of nature." Yet Adorno's thesis is that music is "the enemy of fate": "From time immemorial the power of protest against mythology has been ascribed to it, in the figure of Orpheus as well as in Chinese theory of music."[251]

Adorno is generally known to have assisted Thomas Mann as "helper and adviser" in musical questions during the composition of *Doctor Faustus*. In July of 1943, Mann received, in typescript, Adorno's treatise on Schönberg from him, which later appeared under the title *Philosophie der neuen Musik*. The passages about the relation of twelve-tone music to the cosmos or astrology exhibit traces of Mann's reading in the typescript, as Rosemarie Puschmann has pointed out.[252] Mann's conception of music, to be sure, differs considerably in some regards from that of Adorno. While the latter declares music to be the "enemy of fate," Mann in the novel represents it as a demonic art, one with an affinity to magic, sorcery, astrology, numerology and the arcane.[253]

In his posthumously published *Aufzeichnungen über Berg* (Notes on B.), written in 1955, Adorno spoke rather casually about Berg's penchant for "dalliances" such as the play with the letters/initials AB and HF in the *Lyric Suite*, and indicated that analogous traits in Adrian Leverkühn's music, "which generally are more Bergian than Schönbergian," were modeled on just these dalliances. They bordered, besides, on Berg's predilection for number mysticism and astrology – areas Adorno himself had no great regard for. Adorno therefore added: "Since he [Berg] knew what I thought of these, he hardly ever confessed his penchant for them to me. If Helene nowadays tries to conjure him spiritistically, he probably would not have withheld his endorsement of these doings."[254]

Despite his highly developed rationality, Berg was, indeed, no Enlightenment champion like Freud or Adorno. He harbored presentiments and had a strong propensity for the occult, the hidden and supersensual. He firmly believed that a powerful fate ruled over human beings, determining their course of life, that there were no accidents, and that in certain incidents one could and should recognize secret hints of Fate.

Three examples may suffice. In a letter to Helene of the fall of 1909, Berg uses the terms *wunderbar* and *mysteriös* to mean significant and supernatural. Amazed by an accidental meeting with Helene's sister Carola, an encounter to which he ascribed a deeper, secret significance, he wrote (ABB 145): "This struck me as so wondrous, so mysteriously significant that I must have given the impression of a madman, who gets into a state of euphoria for no reason whatever …". In a second instance, Berg was greatly shocked by the assassination at Sarajevo and its consequences. He followed the reports in the press with intense interest. On July 3, 1914, he wrote to Helene about one news item that it proved his assumption that "the event was no accident but the fulfillment of a specific fate" (ABB 248). And in the third example, Webern, in the fall of 1925, had started to give piano lessons at the Israelite Institute for the Blind on the "Hohe Warte." Greatly moved by the plight of a fourteen-year-old girl, who four months before had become blind, he wrote to Berg, on October 8, that he regarded his work at the Institute as a "mission," as something "deeply significant" in his life. Berg thereupon replied: "This is no accident, not just one of many possible employments and sources of income – this is – I have to say it again – a genuine Webern fate."[255]

Both Schönberg and Berg were so obsessed with the idea of fate that they also imported it into music. Thus Schönberg regarded the musical work of art as an organism, quasi a living being, that undergoes a development. In his Prague speech about Mahler, he voiced the opinion that a theme did not consist merely of a few notes but of the "musical destinies" of these notes. Even more telling is his saying, transmitted by his pupil Erwin Stein, that "music describes the fates of themes."[256]

Music as destiny, the notion that a composition was subject to a fate, was also a favorite idea of Berg's. His chief imperative to his pupils, according to a report by Helmut Schmidt-Garres, was "to vary." When Schmidt-Garres once submitted a sonata movement to Berg in whose recapitulation a motif was repeated "word for word," he provoked the reproof: "How can you do something like that: consider what your themes and motifs have *lived through* in the meantime!"[257] The remark exemplifies the Schönberg School's critique of the recapitulation in the sonata form, with the implicit postulate that the recapitulation was to be replaced by the "developing variation" in Schönberg's sense.

Illuminating is also the formula "suffering fate" (*Schicksal erleidend*) that Berg uses in his 1926 analysis of the Lyric Suite.[258] The changes in the twelve-tone row in the course of the work, he points out, are inessential in terms of the line, but essential in terms of the characters – "suffering fate." And of the characteristic links between the movements he similarly says that they do not happen "mechanically" but likewise in relation to the large development (intensification of mood) within the piece as a whole" – in short, "suffering fate."[259] Interestingly enough, Berg took over this memorable formulation from a review by Julius Korngold, a critic whom he did not at all esteem.[260]

Berg was fatalistic-minded and by his own admission highly superstitious. Egyptian dream books and tarot cards played a prominent role in his marriage, according to his nephew Erich Alban Berg.[261] He feared unlucky numbers and dates like Friday the 13th – the highest holiday of Black Magic

(ABB 387) – and was fully familiar with the custom of knocking on, or touching, wood. An exaggerated caution often prevented him from talking even to good friends about his compositional projects – evidently he feared that something might intervene to impede the progress of his work. The worry that ideas he deemed good and original might be given away to the competition also prompted him to be cautious. On August 1, 1928, he could not even bring himself to tell Erich Kleiber that he was working on *Lulu*.[262] One month later he confided to his teacher Schönberg that he had composed 300 bars of *Lulu* but argued that this was after all only the beginning of the 3000 and more bars that such an opera would have and fretted: "And what fates might not these plans of mine also suffer in the course of the years of work, despite the most rigorous preparations!"[263]

2.5 Numerology

"He always felt drawn to the mysteries of the world of numbers. One of his ancestors must have been an alchemist who knew the secret formulas and dark mysteries of Black Magic. Curious coincidences, enigmatic relations of numbers in time and space were ever present to his restless mind. They have entered into the incredibly complicated and yet simple and logical figures and proportions of his scores." Hans W. Heinsheimer about Berg[264]

"Numbers mean profound symbols to you, the man of strong feelings; to the mathematician, they are abstractions, lifeless tools." Herbert Fuchs-Robettin to Berg, June 25, 1925[265]

2.5.1 Preliminaries

"In these unconscious mental operations with numbers I detect, moreover, a superstitious inclination, whose origin was long foreign to me." Freud, *Zur Psychopathologie des Alltagslebens*

In the late 19th and early 20th century, numerology experienced a boom, at least in Germany and Austria. In the psychological and psychiatric literature of the turn of the century, it became fashionable to analyze "number notions." Alfred Adler, Ernest Jones, Carl Gustav Jung, Wilhelm Fließ and Sigmund Freud all reported about cases of "obsessing numbers."

For some composers of the *Fin de Siècle*, the concept of "Ninth Symphony" had an ominous overtone. In Mahler, as we learn from his wife,[266] the superstition had taken root that no major symphonist would get beyond the "Ninth," wherefore after his Eighth Symphony he composed *Das Lied von der*

Erde. Of Bruckner, too, it is said that he was reluctant to work on his Ninth Symphony.²⁶⁷ Schönberg meditated about the subject in his Prague speech on Mahler:

> The Ninth, it seems, is a limit. He who aims beyond it has to go. It looks as if a Tenth [Symphony] might tell us something we are not yet to know, for which we are not yet ready. Those who wrote a Ninth were already too close to the Beyond.²⁶⁸

Of all composers who worked in the first third of the 20th century, Berg was probably the one most strongly addicted to numerology. Secret number relations play an important role in both his life and his work. He frequently reflected about lucky and unlucky numbers, discussed them with friends, corresponded about them with Schönberg, and was conversant with all number operations, all methods of adding, subtracting, multiplying and dividing numbers.

Numerology constituted a prominent area of his intellectual world. It is probably less well known that Schönberg, too, had an affinity with number mysticism.

2.5.2 Schönberg's Number: The Ominous 13

> "It is really quite peculiar what a role the number 13 plays in your life. After all, the numbers in your life are directly built upon it. Considering this beautiful order, does the number still have its disastrous character for you? Or should it not perhaps be conceived as the generally determining number, the decisive one, regardless of whether lucky or unlucky."
> Webern to Schönberg, September 16, 1913

Schönberg, according to his biographers Jan Meyerowitz²⁶⁹ and Hans Heinz Stuckenschmidt,²⁷⁰ was extremely superstitious. The number 13 had an ominous quality for him: he feared it, although, or perhaps because, he was born on September 13, 1874. His opera *Moses and Aron* offers the most striking example of his superstition: he wrote the name Aron with one a, because the title would otherwise have thirteen letters.²⁷¹

A series of hitherto unevaluated documents confirms the fact that the fear of the number 13 accompanied him practically his entire life and provides new insights into his frame of mind. Thus, as a letter by Webern of December 30, 1913, indicates, he was full of fears throughout the year 1913. He fared similarly in 1926, that is, thirteen years later. "My state of health is not so bad," he wrote to Webern on May 3 of that year. "But I will be glad when this ominous 1926 year is over. For it is the 52nd year since my birth (4 x 13) and the (2 x 13) 26th since 1900, which was the (2 x 13) 26th since my birth year (1874 + 26 + 26 = 1926). And it started right way with my operation!" 1939, too – the 13th year since 1926 – was a bad year for Schönberg. "I have been ill a lot in the meantime," he wrote to the friend of his youth Dr. Oscar Adler, on August 25."I have always greatly feared this my five times 13th year, and it really turned out very bad. In a few weeks now it will be over, and perhaps I will then be healthier again."[272]

It can be inferred from these passages that he divided his life into periods of 13 years and feared every thirteenth year, thus regarding each of the years 1900, 1913, 1926 and 1939 as critical. Webern's statement quoted above as a motto, which at first seems like a cabbalistic pronouncement, thus turns out to be strikingly logical.

When Schönberg turned 76, Oscar Adler gave him the well-meant advice to beware of every 13th of that year, as the digits of the number 76 added up to 13. Schönberg was particularly terrified of July 13, 1951, which was a Friday, and he actually died on that day.[273]

There are several indications that the ominous 13 also plays a role in Schönberg's music. He certainly ascribed a special significance to every 13th measure of a composition as well as to every multiple of 13. His entries in the autograph of the Violin Concerto op. 36 enable us to realize that the 13th page of a manuscript, too, was significant to him.[274] A closer analysis would surely lead to some revealing results. Some interesting observations were made already in 1913 by Webern. On September 16, he told his teacher the following: the main theme of the String Quartet op. 7, he had discovered, was "just 13 measures long (including the 2/4 bar)." In the score of the *Gurrelieder*, he continued, the vocal part began on page 13. The Chamber Symphony op. 9 had on its 13th page the number 13, and in the String Sextet *Verklärte Nacht* op 4, a theme commenced on p. 13 that to him was "of the greatest significance."

2.5.3   Berg's Number: The Fateful 23

> "The number 23 had a special significance for him. The first asthma attack, an ailment that tormented him all his life, occurred on July 23, 1900. He wrote his most important letters on the 23rd of a month and pointed out that he also regularly received his most important news on such a day. He arranged his work on his compositions in such a way that at least the first draft was completed on a 23rd. During his mortal illness he was constantly aware of the decisive significance of the date. His death-struggle began on December 23, 1935. – He prevailed upon his pupil and biographer Willi Reich, who was publishing a small avantgarde music journal in Vienna, to name the journal *23* and personally drew the cover design, a large 23. In this instance, the 23 took on a new meaning: it was the number of the Austrian press law on the basis of which one could compel a paper to correct any erroneous report it had printed. The music journal *23* would thus combat and rectify what was wrong in the realm of music." Hans W. Heinsheimer on Berg[275]

In conversation as well as in correspondence, Berg stated time and again that the number 23 played a decisive, mysterious role in his life. He regarded it as his fateful number. On June 10, 1915, he told Schönberg of his conscription and the peculiar coincidence of the 23 in his life, calling the number "fatal," whereupon Schönberg admonished him to look at things in a more differentiated way.

> Every human being [he argued] has such a number, so that it does not have to be an unlucky one by any means but is just *one* of the numbers pertinent to that person. In combination with other numbers it no doubt has other and more favorable meanings.

And a few lines later, his teacher gave him the advice: "In any case, you will have to take care to render yourself more independent of your lucky and unlucky numbers by making an effort to earn both!"

This letter of Schönberg's evidently hit a nerve in Berg, as on July 20 he made an effort to clarify and rectify his meaning. In this letter, he expressed once again his conviction that the 23, which had always played a major role in his life, was "unchangeable" and appeared "inescapable" to him, "like the events accompanying it." After having struck a kind of balance of his experiences with the fatal number, he conceded that it did not necessarily have to be an unlucky number only but had also appeared in connection with "strokes of luck." Insofar, he added, he should not have called it "fatal" but merely "portentous." In the same letter he spoke with great enthusiasm about a book by the Berlin scientist Wilhelm Fliess, *Vom Leben und vom Tode*,[276] - a "statistical-scientific book," whose central thesis was that the life and the life segments of all living beings unfolded periodically and resulted in periods that "are always divisible by 28 and 23," with the 28 being the number of women, 23 that of men. This book, which, he said, fell into his hands by accident in the summer of 1914, seemed to confirm his "belief of many years" in the number 23.

The more one delves into Berg's numerological penchant, the more it appears that most of the statements Hans W. Heinsheimer made about this subject are correct. Thus Berg suffered his first asthma attack indeed on July 23, 1900 (i.e., at the age of fifteen, a few months after the death of his father on March 30, 1900), not on July 23, 1908 (at the age of 23), as Willi Reich had it.[277]

Berg's notion that the 23 attended his life's events at every turn amounted to an *idée fixe*. Behind the 23 and its multiples he always sensed mysterious connections. He was interested in addresses with the number 23 and in telegrams and dates including this number. He noted that the hotel room in which he had spent the night of January 27 to 28, 1914, in Prague had borne the number 69 (3 x 23) (ABB 242) and that Schönberg had offered him the intimate *Du* on June 23, 1918 (ABB 359). "Yes, there's a lot in that twenty-third!" he wrote to Helene on June 23, 1921 (ABB 470). Among the happy events in his life he also counted the fact that the frequently postponed premiere of the *Gurrelieder* occurred of all dates on a 23rd (February 23, 1913).[278] It also will most likely not have escaped him that it was the year 1923 that brought about a major turn in his life, as in that year he achieved his first real successes as a composer.

In light of all this, it is surely no accident that several of his compositions were completed on a 23rd. To cite some examples: the score of the *Drei Orchesterstücke* bears the final date "Trahütten, August 23, 1914"; the instrumentation of the Chamber Concerto was finished on July 23, 1925;[279] the first movement of the *Lyric Suite* was completed on October 23, 1925; the composition of the *Wine* aria was finished on July 23, 1929 (one month later the writing out of the score was done); and the particello of the Violin Concerto was completed on July 23, 1935.

Finally we might cite an incident that seems to highlight the significance of the 23 as a fatal number. In December of 1935, Berg, who was suffering from furunculosis, developed general blood-poisoning (sepsis) and had to be taken to the Rudolfspital. Despite a blood transfusion given him on December 19, his condition worsened rapidly by the 22nd, so that the physicians gave him up. According to Willi Reich, Berg on the following morning still calmly noted that it was the 23rd and said: "This will be a decisive day!" On December 24 at 1:15 in the moring, he passed away "in the arms of his wife."[280] By contrast, Erich Alban Berg reports that Anna Lebert and Charley Berg, the sister-in-law and brother of the composer, were the last persons to be with Berg and that, knowing about his fears of the 23rd, they conceived the idea of moving the clock forward so that when the patient became awake once more, the hands already showed twenty minutes past midnight. Consequently, Berg actually died already on December 23. To all appearances, this version is the one closer to the truth.

2.5.4 Berg and Numbers

Numerologists are persuaded that numbers – above all the single-digit ones from 1 to 9 – have an influence on every aspect of life and personality. There are numerous indications that Berg was an initiate in the mysteries of numerology. He was fascinated not only by his "fateful number" 23 but by the world of numbers in general. Naturally he was familiar with the ancient general symbolism of numbers going back to Pythagoras. But not content with that, he searched for secret relations between numbers and frequently endowed the numbers with a private symbolism.

For the 60th birthday of Adolf Loos, on December 10, 1930, he wrote an artful poetic homage, which also provides insight into his relation to numbers.[281] The poem, composed in elegiac distichs, has nine lines and contains two acrostics that imply his close connection to the famous architect: the initial letters of the lines spell the name of Adolf Loos, while the final letters add up to the name Alban Berg. He will have been struck by the identical structure of the two names: both having nine letters and three syllables each, with both given names containing five letters and both surnames four. The poem makes reference to these peculiarities of Loos's name (Berg does not refer to his own): the nine letters seem to him "symbol and simile" of the number of the Nine Muses of Apollo, the god of light. The four letters of the surname suggest a comparison with the life-giving Four Elements, Fire, Water, Air and Earth. The five letters of the given name he compares to the five senses, and in the triad of syllables he intuits something magical: "Or do the syllables work – like the three Graces – magique?" The poem concludes with the lines:

> Repeatable – e'en in jest – were the play of the finite numbers. -
> But all joking aside: endless goes onward your path.²⁸²

What Berg here calls a joke and a "play of numbers" he pursued at times in earnest. As already indicated, he received major impulses for these operations with numbers from Wilhelm Fliess's *Vom Leben und vom Tod* – a book he had come across in the summer of 1914.²⁸³ Fliess's theories had impressed him deeply. He evidently learned from the book that even significant complex numbers could be reduced to important basic ones, and he was stunned by Fliess's "proof" that the two numbers 28 and 23 not only determined the life of plants, animals and individual human beings but also applied to birth and death dates, life periods, or phases of sickness of entire families, entire generations, even entire nations.

We have several documents for Berg's downright idolatrous veneration of Schönberg. One of the most touching is the letter in which he congratulated Schönberg, on September 13, 1926, on his fifty-second birthday. "On this hand-made paper," he wrote to Schönberg, "I should have congratulated Shaw on his 70ᵗʰ birthday." If he did not do so and instead sent his best to Schönberg, he hoped this substitution would not be held against him, all the less so as the number 52 was somehow linked to the 70:

$(5 + 2 = 7)$

$(10 \times 7 = 70)$

$(5 \times 2 = 10)$

In this "word and number jest" Schönberg should read that "all the 50-, 100- and 1000-year celebrations of all living and dead poets and men of letters did not concern him as much" as any one of Schönberg's, "without whose birth I, too, or at least the part of me that was worth being born, would not have come into the world" [!].

Berg took special pleasure in finding secret number relations not only in names but also in addresses and telephone numbers. In an especially instructive example, Schönberg, on April 4, 1928, sent him his new Berlin address: "Charlottenburg 9, Nussbaum-Allee 17, telephone Westend 2266." Berg initially seems not to have recognized the "numerological" dimension of the address, which is reducible to Schönberg's number 13. Only much later, in a letter to Schönberg of July 22, 1930, he came to gloss it with the following commentary: "Charottenburg 9 and Nussbaum-Allee 17: 9 + 17 = 26, Nussbaum-Allee has 13 letters, not to mention the telephone number 2266! There I much prefer 4466, which contains my number (23)!"

Along with the verse homage to Adolf Loos, this passage makes impressively clear that Berg extracted significant numbers also from the sums of letters in names and addresses. Thus it can be explained why in the famous annotated copy of the *Lyric Suite* he cites 10 as the number of his beloved Hanna.[284] The name Hanna Fuchs contains ten letters. Besides, Hanna was born on July 10, 1894. It also makes clear why the 5 is given as a basic number in the sketches to the *Lyric Suite*, the name "Hanna" being composed of five letters.

In this context, one should ask about Helene's number. Judging from all we know about Berg's "numbers mania," it may be regarded as certain that Helene, too, had her own number, or that Berg had supplied her with one. Regrettably we have not found any indication of that in any document. Might the ten have been Helene's number as well? It is at least conceivable, as the name Helene Berg has exactly ten letters.

As several past studies have shown, numbers play a fundamental role also in Berg's musical creations.[285] The composer frequently worked like a medieval cathedral architect, who calculates every detail and leaves nothing to chance. Not without self-irony, he spoke of his "reputation as a mathematician."[286] Thus the number 23 proves to be a major factor in many of his works. The construction plan of the Chamber Concerto is based on the three and the five. The 23 and the 10 dictate the tectonics and agogic of the movements of the *Lyric Suite*. And strikingly, the construction plan of the Bible scene in *Wozzeck* is based on the holy number seven. The more one delves into Berg's works, the more hidden symbolic number relations become evident. More about that in part three of this book.

2.6 Tone Ciphers

> "[Twelve-tone composition], my Hanna, has also yielded me some other liberties! E.g., that of again and again secreting our letters H, F and A, B into this music; setting every movement in relation to our numbers 10 and 23." Berg in the annotated copy of the *Lyric Suite*

> "He pursued the affair with an endless amount of secret-mongering, ostensibly so that his wife would not catch on, but in verity probably because he enjoyed the secretiveness itself." Adorno about Berg[287]

In addition to his penchant for numbers and number combinations, Berg had a special predilection for tone ciphers and hieroglyphs. Like virtually no other composer of the 20th century, he semanticized his music by means of tone anagrams and cryptograms. He took great pleasure in musically symbolizing names by means of tonal letters. Nearly every single person who played a special role in his life is represented by anagrams and cryptograms in his music: Arnold Schönberg (a-d-es-c-h-b-e-g), Anton Webern (a-e-b-e), Mathilde Schönberg (a-h-d-e), Helene (h) and Hanna Fuchs (h-f) – with es being the German notation for e-flat, h for b and b for b-flat. His own musical anagram is a-b (Alban) or else a-b-a-b-e-g (Alban Berg).

The anagrammatic technique has a long tradition in German music, going back to Johann Sebastian Bach. Bach, we remember, eternalized his name in the last, unfinished fugue of the *Kunst der Fuge* by a theme that begins with the notes b-a-c-h.[288] That b-a-c-h motif became history and exerted an extraordinary fascination on posterity: the number of works that incorporate or use it is a large one. I shall mention only works by Schumann (Six Fugues, op. 60), Liszt (*Prelude and Fugue*), Reger (*Fantasy and Fugue* op. 46) and Schönberg, whose Variations for Orchestra op. 31 were completed in September of 1928. All these works want to be understood in one way or another as homages to the great cantor of St. Thomas and the spirit of his incomparable polyphonic art.

The maxim "art as autobiography" applies to a large part also of Schumann's instrumental music. Like Berg, Schumann had a penchant for the mysterious and esoteric and a predilection for encryption through anagrams. Of all the composers of the nineteenth century, he used the anagrammatic technique most frequently and developed it most fully. He particularly liked working with anagrams derived from names or other words. His very first work, the Piano Variations on the name Abegg op. 1, is indebted to that technique. But the technique attains its fullest mastery in the *Carnival* op. 9 of 1834/35, a sequence of *Scenes mignonnes sur quatre notes*, as the subtitle has it. Those four notes appear here as three "sphinxes" in three different constellations:

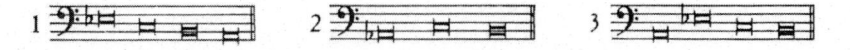

In a letter to Henriette Voigt of September 13, 1834, Schumann unveiled the secret of these "sphinxes," telling her that Asch, the hometown of his secret fiancée Ernestine von Fricken, was "a very musical place name," whose four letters were also contained in his own name and were "the only musical ones" in it (i.e., a-es-c-h).[289] Asch is thus the town whence Ernestine hailed and at the same time a cipher for Schumann himself. Such discovery of recondite connections is especially characteristic of Schumann, as it is of Berg.

In looking closely at the way Schumann works the four notes in *Carnival*, one is reminded of the later serial technique. By varying the order and rhythm of the four or else three notes – in the "sphinx" no. 2 the first two letters of the name Asch are represented by the single note *as* (a-flat) – he obtains different beginnings of the pieces and numerous characteristic turns to boot.

As in *Carnival*, so in Schumann's later works, tone anagrams have not only a constructive but a poetic-esoteric function. Thus the "Nordic Song" from the *Album für die Jugend* of 1848 op. 68 is an homage to the Danish composer Nils Gade, in which the g-a-d-e motif is literally a cornerstone of the piece, being not only harmonized in different ways but also transposed to the fifth degree. In the late violin sonata, Schumann similarly treats the anagram FAE, which stands for the motto *frei aber einsam*, "free but alone."[290]

The more one delves into Schumann's music and way of thinking, the clearer it becomes how much he "encoded" in his works. Many of his compositions contain cryptograms waiting to be deciphered. For example, it seems to have remained hitherto undetected that the head and main motif of the Piano Concerto, the familiar C-h[b]-a-a motif, is a cryptogram for Chiara, i.e., the adored Clara Wieck, for whom Schumann wrote the famous "Schwärmbriefe" (rave letters):[291]

Berg devoted an analysis both detailed and insightful to Schumann's famous *Träumerei*.[292] He greatly valued the *Kinderszenen* and generally seems to have had an affinity with Schumann. Very likely he received major impulses from the latter's anagrammatic technique. In any case, one cannot but be struck by the close similarity between the Abegg motif from Schuman's Piano Variations op. 1:

and Berg's own anagram in the Chamber Concerto of 1923-1925

[musical example: A B A B E G / Alban Berg, mit Dpf., p]

And one may note that Schumann's motif, like Berg's, appears also in retrograde motion:

[musical example, mf]

and that at one time (in the finale) it is treated in serial fashion:

[musical example, ad libitum]

Incidentally, the first "sphinx" in the *Carnival*

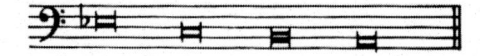

[musical example]

seems like a germ of Berg's Schönberg anagram in the Chamber Concerto:

[musical example: A D / Arnold — S C H B E G / Schönberg — verklingen lassen]

Especially illuminating for the autobiographic and poetic aspect of Berg's art is the manner in which he relates the various tone anagrams to each other. In the *Lyric Suite*, for example, the notes signifying the initials AB and HF, stan-

91

ding for Alban Berg and Hanna Fuchs, move together already in the *Andante amoroso* and then enter into a mystic union in the *Allegro misterioso*, at whose start we hear three four-note motifs (in the German letter notation):

b-a-f-h, a-b-h-f and a-b-f-h

Berg had tried out that kind of symbolism already much earlier – in the years 1908-1910, when his love for Helene had reached a boiling-point. At that time he took special pleasure in linking his name with hers. If in 1908 he had signed a letter with the mere note anagram

(=Alban) (ABB 59), on September 5/6, 1909, he signed another letter "Helenealban" (ABB 139), and on September 3, 1910, he drew two linked hearts in lieu of a signature as a symbol of their mystic union.

From this time also date the Four Lieder op. 2 after poems by Hebbel and Mombert.[293] At least the second of the Mombert songs has a strong autobiographic connotation: the background against which it is to be viewed is Berg's love for Helene. The poem reads:

> Nun ich der Riesen Stärksten überwand,
> (Now that I felled the strongest giant,)
> mich aus dem dunkelsten Land heimfand,
> (found home from out the darkest land,)
> an einer weißen Märchenhand,
> (led on by a white fairy hand,)
> hallen schwer die Glocken;
> (bells are tolling heavy;)
> Und ich wanke durch die Gassen schlafbefangen.
> (And I stagger through the streets beset by sleep.)

Berg alluded to just this poem and this song when he wrote to Helene in the fall of 1910 (ABB 210): "I yearn for your voice – – – for your beauty – – – for your while fairy hand – – for your deep nature – – – – – come, beloved!"

Adorno remarked about this song that it contained "the earliest model of that letter symbolism Berg clung to so superstitiously. The words 'an einer weißen Märchenhand' are accompanied by the notes a b h – as the initials of the names Alban/Berg/Helene." Building on this remark, one should note that the notes in question in fact signify Alban/Helene and that just before this passage (in mm. 5/6) the voice intones the descending fifth h-e to the word "heimfand" – clearly the full anagram for Helene. From this phrase, Berg then also developed the bell motifs in the right hand of the piano accompaniment (mm. 6-8).

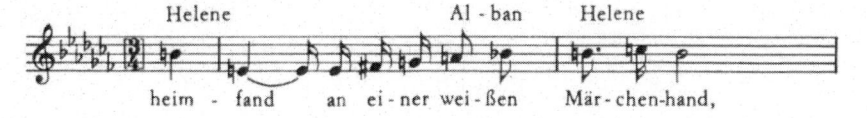

```
        Helene              Al - ban    Helene
    heim - fand   an ei-ner wei-ßen   Mär-chen-hand,
```

It is to be noted that such anagrams functioning as tonal ciphers are found also in Schönberg's work.[294] However, the anagram technique to all appearances is of much greater significance in Berg's oeuvre than in Schönberg's, so that Adorno appears to be right in this connection, too, in saying that Adrian Leverkühn's music in Thomas Mann's Doctor Faustus was more Bergian than Schönbergian.[295] In any case that is true of the tone cipher h-e-a-e-es used by Leverkühn in his 13 songs on Brentano texts, which is nothing other than an abbreviation of the fatal Hetaera Esmeralda.[296]

2.7 Magic Music

> "Music is a demonic region [...] It is Christian art with a minus sign. It is at once the most calculated order and chaos-pregnant anti-reason, rich in conjurational, incantational gestures, numbers magic, of all the arts the most remote from reality and at the same time the most passionate, abstract and mystical." Thomas Mann, *Deutschland und die Deutschen*[297]

2.7.1 *Doctor Faustus* as Point of Departure

When Thomas Mann wrote the above sentences in May of 1945 for a lecture he would give in Washington, he had been working on his *Doctor Faustus* for two years. Key ideas from the novel were incorporated in the lecture. One of the novel's central themes is the relation of music to magic. Mann transforms Faustus, the 16th-century magician, into a modern artist, specifically a musician, the German composer Adrian Leverkühn, who sells his soul to the Devil for the sake of inspiration.[298] Music – especially twelve-tone music – is a demonic art for Mann, with an affinity to magic, sorcery, the arcane, astrology and numbers symbolism. In a letter to Agnes E. Meyer, he went so far as to call the serial technique a "piece of devilry."[299]

The notion of music as a conjuring, "bewitching" art was widely held already by the ancient advanced civilizations.[300] Mann's reference to music as an art rich in "conjurational, incantational gestures" alludes to that tradition. This is also the Devil's view in the novel when he says that Leverkühn had put the

Bible under the bench and henceforth had made common cause "with the figuris, characteribus and incantationibus of music."[301] Mann, in fact, as Margarethe Puschmann has cogently shown,[302] saw the essence of music specifically in its modulatory techniques, in enharmonic change, in the principle of variation and in the mirror effects of the serial technique, which he paralleled to the Magic Square.

To illustrate: Adrian explains the principle of modulation with the aid of an unusual example, not, say, the turn from C major to F major, but one from F-sharp major to B major. In doing so, Mann writes, he chose "nothing but black keys," thereby moving the circle of fifths − the "compass card of keys" − into the region of black art. He demonstrates that one can "erect a major and a minor scale on each of the twelve tones of the chromatic scale." It is surely no mere coincidence that the twelve major and twelve minor keys together add up to twenty-four, the number of years apportioned to the Doctor Faustus of the Volksbuch after the conclusion of the pact with the Devil and to Adrian Leverkühn after his visit to the hetaera Esmeralda. Adrian was in fact familiar with enharmonic change already as a young man and postulated that music was systematized ambiguity.[303]

Most importantly, however: above his pianino, a magic square is attached, a square of sixteen cells, whose numbers, read in vertical or horizontal columns, always yield the sum of 34 − a number fraught with meaning. The square in question is the Seal of Jupiter, the so-called tabula Jovis, which was regarded as a remedy against melancholy and was also worn as a talisman.[304] In Albrecht Dürer's famous copper engraving Melencolia, it is depicted above the figure of Melancholy. Puschmann made it look probable that Mann regarded this magic square as a symbol of twelve-tone music and serial technique. The question is whether Mann's analogies between twelve-tone music and magic are merely the clever tricks of an ingenious writer or are rooted in music-historical fact. As one looks more closely at Schönberg's, Webern's and Berg's conceptions of the theoretical preconditions of dodecaphonic music, it becomes clear that they were likewise indebted to magical thinking, confirming once again the observation that Mann was very well informed.

2.7.2 Mirror Magic

> "The mirror is our schoolmaster." Leonardo da Vinci

The question as to the relation of time and space in music − a fundamental question of music theory − has intrigued a number of 20th-century composers. Already during his years of teaching at the Prussian Academy of the Arts in Berlin (1925-1933), Schönberg gave thoughts to the subject, which he confided to his assistant Josef Rufer. The following statement considers the time-space relation once from the standpoint of the composer and once from that of the listener.

> Music is an art that unfolds in time. But the conception (= vision = perception = inner listening) of the work of art by the composer is independent of it: time is seen as space. In the act of writing, space is folded over into time. The process is the reverse for the listener. Only after the temporal lapse of the work can he see it as a whole, its idea, its form, its content.[305]

In his frequently cited essay *Composition with Twelve Tones*, a sensational lecture he gave in Los Angeles on March 26, 1941, Schönberg touched on the problem of time more in passing, concentrating instead on that of musical space, which he conceived as a unity. The "law" laid down by him (in small capitals) states: "THE TWO+OR-MORE-DIMENSIONAL SPACE IN WHICH MUSICAL IDEAS ARE PRESENTED IS A UNITY" (S&I, 220/GS I, 77). And he postulates further:

> The unity of musical space demands an absolute and unitary perception. In this space, as in Swedenborg's heaven (described in Balzac's *Seraphita*) there is no absolute down, no right or left, forward or backward. Every musical configuration, every movement of tones has to be comprehended primarily as a mutual relation of sounds, of oscillatory vibrations, appearing at different places and times (S&I, 223/GS I, 79).

The notion that in musical space there was no absolute down, "no right or left," must seem willful and strange if one considers that musical space as generally understood presupposes the differentiation between low, middle and high registers. Schönberg's statements make sense only when one considers that they refer to serial technique, the treatment of the "prime series" and its "mirror forms" (retrograde, inversion and retrograde inversion).

To illustrate, Schönberg uses a diagram (see below) that depicts an image together with its mirror image. In addition, he reproduces the prime row of his Quintet for Winds op. 26 together with its "mirror forms," remarking that the use of these mirror forms corresponded to the principle of the "absolute and unitary perception of musical space" (S&I, 225/GS I, 81).

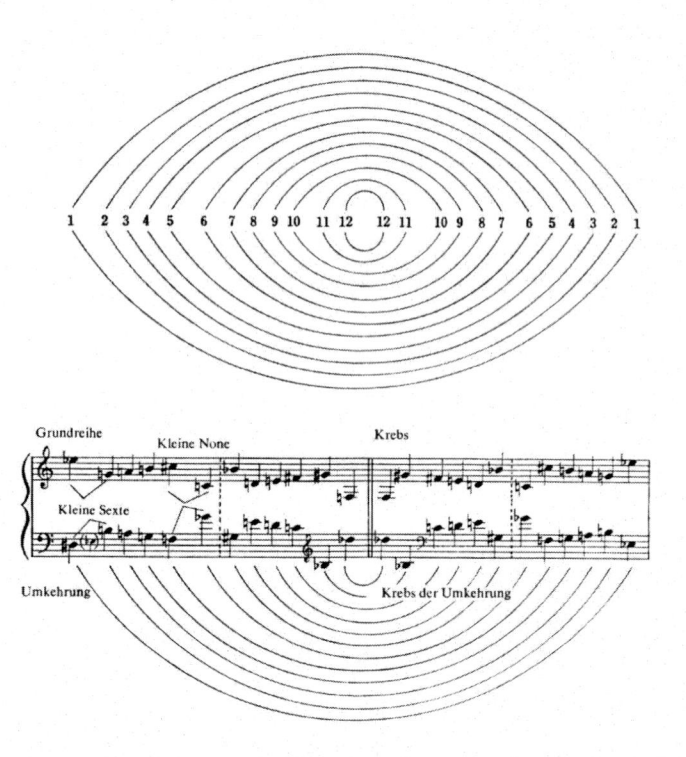

The mirror metaphor serves as the key for a deeper understanding of the relations and connections.

> To the imaginative and creative faculty [Schönberg explains elsewhere], relations in the material sphere are as independent from directions or planes as material objects are, in their sphere, to our perceptive faculties. Just as our mind always recognizes, for instance, a knife, a bottle or a watch, regardless of its position and can reproduce it in the imagination in every possible position, even so a musical creator's mind can operate subconsciously with a row of tones, regardless of their direction, regardless of the way in which *a mirror* might show the mutual relations, which remain a given quality (S&I, 223; GS I, 79 has "Quantität").

More drastically, Schönberg had years earlier explained the nature of the mirror forms of the prime row in a lecture by taking a hat, turning it to all sides and saying: "See, this is a hat, whether I look at it from above, from below, from the front, from the back, from the left, from the right, it is a hat once and for all, even though it looks different from above than from below."[306]

Gustav René Hocke has drawn attention to the fact that at the beginning of modern times, the mirror becomes a symbol of the problems of the "modern" mind.[307] Mirror metaphors were favorites not only with the Mannerists of the 16th and 17th century, but also in the Expressionist and Surrealist art of the 20th. The special fascination that mirror reflections had for Schönberg and his pupils can explain in part their interest in symmetrically constructed twelve-tone rows. In several instances, Schönberg divided his rows into two halves of six notes each (hexachords) and designed them in such a way that the second (*Nachsatz*) presents a mirror form (retrograde, inversion or retrograde inversion) of the first (*Vordersatz*). To put it even more concretely: several series are arranged in such a way that if one transposes the first hexachord to the lower fifth degree, the second supplies all the remaining notes. Here are several examples.

In the row of the Fantasy for Violin op. 47, the second phrase is simply the inversion of the first phrase a fifth lower:[308]

$$b^b - a - c^\# - b - f - g \mid e^b - e - c - d - a^b - g^b$$

The series of the Quintet for Winds op. 26 is structured similarly, except that here the correspondence between first and second hexachord extends only to the first *five* notes:

$$e^b - g - a - b - c^\# - c \mid b^b - d - e - f^\# - g^\# - f$$

In the series of the *Ode to Napoleon* op 41

$$c^\# - c - e - f - a - g^\# \mid e^b - d - f^\# - g - b - b^b$$

the second phrase is simply a transposition of the first. Additionally, the first phrase itself is also symmetrically designed, in that the second group of three notes constitutes a retrograde inversion of the first.[309] In the last of his Vienna lectures on twelve-tone music, Webern revealed that his symphony op. 21 of 1928 was based on a mirror-symmetrical row:

$$f - a^b - g - f^\# - b^b - a \mid e^b - e - c - c^\# - d - b$$

A peculiarity of the row, he added, was that the second half was merely the retrograde ("crab") of the first, making for an "especially intimate connection."[310]

We might add that the all-interval series invented by Fritz Heinrich Klein, on which the *Lyric Suite* is based, is likewise symmetric in structure:

$$f - e - c - a - g - d \mid a^b - d^b - e^b - g^b - b^b - c^b$$

As Berg wrote to Schönberg on July 13, 1926, the second phrase of the series is "the mirror image, lower by a diminished fifth, of the first half."[311]

97

2.7.3 Magic Squares

According to ancient tradition, magic is closely related to astrology. The Middle Ages coordinated each of the seven planets then known with a magic square having particular properties.[312]

As a rule, such squares consist of nine, sixteen or twenty-five squares containing letters or numbers that, read vertically or horizontally, forward or backward, always yield the same words or sums of numbers.

There are indications that at least Schönberg and Webern were fascinated by magic squares. In them they saw parallels to certain compositional procedures, especially to dodecaphonism.

Thus Schönberg, as Josef Rufer tells us,[313] compared the correspondence between simultaneity and successiveness — that is, the relation of the vertical and the horizontal in composition — to the principle of the magic square.

Webern, on the other hand, was greatly interested in the old Latin saying *Sator opera tenet*, a magic square that was used as a protective magic against fire and calamity and was also venerated as a cosmic formula. In a letter to Hildegard Jone of March 11, 1931, he quotes and explicates the square:[314]

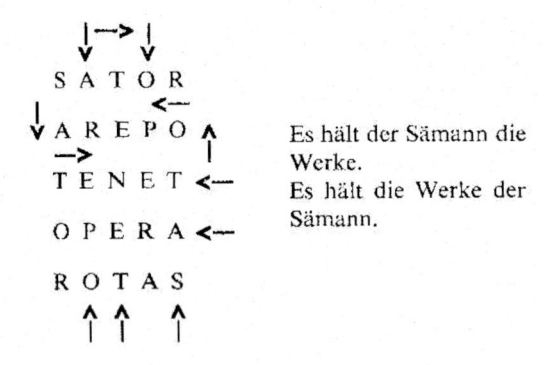

```
   | -> |
   v    v
  S A T O R
  |    <--
  v A R E P O ^
   -->       |
    T E N E T <--

    O P E R A <--

    R O T A S
    ^ ^   ^
    | |   |
```

Es hält der Sämann die Werke.
Es hält die Werke der Sämann.

The arrows indicate that the square is to be read in zig-zag, that is, as a boustrophedon.

Followed horizontally, the text reads:

Sator opera tenet

Tenet opera sator

Webern translates this as: "The sower holds the works. The works holds the sower" and adds that the square can also be read vertically: "from the top down; up; down; up (i.e., tenet twice), down; up. Then again vertically, starting at bottom right: up, down, etc."[315]

The sator square appears to have inspired the dodecaphonic series for Webern's concerto op. 24 of 1931-1934, as the sketches to this work document.

The series divides into four groups of three notes each, of which the last three represent diverse mirrorings of the first:

As one can see, each triad of notes consists of a descending or ascending minor second and an ascending or falling major third.

Incidentally, Schönberg seems to have taken special pleasure in conceiving musical magic squares. By that he meant dodecaphonic series formed in such a way that no octaves result when the row, its retrograde, the inversion a fifth higher and its retrograde are played note against note.

On July 5, 1924, he jotted down the following magic square:[316]

2.8 Symmetry and Palindrome

> "The visual, however, also extended into the compositional proper. He planned more and more according to quasi spatial, symmetric relations. His penchant for mirror- and crab-like formations, too, was probably connected, apart from the twelve-tone technique, to the visual dimension of his responses; musical retrogrades are anti-temporal, they determine music as if it were intrinsically simultaneous." Adorno about Berg[317]

Inversion and retrograde (palindrome) are known to be fundamental techniques in twelve-tone composition. Their application is explainable not least by the fascination the magic of the mirror and the magic square exerted on Schönberg and his pupils. Symmetry and palindrome importantly determined not only the structure of the dodecaphonic rows but also that of entire sections and movements. Berg especially had a soft spot for symmetric structures and retrogrades. The questions we will pursue in what follows are from which artists he received important impulses, and what meanings these techniques had for him.

2.8.1 The Idea of the Retrograde in Schönberg

The palindrome is a musical as well as a literary procedure. Literary palindromes, as the magic squares prove, were known already in antiquity. Musical palindromes we first meet in the Notre-Dame period (1180–1250). Schönberg, Berg and Webern were familiar with examples from the musical history of the palindrome. To all appearances, however, they received major impulses also from literary tradition.

A very instructive example of a mirror-symmetric structure in literature is exhibited by August Strindberg's drama of 1898, *To Damascus I*. The seventeen scenes of which it consists constitute seventeen stations – as modeled on the medieval mystery play – which the "Unknown," the protagonist of the play, has to pass. As the literary critic Fritz Paul has pointed out, Strindberg composed the 17 scenes in the form of "a symmetric crab [retrograde] fugue," in that scenes 10–`17 correspond palindromically to scenes 8–1.[318] The ninth scene ("The Asylum") forms not only the formal pivot of the pyramid of stations but also the climax of the inner transformation undergone by the "Unknown." In a letter to Gustav of Geijerstam of March 17, 1898, Strindberg explains the structure of the drama as follows: "The art consists in the composition, which symbolizes the recurrence of which Kierkegaard speaks; the action unrolls up to the Asylum; there it reaches its climax and then reverts again [...]."[319]

To Damascus I did not appear in German translation until 1912. Schönberg, Berg and Webern were eager to get to know the already famous play. Apparently Webern was the first of the three to read it. On September 17, 1912, he wrote to Schönberg: "I have finished reading *To Damascus*. It is something terrifying. It is 'as things really are.' The highest reality, nothing but spectres. I am very anxious to learn what you have to say about it. After all, you promised me to write about it." Evidently all three men were greatly impressed by the play, by its form as well as by its content.

It has been repeatedly observed in Schönberg research that his drama of 1910-1913, *Die glückliche Hand* op. 18, is based on a quasi symmetric design, a deliberately cyclical conception. John C. Crawford, probably the first to draw attention to this fact, thought he could establish a connection between it and the first part of Strindberg's *To Damascus*: Schönberg's libretto, like Strindberg's drama, was divided into "stations" exhibiting a mirror-symmetric construction.[320] Michael Mäckelmann, however, has demonstrated that the similarity had to be accidental, since Schönberg's libretto draft bears the date "late July, 1910."[321]

On the other hand, we can regard it as certain that Strindberg's idea of the palindrome influenced the conception of Schönberg's oratorio *The Jacob's Ladder* of 1915–1917. The text of the oratorio is divided into two parts nearly equal in length, which are arranged mirror-symmetrically and are linked by a grand symphonic interlude. In the first part, souls rise from earth to the light, in the second they descend again to earth, in order to take on a new body as ordered by the Archangel Gabriel. Thus the action unfolds in the interval between death and new birth.

It is symptomatic of the palindromic design of the work that some figures from the first part also recur in the second, although with a different designation and in retrograde order. Schönberg himself referred to these correspondences in the notes to his textbook:[322]

Part 1	Part 2
The Called (p. 42)	~ A third voice (p. 52)
The Rebellious (p. 43)	~ A fourth voice (p. 52)
The Striving (p. 44)	~ Another voice (p. 52)
The Dying (p. 48)	~ A voice (p. 51)

Berg had carefully read and closely studied the libretto of the *Jakobsleiter*. The numerous marginal notes in his personal copy, too, lead us to conclude that the quasi mirror-symmetrical design of the oratorio served him as a model for conceiving the libretto to his *Lulu*: the two parts into which the opera is divided depict the rise and the fall of Lulu, and an orchestral interlude, the famous *Ostinato*, functions as a bridge between the two parts.

It hardly needs emphasizing that the retrograde construction in many of Schönberg's, Berg's and Webern's compositions has a greater relevance than literary palindromes can have. *Der Mondfleck* (The Moon Stain), the 18th of the *Pierrot* melodramas of op. 21, is probably Schönberg's earliest musical palindrome and at the same time the most rigorously constructed one.[323] Of its two parts of equal length, the second, disregarding the piano part, is, note for note, an exact crab of the first. The strictly polyphonic piece is, moreover, constructed in the most complex manner: accompanying a rigorously built double canon performed by two winds (piccolo and b-flat clarinet) and two strings (violin and cello), the piano plays an equally rigorous fugue, which does not share the palindromic structure. An additional artful trait is that the main voice of the piano fugue imitates the succession of notes of the clarinet voice but does so in a freely augmented rhythm.

According to Theodor W. Adorno, the lunatic determination of every note in the *Mondfleck* serves a "poetic intention": it "symbolizes the inescapable circling, whose emblem is the Pierrot, who keeps vainly rubbing on a white spot of moonlight on his black coat "until the early morning."[324]

The *Pierrot* melodramas of op. 21 are among the works of Schönberg that Berg studied most closely. In his personal copy of the score (U. E. 5336, © 1914 by Universal Edition), he noted that the *Moon Spot* had a "crab form" and divided into two parts of 9 ½ measures.

2.8.2 Parallelisms and Mirror-Symmetric Structures in Berg

In the summer of 1924, Berg was preparing the publication of a festschrift for Schönberg's fiftieth birthday. On August 18, he conveyed his thoughts about the sequence of the essays to be included to Webern and suggested a weighting and evaluation of the contributions as the criterion for their order. He had in mind the manner in which Karl Kraus arranged the individual numbers of *Die Fackel*, that is, in "a kind of symmetry" following the schema of poem, glosses, main article, glosses, poem, or else first main article, glosses, notes, glosses, second main article. "Accordingly," he wrote, "one could even put Schönberg's own article in the center." The passage suggests that Kraus's mirror-symmetric ordering of the contributions to the *Fackel*, a journal Berg read regularly, not only impressed but also inspired him.

Berg took special pleasure in ferreting out parallel situations in history, in life and in works of art. An instructive text in this regard is, to begin with, his essay with the confessional title "Credo," published in 1930 in the noted journal *Die Musik*. Convinced as he was that the achievement of his revered teacher Schönberg was comparable only to that of Johann Sebastian Bach, he quoted Hugo Riemann's appreciation of Bach and held that, apart from a few modifications rooted in the nature of the thing, it applied almost word for word to Schönberg.[325]

In another, equally illuminating case, Schönberg, in the summer of 1921, had taken his family, along with a few of his pupils, on vacation to Mattsee, a vacation spot in the province of Salzburg, unaware "that this town had been notorious for a long time for its anti-Semitic attitude."[326] When an "Arian" tourist gave him to understand that his presence was undesirable, Schönberg indignantly quit the town. This incident, which was of major consequences for Schönberg's national and religious self-image,[327] shocked Berg deeply and impelled him to think about the following "parallelism" in Schönberg's life:

Summer 1911	Summer 1921
Schönberg in Ober-St. Veit	Intensive work on the
Intensive work on the *Harmonielehre*	*Harmonielehre*, 2nd edition
(commenced during a violent toothache)	(after 14 days of tooth ache, Schönberg had to have a tooth pulled in Salzburg)
Threatened by the mad engineer	Threatened by National Socialism
Polnauer resides with Schönberg	Polnauer said to have recently gone to
Flight (to Bavaria)	Mattsee. Flight to Mödling?

"That can't be a mere coincidence! – I still hope that it will not come to that final correspondence," he wrote to Helene on June 29, 1921 (ABB 474).

Berg had a nose for parallel situations in the operas he composed. In his 1929 lecture on *Wozzeck* in Oldenburg, he had spoken of the subject more or less in passing, saying that there were notable analogies ("parallelisms") between the final scenes of the two acts. The concluding scene of Act One depicted Marie's seduction by the drum-major; the subject of the final scene of Act

Two was the clash between the jealous Wozzeck and the drum-major – a collision ending with the defeat of Wozzeck. This constellation of events led Berg to the following inference: "The wrestling-match between the two in this scene is musically no different from the one in the previous final scene between Marie and the drum-major, which ends with her rape." Berg indeed used the same music to accompany the two segments depicting the wrestling, with I.5, mm. 693-696, corresponding to II.5, mm. 789-792. Instructive is also his remark that while the rondo form in the *Andante affettuoso* of the seduction scene was merely hinted at, the concluding piece of Act Two was actually "a rondo constructed strictly on the basis of the theory of musical form," specifically a *rondo martiale*.[328]

More frequently than in *Wozzeck*, parallel situations occur in *Lulu*, and Berg utilized them all for a corresponding musical construction. *Lulu* is without doubt one of the richest works in terms of leitmotivic relations. The tracking down of the numerous interconnections is suspenseful and astounding, as we will see in a later section.

Let us now turn to the palindromic (mirror-symmetric) structures. Berg evidently had a much greater predilection, not so say weakness, for them than Schönberg or Webern. Beginning with the *Pieces for Orchestra* op. 6, there is hardly one work in which they are not present.

In literary criticism,[329] the palindrome is defined as a succession of morphemes or words that, read forward or backward, yield the same sense or any sense at all.[330] Palindromic musical structures generally divide into two sections of equal or nearly equal length. The first can be seen as a development toward a certain goal, while the second section retraces the same path in "crab motion" back to the beginning – whether note for note or with modifications.

Lulu offers a prime example of a palindromic design in Berg. The famous orchestral interlude at the beginning of the second act – the much-admired *Ostinato* – divides the opera into two halves and bridges the gap between the final act of *Erdgeist* and the first act of *Büchse der Pandora*. The scenes up to the Ostinato – as Berg explained in a letter to Schönberg – depict the fabulous rise of Lulu, the scenes after the Ostinato her deplorable fall. But it is exactly in the middle of the Ostinato that the *Umkehr* (reversal), to use Berg's own term, begins.[331] Both the prologue and the sextet in *Lulu*, incidentally, are likewise palindromic in design.

How is one to explain Berg's conspicuous predilection for palindromic structures? One reason was the desire for a formal rounding-off and unification. Another, no less weighty one, was the intention of returning, after many complications, to the original situation. In the Oldenburg lecture, Berg spoke in just these terms about the very first scene in *Wozzeck*.

> The rounding off and unity of the suite is obtained, inter alia, by the fact that the little introductory prelude recurs refrain-like at the end of the scene, but in crab motion, that is, note for note retrograde, thus doing justice also musically to the dramatic proceedings of the scene, whose content returns to its starting point.

It is my contention that many of Berg's palindromic structures conceal semantic considerations and intentions, even if Berg wrapped himself in silence about them. A case in point is the palindromic Adagio of the Chamber Concerto. In the piano sketch of the Adagio, he referred to the music of the movement as *midpoint* and *turning-point* and remarked that that had to add up to a *picture*. Berg commented more explicitly, and clearly programmatically, on the third movement of the *Lyric Suite*. In the copy of the score meant for Hanna Fuchs, he elucidated the *Allegro misterioso* with the addition: "for as yet all was secret – secret even to ourselves." He also intimated that the *Trio estatico*, the middle part of the movement, expressed the passionate, though still restrained, confession of love. But then he interpreted the palindromic third part of the movement as a retraction: "Forget it – – –!" In a letter to Schönberg of February 16, 1932, he similarly explained the palindromic structure of the core section of the concert aria *Der Wein*: the retrograde second part of the rather ecstatic song "The Wine of Lovers" led back to the largely desolate mood of the third song, "The Wine of the Solitary," which functioned as a foreshortened and greatly varied recapitulation of the first song.

Additional examples of palindromic structures or predispositions in Berg can be found in the *Prelude* to the *Pieces for Orchestra* op. 6, the *Largo desolato* of the *Lyric Suite* and the *Andante* of the Violin Concerto. Even in the early Hebbel song *Schlafen, Schlafen* (Sleep, Sleep) op. 2 no. 1, the tendency toward formal rounding-off and unifying is already fully formed.

If one seeks to interpret such retrograde structures as a mark of the time, one can bring to bear historical, technical, music-theoretical, generally philosophical, as well as psychological points of view. Hans Ferdinand Redlich saw in them "a phenomenon of the cinematographic age" and compared it to the concept of the technically possible "play-back" fostered by film and radio. But he also argued psychologically, noting that the era of Berg suffered "like no other from fear of the evanescence and unrepeatability of time" – that it was uniquely characterized by fear of the inescapable fact of the *vita fugax*.³³² Twenty years earlier, Ernst Krenek had argued music-philosophically, saying that the idea of the retrograde expressed an "opposition to the lapse of time," that it constituted a characteristic content element of the New Music: "its relation to infinity, its eschatological coloring, its pathos-laden dialectic resulting from the solitary struggle of the individual against the irretrievable evanishment of onrushing time into nothingness."³³³

Berg's own statements about the reason for the retrograde in several of his works help us to recognize his belief that certain developments necessitated a reversal at some decisive point. He seems to have been guided by the more neutral conviction that despite protracted developments, things often took a course that paradoxically led back to the initial, that is, the original situation.

2.9 Tonality, Atonality and Dodecaphony: Transvaluation of All Values

2.9.1 The Atonal Cosmos as Counter-Universe

> "Around 1911, I wrote the *Bagatelles for String Quartet* (op. 9), nothing but short pieces taking two minutes each; perhaps the shortest that has hitherto existed in music. In doing it, I had the feeling: once the twelve tones have run their course, the piece is over." Anton Webern³³⁴

> "Nowhere in nature is there any indication that it would be desirable to play a certain number of notes in a prescribed space of time and within a certain pitch horizon." Paul Hindemith³³⁵

When, in composing the *Entrückung* (Rapture), the finale of his second string quartet op. 10, Schönberg, in 1908, stepped beyond the limits of tonality and opened up a new universe of musical sound, he was not yet fully conscious of the historical significance of his act. Only in connection with the *George Lieder*, completed in 1909, did he speak of a crossing "of every barrier of a past aesthetic." It was inevitable that this repeal of tonality, and the consequent abandonment of numerous traditional norms, would provoke the conservative powers to enter the lists. As late as 1930, the word "atonal;" – as Berg noted in a radio dialogue – was regarded as signaling "non-music" (Schr, 298). And Paul Hindemith wrote in 1937: "Today we know, of course, that there can be no such thing as atonality, that this term applies at most to harmonic disorder."³³⁶

Many composers and theoreticians regarded tonality as a force quasi given by nature. Paul Hindemith compared it to gravitation: "Tonality is a force like the earth's gravitational force."³³⁷ Schönberg, on the other hand, did not deem it in any way a "natural law of music," a "constraint imposed by the nature of music,"³³⁸ but only one kind of musical device, one marked by domination and restriction: there could be no doubt that the tonic exerted "a certain predominance over the formations that derive from it."³³⁹ Elsewhere he defines tonality as "a function of the tonic," that is, "everything that constitutes it emanates from [the tonic] and refers back to it."³⁴⁰

With his first works in so-called free atonality, Schönberg annulled the tonal constraints, freed music of the "shackles of the key"³⁴¹ – but entered a realm that was only seemingly a realm of freedom: he was led by the conviction that certain laws obtained here as well, though as yet he could not name them. In the last chapter of his *Harmonielehre* of 1911, he confessed:

> In composing, I decide wholly by feeling, by form feeling. It alone tells me what I must write, everything else is excluded. Every chord I set down corresponds to a constraint; the constraint of my need to express myself, but perhaps also a constraint of an unconscious but inexorable logic in the harmonic construction. . I am firmly convinced that it exists here as well; at least as much as in the regions of harmony cultivated in the past."³⁴²

As numerous studies in past years have shown, Schönberg and his pupils developed a number of procedures and techniques in their free atonal works that permitted a meaningful way of composing.³⁴³

In closely studying atonal music, one progressively recognizes it as a counter-world to the world of tonal music. Their mutual relation can be reduced to the formula: whatever is allowed and enjoined in tonal music is now forbidden, and what was forbidden in it is now permitted. This can be demonstrated in at least three respects:

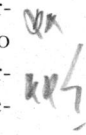

1. In free atonality, constellations are avoided that would produce a relative preponderance of a particular tone. Whereas tonality is characterized by hierarchical structures, a (relative) equality of all the twelve tones is from the start a mark of free atonality. Thus fields of nine, ten, eleven and twelve tones are frequent in atonal compositions. At times one can observe two chords or a section of melody and its accompaniment being in a complementary relation to each other.
2. Triads and tonal accords generally (including octave doublings) are systematically avoided in atonal music.
3. The relation between consonance and dissonance is stood on its head. If in tonal music dissonances were the exception, to be used only under specific conditions, it is now consonances that are generally outlawed.

Speaking about one of his *Pierrot* melodramas, the famous *Moon Stain* no. 18, Schönberg stated – as his pupil Hanns Eisler tells us – that consonances were permitted in it only in passing or on weak beats.[344] From all this we can see that in 1908 Schönberg was intent on thoroughly revolutionizing the tonal world.

2.9.2 Embracing Complexity

> "Density of texture is certainly an obstacle to popularity."
> Arnold Schönberg, "Brahms der Fortschrittliche" (GS I, 49)

In his key essay, "Composition with twelve Tones," Schönberg called the "emancipation of dissonance" a major presupposition of the "method of composing with twelve tones which are related only with one another" (S&I, 218/GS I, 75).

> A style based on this premise treats dissonances exactly like consonances and dispenses with a tonal center. By avoiding the establishment of a key, modulation is excluded, since modulation means leaving an established tonality and establishing another tonality.

He goes on to note that the first compositions "in this new style" (he does not use the word "atonal") were written around 1908 by him and soon afterwards by his pupils Webern and Berg. "From the very beginning," he writes, "such compositions differed from all preceding music, not only harmonically, but also melodically, thematically and motivically" (S&I, 217/GS I, 74). Indeed, as one immerses oneself in these pieces, it becomes clear that one has to speak of the "emancipation," not only of "dissonance," but also of melody and rhythm. Both are distinguished especially by their complexity of texture. Schönberg, Berg and Webern clearly had a great predilection for the complex and artificial: they fancied complex structures in past music and never tired of pointing out such situations in their writings and lectures – no doubt in order to prove the historical legitimacy of their own artistic endeavors.

Thus Berg, in his noted essay "Warum ist Schönbergs Musik so schwer verständlich?" (Why is Schönberg's Music so hard to understand?), sought to track down the reasons for the relative lack of immediate appeal of his teacher's music. Among them he named its complexity, its "immeasurable wealth" and the plethora of "artistic means." He saw in his teacher's work the "combination, the simultaneous presence," of all those qualities "that are usually cited as the very virtues of good music but in most cases are found only *singly* and spread out over different times." After numerous arguments, he concluded "that it is not so much the so-called *atonality* [...] that accounts for the difficulty in comprehending" as it is here, too, the highly complicated structure in general of Schönberg's music – specifically, among other things, a great "diversity in harmony," a melody that "makes the boldest use of the potential of the twelve tones," the "asymmetric and quite free construction of themes," a highly developed art of variation and polyphony, and a "multiformity and differentiation of rhythm."[345]

On April 23, 1930, Berg and the Viennese journalist Julius Bistron engaged in a dialogue on Vienna Radio on the timely topic "What is atonal?" (Schr, 297-306). The text contains a defense of atonal music and Berg's commitment to the "new art." The dramaturgy and argumentation of the dialogue are skillful and convincing. Berg starts from the numerous prejudices about, and objections to, atonal music, which to many was tantamount to "non-music," and disarms them piece by piece.

While it was true, Berg points out, that atonal music could not be referred to any major or minor scale, there had been music also before the existence of the major-minor system. He goes on to show that the slogans "a-melodic," "a-rhythmic" and "a-symmetric" used in the war against atonal music did not really do justice to the matter. He could demonstrate in any measure of any modern score that atonal music, "like any other, is based on melody, a main voice, a theme, and its course is determined by them." He would not deny that in atonal vocal music there occurred "instrumentally chromatic, tangled, notched, large-leap intervals," but similar traits could be found also in Wagner, in Schubert lieder, even in Mozartian voice-leading. He further concedes that the atonal orientation disdained duple and quadruple times and instead favored "the art of asymmetric melody construction," but he submits that already in the 18th and 19th century there was a clear tendency "to abandon clinging to "this duple and quadruple time." In this respect there was "a straight line leading from Mozart via Schubert and Brahms to Reger and Schönberg – two composers who, when speaking of the "asymmetric structure of their melodic lines," pointed out that this could be said to be equivalent to the "prose of the spoken word."

Berg also rejected the term "a-rhythmic" as unfounded. It would be correct, he thought, to speak rather of a refinement of artistic means. Hand in hand with the freedom of melody formation, he explained, goes that of rhythmic ordering. In addition, he praises the "many-voicedness of the new music" (he sees in it the onset of an "epoch predominantly polyphonic in character") and emphasizes the continued use of older forms in atonal music.

As we can see, Berg in this radio dialogue represents the rigorous viewpoint of the Second Viennese School. Many of the opinions he voices derive from ideas of Schönberg's, which Berg here exemplifies. We might think back again to the article "National music" of 1931, in which Schönberg enumerates all of the artistic devices he learned from Bach, Mozart, Beethoven, Wagner and Brahms, among them the "deviation from duple time in the theme and its components" (GS I, 253). And in his radio address "Brahms der Fortschrittliche" (the Progressive), he discusses at length the construction "with phrases of unequal length" in Haydn and Mozart and asymmetry in Brahms. (GS I, 45 ff.).

2.9.3 Berg's Specialty: Tonal Elements in Dodecaphony

> "I tell you this whole clamoring for tonality springs not so much from the need to be able to relate to a key note, as rather from the need for familiar consonances, let's be honest, for the triad – and I maintain that, so long as it contains a sufficient number of such triads, a music will not give offense, no matter how much it might otherwise violate the sacred laws of tonality." Berg, "What is atonal?" (1930)[346]

Schönberg and Webern were purists inasmuch as, after taking the step to atonality and later to dodecaphony, they turned their back for a long time, or even once and for all, on tonality: both of them (Schönberg at least until his emigration) were bent on avoiding every tonal reminiscence in their works at any price. Berg, for all the boldness of his music, proceeded less radically; even after turning to dodecaphony, he did not completely break with tonality. Characteristic of some of his works (e.g., *Wozzeck*, as well as the Chamber Concerto) is a peculiar symbiosis of tonality, free atonality and dodecaphony. Atonal and dodecaphonic movements coexist n the *Lyric Suite*, and the Violin Concerto contains in its adagio finale a homage not only to Johann Sebastian Bach but also to tonality.

Entries in his sketches document that even in his twelve-tone works Berg thought partly in tonal categories. Triads, the landmarks of tonality, can be found repeatedly in his dodecaphonic compositions, the twelve-tone series of the Violin Concerto is a prime example of a tonally colored row, and a careful analysis of his compositions will yield frequent violations of the strict rules of dodecaphony.

In a hitherto largely ignored conversation with Schönberg, Berg justified his soft spot for tonal formations in his operatic works by referring to the necessity of "contrasting characterization." In his draft for a foreword to the Berg book by Willi Reich, Schönberg wrote as follows:

> I do not know if it is generally known what Alban once replied when we talked about the admixture of key-oriented groups in the free style. He said that as a dramatic composer he thought he could not altogether relinquish the possibility of contrasting characterization with the occasional aid of major and minor. Although I myself have never encountered this problem in my stage music, his explanation seemed perfectly plausible to me.[347]

In an important letter to Erwin Stein of March 17 and 19, 1936, Schönberg spoke more critically about Berg's stylistic peculiarities. There he declared himself unable to comply with a request of Stein's to attempt to complete and orchestrate the third act of *Lulu* (Stein had sent him the particello of the third act). As a major reason he cited fundamental differences between his way of writing and Berg's style. Whereas he, he explained, invented "orchestral parts combined absolutely for a joint effect," Berg's "way of thinking was really decidedly pianistic." In certain places, the basses seem like "the left hand of a piano setting." Besides, Berg proceeded very differently in the use of rows than he did.[348] In this context, Schönberg mentioned specifically Berg's predilection for octave doublings" – something not reconcilable with the rules of the twelve-tone technique devised by Schönberg.[349]

In looking closely at the score of *Lulu*, one will repeatedly notice pseudo-tonal formations. Sometimes, longer passages are tonally colored. The large orchestral interlude (Grave) between the second and third scenes of the first act (mm. 957-992) and Alwa's Rondo in the second scene of Act II (mm. 1001-1015) offer two instructive examples.

In both segments, triads form the basis of complexly structured sounds. Several bars from the piano score will illustrate the technique and its underlying chord progression:

E   A   Cis   D   Gis   H₇   B   Es   F

A few concluding remarks about Schönberg. The oeuvre he produced in his American exile is full of surprises: not only because it includes several tonal pieces (the Variations for Winds op. 43a, the second Chamber Symphony and the Suite for String Orchestra), but also because even the works written in the twelve-tone technique reveal almost everywhere a loosening of the strict dodecaphonic rules. Tonal elements and reminiscences are now also noticeable in the late Schönberg. He himself explained his tonal works as the result of a longing having been in him "to return to the older style."[350] Adorno hazarded the guess that all his life Schönberg "took pleasure in heresies against the 'style' whose inexorability was of his own making."[351] I think it conceivable that in Schönberg's decision to revise his rigorous principles Berg's compositional manner may have played a role as well.

2.9.4 Transvaluation of the Tritone

Medieval music theory, we know, distinguished two degrees of consonance: the perfect and the imperfect. Octaves and fifths were "perfect," thirds and sixths were "imperfect." In tonal music, the pure fifth fulfilled the function of the dominant. The diminished fifth, the tritone, on the other hand, was ever since the Middle Ages regarded as a dissonance and as *diabolus in musica*, that is, the personification of the Satanic in music.[352]

A transvaluation of all values takes place in atonal music insofar as in place of the pure fifth, which is avoided, the tritone becomes the quasi dominant interval, taking on a privileged position within the tone system – also because it divides the octave into two exact halves. Marie Louise Göllner has outlined the position of the tritone in the New Music aptly as follows: "Within the new referential systems, in which the concepts of consonance and dissonance no longer hold sway, the tritone at last appears as an independent 'dyad,' as embodiment of structure and symmetry."[353]

The tritone and tritonic formations play a major role in the twelve-tone compositions of the Second Viennese School. Many series include one or more tritones, and tritonic relations are likewise common. Schönberg's Piano Suite op. 25 of 1921, his first major work in twelve-tone technique, offers an instructive example. Its basic row

$$e - f - g - d^b - g^b - e^b - a^b - d - b - c - a - b^b$$

contains two tritones, with the two corner notes adding up to yet another. No less remarkable are the row forms Schönberg uses in composing the six-movement work: they include, besides the basic form and their mirror images (inversion, retrograde and retrograde inversion), only the transpositions into the tritone.

The result is, as Wolfgang Rogge justly remarked, a "close uniformity of sound,"[354] for one thing because in tritone transpositions each tritone interval returns as the same in a different position, owing to its symmetric partition of the octave, and for another because the g-d♭ interval appears in the same place even in its inversion.

$$b^b - a - g - d^b - a^b - b - f^\# - c - e^b - d - f - e$$

Schönberg himself noted that in the "Prelude" to the Suite he had employed the basic form of the row for the theme and the tritone transposition for the accompaniment in order to avoid the forbidden octave doublings.[355]

As the illustration below shows, the four first notes of the theme are instantly imitated by the left hand – albeit inexactly in its rhythm and in the tritonic relation, probably the most important tonal relation in the entire suite.

Tritone relations predominate also in the adagio finale of Alban Berg's Violin Concerto of 1935, in which Bach's chorale setting *Es ist genug* undergoes two variations as artful as they are expressive. In the first variation (mm. 158-177), the chorale's melody is intoned in its basic form but in tritone transposition, with the echo-like repeated phrases being again displaced by a tritone.

The design of the second variation is similar (mm. 178-199), although here the chorale melody appears in its inversion. One will better understand why Berg here assigned such outstanding importance to the tritone when one realizes that the beginning of the chorale melody (b♭ –c – d – e) is in fact a diatonically filled-in tritone (the musical-rhetoric figure of *parrhesia*).

2.9.5 The Tonal as Symbolizing the Abnormal and Trivial

As a rule, tonal elements are so organically integrated into Berg's dodecaphonic musical language that they hardly sound like foreign bodies or seem like admixtures.

It is otherwise with tonal enclaves like the fairytale narrative in the Bible scene in *Wozzeck* and with isolated fifths, triads or diminished seventh chords that leap out from their atonal environment and thereby call attention to themselves.

It can be shown that Berg in many such cases employed such conspicuously tonal elements for specific symbolic reasons. Here are some examples.

As already evident from the sketches to *Lulu*, Berg characterized the Countess Geschwitz by empty fifths and by pentatonics. In tonal music, the pentatonic scale represents an exotic tonal system. Berg evidently chose it purposely to symbolize the abnormal disposition of the Countess. Already during her first entrance (Act II, mm. 508), moreover, her pentatonic leitmotif appears in parallel empty fifths:

In the first scene of the second act, spectrally sounding, long-held empty fifths sound whenever the concealed Countess becomes visible (e.g. mm. 427-441) or steps out of her hiding-place (mm. 605-608). Seeing her, the mortally wounded Dr. Schön rears up stiffly and execrates her as "the devil."

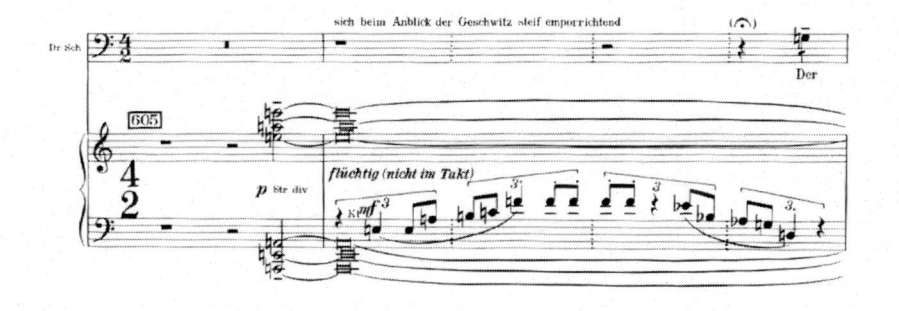

The eery effect resulting from these spookily soft parallel fifths is certainly intentional.

According to Chr. Fr. D. Schubart's classical aesthetics of musical keys, C major is "altogether pure."[356] The concert impresario Johann Peter Salomon gave the sobriquet *Jupiter* to Mozart's last, C-major symphony, perhaps in order to signal two aspects of the work, its majesty and its radiance. Alban Berg uses the C-major triad in both of his operas to symbolize the triviality of money. Wozzeck's lines, "There is money again, Marie, my pay and something from the captain and the doctor" in scene 1 of the second act (mm. 116ff.), are accompanied by a long-sounded C-major chord, according to Berg himself a sound symbol for the "matter-of-factness" or "prosiness" of money.[357]

In scene two of the first act of *Lulu*, the same triad underlines the segment of the dialogue between Schigolch and Lulu that turns on money: (Lulu: "How much do you need?" – Schigolch: "Two hundred, if you have that much in cash. Or three hundred, for all I care.") (mm. 467-469). And it is surely no accident that a C-major triad concludes this long dialogue between Lulu and Schigolch – a finely worked piece of chamber music (mm. 531-532).

Photograph 6: Helene Berg

(with kind permission of the Alban Berg Foundation Vienna)

3 Part Three: Life and Work

"Art is mute to him, who has not lived; as it is meant to transfigure life, life must therefore precede it." Hieronymus Lorm, *Die schöne Wienerin* (Quotation Collection, no. 421)

...should I remind you of Ibsen, Wedekind, Peter Altenberg, of Strauss and Pfitzner? Need I tell you that having mastered the technique of drama and the theory of composition hardly suffices to write such works, to produce such divinely ideal thoughts – that all of these great ones have preserved for themselves, besides an 'open eye,' an evergreen idealism, the belief in Love?" Berg to Helene, June 2, 1907 (ABB 13)

3.1 Helene and Alban: "The Story of a Great Love"

"O shield me, Helene, only you can –" Berg to Helene, summer 1908 (ABB 25)

"O Helene, we can never let go of each other." Berg to Helene, July 14, 1909 (ABB 68)

"O, write soon again, my one and only, your letters are better than any medicine." Berg to Helene, July 14, 1909 (ABB 69)

"Ah, to get up to you quickly: there blooms salvation, life and eternity for me." Berg to Helene, July 25, 1909 (ABB 91)

"All the more I know, in a word, THAT WITHOUT YOU I CANNOT LIVE." Berg to Helene, January 18, 1911 (ABB 213)

"I will always be a faithful companion to you, a lover and support – here and yonder in the 'other world'."

"I extinguish myself and want to be there only for you. Now we will always stay together!" Helene to Berg, May 2, 1911 (ABB 215)

"So, my little peach, come, come soon, I need you more than ever! I am uprooted! Peachy, my longing for you is immeasurable!" Berg to Helene, October 4, 1915 (ABB 293)

"If I did not have you, my one and only, I would kill myself!" Berg to Helene, July 9, 1918 (ABB 371)

"Only YOU are missing – and hence, for me, everything!" Berg to Helene, February 28, 1932 (ABB 599)

On August 2, 1909, Berg told his beloved Helene Nahowski about his life on the Berghof. He found little time to read, he wrote; his days were passing "quickly" and "inactively." One reason for that was that he slept relatively much and "during my waking hours lead purely a writer's life, every day writing one or two chapters of a great novel" entitled:

"Helene and Alban

The Story of a Great Love"

"At the end of a dreary summer," he went on, "when some 70 to 80 letters of 8 to 16 pages each will have come together, the book would make a nice gift, a surprise for your Old Man! Something like that should surely convert him!" (ABB 99f.) The passage indicates, among other things, that Franz Nahowski, Helene's nominal father,[358] who vehemently opposed a union between his daughter and Berg, did not as yet have any real sense of the intensity of Alban's feelings for Helene.

To retell the story of Berg's love for Helene is difficult for several reasons: for one, because the written documents about it are not by any means all accessible as yet (Berg wrote far more letters to Helene than the 569 published ones, and her letters to him are, with very few exceptions, unpublished to date), and for another, because, of course, even written documents cannot always provide sufficient information about complex psychological processes.

According to Hermann Watznauer,[359] Berg first saw Helene at the Vienna Opera in 1906/07 and seems to have been instantly smitten by her. He first actually met her on Good Friday of 1907.[360] Together they attended several performances of Richard Wagner's *Tristan und Isolde* (ABB 11), a work that deeply moved them because they identified with Wagner's protagonists (ABB 25).

Berg loved Helene – that much emerges from the letters – for her beauty, her humanity and, not least, her stable, poised personality. He saw in her the "archetype of the most perfect humanity" (ABB 94) and above all a woman who could give him protection, support and security.

In pursuing the story of this love, taking into account the most crucial biographic events, one can distinguish three separate phases. The first comprises the time between 1907 and their wedding on May 3, 1911, and is naturally the most passionate. Berg's deep affection for Helene rapidly grew into an overpowering, immeasurable longing. On August 28, 1910, he spoke of "Sehnsuchtsqual," "torment of longing," and "frenetic love passion" (ABB 187) – a passion, he analyzed, that "creates an equal amount of suffering" (ABB 191).

His longing for Helene seems to have been an emotion that totally dominated him from the start.[361] The hundreds of letters he wrote to her sprang from an urge to communicate with her, to bridge the painfully felt distance from her spiritually and emotionally. Time and again he confessed that he missed his beloved, that he fervently longed for her. Here are some examples.

Photograph 7: Alban and Helene

(with kind permission of the Alban Berg Foundation Vienna)

A letter of August 19, 1908, closes: "I greet you full of anxious love and the most genuflectingly suppliant longing!" (ABB 38). Under the date of July 14, 1909, we read: My love and longing for you is so great that in writing this I just now got completely well and do not feel anything untoward" (ABB 69). On July 15, 1909, he proclaims: "I am crazy, insane with love and longing for you, Helene" (ABB 70). And with similar ardor he confesses on July 21 and 25: "I was quite crazy again with longing and anxiety and just wrote in my soul's agony." "But that's exactly because today, tomorrow and the day after there is no longer anything for me but the longing for a token of love, for a sign of life from your love ..." (ABB 78, 88).

When he had to be separated from Helene for any length of time, he was deeply depressed, feeling the separation as a "gigantic sacrifice" (ABB 172). Each day he longingly waited for mail from her, having "the unquenchable need" to be in constant contact with her (ABB 88), and could not bear not to receive a "loving word" from her (ABB 187). If mail from Helene failed to arrive, he felt miserable, downright lost, and waited impatiently for any letters, postcards or telegrams. A torturous feeling of waiting, disorientation and helplessness overcame him, and he seems to have suffered unspeakably when in such straits. Fits of despair are thus not infrequent in the letters of this first period. On July 29, 1909, he wrote to Helene: "Your last letter just arrived!! I cannot come up to you, for six more weeks I am to wait – wait – wait, until I can finally see you again.! How am I to bear that!!!! Help!! Help!! In this direst need!!!!" (ABB 97). And in a letter of August 21, 1910, we read: "The summit of my suffering has been traversed – – it has!!! Down I go now in dreadful haste, toward the end: today there was not even a letter from you" (ABB 178).

In the light of these passages from the letters, one begins to understand why Berg was able to express the experience of waiting so convincingly. In the text of the fourth Altenberg song, "Nothing has come for my soul. I have waited, waited, oh waited," he found a situation described that he knew only too well from his own experience, and it is surely no accident that waiting is a state that especially characterizes Marie in *Wozzeck*. The empty fifths that symbolize this waiting are among Marie's personal leitmotifs, and Berg explained in the Oldenburg lecture that there was something fateful about this "waiting aimed at the indefinite," since it found its "end" only in Marie's death.[362]

It likewise emerges from Berg's letters to Helene that in the period before their wedding, and for some time thereafter, Berg, racked by the experience of his love for her, reflected time and again about questions of the philosophy, specifically the metaphysics, of love. He wrestled with the literature on the subject and took a lively interest in views that corresponded to his own highly idealized conception of love. He was especially taken with Balzac's *Physiology of Marriage*. On July 14, 1909, he conveyed his impressions of this "*very ingenious book*" to Helene. Of the many sentences of Balzac's he quotes there, the following deserve special attention, because to Berg they seemed directly "aimed" at his relationship with Helene: "The duration of the passion of two people who are capable of love depends on the strength of the resistance put up either by the woman or by the obstacles that the accidents of social life oppose to the happiness of the lovers … The realization of this basic law shaped the amatory fables of the Middle Ages: the Amadis, the Lancelots, the Tristans (!! Helene !!) were all witnesses to this truth" (ABB 68). (One will note the exclamation marks here after "Tristan").

Photograph 8: Helene Berg (1916)

(with kind permission of the Alban Berg Foundation Vienna)

The following passage from a letter of July 30, 1909, indicates that Berg had adopted Wagner's idea of the *liebestod* from *Tristan*: "Oh Helene, sometimes, as just this moment, it comes over me with ferocious force: the longing to have you at my side at least for a second – and to die loving you – the love death" (ABB 99).

Additional proof of that is found in a letter of February 25, 1912. Here Berg tells his now wife that while on a train he read a newspaper review of a lecture about "metaphysical eros." The lecturer's ideas as reported in the article must have strongly impressed him, as he quotes a lengthy section from the report, commenting on it with the words: "I liked that very much, and you will like it, too." The section quoted by Berg runs as follows:

> ...Lucka posited that there have been three stages in the relation between man and woman, and that our way of experiencing love is the third and probably definitive one. ... The more highly differentiated the lover is, the harder it becomes for his beloved to be replaceable by another. Modern love is inseparably bound up with the need for the unique and definitive. It carries with it the highest felicity and the greatest suffering. The lover wants to unite inseparably with the beloved. Since this is not possible within earthly existence, such love leads in its ultimate consequence to the ideal of the love death, as Wagner has embodied it so incomparably beautifully and profoundly in *Tristan und Isolde*. With a reference to the tragic character of modern love, which in its highest development transforms itself into a metaphysical eros, Lucka concluded his stimulating and psychologically profound lecture, for which the large audience thanked him with lively applause (ABB 222 f.).

This letter, too, thus suggests that Berg identified with Wagner's philosophy of love. In the light of what has been said, it would be odd if Berg's love for Helene had not precipitated out in his work. In fact, several of the compositions that came into being between 1907 and 1912 refer to his beloved. This is true especially of the songs "Traumgekrönt" ("Crowned by Dreams," text by Rainer Maria Rilke), "Schließe mir die Augen beide" ("Close my eyes, one and the other," after Theodor Storm) and "Nun ich der Riesen Stärksten überwand" ("Now that I felled the strongest giant," after Mombert) op. 2 Nr. 3, as well as of the String Quartet op. 3. In his letters to Helene, he quotes the poems or lines from them: evidently he was searching at the time for love lyrics that he thought expressed his feelings for her. On August 15, 1907, he sent her the complete text of the poem "Traumgekrönt" and emphasized that the musical setting of the lyric was completed the day before, after he had received a letter from her (ABB 14f.). Using lines from the same poem, he reminded her a little later of a special event: the day on which he had kissed her for the first time (ABB 19f.).

There can be no doubt that several of the lieder written during this time were directly related to Helene in Berg's mind. In fact, he dedicated them to her several years later. Among the papers in his estate was found a manuscript of ten songs entitled "Ten Lieder from the Year 1907. For my dear wife on the 3rd of May, 1917."[363] The volume contains the songs "Die Sorglichen" ("The Solicitous," after Gustav Falke), "Frau, du Süße" ("You, sweet woman," after Ludwig Finckh), "Schließe mir die Augen beide," "Sommertage" ("Summer

Days," after Paul Hohenberg), "Die Nachtigall" ("The Nightingale," after Theodor Storm), "Liebesode" ("Ode of Love," after Otto Erich Hartleben), "Im Zimmer" ("In the Room," after Johannes Schlaf), "Aus den Schilfliedern" ("From the Reed Songs," after Nikolaus Lenau) and "Nacht" ("Night," after Carl Hauptmann). The overall dating of the songs "from the year 1907" is not quite accurate, as some of them were composed before 1907 and some of them ("Nacht," "Schilflied") not until 1908.[364] In 1928, Berg decided to published six of these songs, together with the above-mentioned "Traumgekrönt," under the title Sieben frühe Lieder.[365] Both the printer's copy and the printed edition bear the telling dedication "For my Helene."

Helene's life motto, according to Erich Alban Berg, was "Family is nothing, being soul-mates is everything."[366] There were light elves and black elves, she noted – Alban belonged to the first category, everyone else to the second. The (Wagnerian) theme of *Lichtalben* and *Schwarzalben* crops up repeatedly in Berg's and Helene's correspondence and indicates that a feeling of belonging together and of a mental and spiritual communion had quickly grown between them. Berg thought about the etymology of their names. Helene meant as much as "Sun Bright" and "Radiant One"; his own name Alban he translated as "the White One" (ABB 118). He seems to have been conversant with both Greek and Norse mythology. As a twenty-four-year-old, he ironically identified with Siegfried, wishing to be as strong as Siegfried, so as to be able to overcome the *Schwarzalben*.

> If once upon a time value was placed on physical strength [he wrote to Helene on July 16, 1909], now it is on the mental, spiritual, and I compare myself to 'Siegfried' in that sense. What mattered most, after all, was my struggle against the Black Elves, to whose striving for wealth, learning, fame, external power I wanted to oppose my striving for the highest, for Brünnhilde-Helene, the emblem of spiritual and moral perfection (ABB 71).

After reading Strindberg's novel *Black Flags*, he thought, on August 17, 1909, that he had found a comrade-in-arms against the Black Elves in the Swedish writer (ABB 118), and he boasted as late as 1921 that Helene's spirit was victorious even over the Black Elves" (ABB 464)[367]

A second phase in the story of Berg's love of Helene can be said to extend over the roughly fifteen years between the contraction of their marriage and the severe marital crisis provoked by Berg's affair with Hanna Fuchs in 1925. Judging from Berg's letters, the marriage seems to have been intact during those fifteen years, and Berg's love for Helene did not lose any of its intensity.

The exaltation, to be sure, that had characterized his emotional life during the years before the wedding gradually yielded to sentiments of tenderness and intimacy. As before, Helene remained Berg's point of reference. He was so firmly fixated on her that he could never bear to be without her for any length of time. If they were apart for a few weeks, he invariably felt lonely and uprooted. As late as February 8, 1920, he wrote to her that the thought of her suffering half as much from their separation as he himself did was unbearable to him (ABB 441). He reproached her generally for leaving him alone so often.

Erich Alban Berg seems to be correct in asserting that in his original veneration for Helene his uncle seems to have been "totally subordinated" to her in their daily married life. "Alban was of a pliable nature, Helene was the strong-willed one."[368] To outsiders, the marriage seemed exceptionally harmonious: Alma Mahler-Werfel, for one, spoke of a "beautiful marriage," as Berg was very gratified to report to his wife at one point (ABB 503). Interesting in this connection is Helene's saying that in their marital life she left her husband a good deal of latitude. "In our life in Vienna," she reported to Alma Mahler in a hitherto unpublished letter of November 28, 1936, "he went out alone much more often than with me: to concerts, the theater, meetings, parties, suppers (sometimes also to you and Zolnay alone)." And she added by way of explanation: "I, who hate winter and cold, much preferred to go to bed with a book, or listened to the concert on the radio."

That the marriage was not altogether without problems seems to be signaled by a letter of Berg's to Helene dated November 29, 1923, indicating that Helene had consulted an internist about an illness, who in turn referred her to a psychoanalyst. During several "sessions," the latter spoke to Helene about sexuality and frustrated desires. The vehemence with which Berg reacted to Helene's account suggests, for one thing, that he had reservations about the analyst, who was unknown to him (he laudably mentions Freud and Adler in this connection), and, for another, that Helene's narrative evidently hit a sensitive spot. But he tried to assuage Helene by saying: "After all, it takes two to make an unhappy marriage! For me it is a happy one, the happiest I have ever seen!"

In May of 1925, Alexander von Zemlinsky performed Berg's *Three Fragments from Wozzeck* at the Third World Music Festival of the International Society for New Music in Prague. Berg made a special trip to Prague for it. He spent the night at the home of Herbert Fuchs-Robettin, a Prague industrialist, and fell passionately in love with the latter's wife Hanna Fuchs (1894-1964), a sister of Franz Werfel, who was then 31 years old. The love was as charged with pathos as it was mutual but was hopeless from the start, because – as Adorno remarked [369] – Berg did not want to leave his wife, nor Hanna her husband and their two children. Nevertheless, Berg's feelings for Hanna plunged him into a severe crisis. For years, love letters traveled from Vienna to Prague.

The situation was paradoxical in that Berg saw in Hanna the ideal beloved but also could not live without his wife, whom he continued to surround with tender affection. When on trips, he never stopped writing loving letters to his wife, whom he missed sorely.[370]

The affair with Hanna Fuchs was undoubtedly one of the most momentous events in Berg's life. In the emotional realm, it led to a reorientation. If Berg had once dedicated the Storm lied "Schließe mir die Augen beide" to Helene and had written the first String Quartet for her, he now composed a second setting of the Storm poem and the second String Quartet, the *Lyric Suite*, for Hanna, who now took the place in his inward life once held by Helene.

Both friends and pupils were let in on the affair. Helene, too, knew about it almost from the beginning. On the outside, the Bergs still gave the impression of leading an exemplary marriage. Thus Willi Reich was able to write in 1930 in an article on Alban Berg published in the noted journal *Die Musik*:

> Well beyond her gratifying relationship with the human being Alban Berg, Frau Helene is not only her husband's constant companion in all his artistic travels but also, with the most refined development of heart and mind, the most critical counselor in his work. Her presence gives the artist the peace of a comfortable home and thus the quiet needed for undisturbed creative work.[371]

Hanna Fuchs was Alban Berg's "immortal beloved." In a letter he wrote in 1931, that is to say, six years after his first visit to Prague, he addressed her as his "one and everlasting beloved" (*Einzig- und Ewiggeliebte*) and confessed to be leading a kind of twofold existence. His life with his wife was only seemingly happy – a façade, which reflected only the "outward being." The real Berg, the "other being," was with Hanna in thought:

> Not a day goes by, not a night, that I am not thinking of you, not a week when I am not overwhelmed by a longing that wraps all my thinking and feeling and desiring into a fervency that to me is not a whit fainter than the one in May of 1925 – except that it is shadowed by a sadness that ever since then has reigned over me and long since has turned me into a twofold or, more properly, a divided being."[372]

It is astonishing to read in this letter that as late as 1931 Berg was still hoping for a union with Hanna.

Adorno was thus evidently mistaken when he remarked that the matter of Hanna Fuchs had not been "central" to Berg, that it was not so very hard for him to get over her.[373] The truth of the matter is that the affair had traumatic repercussions for both Berg and Hanna, who still met occasionally in later years. Hanna Fuchs is said by Helene to have broken into a helpless crying fit when glimpsing Berg once at the Vienna Opera or a Viennese theater.[374] And Berg in turn was supposedly always quite stricken after occasional meetings with Hanna in a coffeehouse.[375]

Letters recently unearthed indicate that during his last years Berg maintained relations also with other women. Thus he addressed desperate love letters to Anna Askenase, the wife of his friend, the pianist Stefan Askenase, who lived in Brussels and visited him in Carinthia.[376] In 1933 he hoped to spend a few spring weeks with her. On March 23, 1932, he wrote to her that nothing had changed in his love for her, "except that an ever-growing, unappeasable longing" had been added to it. Helene seems to have been cognizant of this attachment of her husband's as well. On October 27, 1932, Berg wrote to his distant beloved that the last degree of freedom that had remained to him in his marriage had "disappeared totally since that catastrophe." Everything, everything was now buried: he was unable to work, everything connected with questions of livelihood had become wholly indifferent to him, he hated all human beings and himself as well, "who would deserve to be made away with"! He had another tender love relationship with the actress Edith Edwards (1899-1956), who worked in Zurich for some time.

Adorno seems to have been right, therefore, in saying that Berg's numerous love affairs always ended unhappily: "the unhappy end was, as it were, composed into them, and one had the feeling that with him these affairs were from the start part of his productive apparatus, that, very much in the sense of the Austrian joke, they were desperate but not serious."[377]

Helene voiced similar explanations for her husband's escapades. After Berg's death, she discussed the Hanna affair with her friend Alma Mahler-Werfel. On November 28, 1936, she wrote to her that there was only one explanation: "Alban searched for an excuse to keep this poetic love within the boundaries he wished for himself!" He himself had constructed obstacles and thereby created for himself the very Romanticism he needed. Perhaps it also was a "subconscious caution": "he did not want a closer, all-too close contact with this woman (whom he endowed with his incredibly flourishing artist's imagination), out of fear of disappointment (for Alban was spoiled, both mentally and physically!)," and so evaded her. Admittedly, Helene believed that only thus the *Lyric Suite* could come into being. She had, she said, to acknowledge the "deeper meaning" of everything that happens and be silent.

3.2 The String Quartet for Helene

> When, during my morning's toilet, ideas for composition come to me – not what it then turns into, the product of my mental labor, but the first, original thought: a theme, a mood, often just a particular chord, or at most a longer melody – then I always have the feeling as though this came winging to me from you – as though something like that could never come into being if you didn't exist!!" Berg to Helene, spring 1909 (ABB 62f.)

> "Tonight your quartet! Oh, if only you could be there!!" Berg to Helene, August 2, 1923 (ABB 520f.)

> "People should see what you look like, you who owns the quartet, who has born it." Berg to Helene, August 3, 1923 (ABB 522f.)

3.2.1 The Autobiographical Background

On August 2, 1923, the Havemann Ensemble in Salzburg played Berg's first string quartet. The performance, which was attended by numerous critics, was an overwhelming success. On the following day, Berg gave his wife a detailed and enthusiastic account of the performance, and the response of the audience, and regretted that she had not been there – she to whom the quartet "altogether belonged," nay, who had "born it." These utterances and the dedication of the printed score "To my wife" make us realize that this work, written in 1909/1910, has to be viewed against an autobiographical background.

To begin *in medias res*: the lovers' happiness of Alban and Helene during the years 1908, 1909 and 1910 was overshadowed by the objections Helene's parents had to the union of their daughter with the young composer. Franz Nahowski was concerned about his daughter's future and feared that the sickly musician would not be able to provide her with a livelihood free from care. He thus opposed the union peremptorily, insulted Berg wherever he could, even forbade his daughter to see him, and thereby hit him in a very tender spot: for Berg suffered unimaginably from the separations imposed upon him. In a famous letter of July 1910, he sought to refute the charges brought against him by his prospective father-in-law, "intellectual inferiority,

127

"pecuniary destitution," supposedly "ruined health" and "depravity" of the members of his family (ABB 160-172).

Helene herself was initially torn between her love for Alban and respect for the will of her parents. In a letter to Alban of July 23, 1909, she reproached him for his "imprudent way of life" and asked him:

> Don't you realize that our future depends on whether or not your health improves? My parents are not altogether wrong from their standpoint in rejecting you because they are afraid that I would never be able to stop worrying about you and would be unhappy with you.

Even so, she averred: "No, Alban, no, I will not give you up!" (ABB 85)

Meanwhile, the lovers were able to gain Helene's mother and her sister Anna as allies in their cause. With their help, Berg hoped Helene would be able to persuade her father to agree to a meeting with Berg, even to visit him at the Berghof. On August 18, 1909, he pressured Helene to prevail with her father and put the painful question to her: "Or does the grumpy face of your father mean more to you than the immeasurable, unbearable agony of your beloved?" (ABB 119)

This and similar utterances indicate that Berg had to cope with numerous anxieties during this period. He had to fear that he might lose Helene to another man (ABB 158) and was afraid that he might become estranged from his beloved (ABB 186). When he realized that Helene had remained his, he triumphed all the more. On September 3, 1910 – long after the completion of the String Quartet – he wrote to her: "Oh, how mistaken your Old Man was to think again that a month-long separation would wear us down!! On the contrary! Now we know all the more, now we really feel it, how inseparable we are" (ABB 203).

How much Berg suffered from the periodic separation from Helene, the following passage from a letter of September 9, 1908, makes clear:

> Soon I will not find words any more about the baseness of the world order that separates us two!!! It is unheard-of!!! Sometimes I think I shall go mad with pain – another time, frantic with rage! And the infamous feeling: 'nothing is any use'! I have to put up with it all!!!

On March 12, 1986, I met Frau Fritzi Schlesinger-Czapka, a confidante of Helene Berg's, at Trauttmansdorffgasse 27, the locale of the Alban Berg Foundation. She kindly answered many of my questions and told me many valuable things about the relationship between Helene Berg and her husband. She not only showed me *Wozzeck* sketches in her possession but also told me about a program to the String Quartet op. 3, a program Helene Berg dictated to her sometime after they established a closer contact in 1949. That program runs word for word as follows:

> The inspiration for Berg's opus 3 derived from the following incident:
>
> He was at my parents' home in 1908. Many young people frequented it, for my sister and I were merry girls. There were many suitors, among them also Alban Berg. None of the young men appealed to me, except Alban! When my father noticed that, he forbade further visits from Alban Berg, for Alban was sickly (asthmatic ever since the age of 14) and had a profession – musician and composer – that did not suit my level-headed and practical father. Besides, he feared that owing to the chronic illness of asthmatic persons, I would have a life full of worries. The separation hurt Alban and me deeply. Thus opus 3 came about. It speaks of love and jealousy and outrage about the injustice done to us and to our love. – Helene Berg

This program, first published here, is a second-hand source, yet it seems authentic. The diction is without doubt that of Helene; the biographic events referred to are correctly given, and the statements about the feelings the work gives expression to closely fit the character and gesture of the work.

3.2.2 Genesis of the Work: From Tonality to Free Atonality

According to Hermann Watznauer, Berg's earliest biographer, the Lieder op. 2 were written in 1908.[378] Watznauer lists them in the following order: "Nun ich der Riesen Stärksten überwand" (op. 2, no. 3), "Schlafend trägt man mich" (I am carried sleeping) (no. 2), "Dem Schmerz sein Recht" ("Schlafen, schlafen, nichts als Schlafen") (Sleep has its rights [Sleep, sleep, nothing but sleep]) (no. 1), and "Warm die Lüfte: (Warm the breezes) (no. 4), and gives them opus numbers from 82 to 85. (He makes one mistake here: the author of "Schlafen" is not Paul von Hohenheim but Friedrich Hebbel.) In a questionnaire sent by Watznauer to Berg, the latter gave the date of the songs' composition as "1908 to 1909."[379]

The String Quartet, according to Watznauer, is the last work Berg composed under Schönberg, the work having been completed in April of 1910 at the latest.[380] The printed score, however, bears the date "Vienna, spring of 1910." Letters written by Berg to Webern, too, indicate that work on the quartet was probably not completed until June or July. On May 30, 1910, Berg told Webern that he "didn't even get around to finishing the quartet."[381] A later letter, on the other hand, reads:

> I am almost ashamed of the old things of mine I sent you (op. 1 and 2) and have the one consolation that you will like my newest, the quartet, much better – whose first movement you already know, and which, as I surmise, has greatly improved in its subsequent parts – (we have rehearsed it in its *entirety* in Vienna, and I would have loved to see you there...

There is much to suggest that Berg began work on the quartet in 1909 at the latest.

Stylistically and in terms of compositional technique, the Four Songs op. 2 and the String Quartet op. 3 deserve special attention, inasmuch as they embody the transition from tonality to free atonality. While the first three lieder of the opus 2, in spite of their boldness of conception, are still tonally anchored, the last Mombert song, "Warm die Lüfte," is regarded as the first atonal lied composition. Several observations suggest that Berg had first closely studied the transition from tonality to atonality on Schönberg's George lieder op. 15 and his second string quartet op. 10. Altogether new insights into both the dating and the genesis of op. 2 and op. 3 emerge from a study of the sketches. The sketchbook F 21 Berg 7 is particularly instructive in this respect. It numbers 74 pages and contains sketches not only to string quartets but also to three songs. Its contents are as follows:

p. 3:	Draft of a theme
pp. 5-9:	Sketch of the Hebbel song "Sleep, sleep, nothing but sleep"
pp. 10-41:	Sketch for the first movement of the string quartet and to other, unexecuted quartets
pp. 42-45:	Sketch for the last Mombert lied, "Warm the breezes"
pp. 46-68:	Sketch mostly for the second movement of the quartet
pp. 69-70:	Sketch of another, unexecuted lied
pp. 71-74:	Sketches for the quartet

This outline indicates that Berg, probably in 1909, alternated between lied compositions and work on the string quartet. First he sketched out the Hebbel song "Sleep, sleep," then – after diverse drafts for quartet openings – the first movement of the quartet op. 3 and, following that, the Mombert lied "Warm the breezes" and the second movement of opus 3. These data lead to the conclusion that Berg's first atonal composition was not the Mombert lied "Warm the breezes," as is commonly assumed, but the opening movement of the string quartet op. 3. The genesis of that work, however, is as complex as it is instructive. Close study of the sketches reveals that Berg's earliest draft for a string quartet was a composition in enlarged tonality! He found his way to free atonality only via diverse experiments and detours. To clarify the situation, one should note, to begin with, that the quartet openings on pp. 3, 10/11 and 12 (one in 4/4, the other in 3/4 time) are not directly connected to the opus 3.

Berg evidently liked these ideas and made clean copies of them. He wrote them down on several sheets of music in a 16-line score format (F 21 Berg 49), developed them further and wrote them out in a four-voice set. The draft noted down in 4/4 time is in F minor (the key signature has 4 b's) and works with motifs that remind of mm. 137 ff. of Schönberg's *Transfigured Night*. More interesting with regard to the genesis of the opus 3 is the second idea noted down on p. 12 of the Sketchbook. This is a nine-bar theme for the first violin, which is composed of four motifs ($x + x^1 + x^2 + y$), with the last motif (y) intended to be imitated by the second violin, the viola and the cello. One should note that the theme contains the tonal letters for the names Helene (h [=b] and e) and Alban Berg (a, b [=b♭], e and g).

From this idea Berg developed a complete main group, notated in G minor (!) and existing in no fewer than three four-part versions (F 21 Berg 49, fol. 1 verso, fol. 4 and fol. 6 verso/7). Here is the note text of the first version:

This draft, too, remained a fragment, however – probably because it was a tonal conception.

Berg's endeavor, at this time, seems to have been to go beyond the limits of tonality. Thus he decided to develop yet another idea, which is notated on p. 13 of the sketchbook (F 21 Berg 7) and is built on descending fourths:

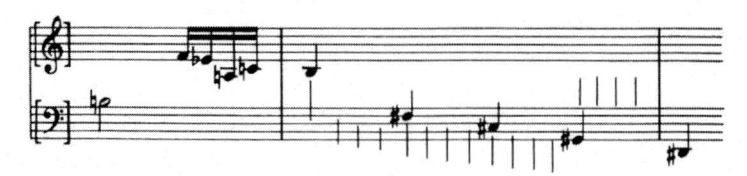

Evidently Berg was not yet satisfied with this idea. He modified it and from that developed a figure (F 21 Berg 49 fol.2) that comes pretty close to the final form of the principal theme of opus 3 – and, moreover, harbors the total chromatic scale within itself.

Another notation of the main theme (F 21 Berg 7 p. 14), moreover, presents the next stage in the development. Here the theme is clearly divided into a first and second phrase, the latter exhibiting a whole-tone coloration:

Upon closer inspection, this version turns out to have been gained, through transformation and estrangement, from the rejected head motif, initially conceived in E minor:

The genesis of the String Quartet op. 3 has thus a special relevance, inasmuch as it can cast a light on the momentous transition from tonality to atonality in

Berg's oeuvre. In its final form, the work is treated in free atonality. There are no tonal enclaves, and seemingly tonal parts are rare.[382] Wherever one looks one meets with fields of ten, eleven and especially twelve tones. "Lists" of tonal letters on pp. 49 and 64 of the sketchbook show, moreover, that Berg was operating consciously with twelve tones here. He wrote down columns of the twelve tones from b natural down to c and then crossed all or most of them out, apparently so as to check the extent to which all twelve tones had been used in a particular passage. Similar controls of the twelve-tone character of his "atonal" compositions occur repeatedly also in the sketches to later works.

3.2.3 Tectonics

In 1909, Anton Webern composed his *Fünf Sätze für Streichquartett* (Five Movements for String Quartet) op. 5. They take ca. five minutes to perform, have a fragmentary character and are regarded as early examples of Webern's aphoristic style. The longest of the five movements (which the composer himself regarded as belonging together[383]) is the first with its 55 measures; the shortest ones, on he other hand, the second and fourth, have only 13 bars each. Rudolf Kolisch aptly observed that by an extreme condensation and foreshortening, Weber wrested highly concentrated and un-rhetorical, lyrical forms from his material.[384] A special characteristic of the *Five Movements* is the fact that they exhibit neither themes nor motivic-thematic work in the traditional sense.

Berg's opus 3 differs radically from Weber's movements in the breadth of its design, the astonishingly close-meshed polyphonic texture and the stringency of a motivic-thematic working along traditional lines. Berg's quartet, too, however, departs from the generic tradition in that it is in only two movements. Probably that seemed sufficient to Berg at the time. Only shortly before his death, in the spring of 1935, as we learn from a letter to Rudolf Kolisch, he had considered "composing in" a brief additional movement between the two original ones.[385]

A closer look at the work reveals an amazing boldness of conception, a heightened expressivity and individual form. While the first movement shows the scaffolding of the sonata form, it exhibits numerous peculiarities. Let us begin with a rough outline of the work's structure.

Exposition

mm. 1-40		Main movement
	1-9	Main subject (divided into first and second phrase) (tempo I)
	10-27	"Contrasting idea" (Tempo II): crescendo passage

	27-40	"Stretching" of the main subject, which is occasionally intertwined contrapuntally with the contrasting idea; climax of the crescendo passage (*fff*), followed by gradual decrease
	41-57	Secondary movement
	58-80	Concluding group, presenting a new motif (*flüchtig* [fleetingly]) and quoting or varying material from the secondary movement.

Development

mm. 81-105   Treatment of motifs from the concluding group and the secondary movement in the form of a tremendous crescendo passage, which climaxes in m. 98 and then subsides

Recapitulation

mm. 105-119   Main theme (strongly varied)

119-152   Contrasting idea (repeatedly incorporating the head motif of the main theme)

Coda

mm. 153-187   Material from he concluding group; working of head motif of the main theme

The more closely one analyzes the music in its detail, the clearer it becomes how complexly it is shaped. To begin with, the development is "total,"[386] that is to say, it takes hold already in the exposition. Thus the actual contrasting idea is introduced in mm. 10-13 and then regularly developed, i.e., treated in inversion, sequenced and given a tremendous crescendo (mm. 14-27). Then the main theme, in being resumed in mm. 27-40, is not only stretched by diverse means but also intertwined contrapuntally with the head motif of the contrasting idea.

In light of this, it is understandable that the development section proper is rather brief. Whereas the exposition consists of 80 bars and the recapitulation plus coda has 82 bars, the development is limited to a mere 25 bars.

Adorno, who set forth a detailed formal analysis of the first movement, drew attention to another important aspect of the work. He spoke of the "liquidation of the sonata," the disintegration of the "sonata system," and thought that the quartet – at any rate its second movement – no longer contained any "themes in the old static sense": a "permanent transition softens any firm shape, opens it up to what goes before and what comes afterwards, maintains it in a constant flux of variants, subjects it to the primacy of the whole."[387] For proof of this observation one only needs to compare the secondary group with the concluding one: though the latter commences with a "fleetingly" recited new motif, it also picks up thematic material from the secondary group. Thus mm. 47-52 and 72-77 correspond to each other.

The second movement is constructed even more irregularly and freely. Adorno calls it a rondo that dissolves into unbound prose.[388] It appears to me, however, that in conceiving this movement Berg still had the ground plan of the sonata in mind, which he enriched with rondo-like elements. The following schema provides a rough orientation, though it cannot convey an impression of the full complexity of the movement.

Exposition

mm. 1-3   Introduction (moderate quarter notes): *sehr heftig* [very vehement]

    4-33   Main movement

34-53	Transition, exposing several heterogeneous motifs (incl. an important tritonic one)
54-60	Secondary movement, lyrical in character (*breit* [broadly])
61-72	Transition (in mm. 60-63 the vehement motivic gesture of the beginning in the cello)

Development

72-118	New composition, using material exposed at the beginning: initially fugato; entries of the leading motif in perfect fifths: on a^b (m. 73, 2nd vl.), on e^b (m. 74, 1st vl.), on b^b (m. 75, vc.), on f (m. 82, 1st vl.), finally on $b^\# = c$ (m. 99, 1st vl.)

Episode

119-142	*Sehr ruhig und mäßig* [very calmly and moderately]
142-150	Transition

Free recapitulation

151-174	similar to main movement; in mm. 154-172 a pedal point or constant $c^\#$
175-199	Transitional section
200-207	Secondary movement, lyrical in character (*Breit*)
208-216	Transition (with head motif of main movement)
217-232	Conclusion with the tritonic motif, the very vehement gesture of the beginning and a reminiscence of the start of the first movement

Adorno thought that the thematic relations of this movement were complicated by the fact that the themes echoed back to those of the first movement, the latter at times being actually quoted, the figures, however, being throughout variants, derivations of its themes. Now, the head motif of the first movement is indeed quoted in mm. 168-170 and 227-231, and several additional reminiscences of the first movement are in fact unmistakable.[389] The statement, however, that the figures of the second movement are "throughout" variants, derivatives of those of the first cannot be upheld as a generalization — though Adorno evidently overlooked the fact that the main motif of the second movement is indeed a variant of the second phrase of the first movement's main theme:

Kopfsatz, T. 7–9

II. Satz, T. 5/6

An instructive example of Berg's technique of the *evolving variation*, we might add, occurs in mm. 23ff. of the second movement. By splitting off the last three notes of the motif just quoted, Berg obtains an independent motif, which is consistently developed and thereby diastematically transformed.

One could describe the music of the string quartet as a seismogram of complex psychic processes, one extending between the poles of apathy and supreme excitement, calm and paroxysm, tenderness and vehemence. Even the frequent expression marks will convey a vivid impression of the alternating characters. In contrast to the "very vehement" beginning of the second movement, we later get figures to be performed *espressivo, grazioso* and *very tender* (mm. 37ff.). Yet later – towards the middle of the movement – the *very calm* episode (mm. 119ff.) forms a sharp contrast to the *very agitated* (m. 72) and *very excited* (m. 81) development.

Perhaps even more characteristic than such contrasts is the fact that the music frequently proceeds in long crescendos, which reach one or several climaxes and then gradually subside, sometimes dying away completely. The agogics and external dynamics are often subjected to extreme fluctuations. Accelerandos and crescendos, as well as ritardandos and diminuendos, frequently determine the course of the music. To cite only one example: the development of the head movement (mm. 81-105) is devised as a mighty heightening arc – a crescendo from triple piano to fourfold forte, one that is paralleled by an accelerando and which after reaching a climax in m. 98 is followed by a gradual diminuendo down to pianissimo.

Great effects by means of long crescendos were achieved in the 19th century, as is well known, by Richard Wagner, especially in his *Tristan* (1859). Bruckner, in his symphonies, took up from Wagner,[390] as did did Schönberg in his early programmatic instrumental works – the *Transfigured Night* op. 4, the symphonic poem *Pelleas and Melisande* op. 5 and the first String Quartet op. 7. Berg's dynamics takes its departure from both Wagner and Schönberg. The latter's technique of heightening differs substantially from Berg's, however, in that Schönberg loves to break off his crescendo waves abruptly upon reaching the climax.

3.2.4 Semantics: Echoes of Schönberg's *George Lieder* and Wagnerian Motifs

Comments of a non-technical nature are sparse in Berg's sketchbook *F 21 Berg*. Besides the catchwords "Marsch" (p. 7) and "Reminiscenz" (p. 68), one will search in vain for any hermeneutic references. But it would be a mistake to conclude from that that the String Quartet has no program. A series of new observations leads to the conclusion that Berg semanticized his music by means of quotations and allusions.

During the years 1908, 1909 and 1910, Berg was fascinated by Stefan George's *Buch der hängenden Gärten*. George's unusual love poems suited Berg's emotional frame of mind. In several letters to Helene, he quoted or paraphrased verses from the book. On October 6, 1908, he wrote:

> You must know that this afternoon my longing for you had once again become immeasurable, for I had hoped with all my might to be able to see you this evening, and it seemed to me that "if I" (as some divine lyricist says) "could not touch your body today, my soul would have to tear with utter force"! You may think that one does not die of that, but you will forgive me, won't you, if in matters of love I regard the poets as more competent – for the time being at least - -(ABB 50).

Two days later he wrote to his beloved that he was "suffering unutterably" (ABB 51) – possibly in allusion to George's "me, who suffers since I have been yours." In a letter of the autumn of 1909, we read that his heart had wavered "so much between fear and hope" (AQBB 144) – evidently an allusion to the seventh poem of the *Hanging Gardens*:

Angst und Hoffen wechselnd mich beklemmen,
(Fear and hope in turn oppress me,)
meine Worte sich in Seufzer dehnen,
(all my words to sighs are turning,)
mich bedrängt so ungestümes Sehnen,
(I'm assaulted by such yearning)
dass ich mich an Rast und Schlaf nicht kehre,
(that I find no sleep or leisure,)
daß mein Lager Tränen schwemmen,
(that my bed with tears is churning)
daß ich jede Freude von mir wehre,
(that I ward off every pleasure,)
daß ich keines Freundes Trost begehre
(no friend's comfort can access me.)

Even more significant than these lyrical allusions is that Berg at two places in the second movement of the string quartet (mm. 54-61 and 200-203) quotes or paraphrases melodic phrases from two of Schönberg's settings of the George Lieder op 15, song no. 7 "Angst und Hoffen" (Fear and Hope) and song no. 4 "Da meine Lippen reglos sind" (Since my lips are all unmoving):[391]

Berg deemed the renowned *George Lieder* of his teacher, which he had heard already at their Vienna premiere on January 14, 1910, "most glorious."[392] His numerous annotations in his personal copy of the first edition[393] make clear that he had minutely analyzed the songs, evidently taking special pleasure in detecting tonal centers in several of the settings. How much he valued the latter one can also see from the fact that he copied the first four songs by hand.[394]

Returning to the quartet, some other relevant observations are to be made in the middle part of the second movement, specifically in the section *Sehr ruhig und mäßig* (mm. 119-142), which has an exterritorial status insofar as it does not recur in the course of the movement: it is something "said once only."

Both in its "tone" and in its "flow" (note the similar sequencing), the music notably recalls the great love scene in Wagner's *Tristan und Isolde*:

WAGNER, *Tristan und Isolde*, II. Aufzug, 2. Szene

BERG, Streichquartett op. 3, II. Satz, T. 119 ff.

Following this passage, we find significant variants of the so-called "Gaze motif," whose characteristic interval is the descending minor seventh:

WAGNER, *Tristan und Isolde*, Vorspiel, T. 25–28

zart

BERG, Streichquartett op. 3, II. Satz, T. 129–132

Vc.
p ma espress.

Berg loved Wagner's *Tristan* above everything. Especially the great love scene in the second act seems to have had a profound personal meaning for both him and Helene.[395] We can therefore presume that the echoes cited are intentional.

A special relevance for the semantic decipherment of the second movement, finally, is to be accorded to the tritonic motif that is first sounded three times in the transition to the secondary group (mm. 34-36). It is treated ostinato, recurs countless times in the course of the movement, and positively dominates the conclusion of the work (mm. 217-232). A similar tritonic motif characterizes the giant Fafner in Wagner's *Ring of the Nibelung*, who has killed his brother Fasolt for the sake of the Nibelungs' gold and now guards the legendary treasure as a dragon ("I lie and possess"). Fafner's unmistakable personal motif occurs not only in the *Rheingold* and in *Siegfried* but also in *Götterdämmerung*, in that eerie scene between Alberich and Hagen, when they recall the fallen giant:

WAGNER, *Götterdämmerung*, II. Aufzug, 1. Szene

BERG, Streichquartett op. 3, II. Satz, T. 217–220

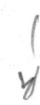

Vc.
fff marcatissimo ff   *f sempre marcato e f*

Would it be presumptuous to think that the tritonic motif here was to characterize, and cut to the quick, those "Schwarzalben" whom Berg opposed so vehemently and who stood in the way of his union with his fervently beloved Helene?

3.3 March of an Asthmatic: The Third of the Orchesterstücke op. 6

> "My asthma, too, has returned along with the spring – thus enough of a precondition for writing something merry for a change. But maybe things go the other way round for once: if what I write is not what I have experienced, perhaps my life will for once follow my compositions, which would then be sheer prophecies. But I fear I lack those powers, like so many others, and even if I am at the greatest pains to avoid 'the tears,' the result may not, after all, turn out to be the march of an upright man, who marches along cheerfully, but at best – and then it would at least be a *character piece* – a 'march of an asthmatic,' which is what I am and, it seems to me, will remain forever." Berg to Schönberg, April 10, 1914

3.3.1 Genesis and Autobiographic Occasion

In early March of 1914, Berg traveled to Leipzig to attend a performance of Schönberg's *Gurrelieder*. From there he went to Amsterdam, where works of his teacher (among them the *Fünf Orchesterstücke* op. 16) were performed. During their return trip, which took them through Berlin, Schönberg told Berg point-blank that he was not at all satisfied with the latter's artistic development and creativity. He encouraged him to tackle a larger composition and had no qualms about telling him that for his 40th birthday (on September 13, 1914) he wished for the dedication of new pieces. Several months later, on July 11, 1914, Berg told Helene that he owed the impulse for his *Drei Orchesterstücke* to his having heard Schönberg's pieces and to the latter's "admonishing advice to write character pieces" (ABB 253f.). He made it clear in the same letter, however, that his orchestra pieces would not be "modeled on" Schönberg's, but, on the contrary, would be "totally different."

On September 8 – still in time for Schönberg's round birthday – Berg sent him a "roll of music" containing two of the *Three Pieces for Orchestra*, the first and the third. The second piece, *Reigen* (Round Dance), was not yet finished at that point. In an accompanying letter, Berg told his mentor that it had been his wish for many years to dedicate something to him. The pieces he had written under him – the Piano Sonata op. 1, the *Vier Lieder* op. 2 and the String Quart t op. 3 – he could not well inscribe to him because they had been "directly received" from him, and his hope of writing "something independent and yet of equal value with the foregoing things," which he could inscribe to him without irking him, had "for some years unfortunately" proved deceptive. Only Schönberg's challenge had at last given him the courage to attempt a work that he would not have to be ashamed to dedicate to him.

Berg went on to say that the composition of his pieces had been preceded by "intensive study" of Schönberg's orchestral pieces. He had fairly concrete ideas about the as yet unfinished second piece at the time – "a piece in the character of a dance with a (very approximate) length of 100 measures, that is, longer than the *Praeludium*, shorter than the *Marsch*." (In the printed version, the *Prelude* has 56 bars, the *Round Dance* 127 and the *March* 174.)

In a later letter of late November, Berg wrote Schönberg that the *Three Pieces for Orchestra* had sprung from the "most strenuous and holiest endeavor" to "create character pieces" in the form asked for by his mentor – "of normal length, richly thematic work, without an addiction to producing something absolutely 'new'" – and to give his best with this work.[396]

Berg's letters to Schönberg and Webern show that he started to work on the *March* in April of 1914: "the design and many parts" were already done by April 10.[397] During the summer in Trahütten, he finished the *Praeludium* and started to write out the *Marsch*, which he had completed while still in Vienna, in score form.[398] The last part to be written was the *Reigen*; the score for this piece was executed in the summer of 1915.[399]

The earliest sketches for the *Three Pieces for Orchestra* are contained in a sketchbook preserved in the Viennese Municipal and National Library (Signature MHc 14263). The book comprises counterpoint exercises from the time of Berg's studies under Schönberg (pp. 7-20); a piano sketch of mm. 4-11 and 16-19 of the *Prelude* (pp. 23/24); the earliest drafts for the *March* (pp. 30/31), indicating that one of its themes was to have been in C minor; the characteristic chordal sequences from the *Round Dance* mm. 4/5 and from the *Prelude* mm. 44-46; as well as a twofold partial draft of the second of the four pieces for clarinet op. 5 (pp. 36/37 and p. 41). A note on p. 30 shows that the march was from the outset conceived as the finale.

On July 10, 1914, Berg joyfully told Helene that the *March* on which he was working was rounding off well. After all, though, was thinking of it all day long – even when he was working on other things the production was quietly continuing to simmer (ABB 252f.). The next day he informed her that he would really like to complete a "little piano piece" for her, but regretted that it was not to be (ABB 252). In the same letter, he also made some revealing remarks about the *Three Pieces for Orchestra*. Although he would not be able to dedicate the pieces to her officially, he wrote to Helene, "yet there is a good deal of *Pferscher* [peach, Helene's nickname[400]] in them, and even though [s]he might not like them right away, I know that someday [s]he will love them as much as me, with all my flaws, and perhaps more than your little piece, even if I manage to finish it" (ABB 254).

This important passage proves that the *Drei Orchesterstücke* are autobiographic in concept. Already on April 10, 1914, Berg had written, not without bitter self-irony, to his teacher Schönberg about the third piece that it might not, "after all, turn out to be the march of an upright man, who marches along cheerfully," but, "at best," a "march of an asthmatic," which he was and, as it seemed to him, would remain forever.

Everything, then, points to the likelihood that Berg's tormenting and fearful experiences with asthma entered into the conception of the March. As had been the case repeatedly in the last several years,[401] he was afraid again that some day he would not survive one of his violent asthmatic attacks.

3.3.2 Musico-Semantic Hints

> "Words are a cumbersome system of coordinates for a score that Berg, not without artistic conceit, called the most complicated ever written."
>
> "A gigantic model has been critically reconceived: the Finale of Mahler's Sixth Symphony." Adorno about the *March*[402]

Of the composers of the Second Viennese School, Berg was the one with the closest elective affinity to Gustav Mahler. His musical language often exhibits a striking proximity to Mahler's idiom, something that is especially noticeable in the *Three Pieces for Orchestra* and in the *Violin Concerto*. The *March*, in particular, can be called the result of an equally intensive and productive contention with the symphonic oeuvre of Mahler.

If Adorno thought that in the *March* Berg was critically reflecting the Finale of Mahler's Sixth Symphony (the so-called *Tragic* one), Hans Ferdinand Redlich had earlier sought to concretize Mahler's influence on Berg. Berg's marking *Allegro energico* (Tempo III, at m. 91), he noted, was identical with Mahler's in the Finale of the Sixth Symphony. In both works again, the hammer served as a tone symbol of catastrophe and in both cases was struck three times. Besides, motifs and rhythms sounding simultaneously at the beginning of Berg's march resembled analogous figures in Mahler's symphonies (especially the Sixth and Fifth).[403]

As apt as these remarks are, one must note, on the one hand, that the parallels to Mahler are a great deal more extensive yet and, on the other, that Berg's *March* is nevertheless a piece of unmistakable originality, one whose idiom is already that of Expressionism. Berg heard the Sixth Symphony on November 28, 1911, in Vienna under the direction of Ferdinand Löwe. How powerful the impression it made on him was can be gathered from a letter he wrote to Webern on December 6, 1911. It reads in part:

> Of what significance is all this composing if on the following day one hears the Sixth (I surely don't have to say by whom that is, there is really only one Sixth, in spite of the *Pastoral*). I tell you – or really I don't need to tell you – how forever inexhaustible, never fully to be grasped this work is. How glorious it is, be it never so poorly performed. And it really was that!

Theodor W. Adorno, who, as mentioned before, liked to speak of the "liquidation" of the sonata in early Berg, divided the March into a multi-stage introduction, three "main groups" (mm. 53, 91 and 136) and a coda (m. 149).

Upon closer inspection, however, it becomes clear that the piece is dominated by a principle of contrast.

Thus the character of the march is again and again interrupted by tender, retarding parts that are not at all march-like but are of an altogether different tonal character, an expressive melodic gesture and a reduction in both tempo and dynamics. It would be no exaggeration to say that the peculiar physiognomy of the piece is determined by the constant alternation between robust and tender parts, between martialism and extreme subjectivity, between violence and powerlessness.

Mark DeVoto thought one could make out at least 31 different motifs and themes in the *March*, including major independent variants or inversions.[404] If one were to make an actual list of the motivic-thematic characters in the work, it would make sense to divide them according to the two different aspects described. The category of genuine march includes – besides the four simultaneously sounding motifs of the introduction (according to Adorno, these are "march rhythm, clarinet trill, march-like tone repetition in the English horn" and "oboe fanfare") – above all characteristic motifs won from just that "oboe fanfare."[405] They are sounded in two decisive places in the score: at the beginning of the *Allegro energico* (mm. 90ff) and at the start of the Coda (mm. 148ff.), there with the characteristic marking *marziale*:

A leading role within the march category, moreover, is taken by a characteristic signal that sounds frequently – repeatedly in tritonic coloration – and in one place (mm. 73-75) is even treated imitationally:

Fundamentally different from the aspect of the march is the musical landscape of the second category, which is marked by highly expressive melodic lines (one is tempted to speak of novel "sighing figures"), which are often performed solo and very tenderly. The following table lists only some especially characteristic examples:

T. 29 - 31
Va. Solo

T. 40/41
Vc. Solo
mit Dpf.

T. 99/100
1. Vl.

T. 129 - 131
1. Vl.

T. 166/167
1. Pos. m. Dpf.

T. 168/169
1. Solo-Vl.

Like Schönberg's *Gurrelieder* and Mahler's *Tragic Symphony*, Berg's *Marsch*, too, requires a gigantic orchestral apparatus, including a large percussion group. The latter consists of great and small drum, cymbals, great and small tamtam, two timpani, tenor drum and triangle, great hammer ("with non-metallic sound"), glockenspiel, xylophone and celesta. Some of these percussion instruments – especially the timpani, great and small drum and tenor drum – repeatedly have the job of underscoring the onward-pressing thrust of the march by means of terse, frequently ostinato rhythms, as the examples below will illustrate. The rhythm of the great drum quoted last, incidentally, is modeled on the leit-rhythm of Mahler's *Tragic*.[406]

Not least important for an interpretation of the *March* is Berg's conversance with the contemporary secondary literature about Mahler. He owned the two books by Paul Stefan[407] and the book on Mahler by Richard Specht, published in 1913, which, according to a note on the inside of the book cover, he acquired on December 12, 1913. Numerous reading traces – marginal lines, exclamation marks and annotations – indicate that he read this book attentively.[408] Specht's interpretation of the Finale of the *Tragic Symphony* is instructive in the present context. In that terrible movement disclosing a "ghastly picture of the world," Specht writes, there sounds, "not the whetting of the Grim Reaper's scythe – the hammer of the world's being hurtles down [...] and Death itself sinks under the these blows crushing the entire earth to dust."[409]

There is much to suggest that Berg, too, felt the three hammer strokes in his *March* to be "crushing blows." The first stroke coincides with the climax of the piece (m. 126), the second falls somewhat later (m. 142); the piece ends rather abruptly with the third (m. 174).

A special importance for the semantic decipherment of the piece must be ascribed also to the Coda (from m. 149), in particular the five bars titled *Pesante* (mm. 155-159), because they have all the markings of a compositional type that we know from Mahler. I am referring to the type of *exequies music*, a genre of requiem-like music contiguous to both the funeral march and the chorale, and one for which the participation of the brass and the tamtam is all but obligatory.[410] All this applies also to the five *Pesante* bars, with the one difference that in Berg the characteristic quoted rhythm of the great drum and rolls of the small drum are added to the regular tamtam beats. From what has been said it will be evident that the strokes of the great drum here have a lugubrious, funereal meaning, as they do in Mahler.

Shortly after the *Pesante* bars and toward the end of the piece (mm. 161-164), we come upon another passage that is very striking for its timbre: *calm and always very slow (dragging)*. Its specific feature are chromatically ascending and descending mixtures of woodwinds and strings – parallel tones that form a basis for a three-part canon of the first trumpet, the first horn and the second trombone. This is followed in m. 165 by fleeting figures of the A and E♭ clarinet and the piccolo flute. These mixtures with their strongly coloristic effect remind of the invention over a hexachord in the pond scene in *Wozzeck* (III/4), specifically at the point where Wozzeck drowns. The similarity in sound effect is so striking that I would assume that in the *March*, too, Berg has used tone-painting to depict a fit of choking or asphyxia.

Gustav Mahler shared the belief, going back to Goethe and the Romantics, that in the hours of inspiration the artist is lifted to a higher, anticipatory level of his existence.[411] Paul Stefan formulated this persuasion by saying: "Mahler used to say that his works were anticipated experiences."[412] When Berg was working on the *Drei Orchesterstücke* in 1914, he had appropriated Mahler's maxim. That is the gist of the sentences from the letter to Schönberg of April 10, 1914, cited as a motto to this chapter: "If what I write is not what I have experienced, perhaps my life will for once follow my compositions, which would then be sheer prophecies."

3.4 *Wozzeck* as a Message for Humanity

> "Among operatic works of a radical-modern tendency, works that seek new ways, there is none that equals this 'Wozzeck' in ethical thought and inner purity." A. Stehle in 1930[413]

3.4.1 An "Opera of Social Compassion"?

On May 5, 1914, at the age of 29, Alban Berg attended the premiere of Büchner's drama *Woyzeck* at Vienna's Residenzbühne.[414] The performance impressed him so much that he decided on the spot to turn the drama into an opera.[415] Arnold Schönberg, to whom he announced his intention, advised against tackling the project, as he regarded Büchner's play as "a drama so extraordinarily tragic" that it "seemed to preclude music."[416] Besides, Schönberg took exception to the scenes of quotidian life contained in the play, scenes that in his view were incompatible with opera as then understood.[417] Berg did not let himself be discouraged by the opinion of his teacher and decided to risk the venture. Hampered as he was by illness, military service and manifold obligations, it took him years to adapt the text and set it to music. It was not until April of 1922 hat he was able to complete the orchestration.[418]

In spite of numerous critical voices, the Berlin premiere of the opera under Erich Kleiber on December 14, 1925, gave Berg the long wished-for breakthrough. At least on the German stage, the work quickly entered the repertoire. By the end of 1932, the Berlin premiere had been followed by at least 30 performances.⁴¹⁹ According to Hans Mayer, the literary reputation of Georg Büchner, who had been little known until then, evolved by way of the operatic stage.⁴²⁰ The remarkable successes of the many *Wozzeck* productions spread not only Berg's but also Büchner's name world-wide.

How is this success of the opera, sensational for an "atonal" work, to be explained? Although reception-aesthetic investigations of the matter are still wanting, it seems certain that many critics were taken with the novelty of Berg's musical language and were moved by both the subject and the expressivity of Berg's music. Thus Igor Glebov (pseudonym for Bois Assafiev) wrote, apropos of the opera's Leningrad performance on June 13, 1927, that there was "no more passionate, emotionally truer and more deeply impressive drama" than *Wozzeck*. With it, "the limits of musical-dramatic expressivity of western European opera" had been reached.⁴²¹

Today, *Wozzeck* is regarded as one of the most important operatic works of the 20th century (Wolfgang Rihm called it the "opera of the century"⁴²²), as a milestone in the development of musical theater and a work without which, e.g., Bernd Alois Zimmermann's *The Soldiers* would be unthinkable.⁴²³ But what exactly is its place in the operatic production of the 1920's? Hans Ferdinand Redlich, who in 1957 undertook to answer that question, thought that with *Wozzeck* Berg had created a "new operatic archetype," namely "the opera of social compassion": in the intellectual types of Büchner and Berg, the creative success of a symbiosis of social-critical potency with a corresponding musical talent was anticipated and predetermined from the start.⁴²⁴ The Swedish composer Bo Ullman opined that Berg's music drama did "not betray the social-critical content" of Büchner's drama: "in the tone of his music": Berg had done justice to "the social-critical intentions of Büchner's text and had known how to foreground "the economic situation" of the main figures musically.⁴²⁵

The arguments to which the proponents of this theory appeal seem at first blush convincing. Already in 1926, Rudolf Schafke called Berg a "committed revolutionary and socialist."⁴²⁶ And indeed, some of Büchner's unmistakably social-critical maxims gain in forcefulness in Berg's musical setting: we might think of Wozzeck's exclamations such as "Folks like us are plain wretched in this and the other world. I think, if we got to heaven, we would have to assist with the thunder,"⁴²⁷ and "Nothing but work under the sun, sweat even in sleep. Poor people, we!"⁴²⁸ The "Poor people, we" motif in fact functions as one of the major motifs of the opera.

Even so, we must consider that the *Woyzeck* fragment is exceptionally multi-leveled. It impresses one not only by its pervasive social-critical intention, but also by its reflections on the problem of the freedom of the will and the dualism of Nature" and "Morality," and, moreover, seems to anticipate discoveries of later depth psychology and imparts stunning insights into the basic questions of human existence.[429] A sentence like "Man is an abyss, one gets dizzy from looking into it"[430] gives expression to experiences that are central not merely to the 19th century. Büchner himself spoke about the "ghastly fatalism of history" in a letter of 1833 to his fiancée and posed the compelling question: "What is it within us that lies, murders, steals?"[431]

What, then, was it that fascinated Berg about the *Woyzeck* fragment, and how did he perceive its subject? Regrettably, he has expressed himself about that only in vague hints, both in conversation, in letters and in lectures. Happily, however, we find important clues for an answer to these questions in the earliest *Wozzeck* sketches. The following inquiry is based in part on hitherto unexploited documents.

3.4.2 The Characterization of Three Figures in the Opera: the Captain, the Doctor, and Wozzeck

Some time after the Vienna performance of *Woyzeck* in May of 1914, Berg began with an adaptation of the text for his opera. In his personal copy of Büchner's play, we find numerous entries – marginalia, corrections, transpositions, stage directions – that afford insights into his dramaturgic and musical ideas.[432] Of special interest is a note about Wozzeck's two military superiors. The scene "Forest Path by the Pond" contains the following characterization of the Doctor and the Captain: "Doctor always scientifically matter-of-fact. Captain: superstitious, fearful, philosophical."

The sketches for *Wozzeck* that are preserved in the Music Collection of the Austrian National Library in Vienna (Fonds 21 Berg 13/I-XIV, 28/XXXVII and 70/I-III) have been described and interpreted in detail by Peter Petersen.[433] They comprise isolated textual passages, drafts of entire scenes, rhythmic sketches and the chief leading themes and motifs of the opera. A note on p. 57 of the second sketchbook (Berg 13/II) shows that Berg's opinion about the captain was extremely negative. The note reads: "The Captain. A zero. With a moderate talent for dissimulation [*Verstellungsgabe* is written above the line], of always (?) wanting to seem more – blusterer (a good man) – easily moved about himself – With a remnant of military discipline., which keeps quickly disappearing behind the manner of stolid (complacent) asthmatic upper echelons."

The Captain, in Berg's view, is therefore a hypocrite, a swaggerer and an asthmatic hypochondriac. Berg regarded his talk about the "good man" as mere gas and had correctly diagnosed his hypochondriacal disposition. The Captain fears for his life, is afraid of death and imagines his own funeral. His words about himself, in the street scene in Act II, "But they will say: he was a good man, a good man," are significantly accompanied by the stage direction: "Captain more and more moved" in Berg's score[434] – a comment not found in Büchner's text.[435]

Berg had no sympathy with the Doctor, either. The latter's pseudo-scientific conceit and lack of human warmth must have appeared grotesque, even repulsive to him. Precisely at the time before the composition of *Wozzeck*, he was skeptical, as appears from a letter to Schönberg of May 6, 1913, about a merely dissecting science that claimed to be able to explain everything in purely materialistic terms, even the mysteries of life and death.[436] He had grasped the subtle irony of the doctor's diagnosing "a nice fixed idea, a delicious aberratio mentalis partialis" in Wozzeck[437] while laboring under an idée fixe himself, and aptly gave to the fourth scene of the first act the form of a passacaglia with 21 variations. Long after the composition of *Wozzeck*, according to Willi Reich, he read to his great satisfaction in Riemann's *Musik-Lexikon (Dictionary of Music)* that "The folia (idée fixe!) is evidently one of the older forms of the ostinato."[438]

Berg seems to have regarded both the Captain and the Doctor as relatively undifferentiated characters, as he furnished them with few personal leitmotifs. A sole motif characterizes the Captain, while the Doctor at least got two. For Wozzeck, by contrast, no fewer than six personal leitmotifs are planned in the sketchbook (Berg 13/I pp. 31-34), which bear the following denominations:[439]

> Wozzeck Poor people, we
> Wozzeck thirds, the Upright
> Wozzeck the Hounded
> Wozzeck the Fatalist
> Wozzeck the Outraged
> Wozzeck E^b Minor the Resigned

Quite obviously, Berg wanted thereby to highlight the multiple facets of Wozzeck's personality and predicament musically.

3.4.3 The "Epilogue" to the Opera as "Author's Confession"

In May of 1929, Berg gave his famous introductory lecture in Oldenburg, on the occasion of the revival of *Wozzeck* there. In it he commented also on the orchestral interlude prior to the final scene, calling it the "epilogue" to the opera and referred to it as a "profession [*Bekenntnis*] of the author."

> From the dramatic standpoint, it is to be understood as an "epilogue" following Wozzeck's suicide, as a profession of the author suspending the stage action of the plot, even as a direct appeal to the audience, which, as it were, represents humanity as a whole. From the musical standpoint, however, this last orchestral interlude represents a thematic development of all the important musical figures that have become related to Wozzeck.[440]

A semantic analysis of the music can explicate and concretize what Berg is hinting at here.

The interlude, conceived as an "invention on a key," exhibits a tripartite form with a strongly abridged and varied recapitulation (A – B – A'). The substance of the first part Berg took by and large from an early, unpublished piano sonata in D minor, which in the autograph (Fonds 21 Berg 48 pp. 9-11) bears the number IV. In addition, he based the piece on the chief leitmotifs of the opera. Regarding the sequence of the motifs, one will note that, except for one reminiscence of the motif for Wozzeck's friend Andres (mm. 339-341), the outer parts of the epilogue contain solely motifs related to Wozzeck. At the end of the first part, for example, the motif of the hounded Wozzeck sounds in multiple diminution. The middle portion, on the other hand, works the motifs of the Doctor and the Captain, which are contrapuntally intertwined, and then refers to the seduction scene. That is to say, the music of several bars from the *Andante affettuoso* of the seduction scene (Act I, mm. 656-660) recurs here in artful variation (Epilogue, mm. 352-357). After the intonation of the motif of the Drum Major (mm. 357/8), the middle part culminates in the "Poor people, we" motif and in the famous twelve-note chord, which assumes the function of a powerful dominant before the concluding part. The heavily foreshortened recapitulation once more evokes the plight of Wozzeck and is dominated by his "fatalistic" motif.

Conspectus of the leitmotifs and echoes occurring in the Epilogue

Part 1 (Adagio), mm. 320-345

mm. 339-341 (horns): Andres motif

Hn.(gest.) wie aus der Ferne, aber deutlich

Wozzeck the hounded (motif quadrupled, in multiple diminution)

Part 2

"Considerably more agitated" (mm. 346-351); the two Doctor motifs and the Captain motif contrapuntally intertwined

"Again somewhat more sedate (Andante)" mm. 352-364

Bars 352-357 correspond to the *Andante a affettuoso* of the seduction scene (Act I, mm. 656-660).

Mm. 357/358: the motif of the Drum Major

T. 357/358: das Motiv des Tambourmajors

Mm. 360-364 the motif "Poor people, we" in stretto and the twelve-tone chord quasi as dominant

Part 3 (foreshortened recapitulation *Tempo I* (mm. 365-371)

Leitmotif: Wozzeck the Fatalist

A listener halfway familiar with the opera will not fail to recognize that the music of this last orchestral interlude commemorates Wozzeck as the antihero. It recalls the personages that played a role in the life of the drowned man – his friend Andres, the Doctor, the Captain, the Drum Major – and it recalls above all the crucial scene of the opera, that of Marie's seduction. The epilogue is conceived as a "profession" of the author, that is, it gives expression to Berg's compassion for the tortured man, who, tormented and mortified by his superiors, betrayed by his beloved, humiliated by his rival, derided by the world around him and plagued by delusion, became a murderer.

3.4.4 Excursus: The Epilogue as "Invention on a Key"

In his famous Open Letter of February 9, 1925, to Arnold Schönberg, Berg revealed that there was a special significance to the number three with regard to the construction of his Chamber Concerto of 1923 to 1925. It determined, he wrote, every musical aspect of the work: the instrumentation and the number of players (15), the formal divisions, the proportions of the movements, the "rhythmic forms," the area of meter and also that of "Harmony." Along with "large stretches of altogether dissolved tonality," there were "isolated smaller parts with a tonal touch" and others that corresponded to the laws of "composition with twelve tones" established by Schönberg.[441]

What Berg said about the ratio of tonality, atonality and dodecaphony in the Chamber Concerto applies, *mutatis mutandis*, also to *Wozzeck*. The music of most of the scenes is kept in so-called free atonality. Along with that, however, there are also isolated tonal passages, and there are first signs of a quasi dodecaphonic mode of composition. *Wozzeck* originated at a time (1917-1921) when Schönberg had not yet formulated the rules of the twelve-tone technique completely. Even so, the passacaglia in the first act can be seen as an early stage of serial composition, not so much because the theme of the passacaglia is twelve-toned but because it is frequently, as Redlich's analysis has shown, treated in serial technique.[442]

Berg here already tries on artistic devices that later on became especially characteristic of the serial technique, the most significant being probably the verticalization of the twelve-tone row in the sixth and seventh variation. Outside of the passacaglia, too, however, we encounter numerous twelve-tone sequences and twelve-tone fields in *Wozzeck*. Years ago, Peter Petersen succeeded in tracing four twelve-tone thirds chords in the first three scenes of the opera.[443]

Our particular concern here is with the tonal, or seemingly tonal, enclaves in the opera. Among them we may include the *Quasi Trio* of the military march in the third scene of Act I, the fifth variation of the Bible scene in Act III and the "Epilogue." Regarding the F minor variation of the Bible scene, Erich Forneberg rightly pointed out that its exceptional formation corresponded to a specific intention. For in this scene Marie tells her boy the (foreshadowing) fairytale of the poor child that had no father and no mother. Berg composed this variation in the tonal idiom, because fairytales as such derived from a world other than the "earthly atonal out-of-tune" one.[444]

The Epilogue was called an "invention on a key" by Willi Reichert[445] and an "invention in a key" by Fritz Mahler.[446] Berg himself, in his Oldenburg lecture, had this to say about the tonal conception of the orchestral interlude:

> Its form is tripartite, its unifying principle for once tonality: this D minor, whose harmonically quasi dissolving introduction I have already referred to.
>
> *Piano Score, Act III, pp. 223-224, mm. 319-320*, to be sure, undergoes such a, one can say, limitless expansion, that it was possible to take that all the way to the ultimate tonal consequence. For in the middle part of the piece, at its climax, where its development-like entries condense all the way to strettos, a harmonic consonance emerged as if by itself, which, although it combines all twelve tones, yet has the effect of a mere dominant within the tonal framework, one that in a manner quite natural and harmonically cogent leads back to the D minor of the recapitulation.[447]

A more detailed analysis of this orchestral interlude will show that Berg there indeed stretched tonality, which he conceived as a "form-building means," to its limits and even crossed over the threshold to atonality. Viewed from a distance, the interlude can be seen as a kind of macro-cadence, with the twelve-tone chord in m. 364 fulfilling the function of the dominant. Some specifics on the matter: In the first four measures of the interlude (mm. 320-323), the key of D minor is confirmed. In m. 324, a modulation commences, which leads to an F tonality. The basic harmonic scaffolding of mm. 331-335 is tonally unequivocal: m. 331: C; m. 332: D♭; m. 333: G; m. 334: C_7; m. 335: F-sound (veiled by whole tones). From m. 336 on, the relation to tonality becomes gradually loosened. In the middle part of the Epilogue (mm. 346-364), tonality is dissolved; tonal centers can no longer be made out (except for the tone center of mm. 352-356). The recapitulation (mm. 365-371) is again tonally anchored in D minor.

3.4.5 *Wozzeck* as a Parable

> "There is, after all, also a piece of me in the figure (that of Wozzeck), since I am spending these war years equally dependent on hateful people, bound, sickly, unfree, resigned, even humiliated."
>
> Berg to Helene, August 7, 1918 (ABB 376)

The analysis of the Epilogue has gotten us on the track of Berg's intentions. The question emerges again as to his view of Büchner's play. If one takes into account all of Berg's remarks pertaining to the play, it becomes clear that

Redlich's opinion that *Wozzeck* was an "opera of social compassion" hardly hits the heart of the matter. To wit:

In a letter to Webern of August 19, 1918, Berg explains what had fascinated him about Büchner's play: "What affects me so," he wrote to him, "is not only the fate of this poor man, who is exploited and tormented by the whole world, but also the incredible density of mood in each scene."[448] In the article "Das Opernproblem" (The Problem of Opera) he published ten years later, he remarked, albeit rather vaguely, that the idea of his opera went far beyond the individual fate of Wozzeck.[449]

An important milestone in the reception history of *Wozzeck* seems to have been an article by the Berlin critic Ernst Viebig, who in April of 1923 – i.e., two-and-a-half years before the Berlin premiere – published a very appreciative analysis of the opera in the prominent journal *Die Musik*, having studied the piano score of the work prepared by Fritz Heinrich Klein.[450] In the article, he described the dramatic action of the tragedy by using the words of the literary historian Richard M. Meyer: "The hero is an anybody of the people, poor, weak, despised. For this very reason he becomes a symbolic figure, He is the people itself and his fate that of the people in the hands of their rulers."[451]

Berg was at first very pleased by the article. He marveled at Viebig's apt observations and on April 11, 1923, wrote greatly delighted to his wife: "The content, too, is well retold, in that the *purely human* (the people) is emphasized, not the individual fate" (ABB 508).

Viebig's article, however, seems to have encouraged the notion that *Wozzeck* was a piece about "poor folks," for Berg soon saw himself forced to publish a corrective. In February of 1930, he engaged in a dialogue with Oskar Jancke about *Wozzeck*, which was printed in the *Aachener Anzeiger*. In it he made the following statement:

> There was probably a natural relationship between that work [i.e. Büchner's *Woyzeck*] and me. I want to emphasize, by the way, that my *Wozzeck* is not a mere poor people drama. What happens to Wozzeck can happen to any poor soul, regardless of the dress he may be wearing. It will ever be thus with any human beings who are oppressed by others and cannot defend themselves.[452]

Wozzeck can consequently be seen as the author's profession of a humanitarian ethos and as a quiet protest against all inhumanity. It is a dramatic parable giving expression to the author's compassion for the humiliated, the insulted and defenseless. From this compassionate feeling springs the overwhelming expressivity of the music, which Berg would surely not have composed in the same way if he had not in some way indentified with the fate of Wozzeck. No doubt traumatic personal experiences during World War One precipitated out in the conception of the opera. His letters to his friend August Göttel and his pupil Gottfried Kassowitz strikingly document how much he suffered during the time of his military service.[453] Deeply stirred, he told August Göttel in August of 1916 about the bloody rampage of a crazed soldier – a deed that resulted in casualties of four dead and eleven wounded.[454] The conditions in the barracks, the mindless organization of military life, the unfair treatment he himself was subjected to – all of this provoked his agitation and loathing. Especially illuminating in this connection is a letter written to Kassowitz on Christmas Day of 1915, in which he complained about a military doctor who did not help his patients but made fun of them and threatened them with being detailed to the front.[455]

3.4.6 Some Thoughts about Music between the Two World Wars

Events of world politics have unforeseeable consequences, not only for states and nations, the social order and the economy, but also for the arts. The profound crisis into which the Great War plunged people everywhere also had its impact on the development of music. The musical life between the two World Wars is characterized by an astounding variety of currents. Never before had there been so many simultaneous, competing trends as there were in the 1920s and still in the 1930s: Expressionism and Post-Expressionism, Neoclassicism, Neobaroque, Folklorism, Vitalism, Futurism – a long line of "isms."

According to Ivan Martynov, musical production between the two World Wars extended between two poles, with numerous variants in between. One pole was despair, hopeless dread – the leitmotif of the work of Alban Berg; the other lay in mindless frivolity, superficiality, mere entertainment.[456] Martynov's thesis is untenable in its sweeping generality, but it contains a grain of truth.

Schönberg, Berg and Webern, conceptually linked to Expressionism, cultivated throughout an art given to expressive subjectivity. Their aesthetic creed culminated in the statement: "Music is not meant to be decorative but to be true."[457] Other leading composers, conversely, sought to overcome this very subjectivity, regarded as a legacy of the 19th century, and dreamed of an "objective" music. In 1920, Ferruccio Busoni – a composer of a truly European outlook – wrote a letter to Paul Bekker that would become famous under the title "Young Classicity." In that classicity he included, among other things, a stripping away of the sensual, a renunciation of subjectivism, a reconquest of serenity and, above all, "absolute music."[458] Busoni here expressed what many were thinking and demanding, and what characterized the *zeitgeist*: a break with the art of the 19th century, a liberation of music from the literary, an express rejection of program music, and a reorientation of music toward the art of the Baroque and of Classicism. Concertante music-making, long neglected, the polyphonic forms and techniques of the Baroque, the doctrine of "linear counterpoint" all experienced a renascence and attained an undreamt-of topicality. Béla Bartók and others sought to open up new sources for the New Music by exploring folklore. Alongside, there were experiments with bitonality, polytonality, intricate metrics and polyrhythmics. Elements of jazz and dance music also invaded "classical" music.

Viewed psychologically, Busoni's call for serenity signified a repression of the problematic, a turn to the bright, the Apollinian – an understandable reaction to the shocks the First World War had produced. But it is also understandable that the serious would not be pushed aside but maintained its place. Thus the music between the two wars is Janus-faced: Busoni's *Arlecchino* (1918) was followed by Hindemith's *Marienleben* (1923), Ernst Krenek composed the tragic opera *Karl V.* (1938) after his jazz opera *Johnnie spielt auf* (1927), and when Hindemith's merry opera *Neues vom Tage* (News of the Day) was premiered in Berlin in 1929, Alban Berg was already working on his *Lulu*.

3.5 Berg, Schönberg and Webern: Profiles of a Friendship

> "I am more and more imbued with his paramount importance. His things are so fabulously beautiful, so limitlessly beautiful." (Webern to Berg, January 11, 1912, about Schönberg

> "This relationship of ours with you, as our leader, our guide, is something profoundly beatific to me. You are the bond, the indissoluble bond that unites us. We all live for you. Believe me." Webern to Schönberg, June 9, 1912 (using the familiar pronoun *Du*)

> "This, too, like everything, Schönberg does very thoroughly and skillfully and solves everything *strictly mathematically*, that is, nothing by happenstance, everything by reason." Berg to Helene, September 22, 1918 (ABB 398)

> "After all, the superego arose from identification with the father image." Sigmund Freud

The more intensively one studies Berg's and especially Webern's letters, the clearer it becomes that the so-called Second Vienna School was a spiritual community around Schönberg, the teacher and mentor, whose personality radiated a peculiar fascination. The feeling of a common bond that the members of this community had was a strong one. Most of Schönberg's pupils/disciples believed unshakably in their teacher, admired, venerated and loved him in many cases unconditionally. They lived with the conviction of belonging to an elite group, which was attacked, scoffed at or ignored by any means available solely because they were superior and ahead of their time.

For Alban Berg and Anton Webern, Schönberg was a great deal more than a mere model, not only in an artistic but also in a human respect. One could almost speak of a superego, a father figure. Like Webern, Berg revered his teacher all his life, admiring alike the personality, the genius, the courage, the uncompromising stance and the intellectual wealth of his friend. "No human being on God's green earth means half as much to me as you do," he wrote to Helene in September of 1910, "not even Schönberg. And that is saying something" (ABB 198).

In September of 1910, Webern was hired as conductor's assistant at the municipal theater of Danzig (Gdansk). His initial enthusiasm about the city on the Baltic Sea did not last long. Soon he felt lonely, and most of all he missed the stimulating conversations with his teacher. The empathetic Berg could easily put himself in Webern's frame of mind. "How sad you must be again," he wrote to him, "about having to be so far from all these divinenesses, to have to do without the walks with Schönberg, to miss the meaning and gesture and tone of voice of his speech."

Photograph 9: Berg and Schönberg

(with kind permission of the Alban Berg Foundation Vienna)

Berg stood up for Schönberg whenever he could.[459] At times he literally sacrificed himself for him. Time and again he started actions to help him in his financial distress (conversely, Schönberg, too, was prepared to help Berg financially when able[460]), and he did whatever he could to contribute to the spread of his works and to create the conditions for a better understanding of his art. He authored thematic analyses of several of his works as well as the famous guide through the *Gurrelieder* comprising more than 100 printed pages.[461] More than once he also interceded for him journalistically, and had even assembled materials for a book about Schönberg, in which he wanted to make an "airtight" case for the evolution of his teacher's music.[462] (He found fault with Egon Wellesz' Schönberg study for "curtailing" the "purely musical" aspect.) If he did not complete the book, it was largely because he abandoned the plan of a writer's career in favor of his compositional work.[463]

But as attached as Berg felt to Schönberg, and as cordial as his relation to him was, it would be tendentious to deny that there were occasional tensions. In the course of time, Berg came to know not only the amiable but also the "difficult" Schönberg. He felt led by the nose, patronized, even exploited. As much sympathy as he mustered for Schönberg's financial misery, the latter's "painful cadging affairs" at times bothered him greatly (ABB 442).

For a while, Schönberg, in turn, frequently found fault with Berg. He reproached him with stagnating productivity and "bad time management," and even criticized his epistolary style: Berg, he thought, wrote letters that were much too long and didn't get to the point quickly enough.[464] His criticism was so direct and unsparing that it could not but wound Berg deeply. In letters to his teacher he tried at times to justify himself for pages on end.[465] His reaction to his teacher's criticism of his epistolary style was different, however: he, whose style was the product of a literary training, made it a habit of writing nothing but prosaic, matter-of-fact letters to Schönberg. His experiences, deeper thoughts and feelings he saved for his letters to Webern, by whom he felt understood.

Adorno, as mentioned earlier, summed up Berg's relation to Schönberg by saying that the latter envied Berg's successes, while Berg envied Schönberg's failures.[466] Several of Berg's letters of April 1923 to Helene document that Schönberg registered Berg's first real successes (in April of 1923, Emil Hertzka, the director of Universal Edition, had agreed to publish *Wozzeck* and the Pieces for Orchestra op. 6) with a certain jealousy. "Schönberg was once again insufferable, criticized everything about me," Berg wrote to Helene on April 8: "that I am still working on *Wozzeck*, 'it's Karl Kraus-ish, that eternal correcting!', that I smoke, that I should not think for a moment that I will have any success with *Wozzeck*, because it is too difficult, and, worst, that I am still not working on the wind chamber music" (ABB 505). And in a letter of April 11, we read: "I paid a brief visit to Schönberg, who was critical again, wanted to spoil all my joy about the imminent contract with Hertzka" (ABB 508).

Yet such ill feelings are apt to be found in any friendship. What matters is that Berg had limitless admiration for most of Schönberg's works. Whether it was the symphonic poem *Pelleas and Melisande* op. 5, the first two string quartets op. 7 and op. 10 or the monodrama *Die Erwartung*, he always spoke rapturously about them. Thus he wrote to his teacher on June 15, 1912, that he was once again luxuriating in the *Gurrelieder*. Especially the first part, which he was then studying, seemed to him something of "unheard-of splendor," like "condensed music." In the same letter, he thought he could not even speak of *Herzgewächse*: "words fail. Simply godful – full of god" (*gottvoll – Gottes voll*). After a performance of the *George Lieder* in 1912, he had this to say:

> The George Lieder, which I have always regarded as the most magnificent, and imagined I understood, I now like much, much better still, and I now know that I still have a long way to go to obtain a true understanding of these fabulously beautiful works. That happens to many, I am sure. Our brain and our heart are almost too small for the greatness of such art!

Early in 1923, he studied the score of *Die Erwartung* and was profoundly impressed, above all, by the "novelty" and "concentration" of the work. On January 27, he wrote to his mentor:

> What a work!! What an immeasurable plenitude of the most glorious music – most glorious just for this that each and every sequence of notes stands forth in undreamt-of newness – and the greatest miracle: this immeasurable plenitude condensed to the smallest space and thus in a concentration unequalled by any other music, nay, by the art of any age and any nation.

He received a lasting impression also from the performance, on September 27, 1923, of the D minor quartet op. 7. On the following day, he wrote full of enthusiasm to Helene:

> But then Schönberg's D minor quartet! I tell you, the highest in music! How far everything, everything that is being composed lags behind. Even Zemlinsky! Not to mention the 'young ones'. But Webern, too, of course! And – I! Those 50 minutes of music were the only beautiful ones since you've been gone. And that's saying a lot" (ABB 531).

Extreme expressivity and unexampled concentration: these were evidently the qualities of Schönberg's music that made the strongest impression on Berg. With the phrase "most concentrated music," in any event, Berg also sought to do justice to Schönberg's Suite op. 29.[467] Reading the score of the opera *Von heute auf morgen* (From one day to the next), on the other hand, put him in "a veritably pleasant tranquil mood."[468] And about Schönberg's chorus *Verbundenheit* (Solidarity), he remarked:

> I really have to see you again at long last: when I heard your chorus *Verbundenheit* yesterday (for the first time), I got almost heartsick with longing for you. To be sure, this music is such that even someone other than one so closely linked to you as I am must be filled with profound sadness on hearing those enigmatic triads: I say: enigmatic, for any attempt to comprehend this music analytically is bound to fail.[469]

As for the temporary irritations between Berg and Schönberg spoken of before, there could be no more direct friction after 1925, because Schönberg once again moved to Berlin. Judging by his letters, Berg seems greatly to have missed the commerce with his self-willed mentor. Some letters sound a note of downright yearning. It is touching to read in a letter of December 4, 1930, how the almost 46-year-old Berg calls Schönberg the teacher of his "life." Another letter, of January 25, 1933, is filled with wistfulness, as Berg writes:

> I always knew it, but now I know it better than ever: I need that to live! Every so often I must be able to breathe the air in your room, which always seems to me like a gigantic brain full to bursting, stand at your desk, and partake of the other joys of your home: the warm, matter-of-course hospitality of your dear wife, the sight of the sweetest child in the world, whose being in the world I regard directly as a very great enrichment of my life.

There are, moreover, indications that after completing *Wozzeck* Berg thought of making his friendship with Schönberg the covert subject of an opera about an artist friendship, to be entitled *Vincent* after Vincent van Gogh.[470] For years he had been very interested in the relationship between van Gogh and Paul Gauguin: his library contains several books on the subject.[471] Late in 1923 or in 1924, he learned that the writer Hermann Kasack had dramatized the subject in a five-act play; he read the fourth act of the play in an issue of the journal *Kunstblatt*, was greatly impressed by it and, in a letter to Kasack, asked him to get the publisher (Gustav Kiepenheuer in Potsdam) to send him a copy of the work.[472] Kasack complied with his request: Berg received the desired volume.[473]

Let us, in conclusion, briefly glance at Webern's friendship with Schönberg. It appears to have been steadier than Berg's. Webern seems to have been even more attached to his teacher than Berg and at times to have been in an almost indescribable state of dependency on him – though that does not mean that he, too, did not occasionally rebel against him.[474] On November 24, 1913, shortly before he turned thirty, he wrote him a memorable letter, in which he frankly admitted to needing Schönberg's "leadership." The image and model of his teacher were ever present to him at the time: "I always think of you when I work," he confessed, and one reads with amazement that he did not yet feel "of age." "I cling to your kindly leading hand – in everything." "I implore you, continue to be my guide, give me a good dressing-down again." He asked his teacher to look at all his works critically as the work of his pupil.

3.6 The Chamber Concerto: Homage to Schönberg, Mathilde and the Schönberg Circle

Though performed much more infrequently than the *Lyric Suite* and the Violin Concerto, the 1925 Chamber Concerto for piano, violin and thirteen wind instruments is one of Alban Berg's boldest and most original works. Theodor W. Adorno called it the archetype of everything Berg wrote thereafter.[475] Indeed, we here already encounter numerous of the traits characteristic of the later Berg in fully developed form: the predilection for anagrams and cryptograms, for number symbolism and for the palindrome, the retrograde architecture; the striving for symmetry, for mathematically determined formal proportions; the incorporation of the rhythmic element in the construction; and finally the unique amalgamation of the first two movements in the Finale. It sometimes seems as if Berg had anticipated endeavors that came into full being only in the serial music of the 'fifties and 'sixties.

Berg dedicated the Chamber Concerto to Schönberg on his fiftieth birthday. In the famous *Open Letter* to Schönberg of February 9, 1925, he explained numerous technical aspects of the composition, though he referred to them disparagingly as "externalities." The concerto, he added, was certainly not lacking in "inner processes" any more than any other music, and he confessed to have secreted a great deal of "human-spiritual reference" into the three movements about Friendship, Love and World – so much that the adherents of program music, "if they still happen to exist," would be "more than delighted." More he did not say. From a study of the sketches and many fresh observations, it now emerges that the Chamber Concerto, too, like the *Lyric Suite* and the Violin Concerto, is based on a detailed program, though one he did not reveal.

3.6.1 Genesis of the Work

Berg worked on the Chamber Concerto, albeit with interruptions, for some two-and-a-half years – from the beginning of 1923 to July 23 (!), 1925. That becomes more understandable when one probes into the uncommonly complex score – a masterpiece of combinatory skill – and above all after having inspected the sketches. The fifteen bundles of papers he filled with drafts, various calculations, formal dispositions, outlines, thematic sketches and a "piano sketch" (Fonds 21 Berg 74/I to XV) demonstrate impressively how deliberately he approached the work and how many difficulties he had with composing on the new terrain.

Berg had finished the instrumentation of *Wozzeck* in April of 1922. He composed nothing for several months after that but occupied himself – much to the chagrin of Schönberg – with making corrections in his opera. No later than the beginning of 1923, however, he conceived the plan of writing a concerto for piano and violin for Schönberg's 50th birthday on September 13, 1924 (the suggestion to write a piano concerto had come from Schönberg).[476] As yet, naturally, neither the tripartite form of the work, nor the number of instrumentalists, nor the eventual length of the work (240 + 240 + 480 bars) had been determined.

On July 12, 1923, he informed Schönberg that for the last 20 months he had composed virtually nothing, and that now he would tackle a concerto for piano and violin with accompaniment by ten wind instruments (brass and woodwind). Though he had so far completed only 50 bars, it was to be "a large, two-part movement, symphonic in character, of perhaps 500 measures."[477] Only six days later, however, on July 18, a plan matured to construct the concerto as a great, tripartite symphonic movement, to be comprised of scherzo variations, an adagio and a finale.[478] Already late in June, Berg had fixed his ideas about the character of the individual variations in catch phrases (74/V fol. 21 verso), and on August 9, he set the number of wind instruments at 13 (!) (74/V fol. 26). On September 1, he reported the completion of the first movement, a variations movement "in the character of a scherzo," to Anton Webern and wrote: "The second movement will be an Adagio. The third – a combination of the first two: a sonata movement."[479] He provided more details in a letter of September 2 to Schönberg:

> Of the one-movement but tripartite concerto, the first part, a variations movement in the character of a Scherzo, is finished. It consists of 200 bars, but bars that contain a lot: 6/4 measures. There is also a great deal of contrapuntal work in it, but without it weighing down the light tone of the whole. Seems to me, at least! The second movement will be an Adagio. The third, a combination of the first two: a sonata movement.

At that point, the work on the concerto was interrupted for almost a year. There were several reasons for this. On October 18, 1923, Schönberg's first wife, Mathilde, died, a mournful event that stirred Berg deeply. In February of 1924, the Viennese music theorist and composer Emil Petschnig published a polemical article on *Wozzeck*.[480] Berg felt obligated to write a rebuttal and composed the essay "The Musical Forms in my Opera *Wozzeck*."[481] He was also occupied by thoughts about the festschrift for Schönberg on his 50th birthday, which he was editing, and for which he was writing the sizable treatise "Warum ist Schönbergs Musik so schwer verständlich" (Why is Schönberg's music so hard to understand?). It was only after he had sent the manuscript of his contribution to Universal Edition on August 8, 1924,[482] that he was able to resume work on the Chamber Concerto. "I want to begin composing at last," he wrote to Webern on August 11, 1924. "How will it go? I am downright afraid of it – as before every new work!" The work seems nonetheless to have progressed well, for on February 9, 1925, his own 40th birthday, he was able to complete the composition – though he needed nearly another six months for the instrumentation. The finished score bears the date 7-23-1925.

3.6.2 Three's a Charm

Berg prefaced the Chamber Concerto with a humorous musico-literary motto. The motto consists of letter-notation anagrams of the names ARNOLD SCHÖNBERG (a-d-es-c-h-b-e-g [= a-d-e^b-c-b-b^b-e-g]), ANTON WEBERN (a-e-b [b^b]-e) and ALBAN BERG (a-b-a-b-e-g [= a-b^b-a-b^b-e-g]) and illustrates the proverbial saying "Aller guten Dinge sind drei," all good things come in threes, or "three's a charm." In the *Open Letter*, Berg mentions that the composition of the Chamber Concerto, dedicated to Schönberg on his fiftieth birthday, was completed on February 9, 1925, that is, on Berg's fortieth birthday. The work, meant for Schönberg from the start, had become "a small monument of a meanwhile twenty-year-old friendship." He also speaks of a "trinity of events" and a "triple anniversary," referring evidently to the fiftieth birthday of Schönberg, his own fortieth birthday and the twenty years of friendship with Schönberg and Webern: Berg first came to Schönberg in about the middle of October of 1904 and there met Anton von Webern, who had recently started to take lessons from Schönberg. The motto thus patently expresses the idea of friendship and solidarity and, more specifically, the concept of a "threesome."

A hitherto unpublished letter of Berg's to Webern enables us to see how important the idea of such a bond of friendship actually was to him. On July 28, 1922, he wrote to his friend that the thought of sheets of music being filled "day in and day out" in Mödling by him and Schönberg was to him "downright festive." He continued regretfully: "To be sure, I must not allow the thought to occupy my head that I could be sitting there as well, composing as the third in league!" Most tellingly, he goes on to say: "More than ever I now feel again the fellowship of just the three of us – in spite of the obvious distance! But it has been a long time that I have been made to feel our peculiarity vis-à-vis all other music being made today with such vehemence."

Reflections about the programmatic conception of the Chamber Orchestra have to start from this cluster of thoughts. In the *Open Letter*, Berg hints at the extra-musical circle of ideas of the three movements with the terms Friendship, Love and World – three key words that recur repeatedly in the sketches.[483] On one sheet of sketches (74/II fol. 2; see the facsimile on p. 175), there is even a synopsis of the program. Berg here not only ascribes the three attributes Friendship, Love and World to the three movements but adds a number of other (partly encrypted) points about the ideational content of the work – points that conceal a detailed program. In what follows I shall suggest how, on the basis of a variety of observations, this program can be deciphered.

3.6.3 Tectonics and Number Symbolism: The Numbers Three and Five

If it may be permissible for the nonce to contemplate the Chamber Concerto against the background, not of the time of its genesis, i.e. the 'twenties, but of the serial music of the 'fifties and 'sixties, it must be accorded a special historical significance. For it represents, to all appearances, the first, albeit timid, attempt to predetermine several dimensions (in Newspeak: several "parameters") of a composition in a quasi mathematical manner. In his *Open Letter*, Berg expressly points out that the number three, corresponding to the "threefold jubilee" to which the Chamber Concerto owes its creation, furnished the basis for the composition. The number three, or its multiple, dictates, he explains, the number of movements, the orchestration of the work, the number of players, the length of the performance and numerous "formal" (rhythmic, metric) and "harmonic" solutions. The number three, that is, or its multiple largely determines the dimensions, proportions and formal division of the movements, the "rhythmic forms" of the Rondo Ritmico, the time signatures and the coexistence of free atonality, tonality and dodecaphony.

To elaborate on the major points of Berg's exposition:

- The Chamber Concerto is composed of three movements: a Thema scherzoso con variazioni, an Adagio and a Rondo Ritmico con Introduzione.
- The work has "a special body of sound" that utilizes the "trinity of instrument genres (keyboard, string and wind instruments)". Two concertante (soloist) instruments, the piano and the violin, are pitted against an accompanying wind ensemble.
- The score prescribes altogether 15 (= 3 x 5) instruments, including the solo piano and violin: piccolo, flute, oboe, English horn, E^b, A^b and bass clarinet, bassoon, contrabassoon, two horns, trumpet and trombone.
- Berg specifies the playing duration of the variations movement as ca. 9 (= 3 x 3) minutes; the Adagio and the Rondo Ritmico take 15 (= 3 x 5) minutes each.
- The theme of the first movement is treated and developed in five variations. The theme extends to 30 bars, the movement as a whole to 240 (= 3 x 80) bars.

- The Adagio is in two parts. Each half is founded on the "tripartite lied" $A^1 - B - A^2$, "with A^2 representing the inversion of A^1." Each part has 120 bars, totaling 240 bars.
- The Rondo Ritmico constitutes "an amalgamation of the two preceding" movements, being treated as a recapitulation of the Variations movement and as "simultaneous" recapitulation of the Adagio. Its total extent is therefore 480 (= 2x 240) measures.
- In the Rondo Ritmico, three "rhythmic forms" play a major constructive role: "a main and a secondary rhythm, plus one to be regarded quasi as a motif."
- The Variations are throughout in "triple meters," in the Adagio "duple meter" predominates, and the Rondo exhibits "a constant alternation of every conceivable even and odd, divisible and indivisible meter."
- The "trinity of events" also appears in the "harmony," where "next to large stretches of altogether dissolved tonality, small parts of a tonal character are found," as well as others that correspond to Schönberg's laws governing the "composition with twelve tones related only to each other."

These data make it obvious that the number three is indeed of major importance for the structure of the Chamber Concerto. But Berg reserved an important role in the disposition of the work also for the five, although his *Open Letter* does not say anything about it. A. Pernye noticed decades ago that the motto with which the Chamber Concerto opens is five bars in length, that the theme of the first movement undergoes five variations, and that the main theme of the second movement (mm. 241-245) likewise extends to five measures. He rightly read that as an allusion to Schönberg's 50th birthday.[484]

Some newer observations now show that the relevance of the number five is even larger than Pernye presumed. It is significant, to begin with, that the five-bar motto containing the three anagram motifs is intoned not only at the beginning of the work but, in modified form, also in two other places: at the end of the Adagio and at the end of the Rondo ritmico.

It has been overlooked until now that the five measures of the piano at the end of the Adagio (mm. 476-480) present the SCHÖNBERG motif in motto fashion, but in such a way that it is dissolved into its "elements" and "built up" in stages. In its complete form it then sounds in m. 480 as upbeat to the *Introduzione* (cadenza) of the third movement.

That these five bars have the function of a motto also emerges from a note of Berg's in the score (p. 105): "These 5 measures of the piano introducing the IIIrd movement: independent of the tempo of the Adagio, which is concurrently concluded by the violin and the wind ensemble" [sic].[485]

It has also gone unnoticed that the Concerto as a whole likewise concludes with the five-bar motto. In mm. 781-785, all three anagram motifs are intoned in varied form. Here, too, a note of Berg's in the score leaves no doubt that these last five bars function as a motto. The five measures are marked off from each other by fermatas. Berg remarks (pp. 187/188): "Extend the five [fermatas] in such a way that the duration of the last (fermata) coincides with the dying away of the piano chord."

It is also worth noting that exactly five tempi are prescribed for the Adagio (more on this later), and that the strokes that constitute the main rhythm of the Chamber Concerto (first intoned in m. 297 of the Adagio) are likewise five:

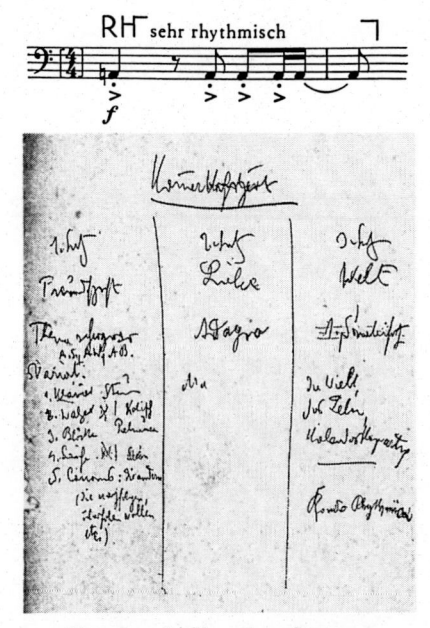

Sketches 1: Chamber Concerto

Draft of the concerto's secret program. Austrian National Library Music Collection, Fonds 21 Berg 74/II fol. 2, by permission of the Austrian National Library

3.6.4 Thema scherzoso con variationi: "Freundschaft." – The Schönberg Circle

The first movement of the Chamber Concerto is, to repeat, a variations movement: a 30-bar theme – a *thema scherzoso* – is varied five times in an extraordinarily imaginative manner. In the *Open Letter* Berg speaks of the "sixfold recurrence of the same basic idea" and remarks:

> That idea, exposed by the wind ensemble as a tripartite variations theme of thirty bars, is repeated in a first variation by the piano solo in the virtuoso character of that instrument (1st recapitulation). Variation 2 inverts the melody of the "theme." Variation 3 is retrograde; variation 4 the inversion of the retrograde (the three middle variations to be seen quasi as the development of this "first sonata movement"), while the last variation returns to the basic form of the theme.

(Berg's account here is erroneous: var. 2 is retrograde, var.3 is inverted.)

From Berg's indications in the above-mentioned program synopsis it is clear that the theme and the individual variations are intended as musical character portraits of Schönberg, Webern and Berg, as well as three (!) other members of the Schönberg Circle, namely Erwin Stein, Rudolf Kolisch and Joseph Polnauer, although it was not always certain from the start whom a particular variation was meant for.

Looking again at the program synopsis reproduced above (Sketches 1), we can make out the monograms A.S., A.W. and A.B underneath the designation *Thema scherzoso*. For the first variation (*Piano*), Berg jots down the name Stein. (Berg's handwriting is not always readily legible, and we know that Eduard Steuermann was the most prominent pianist of the Schönberg Circle. Nevertheless it would be risky to read Steuermann instead of Stein.) For the second variation (*Waltz*), Berg had originally written *I*; but he then crossed out the pronoun and wrote *Kolisch*. The third variation (*Blocks*) was meant for Polnauer. The fourth (*Runs*) was originally aimed at Webern. But Berg again crossed out the abbreviation *Web.* and wrote the name *Stein* next to it. The fifth variation, finally, was characterized by Berg as follows: *Canons: the others (who follow behind, want to overtake etc.* This last remark is yet one more clue to the thesis that in this movement about Friendship Berg wanted to portray the Schönberg Circle musically.

In the *Open Letter*, Berg does not omit to point out that each of the five variations has its own physiognomy, though the scherzo character predominates throughout in this movement. In the letter to Schönberg of September 2, 1923, quoted above, Berg likewise speaks of the "light tone of the whole," unencumbered by the contrapuntal work in it. It will thus hardly be amiss to imagine this movement as a sequence of cheerful scenes at the Schönberg home and/or at the Society for Private Musical Performances.

No less instructive than the program synopsis are the notes Berg made in a sketchbook about the structure and, above all, the character of the theme and the individual variations.[486] The theme was to have a symphonic scherzo character. The first variation, confined to the piano, he imagined "somewhat more veiled and rather dreamy." The second variation he wanted to shape into a swinging waltz. For the third variation he had, as in the program synopsis, "blocks" in mind, adding the adjective *schleudernd* ("flinging" or "skidding") to suggest that the music was to remain in the scherzo sphere. The fourth variation was to be kept "shadowy" and "ppp." The final variation, however, was to end with a great crescendo. Several observations suggest that the characterization of the music serves a programmatic intention.

As Berg explains in the *Open Letter* – and analysis confirms again and again – the number three or its multiple determines numerous dimensions of the musical in the Chamber Concerto. It is thus only consistent for the *thema scherzoso* also to be composed of three sections. These number 15, 9 and 6 measures (their ratio thus being 5 : 3 : 2), and each section has its own tempo (*Tempo I, II and III*). In an article published in 1979, I hypothesized – without knowing the sketches at the time – that the three anagram motives in the theme symbolized the idea of friendship and the mystical trinity, and that the three strongly individualized thematic shapes of the theme were conceived as character portraits of Schönberg (*at tempo scherzando, but somewhat more sedate*), Webern (*With verve*) and Berg himself (*Meno Allegro*).[487] The monograms A.S., A.W. and A.B. in the program synopsis seem to confirm this hypothesis, standing, as they do, beneath the heading *Thema scherzoso*.

However, the movement discloses still further aspects. We must not forget that the Chamber Concerto is a work of homage to Schönberg. As such it contains numerous hidden allusions to works of the latter, such as the Chamber Symphony op. 9 and the Serenade op. 24.[488] Even the number of players is an accolade to Schönberg's Chamber Symphony: in the *Open Letter*, Berg expressly calls the fifteen a "sacred number."[489] He did not mention the fact, however, that the eleven fourth steps that form the bass grounding of the *Verve* section in the *Thema scherzoso* (mm. 16-20) are to be understood as an allusion to the famous theme of fourths in the Chamber Symphony, nor that the whole-tone harmonies at the end of this section (mm. 20-24) refer back to the main theme of Schönberg's symphony.[490] Berg must have thought Schönberg would catch these allusions anyway.

The artful way in which Berg modifies the five following variations beggars description. He understood the first variation, recited by the piano alone, as a "first recapitulation" of the theme, and, indeed, the substance of the theme is left nearly untouched here. Even so, this first modification sounds warmer and more opulent than the theme. Berg's characterization of this variation as "somewhat more veiled and rather dreamy" describes the matter exactly.

The second (retrograde) variation derives its character as a partly slow and partly racy waltz primarily from the typical oom-pah-pah accompaniment in three-fourths meter. The repeated doubling of two alternating chords (mm. 161-168) here produces a semblance of tonal stability:

A particularly conspicuous moment in this variation is the passage with the glissandi in the trombone (mm. 81-85) – a seemingly humorous effect. That this variation was indeed meant for Kolisch seems to be confirmed by the open strings of the violin in mm. 111/112, an instrument otherwise silent in this movement.[491] Kolisch, the first violinist of the famous Kolisch String Quartet, came to Schönberg in 1919.[492] In a letter of June 9, 1921, to his wife, Berg tells her about the most recent Society concert, in which Steuermann and Kolisch performed the Violin Pieces of Webern. The humorous point of the story was that when he was up, the bemused Kolisch – with Steuermann already sitting at the piano waiting for him – appeared at first without his violin and, lost in wonder, asked: "Is it my turn now?"

The third variation, which presents the theme in inversion and is headed *Kräftig bewegt* (Very lively), stands out by its uniquely robust character. The compact, full-chorded piano piece – here and there interspersed by rests – impresses not least by its "chord clusters." The expression marks *martellato* (m. 136) and *schwungvoll begleitend, kurz aber schwer* (accompanying with verve, brief but heavy) (mm. 140/141) are also telling. Berg, moreover, used the terms *Blöcke*, blocks, and *schleudernd* (flinging or skidding) to characterize this variation, which, however, closes with a diminuendo. Hans Ferdinand Redlich called this variation "athletic."[493] There can be no doubt that Berg conceived this variation as a portrait of Dr. Joseph Poldauer (1888-1970). One will have a better understanding of the peculiar shaping of this music after seeing Poldauer's photographs[494] – he was nearly six feet tall and of an athletic physique – and above all after learning that he took on a special task at the legendary concerts of the Society for Private Musical Performances: he had to enforce silence, kept antagonists and potential disturbers of the peace in check and if necessary personally expedited them from the room! Hans W. Heinsheimer, who called him the "Archangel who guarded the gates of the paradise of modern music with the fiery sword of faith and irresistible conviction,"[495] reports that people came to the Society's concerts not only to hear music but to see Dr. Poldauer in action! In a letter to Webern of January of 1911, Berg confessed that he found Poldauer "quite simpatico" – he seemed "immensely honest and true" to him.

In the fourth, very brisk variation, which treats the theme in retrograde inversion, the flitting scherzo character is strongly pronounced. In the piano part, runs (at times in contrary motion), tone repetitions and a staccato articulation stand out. Berg had fixed the expressive radius of the variation originally with the adverb "shadowy" and the dynamic marking *ppp*. In the final version, the *piano* range is overstepped repeatedly – once, toward the end (mm.177/178) even abruptly in a *fortissimo* eruption. In conceiving this variation, Berg, as already noted, had thought at first of Webern and later of Erwin Stein.

Berg regarded the fifth variation, in which the theme reappears in its original form, as a second recapitulation. Two ideas determine the structure of this variation: that of a powerful crescendo, and that of intensive contrapuntal work.[496] The variation opens *piano* and *pianissimo* and concludes in triple *forte*. Moreover, it distinguishes itself in a far larger measure than the other variations by contrapuntal combinations[497] and, above all, by imitational and canon formations,[498] to which Berg attached a programmatic meaning. In the *Open Letter*, he spoke rather abstractly about canons, "in which the voice group entering later seeks to overtake another that started first, indeed catches up with it, outstrips and leaves it far behind." More precisely he indicated in the (private) program synopsis that the canons were meant to symbolize the remaining members of the Schönberg School, "who follow behind, want to overtake, etc." The fifth variation, which corresponds to a Coda, thus stands for the remainder of the Schönberg disciples.

3.6.5 Adagio – Mathilde

Regarding the ideational content of the Adagio, Berg in the program synopsis only jotted down the word *Love*, without providing any further explanation.

The key to a semantic decipherment is the frequently repeated four-note phrase a-h [b]-d-e (in crab motion e-d-h [b]-a), a phrase previously ignored. During a detailed analysis of the Chamber Concerto I conducted in the 1970s, I was struck by it. I assumed that it was meant as an anagram of a specific name, but could not decipher it at the time.

Tableau 1: Mathilde Schönberg (painted by Arnold Schönberg, 1910)

Historical Museum of the City of Vienna

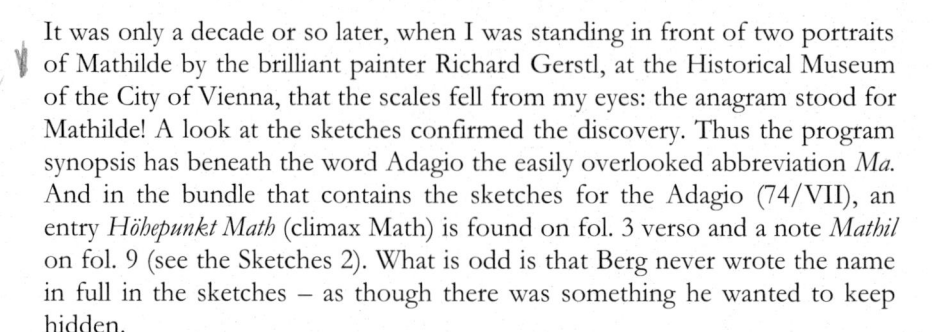

It was only a decade or so later, when I was standing in front of two portraits of Mathilde by the brilliant painter Richard Gerstl, at the Historical Museum of the City of Vienna, that the scales fell from my eyes: the anagram stood for Mathilde! A look at the sketches confirmed the discovery. Thus the program synopsis has beneath the word Adagio the easily overlooked abbreviation *Ma*. And in the bundle that contains the sketches for the Adagio (74/VII), an entry *Höhepunkt Math* (climax Math) is found on fol. 3 verso and a note *Mathil* on fol. 9 (see the Sketches 2). What is odd is that Berg never wrote the name in full in the sketches – as though there was something he wanted to keep hidden.

> Sketches for the Chamber Concerto, Austrian National Library, Music Collection, Fonds 21 Berg 74/VII [A] fol. 9. "Piano Sketch" of mm. 110-124 (= mm. 350-364) of the Adagio, specifically of the "turning

point" or "central point." Above the note "12 strokes" is written the cryptogram *Mathil.*

The Mathilde anagram recurs so often, in diverse rhythmic variants as well as in transpositions, in the Adagio that one can without exaggerating call it the grammalogue or cipher of the movement, as several examples will serve to illustrate:

[musical examples: T. 261-264 (Trp.); T. 300/301 (1. Hn.); T. 314-317 (Pos.); T. 358-363 (1. Hn.)]

To state the upshot of the semantic analysis at the outset: the Adagio is conceived as a musical portrait of Mathilde; the "Love," which Berg does not expatiate upon, is Schönberg's love for his wife.

Mathilde Schönberg, born on September 7, 1877, the sister of Alexander von Zemlinsky, was a smart, musically well-educated woman and an excellent pianist.[499] Oskar Kokoschka once remarked waggishly that she radiated "the warmth of a Russian stove."[500] Schönberg met her in the summer of 1899 and married her on October 18, 1901, in Vienna. The marriage, from which sprang two children, Gertrude and Georg, was overshadowed by severe crises. In the summer of 1908, Mathilde, as previously noted, left her husband and moved in with the painter Richard Gerstl. Upon efforts at mediation by friends – mainly the Weberns – she retuned to her husband – presumably the cause of Gerstl's, from whom Schönberg had learned a great deal as a painter, committing suicide, in a gruesome manner, on November 8, 1908.[501] Mathilde is said to have thereupon been depressed and taciturn for he rest of her life.⁵⁰² Often she withdrew to her room as soon as visitors arrived in Mödling, under the pretext that she did not wish to make any new acquaintances⁵⁰³ - though Alban Berg wrote to his wife in 1918 that on September 13, Schönberg's birthday, he had "spent time in the liveliest conversation" with Schönberg and Mathilde in Mödling (ABB 388).

From the summer of 1923 on, Mathilde was ill and bed-ridden. She suffered from liver and gall bladder ailments and complained about incessant pain. On September 20, she was taken to the Auersperg sanitarium in Vienna, where she died on October 18 of cancer of the kidneys. Both Berg and Webern, as their letters make clear, had followed the course of Mathilde's illness with great apprehension and sympathy.⁵⁰⁴

The Adagio of the Chamber Concerto is divided into two parts of 120 measures each and is designed palindromically, that is, in retrograde form. In his *Open Letter*, Berg states that the two halves of the movement consist of five sections. In my article of 1979, I showed that these details can be stated more precisely.⁵⁰⁵ Three points are important in this connection: first, that Berg prescribes exactly five tempos for this movement; second, that the two halves each divide into six sections; and third, that the corresponding sections in the two halves do not always have the same number of bars, as the following outline will show:

↓ mm. 241-270 (= 30 mm.)		A_1	mm. 451-480 (= 30 mm.)	
Tempo I			Tempo I (from m. 468)	
♩ = ca. 48			♩ = ca. 48	
mm. 271-282 (= 12 mm.)		B	m m. 439-450 (= 12 mm.)	
Tempo II			Tempo II (cf. m. 271)	
Very slow			*Very slow*	
♩ = 24			♩ = 24	
mm. 283-293 (= 11 mm.)		B	mm. 431-438 (= 8 mm.)	↑
Tempo III			Tempo III (cf. m. 283)	

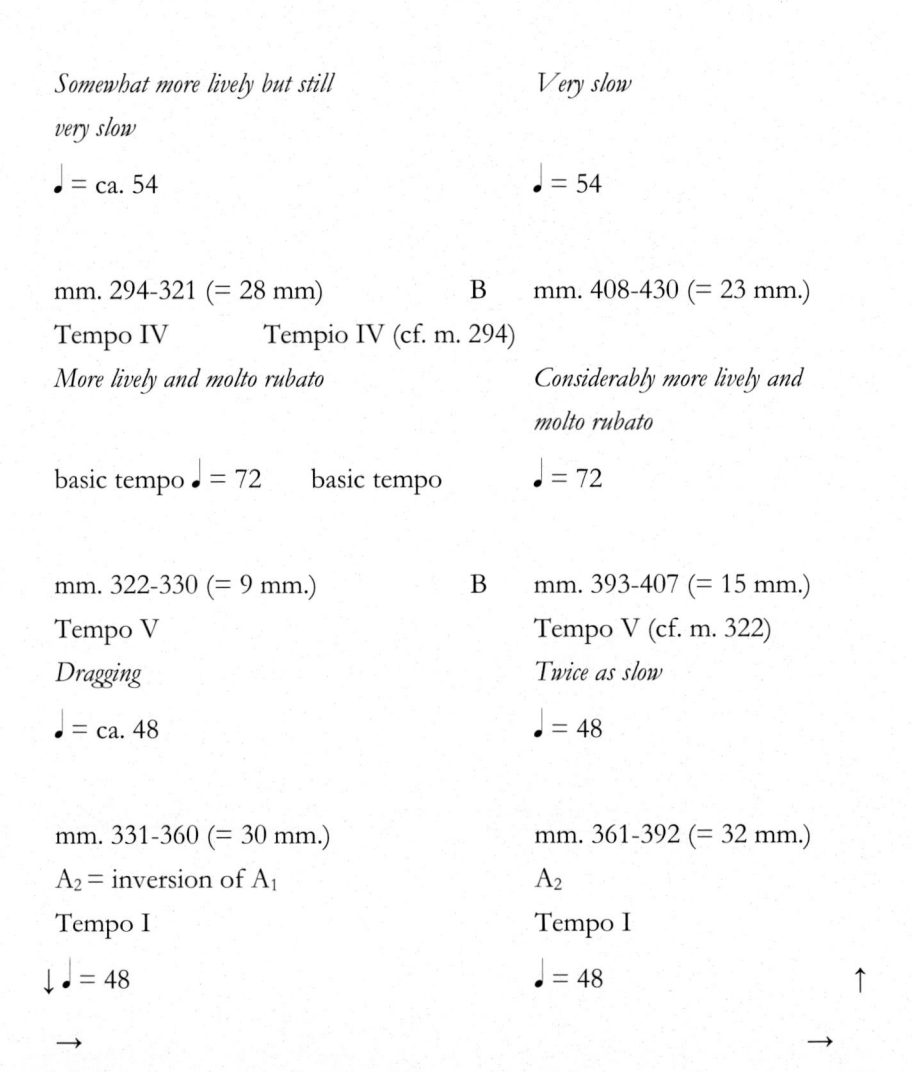

Somewhat more lively but still very slow		*Very slow*
♩ = ca. 54		♩ = 54
mm. 294-321 (= 28 mm)	B	mm. 408-430 (= 23 mm.)
Tempo IV Tempio IV (cf. m. 294)		
More lively and molto rubato		*Considerably more lively and molto rubato*
basic tempo ♩ = 72 basic tempo		♩ = 72
mm. 322-330 (= 9 mm.)	B	mm. 393-407 (= 15 mm.)
Tempo V		Tempo V (cf. m. 322)
Dragging		*Twice as slow*
♩ = ca. 48		♩ = 48
mm. 331-360 (= 30 mm.)		mm. 361-392 (= 32 mm.)
A_2 = inversion of A_1		A_2
Tempo I		Tempo I
↓ ♩ = 48		♩ = 48 ↑
→		→

We can see from this that the retrograde repetition of the movement's first half is by no means a "mechanical" one, but that Berg in shaping the mirror-symmetric second half has taken a good many liberties. In what follows I shall concentrate on discussing those details that are relevant for the semantic analysis.

Whereas the variations movement had ended on a triple *forte*, the Adagio begins *pp* and *ppp* – the contrast could hardly be greater.[506] The muted violin enters with a sixteen-bar theme (mm. 241-256), which is based on a twelve-tone row and is initially grounded by seemingly tonal harmonies in the brasses. Berg's original idea of the passage reads: "broad notes accompanied simply but richly harmonized" (74/IV fo. 13). In mm. 261-264, the trumpet introduces the Mathilde anagram.

The eleven-note theme the violin recites at the beginning of the second section (mm. 271 ff.), accompanied by triplets on the trumpet, is answered by the trumpet a twelfth lower. A close look reveals that the first notes of this theme are derived from the Mathilde anagram:

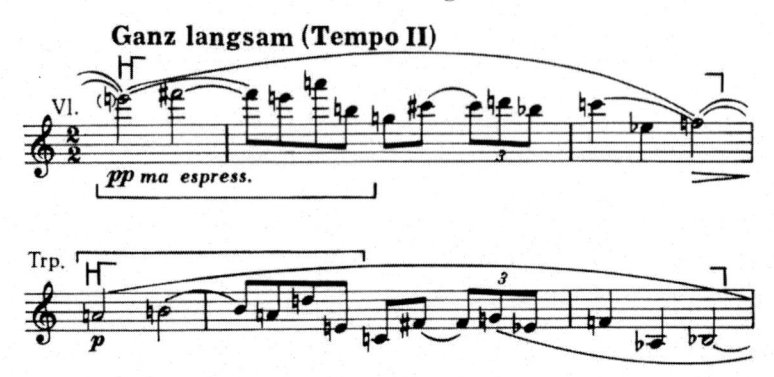

Ganz langsam (Tempo II)

The following entry in the sketches: "triplet accompaniment, above it duet of violin and oboe, a tender song. Horn added" (74/V fol. 26 verso) suggests that Berg in devising this passage was guided by the idea of a love dialogue. At the start of the third section (mm. 283ff.), a new twelve-toned, very *cantabile* theme is presented, which will play a major role in the course of the movement and will appear in every conceivable variation (inversion, augmentation, diminution), as well as being treated in *stretto* (in mm. 303ff.).

Of paramount relevance for the construction of the concert is a new element, the principal rhythm, which is introduced in the fourth section of the Adagio (mm. 297ff.). It is intoned three times in its basic form on the note a (mm. 297-302) and later (mm. 306/7) in augmentation on the note c-sharp. Between the second and third intonation, the horn plays the Mathilde anagram.

This constellation suggests that the chief rhythm refers to Mathilde. The following has to be taken into account. Berg had worked with a principal rhythm already in *Wozzeck*: the tavern scene in Act III is constructed as an invention on a rhythm. Principal rhythms likewise underlie *Lulu* and the Violin Concerto. If we consider that the leit-rhythms in all of these instances have the semantics of a fatality symbol, we may presume that that applies also to the chief rhythm of the Chamber Concerto.

T. 299–301

A relatively short-winded but intense crescendo leads in m. 314 to the *climax*, marked as such, of the movement. The Mathilde anagram appears here quasi in pound notes. Above this firm "foundation," the trumpet, *drowning out everything*, intones the *very cantabile* theme, now in inversion and augmentation:

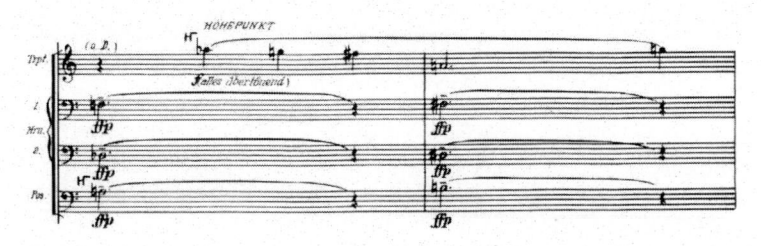

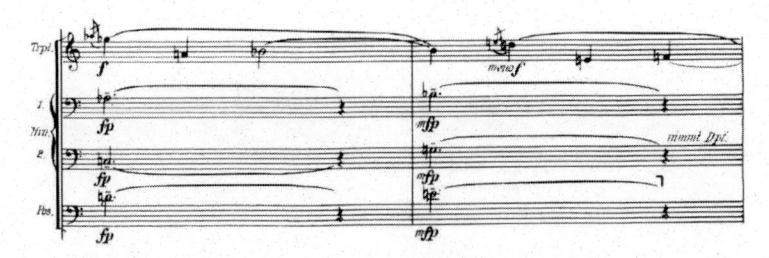

An important hint for a semantic determination of this theme and of the climax generally is found in an early formal disposition for the Adagio in the sketches (74/X fol. 2). After the specification "3 1/4 [bars] *crescendo*," Berg noted "5 ½ [bars] *Melisande*." This notation helps us to realize that he wanted the climax of the Adagio to be understood as an allusion to Schönberg's *Pelleas und Melisande*, a work that, as we have noted, he greatly admired,[507] whose thematic structure he had analyzed,[508] and in which Melisande's leitmotif in fact appears initially in the following form:

The fifth section of the movement (mm. 322-330) with the notable expression mark *Schleppend*, dragging, presents an oddly pale soundscape: the twelve-tone theme, initially intoned by the English horn, is supposed to be recited *pp* and *senza espressione*. Three notes, in a ratio of an augmented and a perfect fourth to each other (c-f#-b) are repeated several times and serve as the "accompaniment."

Sketches 2: Chamber Concerto

Sketches for the Chamber Concerto, Austrian National Library, Music Collection, Fonds 21 Berg 74/VII [A] fol. 9. "Piano Sketch" of mm. 110-124 (= mm. 350-364) of the Adagio, specifically of the "turning point" or "central point." Above the note "12 strokes" is written the cryptogram Mathil.

The sixth section (mm. 331-360), it is to be noted, represents the inversion of the first. In Berg's coding: A_2 = inversion of A_1. This section leads to a "passionately agitated" passage (mm. 350ff.), in which a dodecaphonic theme is played simultaneously in its basic form and in inversion. At the end (mm. 358-360), the muted first horn intones the Mathilde anagram. With that, the mid-point of the movement has been reached.

The second, palindromic half of the movement begins with the retrograde Mathilde anagram. To both forms of the anagram, the piano, which is otherwise silent in the Adagio, twelve times sounds the contra c-sharp. The twelve strokes, according to Berg's conception, were to invoke a *Glockenstimmung*, a bell-ringing mood.[509] The notes that Berg made on this passage in the piano sketch for the Adagio (Sketches 2) are quite instructive. He defines the midpoint of the movement as "center" and "turning-point," and he remarks that it should yield *one* image. He also notes that the passage containing the two Mathilde anagrams and the twelve strokes of the piano should have the effect of an "enclave," though he struck that note out again.

Berg had so great a predilection for palindromic structures that one could speak of a weakness for them. Is the retrograde design of the Adagio to be regarded merely as a structural peculiarity, or does it have deeper significance? Let us consider that Berg called the midpoint expressly the "turning-point," and that he throws out hints with regard to content elsewhere as well (in the piano sketch, we find, for example, the note "Help Help!!" as a presumable commentary on the woodwind sextuplets in mm. 356-358). Let us also call to mind that he wanted the famous palindromic ostinato in *Lulu* to be understood as representing the rise and fall of the title figure. In light of all this, we are almost compelled to assume that the two halves of the Adagio are to suggest the rise and decline of Mathilde, and that therefore the twelve bell stokes signalize the turn in her life. The last section of the movement, in any case (mm. 451-480) – that much is certain – clearly depicts the lingering illness and decease of Mathilde. Let us sketch the chief musical events of the second half. The beginning receives its profile from triadic configurations of the violin playing *pianissimo* and *flautando as if from a distance*. Secondly we notice the retrograde Mathilde anagram being sounded no less than three times: first in the leading E^b clarinet (e-d-h [b]-a), then in the leading oboe (g-f-d-c) and finally in the leading trumpet (b^b-a^b-f-e^b). Thirdly, there are three very striking ascending runs in the violin, which keep rising into ever higher regions and become ever softer (*pp*, *ppp*, *pppp*) – at the end of the Adagio the violin voice is marked *pppp expiring*. The motifs of the woodwinds and the overall sound character of this remarkable passage strikingly resemble the music Schönberg wrote in *Pelleas und Melisande* to create the mood for Melisande's death chamber (Nos. 59-62), as two brief examples may illustrate:

Like Berg in the Chamber Concerto, Schönberg paints the exhaling of the soul with an ascending passage of he muted violin:

3.6.6 Introduzione: "Thunderstorm" – Grief at Mathilde's Death

Judging from the available sources, Schönberg must have greatly loved his first wife, and her grave illness caused him much anxiety. According to a letter of Webern's to Berg of September 12, 1923, he did not leave her bedside for weeks, although he "acted relatively calmly on the outside." After Mathilde's death, he lived for a while with his daughter Gertrud and son-in-law Felix Greissle. He smoked, as Eberhard Freitag reports,[510] sixty cigarettes a day at that time, drank three liters of black coffee and a great deal of liqueur and took codeine and pantopon. In a letter to Helene of November 22, 1923, Berg couched his impressions of Schönberg in the words: "Schönberg was so indescribably ill-tempered that he weighed like a heavy nightmare on everybody" (ABB 526). Schönberg himself wrote about his deceased wife to his father-in-law Alexander von Zemlinsky: "Mathilde was so clear and simple in her dispositions, she managed to untie complicated knots with a few words and everything always quite noiselessly."[511] On August 28, 1924, Schönberg married Gertrud Kolisch in Mödling. He justified his decision to wed again in a letter to Zemlinsky, dated August 21, with these words:

> Must I tell you that I do not comprehend myself how it is possible for me to love another woman after Mathilde. And that I torment myself about detracting from her memory. Will you understand and bear with me? I know that you are much too magnanimous not to see that perhaps precisely because I loved Mathilde so much, this gap has to be filled somehow.[512]

The Rondo Ritmico, the third movement of the Chamber Concerto, commences with a 54-bar Introduzione, which is to be recited by the two soloists, the violin and the piano, *throughout freely in the character of a "cadenza."* Its substance, as well as the entire Rondo, is derived from the two preceding movements, presenting a highly imaginative synthesis of the *Thema scherzoso* from the Variations movement and the first 42 bars of the Adagio (mm. 241-282). [513] In a form outline in the sketches (74/VI fol. 4), the Introduzione is characterized by the key word *Gewitter* (Thunderstorm). At another place, there is a reference to a "distant thunderstorm," which at the beginning of the third movement erupts *fortissimo* in the form of a cadenza, and another note announces that the movement is to be introduced by a "thunderous rumble" of the piano (74/V fol. 22 verso). This note refers to the five measures of the piano at the end of the Adagio (mm. 476-80) – measures that present the Schönberg anagram like a motto and in such a way that the anagram is dissolved into its elements and "built up" piece by piece, while the dynamics traverses the degrees *pp, p, mp, mf* and finally *ff*. This crescendo is in direct opposition to the waning sound of the winds and the violin, whose last run, as previously mentioned, dies away *pppp*:

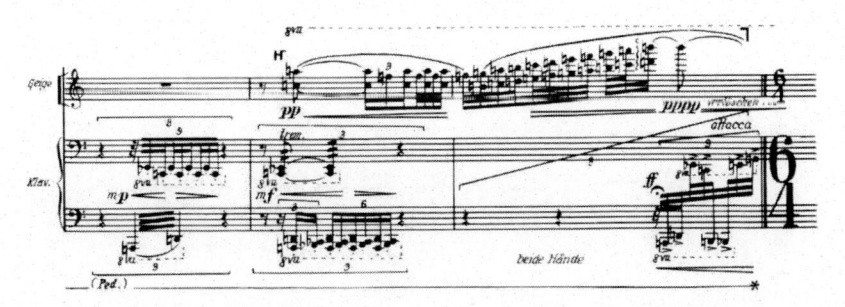

What does all of this signify? After what has been said about the biographic background of the Chamber Concerto and the semantics of the Adagio, it will not require any further explication decide that Berg has here recorded quasi seismographically the shock caused to Schönberg by Mathilde's death. In the same measure as Mathilde's life wanes, her spouse's agitation grows, until the anguish over his wife's death erupts tempestuously in triple forte.

Although the Introduzione, as we have noted, has recourse to "materials" of the preceding movements, the building blocks are put together, i.e., composed, with such originality and imagination that something entirely new is created in the process. The music of the Introduzione has a character and musical manner all its own; it resembles a rhapsody. The notion *ganz wild, rhapsodisch* impressed itself upon Berg while conceiving the cadenza (74/X fol. 5). Not the least symptomatic aspect of this is the agogic: highly agitated passages, at times marked *stormy* in the score, alternate with quieter episodes. Some figures from the *Thema scherzoso*, such as the end of the *schwungvolle Partie* (mm. 20-24), which was more lyrical in character, are now dramatized by means of a new dynamics, opulent ornamentation and a "heaving" accompaniment by the piano (mm. 515-523). Outstanding in the piano part are arpeggios and figurations that estrange tonality or else are shaped in bitonal or polytonal ways.[514]

A detailed analysis of the Introduzione – and of the Rondo Ritmico as such – would require a voluminous treatise. Of special semantic significance is the fact that at the very beginning of the Introduzione, the piano and the violin intone the main rhythm, intended as a symbol of fatality, in metrical displacement, diminution and augmentation (mm. 481-484). Toward the end of the Introduzione, however, Berg achieves the feat of intertwining the last figure of the *Thema scherzoso* (mm. 25-29) contrapuntally with the tender

Mathilde theme of the Adagio (mm. 271-276). The passage provides one more example of Berg's astonishing *polyrhythmics*:[515] the violin plays in 3/4 time, while the piano observes 2/4 time.

3.6.7 Rondo Ritmico: the World as a Kaleidoscope

As a new formal conception, the Finale of the Chamber Concerto is certainly the most original movement of the work. Berg conceived this Rondo Ritmico as an amalgamation (*Verquickung*) of the two preceding movements. In the *Open Letter*, he stated that the peculiar union of the variations movement and the Adagio yielded essentially three kinds of combination:

> 1. the free counterpointing of the respective corresponding parts; 2. the sequential opposition, in duet form, of particular phrases and brief passages [*Sätzchen*]; and 3. the exact addition of entire sections from the two [preceding] movements.

The problem, he continues, was how to "reconcile the discrepant components and characters" of the two preceding movements into a unity (*unter einen Hut*) and thereby to find "a new movement with a fully independent tone" (*tone* was one of Berg's pet terms).

In the repeatedly cited program synopsis, Berg noted in keyword form the ideas that were to shape the conception of the movement: *3rd movement: world, 1st sonata movement. The world, life, kaleidoscope-like – Rondo ritmico*. What he meant by *world* he formulated more precisely elsewhere (74/X fol.7) by the addition of *humanity, humans*; he also referred to Arthur Schopenhauer's *The World as Will and Idea* (74/XV fol. 5 verso). But the world was to be contemplated "kaleidoscope-like," as a motley sequence of images and constant change. Hence the choice of the rondo form: it seemed to Berg to answer the dictate both of *comprehensibility* (through the repetition of ideas) and of colorful *variety* (through the plenitude of shapes and figures). Entries in the sketches (74/XV fol. 3 verso) also demonstrate the thoroughness with which he pondered the matter: to check the validity of his deliberation, he even undertook an analysis of the Rondo from Beethoven's piano sonata in G major op. 31 no. 1.

Berg, however, carried the demand for variety quasi to extremes. The most discrepant characters thus alternate abruptly in the *Rondo ritmico*. Take, for example, mm. 697-702, where a fragment from the Adagio (mm. 431/432) is interpolated between two *scherzando* ideas. In the area of rhythm and meter, too, an astonishing diversity is observable. In the *Open Letter*, Berg notes that through the rondo-like recurrence of three rhythmic forms (a main rhythm, a secondary rhythm and one to be perceived as something of a motif) "a thematic unity" is achieved "that is in no way inferior to the old rondo form."

He also points out that in this Rondo Ritmico "a constant change of every conceivable duple and triple, divisible and indivisible time" takes place.

Berg thought the *Rondo ritmico* exhibited the form of a "first sonata movement." In a tabular outline included in the *Open Letter*, he divided the movement into the Introduzione, a main part bracketed with repeat signs and consisting of an exposition and a development, and a shorter concluding part, which he considered as a "second recapitulation or coda." A more thorough analysis of the movement reveals that it consists in fact of six sections, which correspond to the six sections of the Variations movement and the six large sections of the Adagio.

Introduzione mm. 481-534 (=54 mm.)	~ Theme mm. 1-30 (= 30 mm.) and Adagio mm. 241-282 (= 42 mm.)
Rodo ritmico (exposition) mm. 535-576 (= 42 mm.)	~ 1st VAR. mm. 31-60 (=30 mm.) and Adagio mm. 283-321 (= 39 mm.)
Rondo ritmico (exposition) mm. 577-630 (54 mm.)	~ 2nd VAR. mm. 61-120 (= 60 mm.) and Adagio mm. 322-360 (=39 mm.)
Rondo ritmico (development) mm. 631-670 (= 40 mm.)	~ 3rd VAR. mm. 121-150 (=30 mm.) and Adagio 361-407 (= 47 mm.)
Rondo ritmico (development) Alla Marcia mm. 671-709b (= 39 mm.)	~ 4th VAR. mm. 151-180 (=30 mm.) and Adagio mm. 408-438 (= 31 mm.)
Rondo ritmico (coda) mm. 710b-780 (=71 mm.)	~ 5th VAR. mm. 181-240 (= 60 mm.) and Adagio mm. 439-465 (= 27 mm.)
Conclusion mm. 781-785	~ Beginning (motto)

The juxtaposition shows that the *Rondo ritmico* represents a most ingeniously varied recapitulation of the Variations movement and the Adagio. In what way, however, are the portions from these two movements united in the *Rondo ritmico*, "added" or "amalgamated"? Berg mentions "three kinds of combination" in his *Open Letter* but does not cite any examples. Let us therefore discuss some representative instances.

Mm. 535-539 can serve as an example of Berg's first kind of combination, the "free counterpointing of the respective corresponding parts." Here the beginning of the first variation (mm. 31-37) and that of the third section of the first half of the Adagio (mm. 283-291) are contrapuntally intertwined in the following free and imaginative manner. In mm. 535-537, the winds recite the thematic prefix (i.e., the characteristic first four notes) and the SCHÖNBERG motif from the Variations theme (~ mm. 31-35). There are some significant rhythmic alterations, but the motifs remain recognizable to the listener. There follow, (m. 538) the WEBERN motif (~ m. 35) and the beginning of the BERG motif on the piano, which the contrabassoon completes in m. 538 (~ mm. 36/37). Concurrently (mm. 535-537), the violin, the piano and again the violin play the theme that in the Adagio's mm. 283-286 is blown "very song-like" by the A clarinet and the first horn. The metamorphosis is so radical that the theme is no longer recognized as such by the listener. The same is true of the trumpet's line 537/538 and the line of oboe and English horn (mm. 538/539), which only a careful scrutiny of the score will reveal as a (rhythmic) metamorphosis of the cantabile counter-theme from the Adagio's mm. 287-291.

Let us now look at mm. 698-706 as an example of Berg's second kind of combination, "the juxtaposition of individual phrases and little passages taken over word-for-word in sequence, that is, quasi duet-like." A segment from the Adagio is here followed by a segment from the Variations movement and yet another from the Adagio. Correspondences are as follows: mm. 698-701 (*quasi Adagio*) = mm. 431/432; mm. 702/703 (*scherzando*) = mm. 174-176; mm. 704-706 (*espr.*) = mm. 433-435. A closer look makes clear that the two segments from the Adagio are continuous, so that the measures from the Variations movement are interpolated. Disregarding minor variants, moreover, the three segments are indeed taken over "word-for-word," except that the instrumentation is altered. Of interest is also that the *Adagio* character of the passage is momentarily interrupted by the *scherzando* insertion.

Mm. 524-534, finally, present an example of Berg's third kind of combination, "the exact addition of entire portions from both movements." The passage illustrates how the final phrase of the Variations theme (tempo III, mm. 25-

29) is contrapuntally intertwined with the expressive theme from the second Adagio section (mm. 271-282) without any major rhythmic changes (although the Adagio theme appears in diminution).

Summing up, we can say about the *Rondo ritmico* that it opens up two highly significant aspects. For one thing it shows that Berg has modified the old concept of the recapitulation in a most original manner. The idea to "amalgamate," in the final movement of a work, the two preceding, mutually contrasting movements is a very bold one, of which there are first signs in earlier musical history (in Liszt, Brahms, Mahler and Schönberg)[516] but no really comparable instances. The Chamber Concerto can be called a prototypical work inasmuch as Berg used this method also in his *Lulu*. In terms of thematic substance and its treatment, the third act of that opera is nothing other than a recapitulation of the first two acts.[517]

The other matter the Chamber Concerto documents is Berg's highly developed art of thematic metamorphosis. Numerous thematic figures of the first two movements receive an entirely new physiognomy and an entirely new character through rhythmic and articulatory variation in the *Rondo ritmico*. To cite just one example, the "dragging," theme, articulated legato, of the English horn of mm. 323-325 appears in an astonishing transformation in the piano in mm. 579-582 of the Finale:

Important clues for a greater understanding of the shape, and above all for the semantic decipherment, of the movement are found in Berg's entries in the sketches. In two different places we find the keywords *Schlagwerk Klavier* (percussion piano) (7v4/IV fol. 8) and *Schlagwerk Klav. u. Gg* (and vl.) (74/XIV fol. 2 verso).These specifications refer to mm. 658-662, where the piano and the violin are treated as percussion instruments. The low notes of the piano in the main rhythm, the printed score states, are to sound like a tamtam, while for the violin *col legno geschlagen* (struck with the wood) is prescribed. In all of his works, Berg was ever concerned about musical universality, and since he was dispensing with percussion instruments in the Chamber Concerto, he wanted to compensate for that "lack" at least in this way.

Even more telling are the entries in Fonds 21 Berg 74/IX fol. 3. Here one reads under the date of 12/28 (probably 1924): "characters organ full work / chimes / march / hunting fanfares, specifically quick march 3/4 6/4, festive march 4/4/ 2/4, organ chorale 3/2, fanfares 9/8." These notes suggest that Berg was thinking of a festive march for Schönberg's 50th birthday and of an ovation Schönberg's pupils were to give to their revered teacher. The fanfares were to underscore the festiveness of the events but presumably also to demonstrate the will of the Schönberg School to move resolutely forward.

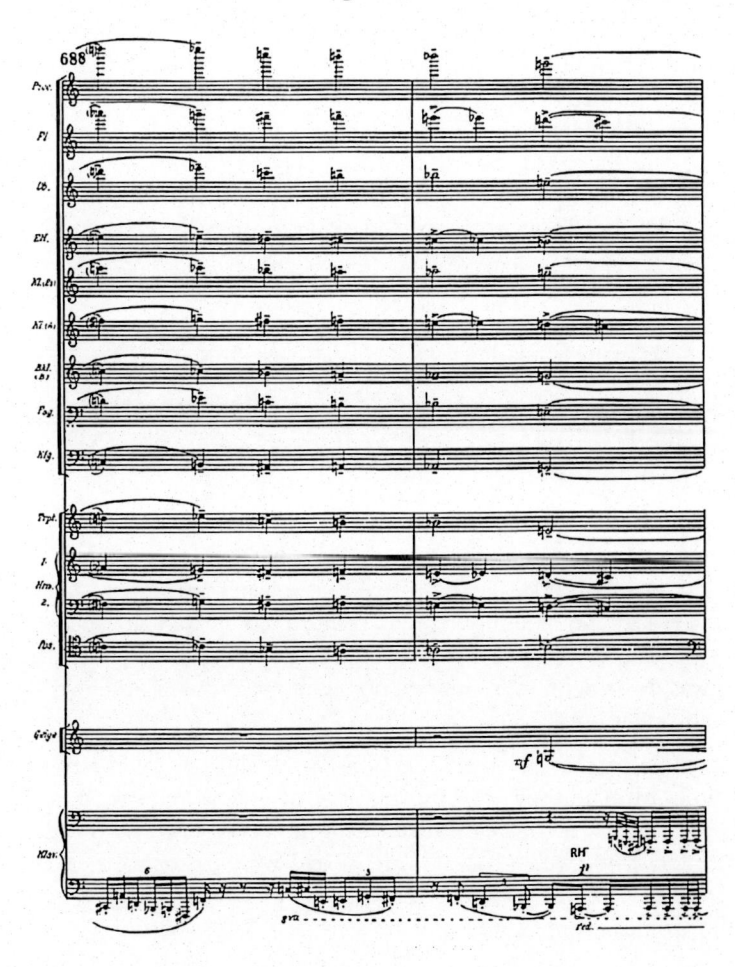

If one familiarizes oneself with the score, one will have to agree that these ideas are strikingly realized. Thus the fourth section of the *Rondo ritmico* (mm. 671-709) is marked *Alla marcia*. In mm. 678-90, then, the piccolo flute, the oboe, the bassoon and the trumpet intone the Schönberg anagram in broad notes, with the remaining winds accompanying in the manner of a chorale.[518] The passage has an organ-like fullness of sound, and one can understand why Berg had originally considered the possibility of including a harmonium:[519]

There are also conspicuous signal- and fanfare-like motifs, such as the one intoned by the first horn in mm. 694/695 and then picked up by the piano and the violin; the section mm. 725-738 at times sounds like a multi-voiced fanfare.

Of particular significance, finally, is the fact that in mm. 775-780 the *Rondo ritmico* issues in the so-called *Mutterakkord* (all-interval chord) invented by the Berg pupil Fritz Heinrich Klein, a famous chord that will later on play a special role in the second version of the Theodor Storm lied *Schließe mir die Augen beide* (Close my eyes, one and the other). In the stretta of the Chamber Concerto, the chord appears in the following form:

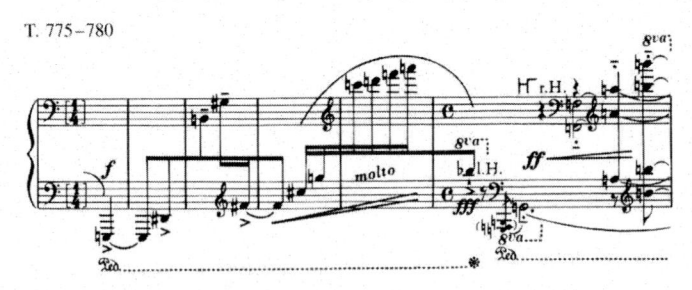

This figure is repeatedly referred to as *Mutterakkord* in the sketches.[520] Berg's pupil Fritz Heinrich Klein had informed his teacher already in March of 1922 in a letter that he had discovered a chord composed at once of twelve different notes and eleven different intervals,[521] commenting that the *Mutterakkord* was downright "the ultimate possibility in the area of chord formation in 12-halftone music."

Why, then, does the stretta of the Chamber Concerto culminate in this all-interval chord? The answer to this question is not far to seek. Berg evidently wanted to say that the development of music was of necessity headed for the composition with twelve tones related exclusively to each other. Already in 1923 and 1924, he was convinced that the future of music belonged to dodecaphonic composition. On September 2, 1923, he wrote to Schönberg:

"Everything you invented in the realm of twelve-tone music and are now using in such sovereign manner, occupies my imagination incessantly."[522]

3.7 From Helene to Hanna: The Two Versions of the Storm Lied *Schließe mir die Augen beide*

> An important character in life is the mobility of the libido, the ease with which it moves from one object to others." Sigmund Sigmund Freud, *Abriss der Psychoanalyse*

> No love can be bound by oath or covenant to secure it against a higher love. In nature, every moment is new; the past is always swallowed and forgotten." Ralph Waldo Emerson, "Circles" (Quotation Collection, no. 644)

3.7.1 Genesis

In 1926, the Universal Edition was to observe the twenty-fifth anniversary of its founding. The staff of the publishing house considered how best to mark this notable event and at first thought of bringing out a yearbook that would at once present a "retrospect of the changes in the new music of the past 25 years" and attempt a "prospect of the next 25 years." On May 13, 1925, they sent a letter to Berg with a request for a contribution. They courteously asked him if "in a kind of autobiographical sketch," he could describe his own development, trace his artistic path during the past 25 years, and set down his impressions and judgments from the perspective of a "retrospective assessment" (F 21 Berg 15/II).

Two months later, on July 13, 1925, the publisher informed Berg about a new plan to celebrate the anniversary by presenting Emil Hertzka, the director of the enterprise, with a portfolio, "in which the most outstanding composers of Universal Edition [would] be represented with a contribution." The idea was "that each composer would submit a sheet, which should preferably contain a piece composed especially for the occasion, or else the hand-written copy of an earlier work, or at least a dedication in words."

Berg met this wish in a particularly ingenious way. He dug up his hand-written musical setting of the poem by Theodor Storm "Schließe mir die Augen beide," a lied he had composed many years earlier in a tonal idiom, and set the text to music anew, this time according to the rules of the twelve-tone technique. Somewhat less than five years later, in February of 1930, he published both versions in the journal *Die Musik*[523] with the following note:

synonymous with the immense journey that music has traveled from tonal composition to that "with 12 notes related solely to each other," from the C major triad to the *mutterakkord*, and which to have accompanied as sole publisher from the beginning is the everlasting merit of *Emil Hertzka*. To him are dedicated the *Two Lieder* overleaf after the same text by *Theodor Storm*, which are to illustrate this journey and which have their *first publication* here. They were composed, one at the beginning, the other at the end of past quarter century (1900-1925), by

ALBAN BERG

In a footnote, Berg stated that the so-called *mutterakkord* was discovered by Fritz Heinrich Klein and explained that it is a twelve-tone chord "that also contains all twelve [actually eleven] intervals."

Although the two settings are thus dedicated to Emil Hertzka, they have in fact a deeper autobiographic significance.

There is, to begin with, a question about the dating of the older version. According to Willi Reich, it was composed in 1907,[524] according to Ferdinand Redlich, already in 1900[525] – Redlich referring to Berg's own dating of the first version to 1900, 25 years before the second version, in his note to the first printing. But the matter is in fact a good deal more complicated. According to Hermann Watznauer, Berg composed the first version of "Schliesse mir die Augen beide" in 1907, right after the Rilke lied "Traumgekrönt."[526] It is also worth noting that this version is included among the "Ten Lieder from the Year 1907" that Berg dedicated to his "dear wife" for the third of May, 1917 (F 21 Berg 67). There are thus several indications that Berg's dating in the Hertzka dedication is not quite accurate but was prompted by his wanting to document his creative development during the first quarter of the 20th century. He may thus have made a "cosmetic" correction by moving the date of the earlier version's genesis up by several years.

How ever that may be: it is certain that in 1907 he closely linked the composition of the first version to Helene. In one of his first letters to her, he quoted the poem to her:

Schließe mir die Augen beide	Close my eyes, beloved woman,
Mit den lieben Händen zu;	By your hands let them be pressed,
Geht doch alles, was ich leide,	All my sufferings at the summons
Unter deiner Hand zur Ruh.	Of your loving touch find rest.

> Und wie leise sich der Schmerz   As wave by wave I feel the smart
> Well' um Welle schlafen leget,   Gently in my soul receding,
> Wie der letzte Schlag sich reget,   As at last it ceases beating,
> Füllest Du mein ganzes Herz .   You fill all my brimming heart.

He added: "My idea about this song has the one plus for me that I can send the letter you disdained yesterday" – a somewhat enigmatic statement that does not make altogether clear whether Berg also sent Helene his composition.

Storm's poem, in any case, seems to have expressed the quintessence of tenderness and shelter to Berg at the time. In a letter of August 20, 1910, to Helene, he compared himself to a morphinist who "from the laying on of a beloved hand falls into a deep, dreamless sleep" (ABB 177). The application of a beloved hand evidently meant liberation from all anxieties and all distress to him.

Berg was working on the completion of the Chamber Concerto in June of 1925 when the second letter from Universal Edition reached him. The artistic issues that interested him at the time concerned the problems of twelve-tone composition, to which in his view the future of music belonged. Psychologically, he was in a severe crisis, into which his passionate feelings for Hanna Fuchs had plunged him. He had become estranged from his wife; inwardly he devoted himself to the distant beloved. In her he put his hopes, from her he looked for salvation.

Thus he conceived the idea to recompose his lied "Schließe mir die Augen beide" and to do it in dodecaphonic style. Storm's poem had a profound personal meaning for him. The older – fairly simple – setting had been in C major, and thus he thought that by a second, exacting and timely one he would he able to convey an impression of the enormous distance the New Music had come during the first quarter of the 20th century.

Berg's sketches and his letters to Webern permit a nearly airtight reconstruction of the twelve-tone poem's genesis. On August 24, 1925, he wrote to Webern from Trahütten, where he was spending the summer vacation with Helene, that he had not managed to do any composing. He was dealing with lesser tasks: *Anbruch* (the yearbook of Universal Edition), the Hertzka portfolio, and the revision of the piano score of his Chamber Concerto. On September 11, he told his friend that "in spite of favorable living and working conditions" he had not yet gotten around "to anything compositional." He was recuperating slowly and, "sort of in between things," writing an article for the Universal Edition Yearbook. On September 18, he reported to Webern that the day before he had finished and sent off a small article for the U Yearbook – an answer to the question "Prospects of the music of the next 25 years." The whole, he said, was more whimsical than learned, "with the irrevocable belief in the only possible answer, namely 'Schönberg,' nevertheless manifesting itself in full earnest." In the sketches for the lied (F 21 Berg 15 pag.2), the title *Schließe mir die Augen beide*" bears the notation "Trahütten, 23.9.25" – an indication that Berg had drafted the lied on that day. The composition was probably completed by early October. On October 12, he told Webern that he had submitted the two "love songs" for the Hertzka portfolio, the "new" lied being his "first attempt at strictest 12-tone (serial) composition."

3.7.2 Dodekaphonics: Fritz Heinrich Klein's All-Interval Row and the *Mutterakkord*

While tackling the work on the twelve-tone version of he lied, Berg reflected again about some fundamental questions of dodecaphonic composition, closely considering especially some discoveries his Linz pupil Fritz Heinrich Klein had come up with in the area.[527]

Klein (1892-1977) was originally a student of Schönberg's but did not get along with him and switched to Berg, probably in 1918. In a letter to Berg of March 12, 1925, he confessed to having a personal aversion to Schönberg: "I hate his Beethoven pose, his genius romps, his 'Schindler' floggings, and because he so long looked down upon and repressed your talent."[528] He evidently felt himself to be insufficiently acknowledged and respected as a twelve-tone composer by Schönberg. There were also disputes about priority, about the question who had been the first to write twelve-tone compositions. Schönberg, Klein complained in another letter to Berg, had "suppressed" the fact that Klein's *Maschine* "was one of the first works in music literature to be constructed in full consciousness with 12-tone transformations."[529]

Klein composed his work *Die Maschine* op.1 in the spring of 1921 for chamber orchestra and in the summer of 1923 adapted it for four-handed piano. In the latter version it was published by the Carl Haslinger publishing house in Vienna with the subtitle *Eine extonale Selbstsatire* (An ex-tonal self-satire) – not under Klein's own name but under the pseudonym Heautontimoroumenos (Self-Tormentor, after Terence and Baudelaire). In 1924, Klein self-published his Variations op. 14 for (two-handed) piano. In a preface he set down the principles of his twelve-tone theory. He stated that he composed altogether "freely," i.e., at will "tonally" or "ex-tonally." He had reached this freedom through his "music statistics," in which he set out from the idea "to search out and systematically represent all the possibilities of music in a mathematico-logical way." Since in his "music statistics" all chords, from the simple triad to the complex *mutterakkord*, were "equal citizens of one sound state," their different consequences, namely tonality and "extonality," were to be regarded as equally valid modes of expression. Accordingly, he had at one time composed a tonal song (like his *Lautenlied* [Lute Song] op. 2) and another time an "ex-tonal" symphony (like his *Zwölfklangphantasie* for large orchestra op. 12).

Central to Klein's twelve-tone theory is the so-called *mutterakkord*, literally mother chord, a twelve-tone cord containing all eleven possible intervals (Klein erroneously speaks of twelve intervals). This is the form in which he presents it:

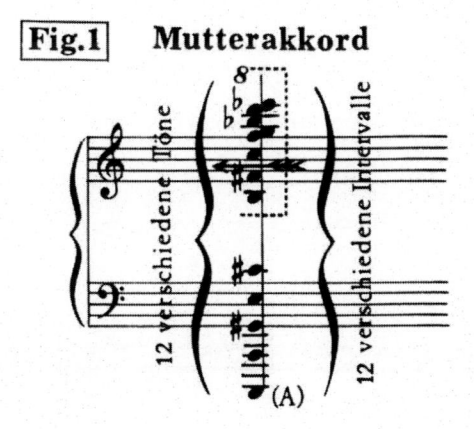

Fig.1 **Mutterakkord**

If one "unfolds" the chord and reads the intervals upward from below, one gets indeed all 11 intervals:

Interestingly, Klein regarded this interval row – he does not use this term but speaks of the "model type II" – as a horizontal projection of the *mutterakkord*:

199

Fig. 2   **Modell – Typ II**
12 verschiedene Töne

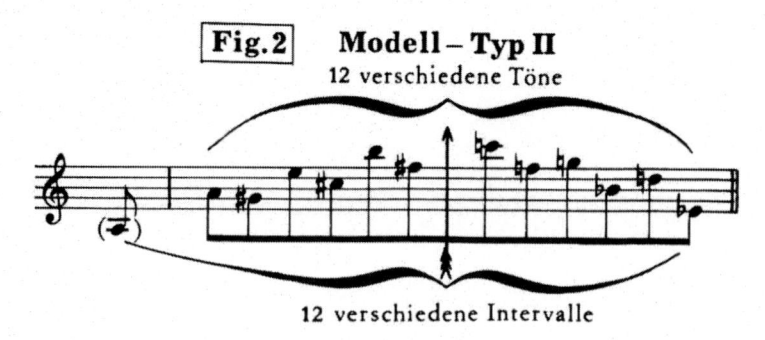

[musical notation]

12 verschiedene Intervalle

He also listed several properties of this row, and of the *mutterakkord*, of which the following are of special significance:

1. The row is symmetrically arranged, i.e, the second half is the "crab" of the first.
2. Both phrases contain one minor triad (C-sharp minor and G minor)
3. If one connects every second note of the row, one gets perfect fourths and fifths.

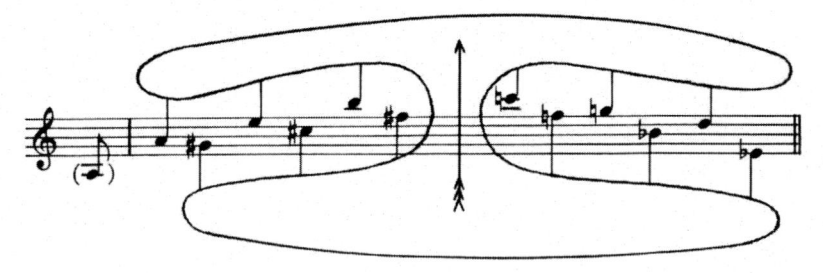

[musical notation]

4. Two-, three-, four-, five-, and six-voiced chords can be derived from the row. Especially interesting is the fact that from the six-voice chords scales of a "tonal" character can also be built:

[musical notation]

No less relevant, finally, is the fact that Klein also obtained a second "form" of the row and the *mutterakkord*, namely by placing the intervals "in reverse sequence":

Fig. 22   I. Form   II. Form

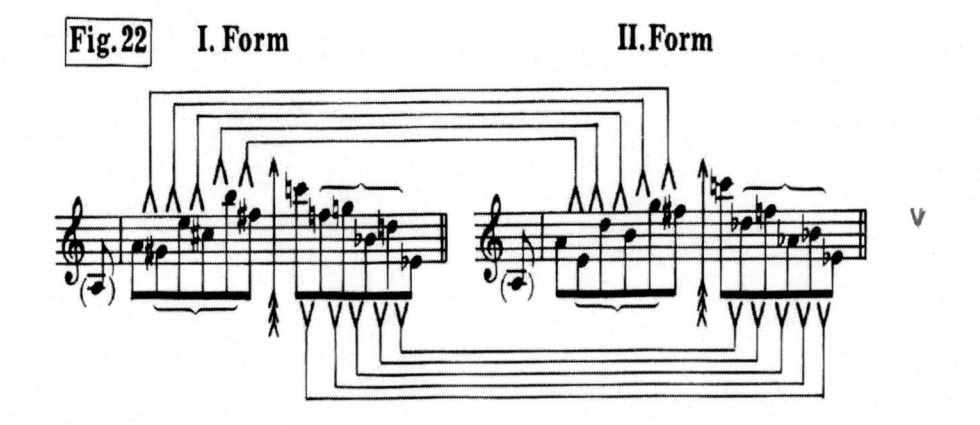

Berg knew Klein's *Maschine* as well as his *Variations* op. 14. Among his effects are personal copies of both works (F 21 Berg 328/1 and 328/2). From a number of annotations in the latter, it also appears that he had studied Klein's preface carefully.

The all-interval row and chord, in any case, provided powerful impulses to him. He based both the twelve-tone version of the Storm lied and the *Lyric Suite* on Klein's row but transposed it downward by a major third, so that it begins with the note f and ends with the note h (b) – the initials of Hanna Fuchs, to whom both works are secretly dedicated.

On July 13, 1926, he told Schönberg that he was working on the *Lyric Suite* and reported to him about his experiences with the "composition with twelve tones." In that context he also came to speak of Klein's row, which he mistakenly regarded as "the only of its kind."[530] His explanations about the properties of the row – this has been altogether overlooked until now – essentially repeat Klein's statements in the preface to the *Variations* op. 14.

What is especially significant now is that the dodecaphonic construction of the Storm lied and of Berg's way of working must remain incomprehensible if one tries to fathom them without reference to Klein's arguments.

Before approaching the composition of the lied, Berg wrote down the two forms of the row, as well as the two forms of the *mutterakkord*, on a music sheet (F 21 Berg 116 fol. 1).

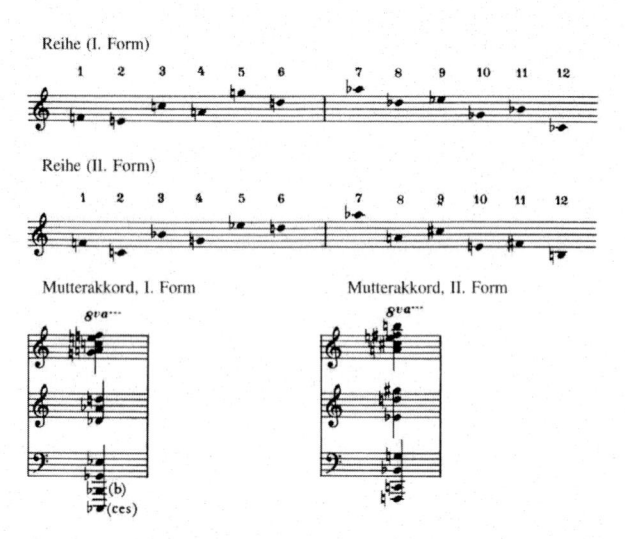

An analysis of the twelve-tone composition shows that Berg is working with both forms of the row. For the vocal part he exclusively uses the first form, which is traversed five times in its original shape. The piano part, on the other hand, relies on both forms of the row. While the first half (mm. 1-10) is confined to the first form, the second half also draws on the second form (see the right hand of the piano part, mm. 11-13). The first half of the song, moreover, closes with the first form of the *mutterakkord* (mm. 10/11), the second half with the second (mm. 19/20).

If Berg borrowed the "twelve-tone material" for his lied from the discussions of Fritz Heinrich Klein, he received major impulses for the shaping of the vocal part from the Petrarch sonnet composed by Schönberg probably in 1923 for his *Serenade* op. 24 There the twelve-tone row is repeated no fewer than thirteen times in its basic form (not completely at the end). Berg makes do with five recurrences, since the Storm poem only contains 60 syllables (12 x 5 = 60). As in Schönberg, the method of setting the words to music is strictly syllabic: each syllable gets only one note.[531]

3.7.3 Comparison of the Two Versions

Regardless of the particular aspect under which one compares the two settings of Storm's poem, the result is always the same: the earlier setting conveys a sense of great simplicity, while the later one exhibits immense complexity.

The *tonal* setting is done in the Romantic or late Romantic style. At first glance one notices the meter (5/4 time), the strictly syllabic composition (only one word, *Schmerz*, in m. 5 is set to a two-note phrase), the even rhythm (eighths are the norm) and the relative simplicity of the harmonic plan. The lied is written in C major, modulates to A minor at the end of the first strophe, and then returns to C major via F major, B-flat major and C minor. Chordal alterations, chromatic turns and suspensions, however, keep the music from being colorless. The vocal line (ranging from b to e₂) and the piano part converge: the melody of the voice is incorporated with the piano accompaniment. The song contains nothing that is merely decorative, nothing ornamental, nothing superfluous: it sounds like a heartfelt prayer.

By contrast, the dodecaphonic setting is in every respect richer and more differentiated. The atonal idiom differs so fundamentally from functional harmony that it does not really admit of a direct comparison. Here, too, the setting is strictly syllabic but exhibits an enormous rhythmic and motivic variety: no measure resembles any other rhythmically. The vocal part (ranging from b to a₂) and the piano accompaniment diverge: the completely independent piano part provides a kind of counterpoint to the voice. Especially worth noting in this respect is the canon between the voice and the right hand of the piano in mm. 4-8 (already envisioned by Berg in the preliminary sketches). The piano part exhibits a tendency to capture all the registers of the instrument, even the highest and the lowest. Noteworthy are also the dyads a/b [b♭] and h [b]/f in m. 16 – very likely a cipher for Alban Berg and Hanna Fuchs.

3.8 String Quartet for Hanna: the *Lyric Suite*

"Now since in my life I have never enjoyed the real happiness of love, I want to erect a monument to this most beautiful of all dreams, in which this love is for once to sate itself utterly from the beginning to the end: I have in my head the outline of a *Tristan and Isolde*, the simplest but most full-blooded musical conception; with the black flag that waves at the end I will then cover myself in order – to die." Richard Wagner to Franz Liszt[532]

"It [the composition with twelve tones], my Hanna, has also yielded me some other freedoms! For example that of secreting time and again our initials H, F and A, B in this music; of bringing every movement and part of a movement into relation with our numbers 10 and 23. I have written this and much else that is suggestive into this score for you (for whom alone, after all – despite the official dedication overleaf – every note of this work was written). May it thus be a small monument of a great love." Berg to Hanna Fuchs in the copy of the *Lyric Suite* dedicated to her.

3.8.1 The State of Reseach

On the surface, the *Lyric Suite* gives the impression of being "absolute music." In reality, however, as we now definitely know, it is based on a secret program. Since it is one of he most personal of Berg's works, one can understand why he would do everything he could to suppress the program and to efface the autobiographic traces of the composition. And he succeeded, too: for fifty years the *Lyric Suite* was regarded as a string quartet sans program. No doubt the much-quoted and much-read essay by Theodor W. Adorno contributed to this view, who surely thought he was acting in Berg's behalf when he categorically denied any connection of the work to program music, saying: "Void of all illustrating intention, it certainly may not be taken as a tone poem in the new German sense. In lieu of that, however, it is a latent opera."[533] In keeping with that opinion, Klaus Schweizer still wrote in 1970 that the *Lyric Suite* may be seen "as the expression of a progressively intensified process of subjectification," which, however, "does not have to be borne up by an extra-musical programmatic theme and its tone-painting depiction, but is completely absorbed without remainder in the representative potential of the compositional processes themselves."[534]

Incidentally, some rather peculiar formulations in the Adorno essay sprang from the wish to divert attention away from the occasion of the work. In a letter to Helene Berg of November 21, 1936, Adorno wrote that by introducing the concept of the "latent opera" he thought he had "objectified" the personal elements to such an extent "that no on will be looking for any private motives. "⁵³⁵

In a longish article published in early 1975, I first proposed the thesis, after detailed study of all the documents then available and on the basis of fresh analytic findings, that the *Lyric Suite* was, after all, based on a hidden program.⁵³⁶ I included the *Lyric Symphony* "for orchestra, soprano and baritone" op 18 by Alexander von Zemlinsky in my investigation, a work completed in 1923 and premiered in 1924 in Prague, which consists of seven "songs" after poems by Rabindranath Tagore. The inclusion of the work was urgently needed, not only because the *Lyric Suite* is dedicated to Zemlinsky, the brother-in-law of Schönberg and friend of Berg, but also because it was linked in two ways to the *Lyric Symphony*: by its title and by a quotation. In the *Adagio appassionato*, Berg in two different places – in mm. 32/33 in the viola and in mm. 46-50 in the second violin – quotes a phrase from Zemlinisky's symphony; that is to say, he both times put the phrase in quotation marks and states in an annotation (note the scholarly punctilio) that it is a "quotation from Zemlinsky's Lyric Symphony". The quoted passage derives from the third movement of Zemlnsky's work, where it forms a vocal phrase sung by the baritone to the words "Du bist mein Eigen, mein Eigen" (You are my own, my own).

In a comparison of the two works, which I made in the 1960s, I discovered that the *Lyric Suite* actually contained three Zemlinsky quotations, which Berg incorporated and paraphrased in more than twenty places in his quartet. I concluded from this that a love poem of Tagore's – the poem *Du bist die Abendwolke* (You are the Evening Cloud), which includes the line "Du bist mein Eigen, mein Eigen" – had served as the program for three of the *Lyric Suite*'s six movements, namely the *Andante amoroso*, the *Trio estatico* and the *Adagio appassionato*.

Of importance for my work were also some fresh observations of the tectonics and the agogic or shaping of the tempi. Thanks to the work of Reginald Brindle Smith,⁵³⁷ A. Pernye⁵³⁸ and Klaus Schweizer,⁵³⁹ it was known that the 23, Berg's personal fatal number, played an important role in the construction plan of the *Lyric Suite*. I discovered, however, that a similar importance attached to an additional number, i.e., the five and its multiple. These two numbers, the 23 and the 5, dictate, down to the last detail, both the tectonics and the agogic of the work, the dimensions and proportions of the six movements as well as the metronomic notations.

205

In the course of my work I noticed another significant four-tone phrase consisting of the notes b [b♭], a, f and h [b]. It plays a decisive role in the *Allegro misterioso* and recurs as a reminiscence in the later movements. It also seemed noteworthy that the *Largo desolato* concealed, besides the known *Tristan* quotation in mm. 26/27, two additional *Tristan* alllusions. Of significance is finally also the scordatura of the cello in the *Largo desolato*, whose C string is to be tuned down to B. I reflected that a similar scordatura of the double basses is prescribed in *Wozzeck* for the scene of the murder (III.2) and that the note b there functions as a death symbol. From all this I concluded that the subject of the *Lyric Suite* was the story of a love that undergoes a great development and finds its ultimate fulfillment in a *liebestod*. At the time I assumed that Berg had written the *Lyric Suite*, like the earlier String Quartet op. 3, for his wife.

3.8.2 Autobiographic Background: Sources and Documents

About a year and a half after the publication of my study, George Perle made a sensational discovery in the United States: among the effects of Hanna Fuchs-Robettin, he found fourteen letters by Berg, along with a copy of the first printing of the *Lyric Suite* with hand-written programmatic annotations by the composer, which went to show that he was in a love relationship with Hanna in 1925, that the relationship inspired him to compose the *Lyric Suite*, and that the work was based on a detailed, composed program here decoded by Berg.[540]

Hanna, wife of the Prague industrialist Herbert Fuchs-Robettin, was born on July 11, 1894, in Prague, as the daughter of the wealthy leather manufacturer Robert Werfel – and sister of the subsequently famous writer Franz Werfel (b. 1890). The Werfels, who had an intense interest in music and theater, were assimilated Jews (their children, who were raised by a Czech Catholic governess, are said to have attended both a Catholic church and the synagogue). When the 23-year-old Hanna told her brother of her decision to become engaged to Herbert von Fuchs-Robettin, he had tried to talk her out of it, but she persisted and in March of 1917 had married the paper manufacturer. Berg fell in love with her in part because of her innate cheerfulness and sweetness and because of a lightness of being that knew no pedantry.[541]

The subject of the *Lyric Suite*, according to Berg, is the story of his passionate love for Hanna Fuchs. The six movements of the work describe the stages of this story, which Berg apostrophizes as a tragedy. His entries indicate clearly that in conceiving the work he was thinking of a diary-like record. Thus he writes of the *Allegro gioviale* that "its nearly inconsequential mood" gave "no intimation of the subsequent tragedy."

The second movement, the *Andante amoroso,* is conceived, according to Berg, as a kind of domestic scene in Hanna's home: the rondo-like movement portrays Hanna and her two children, seven-year-old Munzo[542] and three-and-a-half-year-old Dorothea (Dodo). In the third movement, Berg's love for Hanna advances into the center of events. Berg marks the movement journal-like with the date 5-20-25 and intimates that the middle part, the *Trio estatico,* signalizes the confession of his/their love. The fourth movement, the *Adagio appassionato,* is titled "the next day." Berg explains the frequent imitational passages of the movement, and the twofold exact quotation from Zemlinsky's *Lyric Symphony* ("You are my own, my own"), in terms of an imagined love dialogue, which finally ebbs away "into the completely spiritualized, soulful, celestial."

The fifth movement, *Presto delirando,* he explicates as the description of the "terrors and torments" that now followed. By that he evidently meant the tortured days and nights he spent after having left Prague. The programmatic content of the last movement, finally, is intimated by a reference to Baudelaire's sonnet "De profundis clamavi" from the *Fleurs du mal.* In the score for Hanna Fuchs, several notably cantabile passages in all four instruments are underlaid with the words of Baudelaire's poem in the German translation by Stefan George.[543] Even more telling, almost, than this reference is the annotation that the *Largo desolato* closes "dying away in love, longing and sorrow." From Berg's programmatic entries in the copy for Hanna Fuchs, we also learn for the first time that the musical anagrams H[B]F (= Hanna Fuchs) and AB[B♭] (= Alban Berg) has a special relevance for the construction of the work. We learn besides that he related the quartet's two basic numbers to himself and to Hanna: the 23 is his own number, the 10 that of Hanna (= the twice five letters of her name).

Photograph 10: Hanna Fuchs-Robettin

(with kind permission of Mrs. Dorothea Robettin)

There is no question that these annotations of Berg's are of inestimable value for the interpretation of the *Lyric Suite*. Even so, it would be a mistake to think that they provide complete information about the program of the work. The more one examines these marginalia, the clearer it becomes that they exhaust themselves in hints and allusions. We are dealing, after all, with intimate notes, meant exclusively for Hanna Fuchs. Berg reminds her of past events, alludes to joint experiences and explains only those points of the poetic conception that he thought had to be meaningful to her. He was not intent on providing an exhaustive explication of the musical-programmatic "secrets" of the composition.

As noted, Berg, for obvious reasons, had to keep the affair with Hanna concealed from the public. He could and would not speak about his feelings to his wife. He therefore turned in confidence to close friends, asking them for advice. Two parties recommended that he read *Effie Briest*, the novel by Theodor Fontane depicting the tragic entanglements that can result from a triangular love relationship. Berg could not bring himself to purchase the book and was relieved when Hermann Watznauer offered to lend it to him.[544]

He had also let some of his pupils into the secret of the affair. Among them was Julius Schloß (1902-1972), who had agreed to proofread the *Lyric Suite* for publication. In appreciation, Berg, in the autumn of 1927, made him a present of a copy fresh from the press of the first printing, with the dedication: "For my dear Schloß, who during the days of making corrections truly proved that he also has the key to my music." Evidently he wanted to do Schloß, who had intensively concerned himself with his music, a favor by entering the programmatic annotations in the copy, which is now at McGill University in Montreal.[545] This source, too, is of great value, even though the annotations in it are not as detailed as those in the copy for Hanna Fuchs – not to mention that Berg's handwriting here is often careless and hard to decipher.

Another witness to the affair was Theodor W. Adorno. Berg had let him into the story from the first day on and had used him as a regular accomplice and *postillon d'amour*. The *Aufzeichnungen über Berg* that Adorno set down in early October of 1955 contain a revealing passage that was published only in 1979:

> The Lyric Suite, a program music with a suppressed program, has turned the whole story into a composition with numerous allusions, without, by the way, those allusions – which include the dedication to Zemlinsky and the quotation from the latter's Lyric Symphony – diminishing the quality in the least; on the contrary, this most seductive work obtained its élan from that very background. Of these allusions, I will note only one: in the second movement, the first theme sym-

bolizes Hanna, the second her husband, the third, with its two contrasting parts, the two children. The characteristically repeated note c corresponds in the old solmisation, to a twofold *do*, the older [actually younger] Fuchs child was called Dodo. A hermeneutist taking on the Lyric Suite would have work to do for the rest of his life.[546]

A special place value, finally, attaches to the detailed sketches, which are preserved in fifteen folders (F 21 Berg 76/I to XV). They yield a wealth of information, not only about the genesis of the composition, but also about Berg's creative process, the construction plans and the semantics of the work. A close study makes Berg's programmatic intentions transparent. The sketches pinpoint and supplement his annotations in the copy for Hanna Fuchs and permit weighty inferences as to the semantics of movements and parts of movements not elucidated by Berg in that copy.

3.8.3 Genesis and Overall Conception

> "And now, may I succeed with the most difficult of all leaps – the one into actually starting the composition." Berg to Webern, September 18, 1925[547]

As we have seen, Berg drafted the dodecaphonic lied *Schließe mir die Augen beide* on September 23, 1925. In the sketches to the *Lyric Suite* (76/I fol. 9 verso), we find the date 9-29-1925. Moreover, in the midst of the sketches for the quartet, he wrote down the text of the Storm poem and added notes about the five recurrences of the twelve-tone series in the vocal part (76/I fol. 15). That suggests that for some days or weeks he may have been thinking about both works simultaneously.

The sketches for the *Lyric Suite* show that Berg made notes about every aspect of the projected work. He gave much thought to the number and sequence of the movements, to their form, their "style," their length, their expressive content and their tonal character, as well as to the twelve-tone series and the modifications that series would undergo. He was, besides, interested in the diverse motifs that could be constructed from the tone anagrams. He also sketched the Zemlinsky motifs that were to play such a major role in his work, and diverse forms of the quintuple rhythm of the fifth movement. As was his habit, he pondered every possibility and finally chose the one he regarded as the best solution.

His firm intention from the start was to shape the work in six movements. The tempo markings of the various movements, however, differed in part from the final sequence. One of the earliest drafts (76/I fol. 9) reads: *Allegretto – Andante – Allegretto (Scherzo) – Adagio – Presto – Largo*. Another early draft

(76/I fol. 10) envisions the following structure: *Allegro sonata form (bipartite)* – *Andante Rondo* – *Presto Scherzo (tripartite)* – *Adagio bipartite* – *Allegretto Var.* – *Largo sonata form*. This draft tells us that Berg had planned the fifth movement, which here was to be an Allegretto, from the start as a variations movement. A subsequent draft, which includes indications as to form and "style" of the suite, gets closer to the final version (76/V fol. 8):

str.	I	bipartite (almost sonata)
fr.	II	symmetric, tripartite, may[be] songlike
str. fr.	III	Scherzo Trio
fr.	IV	Adagio
fr. str.	V	Allegro Perpetuum mobile Var.?
str.	VI	Sonata movement

The abbreviations *str.* and *fr.* stand for strict and free and signify that the respective movements or parts of movements are to be done in strict twelve-tone technique or else in free atonality. For the opening movement, moreover, Berg outlines the formal schema $a^1 - a^2 - b$ *transition* – c *side movement* – d *coda* – *reprise* completely; for the second movement he jots down the arc *a b a c a b a* as the formal schema. One may also note that at this stage of the planning he was no longer sure whether the fifth part should be a variations movement.

The expressive content was a problem Berg pondered intensively. For nearly every movement he considered multiple, mostly Italian characterizing epithets. He carefully weighed the pros and contras and eventually picked one. The following early draft will convey a sense of these efforts to find the aptest expression mark for the movements (76/I fo.10):

Allegro comodo and deciso (semplice)

Andante amoroso (gentile giocoso)

Presto ghostly (Scherzo) agitato ardente
        subito impetuoso

Adagio affettuoso passionato

Allegretto delirando inquieto tempestuoso furioso

Largo funebre
  doloroso
  lagrimoso
  lamentabile

lugubre

mesto

76/I fol. 23'

chromatische Form

dazu chromatischer Lauf h ↗ f ↘ h ↗ f

76/I fol. 24'
(Skizze zum Finale)

76/I fol. 25'

76/XII fol. 11'   fol. 14

Table 1: Embodiments of the double anagram in the sketches

Quite early also, Berg had developed fairly definite ideas about the kind of sound he wanted in some movements. Playing *with mute* was envisioned for the third movement, *col legno* for the fifth (76 fol. 8). The last movement was to have a great deal of *tremolo*, and the C-string of the cello was to be tuned down to b (76/XII fol. 14).

He furthermore did much calculating about the size of the movements, and he seems from the start to have decided to base the dimensions of the movements on what were to him the important numbers 23 and 10. In an early draft (76/I fol. 13), he fixed the number of measures of the six movements to be 69 150 138 (= 6 x 23) 100 230 69. In another draft (76/II fol. 6), the figures are as follows: Allegretto 69 – Andante 125 – Scherzo 161 (7 x 23) – Adagio 115 (5 x 23) – Presto 207 (9 x 23) – Largo 123. The total is 800. For comparison, he listed the dimensions of the movements in Schönberg's *Serenade* op 24 and his *Wind Quintet* op. 26 – those of the serenade being respectively 145, 118, 77, 87, 200, 26 and 163 bars, totaling 816, while those of the quintet, which is longer, are 227, 419, 141 and 359 bars, totaling 1146.

From the start, also, Berg planned to form characteristic motifs from the all-important initials AB and HF. Table 1 lists those forms that ended up not being used in the final version. Two of these motifs are especially notable in that they exhibit the head motif of the first string quartet op. 3. Berg will have been considerably astounded to note that the first and last note of that motif represent the initials of Hanna Fuchs!

From the beginning, again, Berg had the definite intention of not only quoting the phrase "You are my own, my own" from Zemlinsky's *Lyric Symphony* but of also deriving characteristic motifs from it and other melodic phrases – variants that I had discovered in my article published in 1975 without having had access to the sketches at the time. Some of these variants in the sketches are as follows:

Sketches 3: Lyric Suite

Austrian National Library Music Collection, Fonds Berg 76/V fol. 10, Row forms for the first movement, References to Fritz Heinrich Klein's serial forms and the mutterakkord, First publication, by permission of the Austrian National Library

A large area in the sketches, finally, is filled with tables of tone rows and dodecaphonic considerations (76/V fol. 8 to 36). They enable us to recognize that Berg proceeded from Fritz Heinrich Klein's all-interval series and his theoretical preface to the Variations op. 14. Klein's name crops up repeatedly in the sketches, as in the note that the "Klein theme" transformed itself from the third movement on, and in the thought that the third movement might use the second "Klein form" (76/XV fol. 8). On fol. 10, Berg then wrote down the serial forms and transpositions that he planned to employ in the opening movement (see Sketches 3). Here we find the "original row" on f, along with its mirror forms and three transpositions, which he calls "dominant form" (row on b), the "lower mediant" (row on d) and the "upper mediant" (row on a-flat). At the same time he sought to interpret the two halves of the "original row" tonally: the first half he reads as C major but also as an F tonality, the second half as G-flat major or B major. In addition he notated Klein's second serial form and commented that of the two forms of the *mutterakkord*, the first contained two minor triads (E-flat and A minor), the second two major triads (A and E-flat major).

The earliest sketches for the *Lyric Suite*, as mentioned before, date from September and October of 1925. On October 12, Berg complained in a letter to Webern that the work was not adequately progressing: "it is not making real headway." Nevertheless, he seems to have completed the first movement by October 23, a date found in the autograph (23/I fol. 5). After that, the work stalled. Berg had to cope with the revision of the *Wozzeck* piano score, and in November/December he traveled twice to Berlin to attend the rehearsals for the premiere of that opera (ABB 541-553). In Vienna, where he spent the first several months of the year 1926, he was apparently unproductive. It was only after arriving in Trahütten on May of 26 of 1926, that he resumed work on the *Lyric Suite*. On June 7, he joyfully reported to Webern that he had finally succeeded in "getting the rusted work cart moving again." On Jun 12, 1926, he completed the second movement (as noted on fol. 15 of the autograph). On June 27, he tells Schönberg that "a movement of my second quartet now in progress represents the attempt to write in strictest twelve-tone music with a strong tonal strain." On July 13, 1926, he reported to him that he was working "in great haste, even nervosity" on "several movements at once," at times "merely sketching." On September 13, the first five movements were finished, and on October 8, the suite was complete in its entirety. Many months later he divulged to Webern that he had been able to finish writing it only "by a supreme effort."[548]

3.8.4 Berg's Analysis of the *Lyric Suite*

Of paramount importance for any discussion of the *Lyric Suite*'s composition is an analysis written by Berg in 1926. Berg composed it for the Kolisch

Quartet, which premiered the work on January 8, 1927, in Vienna. The analysis was known to Stein and Adorno but was published in facsimile by Willi Reich only in 1959.[549] In 1971 it was published again, in both facsimile and transcription, by Ursula von Rauchhaupt, in an indispensable documentation about the string quartets of Schönbeg, Berg and Webern.[550]

Written by hand on nine sheets, Berg's analysis provides data about the overall conception, the serial technique, the forms of, and the "linkages" between, the individual movements. His statements are often detailed but never exhaustive. Berg by no means enumerates all of the thematic "linkages" and "reminiscences." There are only a few hints, which require interpretation, about the semantics of the work.

Let us, to begin with, look at the overall conception of the work. The prime characteristic of the composition is the symbiosis of free atonality and dodecaphony. Half of the *Lyric Suite* is composed in free atonality, and half according to the rules of Schönberg's twelve-tone technique. Although Berg had written dodecaphonic components already for he Adagio of the Chamber Concerto, he did no yet feel sufficiently trained in the "composition with twelve tones" when he began to sketch the *Lyric Suite*. In letters to Webern and Schönberg, he complained several times that he did not get ahead quickly enough, owing to the special difficulties he had with the new technique, and he justified the composition of the movements that are written in free atonality in terms of just this situation. On July 13, 1926, he wrote to Schönberg: "Hence also, so as not to lose heart altogether, the intermittent relapses into my old, familiar free way of writing." (Our analysis will show, however, that this rationale does justice only in part to the true facts of the case.)

The six movements of the *Lyric Suite* are arranged in such a way that, with one exception, a dodecaphonic movement, or partial movement, is always followed by a movement, or partial movement, written in free atonality. According to Berg's specifications, the disposition is as follows:

    I   Allegro gioviale (12-tone)
    II   Andante amoroso (free)
    III Allegro misterioso (12-tone)
         (Trio estatico free)

    IV   Adagio appassionato (free)
    V   Presto delirando (free)
          (the two trios 12-tone)
    VI Largo desolato (12-tone)

(The third movement is tripartite in design, with a trio, the fifth movement is in five parts, with two trios.)

In the preamble to his analysis, Berg had this to say about the principle underlying the movement construction and about the overall conception of his work:

> The series changes in the course of the four movements due to the rearrangement of several notes. (This change [is] inessential with respect to the line, but essential with respect to the characters – '*suffering fate*').

> The linking of the individual movements consists – apart from the fact that the 12-tone row constitutes one such linkage – in the fact that in each case one component (1 theme or 1 row, 1 piece or 1 idea) is taken over into the next movement and the last refers back to the first. Not mechanically, of course, but likewise in relation to the overall development (mood intensification) within the piece as a whole ('*suffering fate*'!)

The overall design of the *Lyric Suite* thus obeys the principle of "mood intensification." The "overall development" takes place between two levels increasingly tending apart. The most obvious expression of the "mood intensification" is the acceleration or else deceleration of the tempo. The tempo of the lively movements becomes progressively faster: *Allegretto* gioviale – *Allegro* misterioso – *Presto* delirando. Correspondingly, the tempo of the measured movements grows increasingly slower: *Andante* amoroso – *Adagio* appassionato – *Largo* desolato. Thus one could say that the two levels constitute a "through-composed accelerando" and a "through-composed ritardano." (Berg illustrates the intended "mood intensification" graphically by a fork with a six-spiked line in his analysis.)

The original and imaginative way in which Berg treats the row is directly connected with the principle of "mood intensification." As noted earlier, Berg based the dodecaphonically constructed movements of the *Lyric Suite* on the "symmetric all-interval row" discovered by Fritz Heinrich Klein and published in 1924. Berg, as we can tell from his remarks, was intrigued by the "mathematical form" of this row, which he mistakenly regarded as "the only one of its kind,"[551] and we are surely not wrong in assuming that he chose the

Kleinian row not least for its immanent potential of forming tonal complexes. (In a letter to Schönberg of July 13, 1926, he weighed the advantages springing from the symmetry of the row against the drawbacks. He regarded it as a "grave disadvantage" that the row "does not have an independent crab form.")

As for the specific dodecaphonic disposition of the *Lyric Suite*, only the first movement, the *Allegro gioviale*, is based directly on the Kleinian all-interval series. In the remaining movements, Berg works with serial transformations, which he lists in his analysis. If we put these "secondary rows" together, we get the following picture:

1st movement		f	e	c	a	g	d	a^b	d^b	e^b	g^b	b^b	b
		1	2	3	10	5	6	7	8	9	10	11	12
2nd movement		a^b	g	e^b	a	b^b	f	b	e	f$^\#$	c	c$^\#$	d
Viola mm. 24-28		1	2	3	10	5	6	7	8	9	4	11	12
3rd movement		b^b	a	f	b	c	g	d^b	g^b	a^b	d	e^b	e
		1	2	3	10	5	6	7	8	9	4	11	12
5th movement		d^b	c	a^b	d	f	a	e	b^b	b	d$^\#$	f$^\#$	g
mm. 86-120		1	2	3	10	4	8	7	6	9	5	11	12
6th movement		f	e	c	f$^\#$	a	c$^\#$	g$^\#$	d	e^b	g	b^b	b
		1	2	3	10	4	8	7	6	9	5	11	12
"half-row"		f	f$^\#$	a	g$^\#$	b^b	b	e	c	c$^\#$	d	e^b	g
		1	10	4	7	11	12	2	3	8	6	9	5

The table shows that Berg is working with (at least) three transformations of the "ur-row":[552] the first transformation, which is formed by the transposition of tones 4 and 10, occurs first in mm. 24-28 of the otherwise freely worked *Andante amoroso* (viola) and forms the series of the *Allegro misterioso*. The second transformation, marked by the transposition of 5 notes, furnishes the basis for portions of the *Tenebroso* trio and of the *Largo desolato*. In the latter, however, Berg also uses a third transformation, the so-called "half-row." It hardly bears any resemblance to the ur-row. The table also reveals that the symmetric structure of the Kleinian row – the second half constituting the transposed retrograde of the first half – is "undone" in all of the secondary rows.

Berg makes it clear in his analysis that the transformations of the "ur-row" are not fortuitous but spring from a particular poetic-semantic intention. That is the meaning of the statement: "This change [is] inessential with respect to the line, but essential with respect to the characters – '*suffering fate*.'" Elsewhere he reveals that he based the *Allegretto gioviale* (originally entitled *Allegretto giojoso*[553]) on the Kleinian all-interval series, because in its "mathematical form" the latter seemed to him especially suited for "this more objective piece." We may conclude from this that the transformations of the row were parallel to the intended process of subjectification. The farther the transformations distance themselves from the "mathematical form" of the original series, the greater will be the distance of the music from the "more objective piece" that opens the work.

The thematic, serial and "ideational" "linkages" between the individual movements, too, however, are in the service of a programmatic intent, as they follow "not mechanically, but likewise in relation to the overall development (mood intensification) within the piece as a whole ('*suffering fate'!*)." It is especially remarkable that Berg used the term "character" several times in his analysis, and the odd formulation "suffering fate" (*Schicksal erleidend*) twice in short succession.

3.8.5 Allegro gioviale (giocoso): "Clinking of Cups"

The two bookend movements of the *Lyric Suite*, the *Allegretto gioviale* (*giocoso* in the particello) and the *Largo desolato*, are the poles of a vast development that ends tragically. There are numerous indications that in conceiving the work Berg had the contrast in thought and mood between the two movements in mind from the start. In an early stage of work on the piece, for example, he wrote down numerous Italian adjectives, frequently with German equivalents, most of which circumscribe the joyful, merry or cheerful character of the head movement. The first list reads: *grazioso graceful – giochevole cheerful, merry – giocondamente boisterous, jolly – giocondo graceful – giovale joyously gay – giojoso*. A second lisit reads *leggiero – comodo – con brio – deciso – semplice – giocoso – facile – gracioso – risoluto – vivace*. What is symptomatic here is that an arrow after *giocoso* points to the last movement (*mesto*).

Berg very likely meant the strictly dodecaphonic *Allegretto gioviale* when he wrote to Schönberg on June 27, 1926, that a movement of his quartet-in-the-making represented an attempt "to write in the strictest twelve-tone music with a strongly tonal strain." A careful analysis shows that he based the movement on the rows f, a-flat and d (along with their mirror forms). Not yet content, he additionally used the scale row and fifths row derived from the original series, thus achieving great diversity:[554]

Scale row:

c   d   e   f   g   a │ g♭   a♭   b♭   c♭   d♭   e♭

Fifths row:

F – c – g – d – a – e │ b – f♯ – c♯ – g♯ – d♯ – a♯

In the copy for Hanna, Berg wrote about the first movement:

> This first movement, whose nearly inconsequential mood gives no hint of the tragedy to follow, perpetually skirts the keys H [B] major and F major. The main theme – the twelve-tone series underlying the entire quartet – is likewise clasped round by your letters."

These explanations were plainly intended for a dilettante and fall far short of the actual complexity of the music. Thus the statement that the movement "perpetually" skirts the keys of H [B] and F major is, of course, a considerable oversimplification.

The truth is that Berg here avails himself of nearly every procedure of the twelve-tone technique, from the simplest to the most complex. An example of a simple technique is the formation of the main theme from the "original row" by means of rhythmic variety, with the eighth note being repeated twice:

More ingenious is the zig-zag-like distribution of the row's notes over two voices:

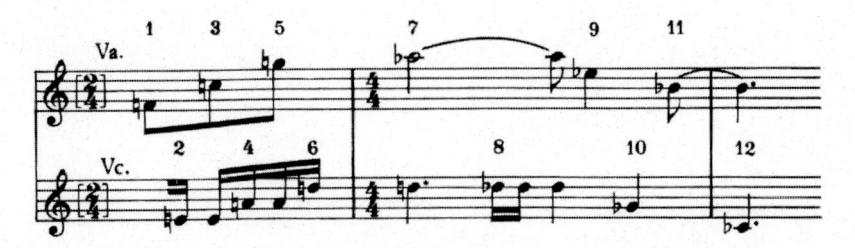

The most complex procedure, by contrast, and one that Berg here uses most frequently, is the quasi contrapuntal combination of diverse serial forms and series. Mm. 15-17 offer an instructive example: in the first violin in mm.

15/16, and continuing in the second violin, the original row appears on f, while its retrograde forms a "counterpoint." The viola plays a transposition of the row beginning with d, while the cello intones this transposition in crab motion.

The *Allegretto goviale*, a fairly regular sonata movement without development, adds up to 69 (3 x 23) bars in the final version. Berg outlined the structure of both exposition and recapitulation before he began the actual composition (76/XII fol. 2 verso and 76/VI fol. 4).

These outlines are instructive in several respects. They reveal that Berg was not thinking in abstract formal categories but always had the concretely musical in mind. Thus he calls the beginning of the transitional passage a "pizzicato idea," talks of "side theme" and "side idea" and aptly refers to the brief concluding group as "coda (stretta)."

We also learn from these drafts that the movement was originally planned for 67 bars, while in the draft of the score it has 66 bars (76/VI fol. 3 verso). Berg later composed three additional bars in order to obtain the significant number 69.

Here is an overview of the structure of the movement in it final version:

Exposition
mm. 1	Quasi upbeat (four chords consisting of fifths)
2–4	Main theme (tempo I)
5–6	somber enclave: *poco pesante* (Berg: "grief")
7–12	continuation of the main theme
13–22	transitional passage
13–16	"pizzicato idea"
23–32	"side theme" *poco più tranquillo* (tempo II), "climax" in mm. 26f.
33–36	coda (stretta): *poco accel.* scale motifs and circle of fifths fourths

Recapitulation
36–37	main theme (now interrupted)
38–39	somber enclave: *poco pesante*
40–48	continuation of main theme
49–52	transitional passage
49–50	"pizzicato idea" (now reduced to two bars)

53–66	"side idea"
67–68	coda (stretta): *poco accel.* (scale motifs)
69	concluding measure

The outline shows that exposition and recapitulation correspond fairly closely. Despite all the maintaining of the analogies, however, the recapitulation, as really goes without saying in Berg, is a new composition. The divergences between the two parts are considerable. Originally, the climax of the exposition was to be possibly surpassed in the recapitulation – a plan that was not executed.

The movement is distinguished by a strong agogic fluctuation. The sole metronomic notation at the beginning is ♩ = 100. Two different tempi have to be distinguished, however, between which there are many gradations. It is surely no accident that the secondary theme enters in m. 23.

In the elucidations for Hanna, Berg spoke of the "nearly inconsequential mood" of the first movement. In the *Nine Leaves*, he called the movement "this more objective piece." In two places in the sketches (76/V fol. 2 verso and 76/XII fol. 14 verso), the movement is characterized by the keyword "Becher-klang," clinking of cups – an expression that suggest the clinking of glasses and a reception scene at the Fuchs-Robettins' Prague villa, whose luxurious life greatly impressed Berg, as he wrote to his wife on May 15, 1925 (ABB 535): "But what made me feel at home even more was the matter-of-course luxury of this life. Oh, if only I could offer that to you!!!"

It also fits the more "objective" character of the Allegretto that a circle of fifths and fourths plays a role, i.e., sequences of pure fifths and fourths, as in mm. 7–9 (vlc.), 34-36 (vlc.), 46-48 (2nd vl.), 61-63 (2nd vl. and vlc,). Berg was conscious of this peculiarity and noted in the sketches (76/III fol. 3 verso) that diminished fifths were to predominate by contrast in the later movements.

The *Allegretto gioviale* is the only movement in the *Lyric Suite* that strikes one as really cheerful and serene. Only four bars seem out of place, mm. 5/6 in the exposition and 38/39 in the recapitulation, which are marked *poco pesante* and seem like somber enclaves. What is striking is that they contain minor and major harmonies: G-flat major and A minor, E-flat minor and A minor in mm. 5/6, E-flat minor and C major, G-flat major and A minor in mm. 38/39. Surely the ominous note in the sketches (76/V fol. 3), "E-flat minor descending grief" refers to these measures. And it is strongly indicative that these *poco pesante* bars are the only ones of the Allegretto that recur as reminiscences in the *Largo desolato*, there with the express marking *pesante* (m. 37) and *di nuovo pesante* (m. 39). One gets the impression that the grief and pain of the *Largo desolato* are embryonically present already in the *Allegretto gioviale*.

3.8.6 Andante amoroso: Hanna with her Children and with Alban

> "After the mid-morning snack, we played nearly all day with the children." Berg to Helene on November 11, 1925, after his second visit to the Fuchs family (ABB 541)

The second and the fifth movement of the *Lyric Suite* are annotated in the greatest detail in the copy for Hanna. That is understandable with regard to the *Andante amoroso*, introducing which Berg wrote: "This 'Rondo' is dedicated to you and your children: a musical form in which the themes (especially yours) – *completing the sweet circle* – recur time and again." Berg did not fail to indicate carefully in the score which theme was meant for Hanna, which for the seven-year-old Munzo and which for the three-and-a-half-year-old Dodo (pet name for Dorothea).

The theme for Hanna stands out for its expressivity as well as its tenderness:[555]

Munzo's theme unequivocally exhibits landler-like traits (*tempo II*):

Dodo's theme (*tempo III*), on the other hand, is a syncopation on the note c (do) repeated ostinato (dodo):

Quasi in parentheses: after his second visit to Prague, Berg, in a letter to Helene, characterized the children of Hanna (who was also called Moppinka) like this: "So, at 1:25 o'clock, Moppinka turne up with the children. The boy is getting on well, but the gal is rather weakly, also looks sickly, thus not even pretty. But nevertheless so sweet that you would surely like her" (ABB 541).

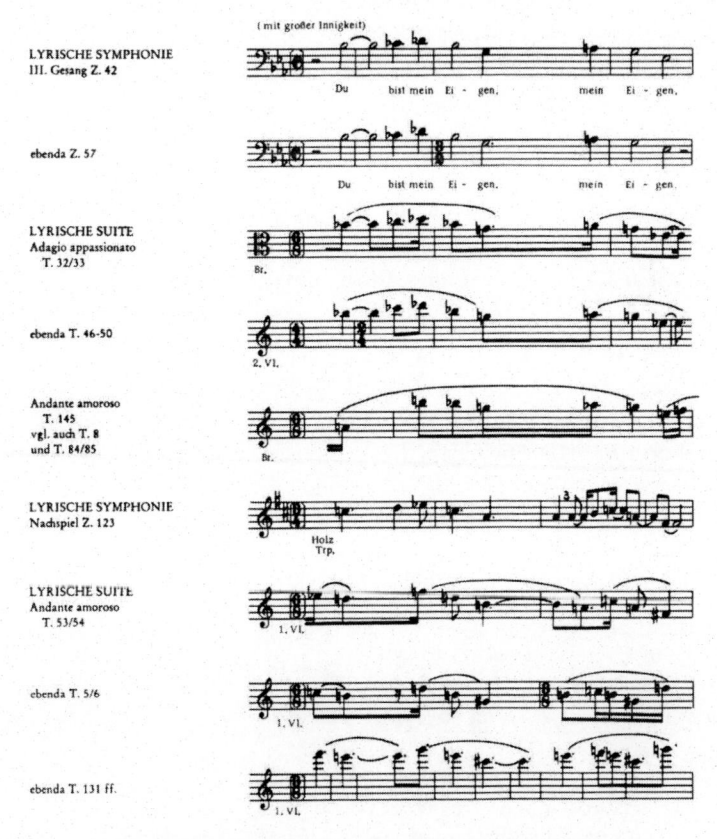

Table 2: The Zemlinsky quotations in the Lyric Suite

Quotation 1: "You are my own, my own"

On the 7th variant, see also *Andante amoroso* m. 10 (1st vl.), m. 47 (vlc.). ad m. 50 (1st vl.), as well as *Adagio appassionanto* mm. 31/32 (1st and 2nd vl.).

For the course of the movement, Berg provided the following programmatic explanations. The adverb "Threateningly" in the viola (mm. 73/74) he annotated: ""Threateningly, but not to be taken seriously. On the contrary." About the duet of the two secondary themes in mm. 101ff., he noted: "Munzo, joined quasi in play by Dodo." The great crescendo in mm. 110 ff. he explicates with the words: "The play turns into earnest." About the entry of the first violin at the climax of the movement, he remarks: "Now you intervene."

Of importance also are his references, in two places (mm. 56/57 and 105) to the ocurrence of the significant initials H [B] F and AB [B♭]).

A careful semantic analysis will show, however, that these annotations by no means exhaust the movement's programmatic connotations. Numerous additional semantemes can be identified, to which Berg, for whatever reasons, did not draw Hanna's attention in the score. These will now command our attention.

One weighty factor is, to begin with, that in thirteen different places the *Andante amoroso* incorporates characteristic variations of the Zemlinsky quote "Du bist mein Eigen, mein Eigen," the quotation with which Berg apostrophizes his beloved in the fourth movement (see Table 2).

Secondly, it is to be noted that in this movement, which is throughout composed in free atonality, the twelve-tone series of the head movement crops up, though in a significant transformation brought about by the transposing of notes 4 and 10. The row, shaped as a thematic character by its rhythm, first appears in the viola (mm. 24-26), then, in incomplete form, in the cello (mm. 27-30) and in the second violin (mm. 30-34). The reason for this transposition and transformation is to let the anagrams AB and HF follow each other in direct sequence, to make them "adjacent":

Ist movement	f	e	c	a	g	d	a♭	d♭	e♭	g♭	b♭	h
	1	2	3	4	5	6	7	8	9	10	11	12
IInd movement	a♭	g	e♭	**a**	**b♭**	f	**b**	e	f♯	c	c♯	d
viola, mm. 24-28	1	2	3	10	5	6	7	8	9	4	11	12

Significant is, thirdly, a – hitherto completely overlooked – characteristic thirds motif, which initially appears very softly in the first violin (mm. 66-70) and then, whether in descending or ascending direction, in all four instruments. It recurs in later movements and reveals itself as a variant of the *Wozzeck* quotation "Lauter kühle Wein muss es sein" (Nothing but cool wine it must be); it can be read as an emblem of intoxication, here the intoxication of love (see Table VI).

All this suggests that besides Hanna and the children, Berg, too, is musically present in this *Allegro amoroso*. Everything that is being narrated musically refers to the standpoint of the enamored narrator. That, in turn, implies that Berg's comment, "The play turns into earnest," is ambiguous: it refers both to the play of the children and to Berg's nascent passion for Hanna.

Formally, the *Andante amoroso* represents an original mode of composition, which in line with Berg's statements in the *Nine Leaves* can best be classified as a two-part, sonatized rondo. The following outline relies in part on the results of the semantic analysis:

Exposition

mm. 1 – 15	Main subject (*tempo I*) 15 bars ♪ = 100	
	1 – 4	Hanna's theme
	5 – 8	variants of the Zemlinsky motif "You are my own, my own"
	9	head motif of the Hanna theme
	10	variant of the Zemlinsky motif
	11 – 15	other motivic material, incl. a descending scale motif
16 – 40	"1st side subject" (*tempo II*) 25 bars ♩= 50	
		landler-like Munzo theme plus the modified twelve-tone row mm. 24-26 (vla.), 27-31 (vlc.), 30-33 (2nd vl.); in mm. 24-36, the 2nd violin intones the head of the Zemlinsky motif
41 – 55	2nd version of the main subject (*tempo I*) 15 bars ♪ = 100	
	41 – 47	Hanna theme
	47 – 55	Zemlinsky motifs, scale motif and other material
56 – 80	2nd side subject (*tempo III*) 25 bars ♪ = 69	
	56 – 65	HF and AB theme with Dodo rhythm
	66 – 73	intoxication motif
	74 – 80	HF and AB theme with Dodo rhythm

Development-like Recapitulation

	81 – 100	1st section (*tempo I, later quasi tempo II*) 20 bars = 3rd version of main subject: Hanna theme,

	Zemlinsky motif, waltz-like motifs, fragments of the twelve-tone row
101 – 150	2nd section (tempo fluctuating) 50 bars
101 – 117	duet between the two side subjects, plus the Hanna theme in the viola, mm. 114-117
118 – 130	crescendo contrapuntal intertwining of the Munzo theme with the intoxication motif
131 – 142	climax followed by diminuendo; contrapuntal intertwining of four different figures: Zemlinsky motif in augmentation (1st vl.) intoxication motif (2nd vl.) Dodo rhythm (vla.) Munzo theme
143 – 150	coda= fourth version of the main movement

The outline makes apparent that, despite Berg's note "150 = 15 x 10" in the copy for Hanna, the tectonics of the movement is dictated by the 5 and not by the 10: the first four sections of the movement have 15, 25, 15 and 25 bars – all numbers that are multiples of five only. The metronomic notations, on the other hand, ♪ = 100 (*tempo I*), ♩.= 50 (*tempo II*), ♪ = 69 (*tempo III*) and ♩. = 46 (m 105) are reducible either to 10 or to 23.

The Allegretto can be called a rondo inasmuch as the main subject recurs three times, albeit each time in a different version. No version is like any other, and the final version (Coda mm. 143-150) is the most remote from the first.

The outline also shows that all the prominent musical figures in this movement are semantically engaged. One need only refer to the climax of the movement (mm. 1131-142), where all the "actors" are musically present: Hanna is represented by the augmented version of the Zemlinsky motif "You are my own, you are my own" (1st vl.), Alban by the intoxication motif (2nd vl.), Dodo by the syncopated ostinato rhythm (vla.) and Munzo by his landler-like motifs (vlc).

The coda is dominated by the Hanna theme, the variants of the Zemlinsky motif and the scale motif. At the end we hear, reminiscence-like, the Dodo rhythm in the cello – "as if from far away," as Berg himself wrote in the copy for Hanna.

Scrutiny of the sketches reveals that Berg had thought very intensively about the musical characterization of Munzo. He originally drafted a "swaying" theme in C minor in the rhythm of a barcarole (6/8 time), with the falling perfect fifth serving as a constructive interval.

Here is the beginning of the tune (76/V fol. 7):

[musical notation: wiegend, Mu, II. Thema, C moll, 6/8, [?]]

But he dropped that plan and sketched the landler-like Munzo theme as we now have it. In an early version (76/II fol. 4 verso), it is in 3/4 time and notated a major sixth higher.

3.8.7 Allegro misterioso: The Confession

> "I am sleepless and full of longing, I am a stranger in a strange land. Your breath comes and murmurs impossible hopes to me." Tagore

In terms of overall format, the *Allegro misterioso* is probably the most perspicuous movement of the *Lyric Suite*: a tripartite scherzo-like movement with a trio. While the two bracketing parts are strictly dodecaphonic, the *Trio estatico* is composed in free atonality. The third part is a palindrome of the first reduced to two thirds; it begins with the latter's conclusion and ends with its beginning. The parts also seem well-proportioned: the first part has 69 (3 x 23) bars, the trio 23 and the third part 46 (2 x 23) bars. The structure of the music, however, is a great deal more complex than these relatively simple relations.

In an early draft, Berg marked this movement *Presto (Scherzo) agitato* (76/I fol. 10). From the start he had in mind a "ghostly" and "mysterious" sound (76/V fol. 6 and 76/XII fol. 14). On p. 31 of the score copy for Hanna, there are annotations "like whispering" and "again quasi whispered." Berg there also headed the movement with the momentous date "20.5.25" and elucidated the word *misterioso* by adding in handwriting: "for as yet everything was a mystery – a mystery even to us." From this and other observations it is clear that this *Allegro misterioso* signalizes the confession of love: the teller of the story confesses, in whispers, his love to Hanna.

The bracketing parts are exceptional in the character of their sound. Their music seems like an ostinato, a perpetuum mobile, a (nearly) uninterrupted movement in sixteenths. The dynamics hardly ever leaves the *pianissimo* sphere, the entire movement is to be played muted, the score is replete with relatively unusual technical directions, such as "at the bridge," "at the fingerboard," "flageolet tones," "flautando" (flute-like) and "col legno" (with the wood). It is thus not surprising that this tonal character has evoked similar associations in a number of critics. Adorno spoke of "whispering,"[556] Redlich of "obscure secret whispering,"[557] Pernye of "Nature's rustling,"[558] and Bouquet of a "cryptic, unreal kind of mood."[559] Berg himself, in a letter of April 13, 1933, referred to the "flitting middle piece" of the *Lyric Suite*.

Of major importance in this movement is the handling of the anagrammatic technique. The initials of Hanna Fuchs and Alban Berg had entered into a mystic union already in the *Andante amoroso*. In the *Allegro misterioso*, however, the double anagram AB/HF becomes practically the signature of the movement. There are few bars in which it does not occur. Berg uses it in every conceivable manifestation, transposition, constellation and metamorphosis, whether horizontal or vertical (see Table III).

He treats it as an ostinato – thus in mm. 26-28 in the viola and in mm. 30-39 in the viola and the second violin – and also in a highly characteristic "chromatic" double form, altogether unrecognized until now and hence requiring special consideration. To explain it we have to go back a bit.

In the *Allegro misterioso*, the four tonal letters corresponding to the initials of the names Alban Berg and Hanna Fuchs dictate the choice of the rows' sequences and other aspects of the twelve-tone technique (in what follows, cf. the facsimile of 76/V fol. 9). Berg himself referred to that fact in his analysis for the Kolisch Quartet, where he spoke generally and abstractly of a "four-note group." The row, he explained there, was used in the outer parts of the movement, but in the form in which it appears in the second movement, and in only four forms:[560]

	b♭	**a**	**f**	**b**	c	g	d♭	g♭	a♭	d	e♭	e
	a♭	g	e	**a**	**b♭**	**f**	**b**	e	f♯	c	d♭	d
	f	e	c	f♯	g	a	a♭	d	e♭	**a**	**b♭**	**b**	**(f)**
Inversion	e♭	e	g♯	d	c♯	f♯	c	g	**f**	**b**	**b♭**	**a**

Of all the twelve transpositions of the series and its inversion, Berg states, the above four forms were the only ones containing a four-note group that "like a common denominator (ostinato) goes through the entire piece." All other rows and inversions did not contain this four-note group.

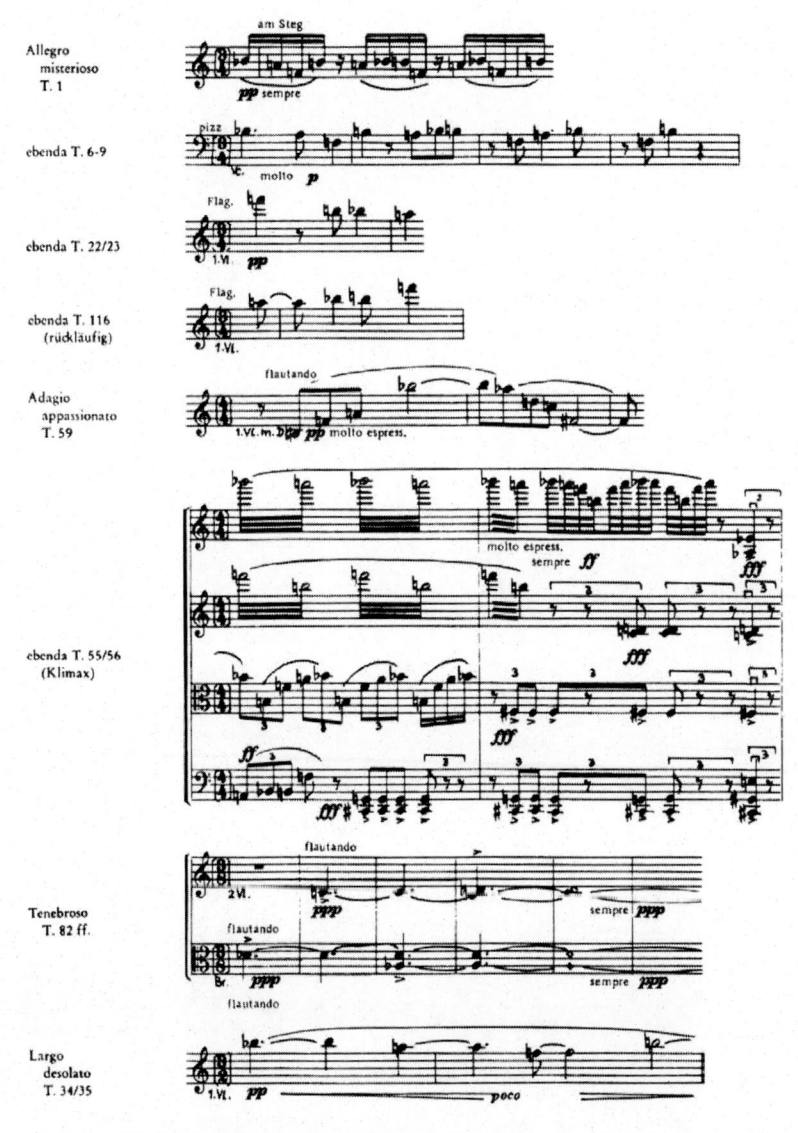

Table 3: The four-note group of the *Allegro misterioso:*

Embodiments and reminiscences

Sketches 4: *Lyric Suite*

Austrian National Library, Music Collection, Fonds 21 Berg 76/V fol. 9, Serial forms for the *Allegro misterioso*. The motivic four-note group composed of the two double anagrams is marked by (horizontal) brackets. The "chromatic forms" of the two anagrams are also notated. First publication, by permission of the Austrian National Library

Berg had expressed himself even more abstractly and generally in his letter to Schönberg of July 12, 1926.[561] Here he announced that in the course of his work on the *Lyric Suite* he had altered the Kleinian all-interval series because it did not have an "independent retrograde form" ("crab form"). "For that reason," he had decided on the following change of the row:

f	e	c	f#	g	d	a^b	d^b	e^b	**a**	**b^b**	**b**
1	2	3	4	5	6	7	8	9	10	11	12

The real reason, however, is that by this manipulation he achieved the "closing up" of the significant letters a b and h f (10, 11, 12 and 1). Besides, the bracketed four-note group represents a transposition of the double anagram b-a-f-h.

From this row and its inversion, he continued, he had gained "the following division into 7 + 5:

something "that yielded, besides the chromatic scale, the following motif and its inversion and a characteristic rhythm and its complement,[562] namely:

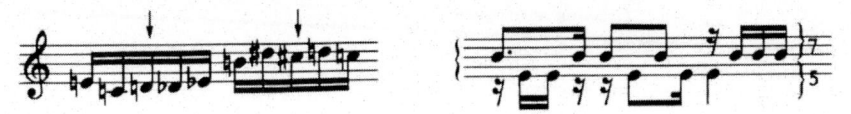

But these rationalizations, too, obscure the true facts: a close look at the two quoted, complementary motifs reveals them to be "chromatic forms" of the two anagrams. The motif f (f#-g-a^b-a-b) h is recognized easily enough as such. But even the three middle notes of the complementary motif turn out to be a chromatic filling-up of the anagram b (g^b-a^b-g) a, here transposed to e (c-d-d^b) e^b.

The augmentation in which this characteristic double motif appears in mm. 10–12 is both instructive and vivid, because it enables us to realize that the chromatic form of the FH motif implies note for note the "Yearning" motif from Wagner's *Tristan und Isolde*, a motif that Berg will quote in mm. 26/27 of the *Largo desolato*.

WAGNER, *Tristan*, Sehnsuchtsmotiv

From this example, too, one can see how many-layered the music of the *Lyric Suite* is.

The more one immerses oneself in the study of the score, the more one must marvel at the imaginative way in which Berg handles the twelve-tone technique in this movement. Three examples may serve to illustrate this.

1. In mm. 6-9 the double anagram (i.e., the notes b-a-f-h or else parallel formations) is intoned in longish notes in the cello. The eight-note figures of sixteenths that the two violins and the viola play along with that are formed of eight-tone series gained from the twelve-tone rows through the "tying off" (Berg uses the term *Abschnürung* in his analysis) of the portentous four-note group.

2. In mm. 19-21, while the cello pauses, the other instruments produce odd tremolo sounds to be played at the bridge, which have an exterritorial status inasmuch as they interrupt the otherwise restless movement of sixteenths, appear like an enclave, and are formed from the above-mentioned eight-tone series that exclude the notes of the double anagram.[563]

3. In the last section of the movement's first part (from m. 46), Berg achieves a contrapuntal masterpiece by treating the twelve-tone rows in stretto.

The *Trio estatico* forms the sharpest contrast imaginable to the *Allegro misterioso*. The four instrumentalists continue to play with mutes, but they leave the *pianissimo* sphere and suddenly "break out" into *fortissimo*. The whispering, murmuring music stops and is replaced by an ecstatic, highly strung music rich in grand gestures and "exclamations." Even so, Berg qualifies the title *Trio estatico* in the copy for Hanna by the addition "but restrained, quasi still with mutes."

Table 4: The Zemlinsky quotations in the Lyric Suite

Quotation 2: "You, who dwells in my unending dreams". Berg varies the theme according to the principle of the "developing variation."

In his analysis for the Kolisch Quartet, Berg made only some quite laconic comments about the *Trio estatico*: The "entirely free" part of the movement, he remarked, functioned as "exposition" for the fourth movement, while also being linked to the second one. A close scrutiny reveals that the thematic content of the Trio is in part supplied by quotations from Zemlinsky's *Lyric Symphony* – references that had remained unrecognized until 1975. Quoted, in artful variants and metamorphoses, are the phrases "Du, die in meinen unsterblichen Träumen lebt" (You, who live in my undying dreams) and "Laß Liebe in Erinn'rung schmelzen und Schmerz in Lieder" (Let love into remembrance melt and grief into song) (see Table 4 and Table 5).

233

Table 5: The Zemlinsky quotations in the Lyric Suite

Quotation 3: "Let love into remembrance melt and grief into song"

The *Trio estatico* furthermore picks up motivic material from the *Andante amoroso*, specifically the scale motif and that portentous thirds motif whose semantics Berg himself helps us to decipher. His note in the copy for Hanna that the motif of the first violin in m. 89 is a quotation from *Wozzeck*, namely Marie's line "Lauter kühler Wein muß es sein!" (*Wozzeck* I.3, mm. 400-403), identifies the thirds motif, which plays a role here as well as in the subsequent movements of the Suite, as a motif signaling intoxication (see Table 6).

Table 6: Intoxication motifs

Chains of ascending and descending thirds and fifths

The presence of these borrowings also explains why Berg wrote the *Andante amoroso*, the *Trio estatico* and the *Adagio appassionato* in free atonality, for the quotations from Zemlinsky's *Lyric Symphony* and from *Wozzeck* hardly admit of a dodecaphonic treatment. Berg's statement, in the July 13, 1926, letter to Schönberg, that the work with the twelve-tone technique did not permit him to progress quickly, wherefore, "in order not to lose heart," he "intermittently" was relapsing into his "familiar free mode of writing," obscures the actul facts of the matter.

The following outline will give an impression of the motivic-thematic substance of the *Trio estatico*:

mm. 70–73 Zemlinsky quotation III, "Let love into remembrance melt";
      in mm. 69/70 the double anagram in the violins

   74–75 Zemlinsky quotation II, "You, who dwell in my undying dreams"

   76–78 Scale motif (~ mm. 13/14 of the *Andante amoroso*)

   79–83 fairly free

   83–84 Zemlinsky quotation III (head motif only) followed by the double anagram in the violins

   85–86 Zemlinsky quotation II

   87–89 intoxication motif with *Wozzeck* quotation (~ mm. 66-73 of the *Andante amoroso*

   90–92 fairly free; in m. 92 the Zemlinsky quotation II hinted at in the viola and the cello

What is probably the earliest conception of the *Trio estatico*, incidentally, was much simpler than the final version. There Berg was thinking of basing that part of the movement on a cello melody to be wreathed around by the other instruments (76/XII fol. 14). Though this plan was dropped, a "remnant" of the conception was retained in mm. 90/91, where the two violins are initially lower than the cello.

The third part of the *Allegro misterioso*, as noted, represents a retrograde repetition of the first part, whose dimension (69 bars), however, is now reduced by one third (46 bars).

The following schema may convey an impression of the ratio between the two parts:

↓mm.   1–28   ~ mm.   110 – 138
          29   ~ approx. 109
          39   ~   108

43	~	107
44–45	~	105–106
46–69	~	93–105 ↑

One should note that m. 109, where the double anagram appears as a chord, corresponds only approximately to m. 29.

In the score for Hanna Fuchs, Berg interpreted the retrograde design of the third part as a retraction of the love confession: "Forget it ---!"

3.8.8 Adagio appassionato: Ardor, Passion, Explosion and Transfiguration

> "Tone: ardor increasing to the highest passion – – –something that also means suffering. (That, too, has to be expressed.) Ditto the other way from ardor to religious (?) transfiguration: with which the movement also concludes." Berg in the sketches (76/III, fol.4)

> "I have caught you and wrapped you, beloved, in the net of my music." Tagore

Berg furnished only a few hints about the *Adagio appassionato* in the copy for Hanna. The mental processes of which this movement treats were too subtle and too personal to be spoken of even in a communication to the beloved. In journal fashion, he headed the movement "The next day," meaning May 21, 1925, the day after the love confession, and he gave to understand that at the base of this Adagio was the idea of a love dialogue, one that finally dies away "into the fully spiritualized, soulful, unearthly." About the "duet" between viola and first violin (mm. 24 ff.) he noted "I and you," about the Hanna theme (m. 30), "Always you (cf. your theme in the 2nd movement)." He also disclosed the meaning of the repeated intonation of the Zemlinsky quotation "Du bist mein eigen, mein Eigen." The first intonation by the viola in mm. 32/33 expresses his voice; the second intonation in the second violin, an octave higher, in mm. 446-50 was meant for Hanna: "Now you say it, too."

We learn a lot more about the conception and semantics of the movement from the sketches, which contain numerous entries, both verbal and musical. Berg could confide his innermost thoughts and imaginations to a paper intended only for himself, without having to make allowances for any other person. Already in the early entry, which we placed as a motto at the head of this section, the route the movement would take is thus traced out, from ardor to passion and from there to religious (?) transfiguration. (The thought that *leidenschaft*, passion, would make for *leiden*, suffering, was in keeping with Berg's personal experience.)

On another sheet (76/XV), he sketched the course of the movement with the words "Duet – Explosion – Transfiguration" and at the bottom of the sheet wrote: "Pedal point 1 9/4 time. [There] follows the explosion rising up from *ppp*." The duet was to comprise 43 + 3 + 1 bars, the explosion 12 bars, and the transfiguration 18 bars.

One can readily confirm that these ideas did indeed largely determine the course of the composition. The *Adagio appassionato* can be divided roughly into four unequal sections: a largely imitationally worked first section (mm. 1-44), which was originally conceived as a "duet"; a second short section marked *Molto tranquillo* (mm. 45-50), which presents the second instance of the Zemlinsky quotation over a pedal point; a third section (mm. 51-88) corresponding to the "explosion" in the sketches, which begins *pp*, rises to a triple *forte* and then returns stepwise to *piano*; and finally a *Molto adagio* (mm. 59-69), which expresses musically what Berg meant by "transfiguration."

Important for the poetico-musical conception of the movement was also the notion of a "billowing" music. The sketches repeatedly include terms like "waves" ["Wellen"] (76/I fol. 13, 76/III fol. 7) "billowing accompaniment" (76/I, fol. 13) and "surging" (76/III fol. 4 verso. 76/XII fol. 14 verso) At one point Berg indicated the course of such waves graphically (76/XV),

Wellen

and another time, he notated the imagined "nocturnal surging" in figures of sixteenths that do not indicate the exact pitches but merely the general movement:

The attentive listener will hardly miss this surging, the up and down, as an earmark from the beginning. In mm. 21/22, unusually large up-and-down interval leaps in all four instruments determine the profile of the melodic movement, and in m. 23, a livelier movement commences that actually resembles a surge. (The ascending and descending figurations in the cello and the second violin are especially characteristic.)

The *Adagio appassionato*, one of the most expressive movements Berg ever wrote, is composed throughout in free atonality. It extends to exactly 69 measures, and its sole metronomic notation is ♩ = 69. Not only the 69 but also the numbers 46 and 23 play a role in the construction of the movement.

Thus m. 23 marks the onset of the lively surging, while in m. 46 the Zemlinsky quotation "Du bist mein Eigen, mein Eigen" enters, muted, in the second violin. According to first calculations, the movement was to consist of 100 or 119 (= 50 + 69) bars (76/I fol. 13). An early written-out version (76/IX fol. 3 verso) had only 65 bars. The recitative intonation of the quotation "Du bist mein Eigen, mein Eigen" here enters at m. 42 (76/IX fol. 2 verso). Berg expanded the composition by four measures in order to obtain the number 69 so important to him. The movement thus illustrates most impressively how Berg, on the one hand, worked like a medieval cathedral architect, who calculates everything, and on the other, was able to invest the music with a maximum of expressivity.

The *Adagio appassionato* borrows its motivic-thematic substance for the most part from the two preceding movements, which at times he quotes note for note. He takes over the three Zemlinsky quotations, the intoxication motif and the momentous double anagram, which now figures in new metamorphoses. It is instructive also to observe how the three Zemlinsky quotations are introduced to the *Lyric Suite*: in the *Andante amoroso*, only one quotation is used, in the *Trio estatico*, quotations 2 and 3 are included, while the *Adagio appassionato* works in all three.

Significantly, the first and the second quotations are contiguous in Zemlinksy's *Lyric Symphony*, where they form the refrain of the third song:[564]

Du bist mein Eigen, mein Eigen,
(You are my own, my own.)
Du, die in meinen endlosen (resp. unsterblichen)
(You, who dwell in my unending [or else
Träumen wohnt
undying] dreams).

After what has been said, it will require no further explanation why Tagore's love poem *Du bist die Abendwolke* served as a major source of inspiration for the *Adagio appassionato*. I will therefore cite it here in extenso:[565]

DU BIST die Abendwolke, die am Himmel meiner Träume hinzieht.
Ich gebe Dir Farbe und Form mit den Wünschen meiner Liebe.
Du bist mein Eigen, mein Eigen, Du, die in meinen endlosen
Träumen wohnt!

Deine Füße sind rosig rot von der Glut meines sehnsüchtigen Herzens,
Du Ährenleserin meiner Abendlieder!
Deine Lippen sind bittersüß, denn sie kosteten aus meinem Leidenskelch.
Du bist mein Eigen, mein Eigen, Du, Bild meiner einsamen Träume!

Mit dem Schatten meiner Leidenschaft habe ich Deine Augen verdunkelt, als sie in meinen
Blick hinabtauchten.
Ich hab Dich gefangen und Dich eingesponnen, Geliebte, in das Netz meiner Musik.
Du bist mein Eigen, mein Eigen, Du, die in meinen unsterblichen Träumen wohnt!

YOU ARE the evening cloud that drifts along my dreams.
I give you color and form from the desires of my love.
You are my own, my own, you, who dwells in my
Unending dreams!

Your feet are rosy red from the blaze of my yearning heart,
You gleaner of my evening songs!
Tour lips are bitter-sweet, they have tasted of the cup of my sorrows.
You are my own, my own, you, image of my lonely dreams!

I darkened your eyes with the shadow of my passion when they plunged into my gaze.
I have caught you and wrapped you in the net of my music.
You are my own, my own, you, who dwells in my undying dreams!

Berg must have thought this love poem gave expression to his feelings for Hanna, and he did indeed "wrap" his beloved's initials in the net of his music!

The following conspectus of the themes and the design of the movement takes into account both Berg's entries in the sketches and the results of our semantic analysis.

1st Section: Ardor and Passion

- Mm. 1–7 Zemlinsky quotation 2 (canonic entry in all four instruments)
- 8–11 Zemlinsky quotation 2; imitation between viola and 2nd violin (the motif is already changed here after the principles of the *developing variation*)
- 12–14 Zemlinsky quotation 3 = *Trio estatico* mm. 70-74
- 14–22 development of mm. 5-7
- 23~83 of the *Trio estatico*
- 24–29 duet between viola and 1st vl. (substance: Zemlinsky quotation 2, then Zemlinsky quotation 3); surging in vlc. and 2nd vl.
- 30–32 Hanna theme and Zemlinsky quotation 1 (reminiscences of *Andante amoroso*
- 32–33 ~80/81 of the *Trio estatico*; intonation of "Du bist mein Eigen" motif in the viola
- 34–39 ~*Trio estatico* mm. 86-91
- 39–44 new idea, whose main motif is made up of the double anagram

2nd Section: Recitative

- 45–50 *Molto tranquillo* in mm. 46-50 in the 2nd vl. muted, "in altogether free recitative," the quotation "Du bist mein Eigen, mein Eigen"

3rd Section: Explosion and Gradual Quieting

- 51–58 crescendo from *pp* to the climax (*fff*) then stepwise decrescendo; the Viola initially develops the head motif of the 2nd Zemlinsky motif; at the climax, mystic union of the initials (horizontal and vertical).

4th Section: Transfiguration

- 59–69 *Molto adagio* (all instruments muted); the motifs are initially developed from the double anagram; at the end a diatonic triad motif (the head motif of the "Du bist mein Eigen" quotation) rises progressively higher; the conclusion is a seven-note chord, which is in fact a segment of the *mutterakkord*.

The drafts for the Adagio appassionato make it clear that Berg thought a great deal specifically about the finale of this movement. From the start, he intended for the "Recitative" (76/I fol. 13, 76/III fol. 7) to be followed by a "wild unimpeded crescendo" (76/XII fol. 14 verso), whose climax was to be the "*chord ABHF*" (AB♭BF) (76/IX fol. 2); the relaxation after reaching the climax was to proceed by stages. In the final version, the dynamics decreases by steps: *fff* (m.56) – *ff esp.*, *ff* and *f. espr.* (m. 57) – *mf, mp, ma espr., p* (m. 58) – *pp* (m. 59). Concurrently, the number of notes of which the chords in mm. 56-60 are composed decreases continuously.[566] An early entry also envisioned that the movement should end on the *mutterakkord* and muted (76/I fol. 13).

3.8.9 Presto delirando: Terror and Torment after the Parting

> "Not one chromatic step in the entire piece." Berg in the sketches (76/X)

In May of 1925, Berg traveled to Prague alone. Receiving him cordially, the Fuchs family regretted that Helene had not come along (ABB 538). Helene probably did not remain unaware of her husband's infatuation with Hanna. Berg was afraid she might come after him and wrote her on May 19:

> Goldie! I am surprised not to have received any news from you today. How should I interpret that? You are not on your way to Prague, are you? But you will surely announce yourself! The thought of if makes my heart pound like crazy. But may I even wish for it?! It would be madness, though a lovely madness!

Perhaps Berg did not yet foresee at this point that as soon as he left Prague and the Fuchs villa he would indeed lapse into a madness-like state of mind. That state is described by the five-part *Presto delirando*, and Berg sought to give Hanna an impression of it in the copy of the score intended for her by explaining the movement programmatically in detail and writing:

> This Presto delirando one can understand only if one has an idea of the terrors and torments that now followed – of the terrors of the day with its racing pulses, of the tormenting tenebroso of the nights with their dozing hardly to be called sleep.

On the third part of the movement, he commented: "And once again another day with its insanely racing heartbeat." Of the transition to the fourth part (mm. 201-210), he observed: "As though the heart might calm down."

Sketches 5: Lyric Suite

Austrian National Library, Fonds 21 Berg 76/X last page Drafts for the *Presto delirando*. First publication by permission of the Austrian National Library

The fourth part he explained thus: "(*di nuovo tenebroso*) with its heavy breaths that yet hardly suppress the tormenting restlessness"; about m. 261 he noted: "as if for a few moments the sweet consolation of a real, all-forgetting slumber were to descend on one." The transition to the fifth part (mm. 306-320), he concretized thus: "But already the heart makes itself felt." The concluding part, finally, he interpreted by saying: "And once more day and so on, without cessation this delirium."

This commentary, in which the symbolism of day and night play a major role, constitutes the (nearly airtight) program of the *Presto delirando*. Don McLean may have been right in thinking that in formulating this text Berg may have received impulses from Baudelaire's "Autumn" sonnet, a poem Berg copied out by hand. (The copy is in the Schloss Collection of McGill University in Montreal.)[567] Like Berg's commentary, the Baudelaire poem, too, speaks of terror and torment.

Berg's analysis of the *Lyric Suite* for the Kolisch Quarte contains no programmatic statements for the *Presto delirando* but solely pointers about structure and compositional technique. Fundamentally, Berg states that the movement had the form $A_1 - B - A_2 - B_2 - A_3$, with the parts getting progressively longer: 50 + 70 + 90 + 110 + 140 = 460 bars. The movement, he wrote, was "nearly throughout" divided into "5-bar" units, "especially in the trios"; the A parts were composed in free atonality, while the B parts were strictly dodecaphonic, based on the row that was further transformed here and thus reached the shape it has in the Finale.

As with the other movements, so here, too, the sketches yield rich insights into the genesis, structure and semantics of the *Presto delirando*. Interestingly, to begin with, Berg had initially wavered whether to call the movement allegretto, allegro or presto, and had considered several adjectives to characterize the mood: *inquieto, delirando, elegiaco* [?], *furioso, tempestoso, extatico, feroce* (76/X) . Eventually he settled on *Presto delirando*.

Careful scrutiny of the sketches reveals that the number five (not the ten) plays a crucial role in the structural plan of the movement. One is tempted to speak of an "obsessional" use of the number; the five, in this movement, altogether or largely determines the dimensions of the parts, the agogic, the metric divisions and in part also the rhythm.

The earliest calculations in the sketches concern he tempo, the extent and duration of the movement. Berg initially set out from the metronomic setting of ♩. = 120 and figured that if the piece were to consist of 240, 360 or 460 bars it would take respectively 2, 3 or 4 minutes (76/III fol. 9). The length of 360 bars and a 3-minutes' duration seemed adequate. The individual parts were to comprise 35 + 50 + 70 + 80 + 125 = 360 bars. Probably somewhat later he thought of giving the movement some traits of an ostinato and modified the metronomic notation to "♩. = 115 (= 5 x 23)," annotating two pulse motifs with the remark: "Pulse 115" (76/I fol. 16). The symbolic intention here is unmistakable, as the 115 does not actually exist on the metronomic scale.

Notes written even later indicate that Berg had considered basing the construction of the movement on the numbers 5, 23 and 115. He jotted down the formulae 23 x 5 and 115 x 5 and then decided on the extent of 460 bars and a four-minute duration. As yet, however, he remained undecided about the dimensions of the individual parts of the movement. Initially, he looked at a division into 46 (2 x 23) + 69 (3 x 23) + 92 (4 x 23) + 92 (4 x 23) + 161 (7 x 23) = 460 bars. He made several other computations but rejected them all in favor of the final division into 50 + 70 + 90 + 110 + 140 = 460 bars. Incidentally, he reduced the 460 to a 4 by dividing it by 115. He had already intended a metronome notation of ♪. = 120. But he struck the 120 and wrote a 115 above it (see Sketches 5).

The *Presto delirando* not only consists of five parts but to a large degree is also divided into groups of five bars. That is true at least of the two *Tenebroso* parts which bear the notation "fünftaktig" in the score. Disregarded until 1975 was Berg's important notice in his analysis for the Kolisch Quartet that the formal articulation (grouping of bars; Berg speaks of a "rhythm") in the *Tenebroso* trios frequently follows the arithmetic series 1 2 3 4 5 (also retrograde: 5 4 3 2 1). The trios in fact contain several 15-bar "periods" that are formed of the addition of groups of one, two, three, four and five bars.

According to Berg's drafts, this significant arithmetic row was to determine also rhythmic processes. Thus he noted the following series of durations consisting of five, four, three, two and one quarter-notes or eighths:

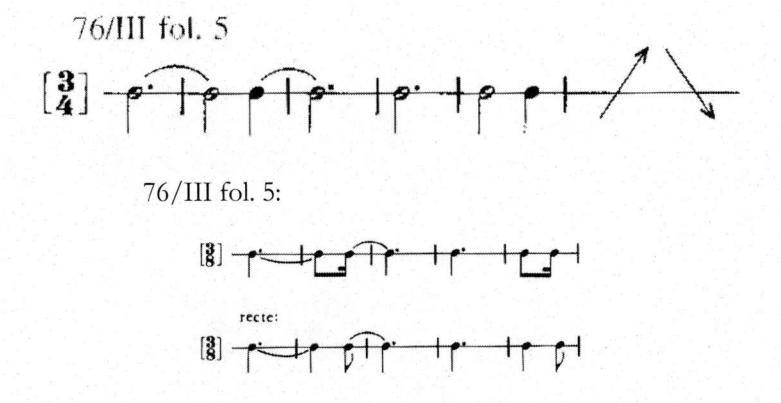

He evidently was thinking of a quasi-serial treatment of the durational sequences. However, these drafts were not made use of in the final version of the composition.

Two pithy rhythms were likewise related to the number five from the start: the *Pulsrhythmus* and the *Fünferrhythmus* (pentadic rhythm) (Berg's terms). The original pulse rhythm took the following form (76/I fol. 16):

Puls 115

[musical notation]

That was to be turned into "chords of up to four voices." But Berg rejected this figure in favor of the following:

[musical notation]

In that form the rhythm crops up in 76/III fol. 5, with the express notation "5 times":

[musical notation]

From that metamorphosis, it is not far to the definitive figure:

Presto delirando, T. 15–19

[musical notation]

Berg had also planned his so-called *Fünferrhythmus* for the fifth movement (76/X),

[musical notation]

which was to be played *furioso* by two instruments and to be adapted to eighths, quarters and "whole measures" but was not included in the final version.

In the sketches, too, Berg schematized the form of the *Presto*, which he conceived as a variations movement, as a^1 b^1 a^2 b^2 a^3 (76/X). We should not, of course, think of conventional variations. We have to do, instead, with an altogether new, bold and original form of variation. The last three parts are newly composed from existing elements, and the first and third part are enormously intensified by comparison with the first. Let us look at the individual parts.

The omnipresent five is to all appearances the number of elements of which the first part is constructed. The following five elements are to be distinguished:

1. The four-bar main theme (mm. 1-4), which is intoned in unison, is twelve-toned (if one includes the *e* of the cello in m. 4) and exhibits a zig-zag motion (the term *Zickzack* crops up in the sketches, as in 76/III fol. 10);
2. the shrill, ascending glissandi of the violins and the viola in mm. 4-7;
3. the intoxication motif, intoned by the cello in mm. 4-8 in rising and falling thirds and subsequently picked up by the other instruments;
4. the pulse rhythm, occurring five times (mm. 15-19), which, first intoned by the cello, gradually takes on the form of a two-, three-, four and finally five-note chord;
5. a characteristic seven-note motif, which first appears in the cello and then – in altered interval sequence – is imitated by the viola, the second and the first violin (mm. 20-30).

Some earmarks of the *Presto delirando*'s main parts are jotted down in catchphrases in early drafts. Thus we read in 76/III fol. 10, "zig-zag" and "leaps" and on the verso side of the sheet, "downward glissandi" and "unisono and in thirds and fourths." The ways in which musical processes are notated here in the form of graphs or diagrams are extremely revealing of Berg's musical way of thinking:

The second part (*Tenebroso*) contrasts with the first as night with day, as a "dozing on" (Berg) does with the greatest unrest. If the main part closes with a fortissimo, the tenebroso is located on the *piano* and *più pianissimo* level. The mode of playing, too, is different: initially *flautando* sounds are prescribed, while the tremolos later on are to be played "at the bridge." The physiognomy of the *Tenebroso* is formed by long-held tones that supersede each other in such a way that a new note enters quasi unnoticed while the previous one still reverberates. The mode is unmistakably orientated on the third of Schönberg's renowned *Five Pieces for Orchestra* op. 16.

As noted, the A parts of the movement are written in free atonality, while the B parts are worked dodecaphonically. The *Tenebroso* is based on the following series:

basic form: d^b c a^b d f a e b^b b $d^\#$ $f^\#$ g
inversion: e f a e^b c $g^\#$ $c^\#$ g $f^\#$ d b b^b

Compared with the row of the *Allegro misterioso*, this series represents a transformation through transposition of several notes – a transposition that serves a programmatic purpose, namely to separate the all-important initials from each other. The new row thus symbolizes the spatial separation from the beloved, and it follows logically that the double anagram appears nowhere in this movement. Only in mm. 82-85 is it evoked in the transposition d^b-c-a^b-d.

It remains to mention that the formal articulation of this first *Tenebroso* trio can be reduced to the following formula: 2 x ([5 + 4+ 3 + 2 + 1] + [1 + 2 + 3 + 4 + 5] + 5)!

The third part is related to the first as a fully composed version to a draft. Not only is it longer (90 : 50 bars), but it also incorporates the latter's building material in a new way. The elements are "put together" differently, the sequence is not always maintained. The following alterations are among the most important. The twelve-tone main theme (mm. 121-124), initially intoned without change (but now struck *col legno*), appears in a different shape at a later recurrence (mm. 148-151): its twelve notes are transposed (1 2 3 4 8 12 5 7 6 11 10 3), with the ninth note being omitted. The characteristic pulse rhythm is at first (mm. 124-129) rhythmically shifted – Berg interpreted it as "madly racing heartbeat." The intoxication motif, which in the first part occurred predominantly in thirds, now appears both in thirds (mm.

161-166 in the vlc.) and in fourths (mm. 133 ff.), in conformity with the principle of the "developing variation" (see Table VI). The glissandi, originally ascending, now (mm. 161-164) go downwards. The characteristic seven-note motif, finally, is here (mm. 184-1194) counterpointed with the pulse rhythm.

The fourth part (*di nuovo tenebroso*) is longer by 40 bars than the second (110 : 70) and is divided quite noticeably into four sections. The first (mm. 211-260 = 70 bars) implements in a new way the idea of the slowly and unnoticeably changing chord. Interestingly, Berg understood the oscillating sounds as "great *col legno* arpeggios" and derived them from the "eighth arpeggios" of the beginning (76/III fol. 3). In the second section (mm. 261-280 = 20 bars) a new, canonically treated motif is introduced, which, following Berg's notes in the copy for Hanna, can be called "slumber motif," and which will return in the *Largo desolato*:

Presto delirando, T. 266–272

Largo desolato, T. 41/42

"Hanging," slowly changing chords also determine the structure of the third section (mm. 281-305). The texture is denser, however, for one thing because the otherwise avoided chromatic progressions play a role here, and for another because the cello recites salient melodic "auxiliary voices." The fourth section (mm. 306-320) is intended as a crescendo transition back to the "day." Five intonations of the pulse rhythm signal: "But already the heart makes itself felt and once more day" (Berg).

The fifth part, comprising 140 bars, offers the fullest sound and brings the greatest intensification. To achieve this, Berg applies every conceivable musical means: the chords erected on the pulse rhythm consist initially of eight notes (mm. 321-325) or else are gradually increased to eight notes (mm. 329-337). Glissandi, hitherto either ascending or descending, now go in both directions and at once (mm. 411-414). If before two elements might be intertwined contrapuntally, now at times three are so: in mm. 415-420, for example, the first violin and the cello play the intoxication motif, the second violin plays a variant of the main theme, and the viola intones the shifted pulse rhythm. An example of contrapuntal condensation occurs when the intoxication motif appears as a four-part canon in the octave at intervals of one eighth (mm. 386-400).

Most important, the music resumes ostinato-like traits: Berg evidently regarded the ostinato as an appropriate technique for musically expressing an obsession approaching madness. Delirium, as defined by medical dictionaries, is a clouding of consciousness combined with great excitation, delusions and fixed ideas.

After a unison intonation of the main theme at the beginning of this part (mm. 326-329), persistent ostinato rhythms and figurations dominate the picture over large stretches. The shifted pulse rhythm sounds no fewer than twelve times in the cello (mm.c329-340). On the basis of ostinato figures in the cello, the next thirty bars (mm. 341-370) can be divided into six five-bar groups. In mm. 342-345, the twelve notes of the main theme are subdivided into groups of 3 + 4 + 5 (2nd vl., vla., 1st vl.). In mm. 356-379 the main theme takes on an astounding form, appearing here in gigantic ascending and descending intervals (thus evoking the "surges" of the fourth movement) and augmented in durations of mostly four eighths, tremolos "at the bridge" being at times prescribed. In the Nine Leaves on the Lyric Suite, Berg pointed out that these fifteen bars were to be read as a reminiscence of the fourth movement, specifically of the viola voice in mm. 45/46. This reminiscence has undoubtedly a profound semantic and psychological significance, as it plainly reminds of the passionate love scene of the Adagio appassionato and invokes the image of the beloved. That the passage had indeed great import for Berg can also be gathered from the fact that according to the original drafts it was to form a period of 23 measures conjointly with the four following bars (mm. 371-374), which intone the main theme (76/XIII fol. 4 verso).

In the last forty bars, the ostinato structures become more and more condensed. At first, a multiply repeated twelve-tone chord is formed from the transposed dodecaphonic main theme (mm. 421-429). Then the first violin insists on the seven-note motif, which recurs altogether four times (mm. 430 - 440). In the coda (mm. 441-460), the twelve notes of the main theme are again divided into groups of 3 + 4 + 5 notes (2nd vl., vla. and 1st vl.), which sound permanently and in such a way that a 3/8, a 4/8 and a 5/8 rhythm are superimposed upon each other. The cello intones the pulse theme five times in the original form and four times in the metrically shifted one. Berg's early conception of a "strong wild conclusion" (76/I fol. 16) was thus carried into impressive effect.

3.9 Largo desolato: Sleep and Death – *Liebestod*

> "Now banish all dreading, gracious death, / Yearningly longed-for lovers' death!" Wagner, *Tristan und Isolde*, II.2

> "I envy the vile animals' lot, who leap / With scarce an effort into stupid sleep! / So torpidly time's spindle winds its skein!" Baudelaire, *De profundis clamavi*

As with several of the other movements of the *Lyric Suite*, Berg, probably at an early stage of conception, also had numerous debates with himself about an adequately expressive title for the Finale. A pretty long list of adjectives in the sketches (76/XII fol. 3) reads: *largo funebre – addolorato – doloroso* (underlined) *– lagrimoso – lamentabile – lugubre – mesto –* [word illegible] *– elegiaco – desperato*.[568] An arrow after *mesto* points to the adjective *giocoso*, probably meaning the *Allegretto giocoso* as the opposite pole to the Finale. The term *Largo desolato* Berg seems to have come up with later. "Disconsolate mood" and "plaintive solo violin," at any rate, are two characteristic key phrases that gesture toward the emotional climate of the *Largo desolato* (76/XII fol. 11). An early scored version of the movement in the sketches (76/XII fol. 13), however, still bears the tempo and expression mark *Largo doloroso* and the metronome notation $\rfloor = 46$.

In the score copy for Hanna, the Finale is headed *De profundis clamavi*, The words of the poem with the same title by Charles Baudelaire (in the translation by Stefan George), are underlaid at a number of noticeably cantabile passages in all four instruments, without the poet being named. From this subtexting and numerous other observations in the sketches – in 76/XII fol. 11, for example, the first two verses of the poem are supplied with the rhythmic and graphic notations so typical of Berg – it appears that Berg actually set the poem to music but suppressed the words upon publication. No les significant than this subtext is the statement that the movement ends "dying away in love longing and sorrow."

Besides the cry to the beloved, Baudelaire's sonnet connotes icy coldness, desolation and horror.

> Zu Dir, du einzig Teure, dringt mein Schrei,
> (To you, o sole beloved, go my cries,)
> Aus tiefster Schlucht, darin mein Herz gefallen.
> (Out of the abyss, down which my heart has fallen.)
> Dort ist die Gegend tot, die Luft wie Blei
> (It is a mournful world of leaden skies,)

Und in dem Finstern Fluch und Schrecken wallen.
(Whose night with dread and blasphemy is crawling.)
Sechs Monde steht die Sonne ohne Warm,
(Where for six months a frozen sun impends,)
In sechsen lagert Dunkel auf der Erde.
(And six months' darkness covers all the earth,)
Sogar nicht das Polarland ist so arm.
(A land more naked than the polar fens)
Nicht einmal Bach und Baum, noch Feld noch Herde.
(Sans beast and brook, sans wood and verdant growth.)
Erreicht doch keine Schreckgeburt des Hirnes
(No monster by delirious fancy spun)
Das kalte Grausen dieses Eisgestirnes
(Can match the horror of that icy sun)
Und dieser Nacht! Ein Chaos riesengroß!
(And that vast night, like ancient Chaos' reign!)
Ich neide des gemeinsten Tieres Los,
(I envy the vile animals' lot who leap)
Das tauchen kann in stumpfen Schlafes Schwindel,
(How easily into their stupid sleep!)
So langsam rollt sich ab der Zeiten Spindel.
(So torpidly time's spindle winds its skein.)

Berg obvious selected this poem, from Baudelaire's *Flowers of Evil*, a poetry volume he greatly esteemed, because it could express the state of mind in which he found himself at the time.

A careful study reveals the *Largo desolato* to be the most multi-layered movement of the *Lyric Suite*. The Baudelaire poem is a first layer of signification. A second is constituted by the quotations from and allusions to Richard Wagner's *Tristan und Isolde*, a work with which, as we have repeatedly said, Berg had a special affinity.

We might note to begin with that, in mm. 26/27, the *Largo desolato* quotes the first three measures of the Prelude to *Tristan*. Apart from a few orthographic imprecisions, the pitches are faithfully reproduced, though the rhythmic values are foreshortened. The beginning of the Prelude combines, as is generally known, the motif of "Suffering" with the chromatically ascending four-note motif of "Yearning." [569] Immediately following the complete quotation, Berg cites the "Yearning" motif again, now a minor third lower (mm. 27/28, 1st vl.). The (probably) earliest notation of the Prelude's beginning in the notebook 479/30 fol. 28 verso,

6 Töne

prompts the surmise that Berg quoted it because, among other things, it contains – is bracketed by – the anagrams AB and HF (actually AF and BH [B♭B])! Besides this fraught *Tristan* quotation, which might have remained unrecognized in its dodecaphonic surroundings had Berg himself not drawn attention to it in his analysis for the Kolisch Quartet, two further *Tristan* quotations and one allusion occur in the *Largo desolato*, which did remain unrecognized until 1975. Let us take a close look at them.

Already in the sketches, Berg had planned "tremolo" and "much tremolo" for the final movement (76/I fol. 25 verso and 76/XII fol. 14). Tremolo sounds occur in mm. 9-12 of the *Largo*'s final version, with the expressive motif of the leading first violin being sequenced twice, each time a minor third higher. The passage exhibits a striking similarity to the Tristan's "So stürben wir um ungetrennt" (So we'd die to be unrent) – the famous incantation of the *liebestod*, which is accompanied by tremolos and is likewise structured in sequences:[570]

WAGNER, *Tristan und Isolde*, II. Aufzug

BERG, Lyrische Suite, *Largo desolato*, T. 10–13

The middle of the *Largo desolato* (the movement has 46 = 2 x 23 bars) is marked by a notable pedal point. One note, the contra-B [H!], is held, excepting some short rests, for five long measures (last quarter of m. 20 to m. 25) by the cello, whose C string has "to be tuned down to B" in this movement. The start of the pedal point coincides with the first dynamic climax of the movement: at this point, headed *pesante e rit.*, the first violin and the viola intone eleven times, in characteristic syncopated rhythm, the augmented triad g^b-b^b-d above the interval B/g of the cello.[571] Concurrently, the volume decreases by stages from triple forte to piano.

Upon closer inspection, the pithy rhythm reveals itself as a quotation of the famous syncopated rhythm informing Tristan's *nachtgesang*, "O night of love, sink down upon us" (*Tristan*, II. 2) (see Table 7).

Another *Tristan* motif occurs in m. 30 (*Meno largo*). Here the first violin and then the viola quote the so-called "Doom" (*Verhängnis*) motif, one of the most important leitmotifs in the *Tristan* score along with the motifs of "Suffering" and "Yearning."[572]

The place to which Berg alludes here is the beginning of the fifth scene of Act I, the first dialogue between Tristan and Isolde. To Tristan's "Demand, Lady, what you wish," Isolde replies:

"Must you not know what I desire, since fear of fulfilling kept you far from my gaze?" Berg twice quotes the "Doom" motif in the form in which it is sounded at that moment (see Table 8).

Admittedly, the quotation in both instances is relatively free: Berg has diminished the rhythmic values and altered a few notes (f for e, g$^{\#}$ instead of g), evidently because the dodecaphonic semi-series at the base of this passage required it.

Table 7: The Tristan quotations in the Lyric Suite

Quotation 1: "O sink hernieder, Nacht der Liebe" (leit-rhythm)

Table 8: The Tristan quotations in the Lyric Suite

Quotation 2: In mm. 26/27 of the *Largo desolato*, Berg quotes the beginning of the *Tristan* Prelude (motifs of "Suffering" and "Yearning") **Quotation 3:** "Must you not know what I desire" ("Doom motif")

At four important moments in the *Largo desolato*, Berg has thus quoted or paraphrased four important motifs from Wagner's *Tristan und Isolde:* the Love motif, the rhythm of the Night Song, the motif of Suffering intertwined with the Yearning motif and the motif of Doom. These quotations and allusions have to be viewed against the background of Wagner's philosophy of love. As he had done in his youth, Berg now, too, identified with Tristan. But the ideal beloved he now saw in Hanna, to whom he assigned the role of Isolde.

A further peculiarity of the *Largo desolato* is of material importance for its semantic analysis: the prescription of a *scordatura* for the cello. The score has the note: "In this movement, the C string of the cello has to be tuned down to H [B]."[573] In the copy for Hanna, Berg carefully drew a little box around the H in order to highlight the letter, Hanna's initial. Yet one must ask why he needed the Contra-B of all things for the Finale – a composition written dodecaphonically, not in a B tonality.

For a precise answer to this question, we must first remember that in *Wozzeck*, the note H [B] recurs at many symbolically important moments in the score. It not only appears as the last note of "the portentous final cadence of the second Act" (Berg), but is also at the base of the murder scene in Act III, which is shaped as an "invention on one note," namely the note B. In his *Wozzeck* lecture of 1929, Berg himself has demonstrated that the B appears as "coherence-building principle" of the murder scene "in the most diverse manner imaginable," namely "as pedal point, as continuous middle and upper voice, multiplied in one or several octaves and in all conceivable positions and timbres."[574] Berg, so far as we know, did not speak about the concrete symbolic meaning of the "H," perhaps because he deemed that superfluous: it is evident that the note here functions as a death symbol.[575]

For our question, it is significant, that for the murder scene, Berg required a *scordatura* of the double basses. In the orchestral postlude to the Bible scene he lets the double basses pause for four measures (mm. 67-70). A note in the score reads: "Db tune the C string down to B." The pause is needed so that the basses ("All with low B") can intone the crucial note B at the beginning of the murder scene (mm. 71/72).

What has been said suggests that the low B also functions as a death symbol in the *Largo desolato*. One might consider that B major is also the key of the ecstatic love scene in Act II of *Tristan*, and that Isolde's *liebestod* likewise closes in B major. Yet the B [H] inevitably also evokes Hanna's name.

A third level of signification in the complex *Largo desolato* consists of the motivic reminiscences from the previous movements. In his analysis, Berg merely noted the links to the opening movement. His specifications read: "Cp., to begin with, m. 10 vlc with 1st movement m. 6 2nd vl. But then: 6th movement mm. 37 and 39 with 1st movement mm. 5/6 or 38/39." A detailed thematic analysis can show, however, that the Finale is linked with almost all the preceding movements:

List of reminiscences

Largo desolato

mm. 7/8 (1st vl.)	= variant of the first theme of he *Trio estatico* mm. 69-74 and the *Adagio appassionato* mm. 27-29
m. 10 (vlc.)	~ *Allegretto gioviale* m. 6 (2nd vl.)
mm. 13-15 (vla.)	= variant of the first theme of the *Trio estatico* mm. 69-74 and the *Adagio appassionato* mm. 27-29
mm. 34/35 (1st vl.)	~ *Allegro misterioso* main motif (= double anagram)
m. 37 (*pesante*)	~ *Allegretto gioviale* m. 38
m. 39 (*di nuovo pesante*)	~ *Allegretto gioviale* mm. 5/6 and 39
mm. 41/42 (1st vl.)	~ slumber motif from the 5th movement mm. 261 ff.

What Berg in his analysis calls the "main motif" of the *Largo*, i.e., mm. 7/8 (1st vl.) and mm. 13-15 (vla.) proves upon closer inspection to be a variant of the first theme of the *Trio estatico* mm. 69-74 and the corresponding passage in the *Adagio appassionato* mm. 27-29 (see Table V). With its expansive and extravagant character, the theme was well suited to express the cry of the first lines of the Baudelaire sonnet. The *flautando* motif of the *Largo* mm. 34/35 (1st vl.) is then a reminiscence of the main motif of the *Allegro misterioso* (see Table III). The Slumber motif also links the *Largo* to the *Presto delirando*, more specifically to the *Tenebroso*. A study of the sketches makes clear that these linkages between the bracketing movements were planned from the start (76/I fol. 17 and 76/XII fol. 11). Turning now to the twelve-tone aspect, the strictly dodecaphonic *Largo desolato* is based, as Berg notes in his analysis, on the series of the fifth movement and on a very characteristic transformation, which he calls "halbreihe," half-row or semi-series.[576]

With some pride he states in the *Nine Leaves*: "The entire material of this movement, even the tonal (triads, etc.), as well as the Tristan motif 26/27, has resulted from strict adherence to the twelve-tone rows (in the above four forms incl. transpositions)."

If we take a close look at the dispositions of the rows and analyze their use in the composition, we can make three instructive observations:

1. The "half-row" is marked much more strongly by chromatic steps than the "row."

2. Chromaticism is an essential factor in the fabric of the *Largo*. In this respect, the *Largo* contrasts strongly with the fifth movement, in which chromatic steps are very rare.

3. The first and last note of the *Largo* form Hanna's initials. At the same time, it is important to note that, in contrast to the *Andante amoroso* and especially the *Allegro misterioso*, the tonal letters corresponding to the anagrams AB and HF no longer occur adjacently; only once, in mm. 34/35 (1st vl.), does the double anagram b-a-f-h (b♭-a-f-b) occur in the *Largo*. However, we learn from the sketches that Berg had originally planned to let the recitative of the cello in m. 10 begin with that phrase (76/XII fol. 13):

According to early drafts, the movement was also meant to close with the double anagram, thus (76/XII fol. 11)

or thus (76/I fol. 19)

We have not yet exhausted the information to be gleaned from the sketches, however. Additional important data include the following:

The pizzicato introduction (mm. 1-6) was conceived originally as a musical "motto" (76/XI fol. 1 verso and fol. 10 verso.): the tremolos already discussed (mm. 9-12 of the final version) formed the real beginning of the movement. They are notated no fewer than four times in score form, though a tritone or else a minor third higher than in the final version (76/XII, fols. 2, 4, 6 and 13). They are distinct from each other in their metric division and extend to four or five bars. One of these versions (76/XII fol. 13) deserves to be thrown into relief, because Berg headed it *Largo doloroso*, and because it was five bars in length and was written in 3/2 time. Berg, it seems, regarded it as significant that it consists of 15 half notes, since he made a note of it in the margin. On another sheet (76/I fol. 25 verso), the chordal sequence these tremolos constitute is marked *schlafakkordfolge*, sleep chord sequence – a rubric significant also for the semantic interpretation of this symbolically fraught *Largo desolato*.

It remains to mention that Berg understood the penultimate section of the movement (mm. 36-40) as "quasi Coda" (76/XII fol. 3 verso) and even at an early conceptual stage had planned "the ceasing of all the instruments, viola last" (76/XII fol. 3 verso). "Fading away," the instruments were to stop playing one after the other (76/XII fol. 6 verso).

In view of the many quotations and reminiscences, which enabled us to tease out several levels of signification, it is understandable that to Erwin Stein – and nearly all later critics – the form of the *Largo desolato* seemed "quite free, downright rhapsodic." The rather laconic statements Berg himself made in his analysis of the movement's form are such that they might seem to support Stein's description. Berg wrote:

> Something about form: 1-6 Introduction, 7/8 main melody suggested, 9-12 introduction again and from 13 on main melody (vla.). Recurrence of the rhythm of the main melody in 31/32 through tone-altering entries of the instruments.

Upon closer inspection, however, the form of the *Largo* turns out to be not at all "free" but as stringent as can be.

The movement is divided into two halves of identical length (23 + 23 bars), which, with few exceptions, are mirror-symmetric, albeit not in a sense of strict crab motion: only mm. 24/25 (~ mm. 23/22)) are strictly retrograde, as Schweizer already pointed out.

The following outline, registering all of the quotations and reminiscences, can demonstrate the mirror-symmetric tectonics of the movement more succinctly than lengthy paraphrases:

mm. 1-6 (*tempo I*)
Berg: "Introduction"
(in the sketches: "Motto")

mm. 36-46 (*tempo I*)
(in the sketches: "Quasi Coda")
mm. 37 and 39 reminiscences of
the first movement, mm. 5/6 or 38/39

the 4 instruments enter successively

the 4 instruments stop successively;
mm. 41/42 (1st vl.)
reminiscence of the slumber motif
in the *Tenebroso*

mm. 7/8 (*tempo II*)
Berg: "main melody suggested"
1st vl.: variant of the theme of
the *Trio estatico*
vlc.: four-tone motif recalling the
Allegro mistrioso

mm. 34/35 (*tempo II*)

1st. vl., vla., vlc.: *flautando* reminiscence of the *Allegro misterioso*

mm. 9-12 (*tempo I*)
Berg: "introduction again"
1st and 2nd vl., vla.: Tremolos =
'reminiscence' of the
Liebestod of *Tristan und Isolde*
(in sketches: "sequence of sleep
chords") Vlc.: reminiscence of first
movement m. 6 and the leading
rhythm ("Night of love")

mm. 13-15 (*tempo II*)
Berg: "main melody"

mm. 31-33 (*tempo I*)
Berg: "recurrence of the main

Vla.: variant of the theme from the *Trio estatico*	melody's rhythm in 31/32 through the tone-altering entrances of the
4 instruments"	
mm. 16-20 (*tempo II*)	mm. 28-30
mm. 18-20 *accelerando*	mm. 28/29 *subito molto accelerando*
	m. 30 "Doom motif" of *Tristan*
mm. 20/21 (*pesante e retard.*) 1st vl. and vla.: leit-rhythm of "O sink hernieder, Nacht der Liebe" vlc.: "death" B	mm. 26/27 (*molto rubato*) Berg: "Tristan motif" (= quotation of the beginning of the *Tristan* Prelude)
mm. 22/23 (*tempo II*) *cantabile* "death" B as pedal point	mm. 24-25 (*tempo II*) *sempre cantabile* (retrograde) "death" B as pedal point

In its tersest form, the results of the semantic analysis would read: the "sleep chord sequence" (mm. 9-13) and the slumber motif (mm. 41/42) connote the yearning for sleep and forgetting in accordance with the last three lines of the Baudelaire sonnet. The numerous allusions to Wagner's *Tristan*, however, concretize Berg's conception of the *Largo desolato* in terms of the idea of the *liebestod*.

3.10 Aspects of *Lulu*

3.10.1 Berg's Reading of Wedekind's *Lulu* Tragedy

> "Now that I have a complete grasp of it, I am all the more convinced of the play's profound morality." Berg to Erich Kleiber, February, 1920[577]

Frank Wedekind has entered theater history as a dramatist who dared to take on certain social taboos: the touchy problem of sexuality, the war of the sexes, egotism as a powerful human mainspring and, above all, the moral double standard of bourgeois society. Long after his death, his stage plays, which caused sensations during his lifetime, seem to have had a sustained influence on modern drama. According to Wilhelm Emrich, Wedekind gave drastic and shocking expression to the problematic nature, impossibility and negativity of so-called absolute values – and set precedents thereby. In the "Lulu" tragedy, Emrich sees "all the essential elements of later tragedies established in embryo," including the tragedies of Jean Paul Sartre.[578]

At the start of the 20th century, Wedekind was both famous and notorious. Oddly, his growing popularity was due to the fact that he had become a victim, and thereupon an adversary, of censorship. In 1904, his *Büchse der Pandora (Pandora's Box)* was published by Bruno Cassirer and instantly prompted the state prosecutor to enter the lists, who confiscated the edition and brought charges against both Wedekind and his publisher for distributing obscene writings. The Royal Berlin Regional Court confirmed the confiscation in 1905 but acquitted the accused. Wedekind thoroughly reworked his play in order to obtain its release for the stage, but his efforts were virtually without success: there were very few productions during his lifetime, most of them so-called "subscription performances."[579]

One such non-public performance of *Die Büchse der Pandora* was given on May 29, 1905, at Vienna's Trianon Theater, "before an invited audience";[580] it had been organized by Karl Kraus, who followed Wedekind's work with consummate interest. The cast of this memorable event included Wedekind's wife Tilly Newes, Wedekind himself, the cultural philosopher Egon Friedell and Karl Kraus. In his renowned introductory address, Kraus indicted the double standard of men, spoke of "the hounded, eternally misunderstood grace of woman, whom a miserable world allowed to climb only onto the Procrustean bed of their moral dictates," praised Wedekind's language, and sought to illuminate the play psychologically from every angle.[581]

Both the performance and Kraus's address left a lasting impression on Berg. According to Willi Reich, he identified "completely" with the conception of the Lulu tragedy set forth in Karl Kraus's speech.[582] More than twenty years would pass, however, before he decided, late in 1927, to turn Wedekind's Lulu story into an opera.

For some time, he had wavered whether to set Gerhart Hauptmann's glassworks fairytale *Und Pippa tanzt* (Pippa Dances) or the Lulu tragedy to music. His friends Soma Morgenstern and Theodor W. Adorno, whom he had asked for advice, counseled differently. While Morgenstern was in favor of *Pippa*, Adorno argued for *Lulu*[583] – which decided the issue. A letter to Morgenstern dated November 17, 1927, indicates that Berg had dialectically weighed all the pros and contras. He was conscious that something even more intense would be expected of him after *Wozzeck*, and he felt that the Lulu tragedy was a strong piece that promised such a heightening, whereas *Und Pippa tanzt* "in purely human and generally artistic terms would not be an escalation vis-à-vis Wozzeck but rather a retrenchment in these matters," practically "a retraction of the front."[584]

In dealing with Berg's *Lulu*, one is initially confronted with two fundamental questions: what was it that fascinated Berg about Wedekind's two-part tragedy, and how did he interpret the action?

To answer these questions, one needs to point out that the various interpretations of the tragedy place their emphases differently. While some critics foreground the social and moral criticism of the plays, others focus on elucidating the psychological dimension. To cite only two examples:

Karl Kraus evidently was mainly interested in the social and moral aspects. Already in 1902 – two years before the publication of *Pandora's Box* – his article "Sittlichkeit und Kriminalität" (Ethics and Crime) had appeared in *Die Fackel*, in which he pilloried the moral double standard of bourgeois society.[585] The leading Wedekind biographer Arthur Kutscher, on the other hand, makes depth psychology the focus of his interpretation. For him the central idea of the tragedy is the "vision of the female sex drive as the principle of destruction." Lulu, according to Kutscher, is "not a human individual, but the "personification of the female sexual urge, which is the center of life, the Earth Spirit, who drags down, an annihilating demon." "Egotism is its foundation and here finds its most indurate manifestation." An important role, for Kutscher, is also played by the idea of the war of the sexes. "The demonic sexual force of woman collides of natural necessity with the polar power of the man, and since it lives in ruthless egotism only for itself, a murderous struggle ensues (Nietzsche's mortal enmity of the sexes)."[586]

Wedekind himself interpreted his tragedy differently, in more cautious terms, placing the emphases in other ways. In the preface to the new, 1906 edition of the *Büchse der Pandora*, he made a fundamental distinction between civil (bourgeois) morality, "which the judge is called upon to protect," and human morality, "which is beyond all earthly jurisdiction," He added that in all the critical judgments of his play, venal love was branded as immoral and its practice as fornication – a term that seemed to him "quite accurate from the standpoint of bourgeois morality." Together with "venerable poets" of all the ages, however, he felt called upon "to defend the unhappy victims of prostitution [*käufliche Liebe*] against the general ostracism." And he invoked Jesus

Christ, "the founder of our religion," who had built the kingdom of God for those "that labor and are heavy laden, not for the rich, for the sick, nor for the healthy, for the sinners, not for the righteous." He passionately pleaded for a "human morality" and postulated that "if the human morality is to be elevated above the civil one, it also has to be grounded in a deeper and more comprehensive knowledge of the nature of the world and of man."587

Berg was greatly impressed by Wedekind's commentary. On Good Friday of 1934, he wrote to his friend Erich Kleiber he thought it so wonderful that he would dearly love to have it preface his *Lulu*.588 The marginal markings and underlinings in his personal copy589 likewise support the conclusion that he largely identified with Wedekind's conception of the tragedy.

Berg seems to have had a differentiated view of Lulu herself. On the one hand, he viewed her as a demonic being, the spoiler or corrupter, the principle of destruction as such. In a letter to Erich Kleibert, he likened her to Don Juan, who is likewise "taken by the Devil."590 As reported by Willi Reich, he shared the opinion of a critic that Lulu was

> a heroine of outsized power of experiencing and suffering, destroying everything around her that, bewitched by her, gets near her, a piece of nature beyond good and evil, and hence a self-closed cosmos remote from everything conceptual, to be unraveled only by music."

On the other hand, he saw in her a beautiful woman, who at times lived in a sphere of unreality. The frequent coloratura passages in Lulu's part, according to Reich, were to "hint, by means of stylization, at that unreal sphere in which the heroine of the opera – a *somnambulist of love*, as Karl Kraus called her – moves in dreamlike virtuosity."591

Berg, we know, created the libretto by "pulling together" the two Wedekind plays, *Erdgeist* and *Büchse der Pandora*, into a three-act opera libretto.592 In arranging the text, he had to sacrifice 4/5 of Wedekind's originals.593 Numerous scenes, characters, and passages of reflection were omitted. Berg was concerned not to destroy Wedekind's "peculiar language." Even so, he made major changes in certain places. Adorno aptly remarked that he virtually ignored the "cynical dimension" of the original, and Hans Ferdinand Redlich spoke equally to the point of a "stylistic ennoblement" and "overall musicalization."594

Above all, however, Berg by his music endowed his opera with an emotional depth lacking in the source. This is especially clear in those sections of a solemn, measured character, in which he cultivates and enhances the *espressivo* of Bruckner and Mahler in new ways. I am referring especially to the *Lento* (i.e., the coda of the sonata) expressing Lulu's bond with Dr. Schön (Act I, mm. 615-624) and the *Grave* at the end of the opera, the monologue of the dying Countess Geschwitz (Act III, mm. 1315-1325).

3.10.2 Lulu's Rise and Fall

"From the brackets (left and right) you can see how what is *separated* in Wedekind – into two plays – is purposely united in my text (by means of my second act). The interlude that with me bridges the gap between the last act of *Erdgeist* and the first of *Pandora's Box* is, after all, the central point of the whole tragedy, in which after the rise of the preceding acts (or scenes) the fall of the following scenes – the reversal – sets in. (By the way: the 4 men who visit Lulu in her garret are to be performed in the opera by the same singers who represent the men who become Lulu's victims in the first half. (In reverse order, however) ..." Berg to Schönberg, August 7, 1930[595]

"Now that I have a complete grasp of it I am all the more convinced of the profound morality of the play. Lulu's rise and fall counterbalance each other; in the middle the great reversal, until she is at last – like Don Juan – carried off by the Devil. I say on purpose – like Don Juan – not, God forbid, to compare myself to Mozart, but *only* in order to juxtapose the two figures 'Lulu' and 'Don Juan.' On the question where you might be able to do the *Lulu* if Berlin, and thus Germany, should fail, another time. Perhaps – hopefully – it will not become acute, this question." Berg to Erich Kleiber, probably February 1924[596]

On August 7, 1930, Berg reported to Schönberg about his work on the first act of *Lulu*. "Besides the composing, whose 12-tone style still prevents me from working quickly," he wrote, "the libretto is also holding me up." Concurrently, he specified for him the relation of his operatic version to Wedekind's two plays, as quoted above, and made it graphic by the following itemization:

	The two Plays	The Opera
Earth Spirit	Act I. Studio, where Dr. Goll, Lulu's husband, dies of a stroke	Act I, 3 scenes
	Act II. Apartment of Lulu and her second husband, who commits suicide	
	Act III. Dressing room of the dancer Lulu, to whom Schön promises marriage	
	Act IV. Apartment of Schön, whom Lulu murders. She is arrested.	Act II. 1 scene divided by an extended interlude
	Freed from prison, after 10 years incarceration, by Alwa (Schön's son) and Geschwitz, Lulu in	
Pandora's Box	Act I. returns to Schön's apartment (scene as before). She becomes Alwa's mistress.	
	Act II. Gambling casino in Paris. Lulu has to flee.	Act III, 2 scenes
	Act III. In the garret in London	

In this connection, he clearly intimated that the central vantage point from which he saw and interpreted the two plays was Lulu's fabulous social rise as the wife of the prominent editor-in-chief Dr. Schön and her subsequent fall, ending as a whore in a London slum. This interpretive pattern prompted him to construct his opera nearly mirror-symmetrically, both formally and musically. Thus the long mirror-symmetrically structured orchestral interlude in the first scene of the second act bridges the two Wedekind plays and at the same time marks the mid-point and the "reversal."

Specifically, the three scenes of the first act present the stages of Lulu's social ascent. Lulu, the wife of the public health officer Dr. Goll, begins an affair with the painter who is painting her portrait. When Dr. Goll realizes what is happening, he suffers a stroke (scene 1). After Dr. Goll's death, Lulu marries the painter, but also continues an affair with Dr. Schön. The painter kills himself after Dr. Schön has bluntly informed him of the situation (scene 2). After the painter's suicide, Lulu works as a dancer at a theater. She forces Dr.

Schön to dissolve his engagement to his fiancée (scene 3) and becomes the wife of Dr. Schön, but also maintains relations with other men (the athlete Rodrigo, the prep-school student, the valet, also Schigolch), as well as with the Countess Geschwitz. When called upon by Dr. Schön to shoot herself, she instead fires five shots at him, killing him. She is arrested (scene 1 of Act II).

The lengthy orchestral interlude that follows in Act II (mm. 652-721) is intended as musical accompaniment to a silent film about the subsequent fortunes of Lulu, her arrest, detention, trial and incarceration, her illness, the medical consultation, her transfer to a quarantine shack and her eventual liberation. In the printed libretto, Berg directs that, corresponding to the symmetric course of the music, the cinematic action should be arranged "quasi symmetrically (that is, moving forward and retrograde)."[597] The result would be the following series of images (in the direction of the arrows):

↓ Arrest	*On the way to de facto*
	Liberation
The three involved	*The three involved*
in the arrest	*in the liberation*
Lulu in chains	*Lulu freed (disguised as*
	Countess Geschwitz)
Detention	in the quanratine shack
In nervous expectation	*In nervouse expectation*
Dwindling hope	*Mounting hope*
↓	↑
Trial	Consultation
The charge	*The illness*
Judge and jury	*Doctors and students*
The three witnesses to the deed	*The three helpers to*
Sentence	*the liberation*
Transportation in the	*Transportation in the*
paddy wagon to the	*ambulance from the*
Prison	Prison

The prison door closes	*The prison door opens*
Initial resignation	*Reviving optimism*
Lulu's image: as a shadow	*Lulu's image: as mirror*
↓ *on the prison wall*	*reflection in a shovel* ↑
→ *One year imprisonment*	→

In the second scene of Act II, which takes place in Dr. Schön's apartment again, Lulu's fall begins. She becomes the mistress of Alwa, the son of Dr. Schön, but her criminal past soon catches up with her. In a Parisian salon, where she presents herself as the center of the demimonde, she is forced to flee from the police (Act III, scene 1). The final scene shows her as a prostitute in a London garret, where she finally becomes the victim of Jack the Ripper.

As is generally known, Berg did not have a chance to complete his opera. Although he was able to finish the score of the first two acts, the third act, of which a handwritten particello and 390 orchestrated measures are extant, remained incomplete. In the late 'seventies, Friedrich Cerha published a fully orchestrated version of the third act, which caused a considerable stir.[598] For a long time, the question whether to prefer the two-act or the completed three-act version remained controversial. Peter Petersen has persuasively argued in favor of the latter, largely on the basis of the noticeable symmetrical correspondence between Acts I and III.[599]

Of the music of the third act, it has been said rightly, if over-inclusively, that it has the character of a recapitulation. Upon close inspection, it turns out to be based to a large extent on material of the first two acts, material that is taken over without change or else varied and developed. But new musical elements likewise play a major role in the third act: Wedekind's lute song, of which Berg composed very artful and imaginative variations, and the theme of the chorale variations.

The mirror-symmetric construction of the orchestral interlude in the second act marks, as noted, the great "reversal" in the fortunes of the heroine. Of the two halves into which this ostinato is divided, the second is the exact palindrome of the first (mm. 652-687). As a concrete instance of the suggestiveness of the musical expression, the ascending "earth spirit fourths" in the first half illustrate Lulu's rise, while the descending fourths in the second half symbolize her ruin:

II, T. 674-678

II, T. 696-700

Naturally, the mirror symmetry that marks the ostinato does not apply with the same rigor to the opera as a whole. For example, as the above-quoted letter to Schönberg of August 7, 1930, indicates, Berg had originally thought of letting the three men who visit Lulu in her garret (at first there were four) be enacted by the same singers who represent her victims in the first half, albeit in reverse order. Lulu's first client, the professor, to be sure, is indeed played by the singer of the public health doctor, the Negro by that of the painter (Schwarz!), and Jack the Ripper by that of Dr. Schön, exactly as Berg had directed, but the planned reverse order had to be dropped. Nevertheless, there are significant musical correspondences. Thus the music for the entrance of the professor refers in many ways to the music that sounded during the first appearance of Dr. Goll in the very first scene. The entrance music for the black man exhibits diverse analogies to the *Monoritmica*, that is to say, the music accompanying the suicide of the painter. Finally, the music that Berg composed for the scene with Jack the Ripper has frequent recourse to the themes of Dr. Schön.

3.10.3 Characterization of Persons, Passions and Ideas

> "I believe I do justice to it [i.e. *Lulu*] by not limiting myself to a single series, insofar as from it I derive a number of other forms (scale forms, chromatic forms, thirds and fourths forms, chord sequences of 3–4 notes etc. etc. etc.), each of which I then regard as an independent row and treat as such (with all its inversions and retrograde forms)." Berg to Schönberg, September 1, 1928[600]

Berg's way of handling the twelve-tone technique in *Lulu* has always been greatly admired. He does not content himself with a single twelve-tone series – as Schönberg does in his 1929 opera *Von heute auf morgen* (From one Day to the Next) – but, applying ingenious methods of selection and permutation, gains several secondary rows that characterize individual figures of the opera. Thus Lulu, Dr. Schön, Alwa, Schigolch and the Countess Geschwitz each get a row. With the help of Berg's own sketches,⁶⁰¹ Willi Reich was the first to present these secondary rows and the related motifs,⁶⁰² and the subject has been elucidated by several later studies.⁶⁰³ Two aspects, however, have hitherto received little or no attention: one, that Berg put the diverse thematic derivations in the service of the leitmotif technique, and secondly, that in characterizing persons, passions, objects and ideas, he uses not only rows but also intervals, themes, motifs, meters, rhythms, harmonies, forms and timbres.

Basic to the leitmotif technique employed in *Lulu* is Berg's musically linking the menagerie animals the animal tamer parades in the Prologue to the main characters of the opera. At the mention of the tiger, for example, the Dr. Schön motif sounds in the orchestra. Schigolch is paralleled with "reptiles [or vermin] from every zone," the Countess Geschwitz with the crocodile. In the middle of the prologue, Lulu is presented as a serpent. The human-animal qualities that Berg thus ascribed to his main characters rub off onto the shape of the themes.

The so-called picture harmonies that symbolize the portrait of Lulu,

have a special significance in that Berg obtains both the Lulu row and the dance-like scale theme of Lulu from them. The latter appears in both its basic and its inverted form:

upper voice   middle voice   lower voice

[musical notation: leggero]

I,T.323/324
Lulu
[musical notation: ei - gent - lich wis - sen?]

Interestingly, the last version exhibits a strong similarity to a motif in Alexander von Zemlinsky's *Lyric Symphony* of 1923:

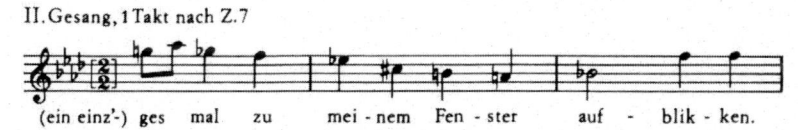

II. Gesang, 1 Takt nach Z.7
[musical notation: (ein einz'-) ges mal zu mei - nem Fen - ster auf - blik - ken.]

In Wedekind, Dr. Schön is a "violent person," a brute, whose nature is marked above all by an immense energy. His series and his theme have a major-mood character – *dur* (= hard) in German. The tenth-leap that especially marks his theme corresponds to the leap of the tiger mentioned in the Prologue.

Allegro energico ♩ = 80
[musical notation]

Alwa, Dr. Schön's son, by contrast, is a delicately strung enthusiast in Wedekind. Berg takes that into account by casting his row and theme in a minor (*moll* = soft) mood:

Andante ♩ = 69
[musical notation]

If we now look at Lulu's satellites, Schigolch is, to begin with, a droll figure in Wedekind. His relationship with Lulu is deliberately shady. To depict him, Berg chose chromatic figures and lines, all derived from the *ur*-series, which lend Schigolch a slinking and sluggish quality that corresponds to his characterization, in the Prologue, as reptilian "vermin of all zones."

By contrast, the athlete Rodrigo is characterized by raw physical strength and clumsiness, which in the Prologue is associated with the nature of a bear. To evoke the "strong-as-an-ox" muscle man by musical means, Berg employs not only chord clusters on the white and black keys of the piano but also a strikingly broad meter (the 9/8 time in the prologue, mm. 25-27, and the 6/8 time in Act II, mm. 99 ff.), as well as the cantabile interval of the minor seventh, which decisively shapes the melodic idiom of Rodrigo.

One of the many sardonic traits of Wedekind's tragedy is that the father of the student, Lulu's youngest beau, is, of all people, chief of police. Corresponding to the impulsive nature of the young man, Berg endows his part primarily with fanfare-like melodies. In two places in the score, we find the expression mark "like a fanfare" (II, m. 104) and "always like a fanfare" (II, m. 118).

In his preface to the new edition of *Büchse der Pandora*, Wedekind described the Countess Geschwitz as the "tragic protagonist" of the play. According to Karl Kraus, she is "no pathological dime-a-dozen creature," but strides through the tragedy like a daemon of joylessness. Berg had no sympathy with the Countess.[604] In the opera, he characterizes her by pentatonic scales and empty fifths. Here, too, the tone-symbolic intention is unmistakable: the exotic tone system corresponds to her "deviant" (lesbian) disposition.

Leitmotifs in *Lulu* signal not only characters but also emotions, passions, states of mind and ideas. Of special importance among them are those conveying Lulu's bond with Dr. Schön, the catastrophe rhythm, the so-called persecution-mania motif and the important, oddly enough hitherto unnoticed kiss motif.

3.10.4 Musical Shaping

> "Until now, it [the work on the libretto and the composition of the opera] has progressed well enough, but still slowly, and only Schönberg's letter (to you) was a consolation. For I, too, spend much, much time on the text and have long since hit upon the same method of work. I could have said every word of Schönberg's about my work myself, and that's a wonderful reassurance to me. The finale of the first act, for example, at which I am currently working, is a development and last recapitulation of a sonata movement, whose repeated exposition occurred much earlier. The difficulty (one of a thousand difficulties!) now is how to work the music prescribed by musical laws into the text prescribed and conditioned by Wedekind's dialectical laws: how to make the two congruent, and to stretch the mighty arc of the plot over everything." Berg to Webern, July 23, 1931[605]

Dramaturgically speaking, Wedekind's *Lulu* tragedy is altogether different from Büchner's *Woyzeck* fragment. While the latter consists of a series of small self-contained scenes, the *Lulu* tragedy is composed of more broadly executed and complexly built ones. Another major difference is that the *Woyzeck* fragment is designed to lead to one catastrophe – the murder of Marie and the subsequent suicide of Woyzeck – while Wedekind's two-part tragedy strides from catastrophe to catastrophe.

What challenged Berg to set Büchner's fragment to music, as we learn from a letter to Webern, was not only the fate of the "poor creature exploited and tormented by the whole world" but also the "immense mood content of the individual scenes." To be able to do justice to just this diversity in the character of the individual scenes, Berg had invented "a large variety in their musical form."[606]

The composition of *Lulu* confronted him with entirely different problems. The many-layeredness of the opera's action results from the multiplicity of relationships Lulu entertains. The result is several parallel action strands, some of them interrupted by insertions, interpolations, episodes and the like and then resumed later on. To solve this problem, Berg based some of the action strands on musical forms that are introduced and then completed at a later time, in accordance with the scenic events.

Viewed from this perspective, Willi Reich's attempt to differentiate the construction of *Lulu* from that of *Wozzeck* categorically seems a generalization that does not do justice to the details. He writes:

If in *Wozzeck* the character of the individual scenes essentially determined the musical forms of the work, the character – the 'total appearance to be carried through' (Berg!) – of each of the now much more broadly developed dramatis personae is decisive for the musical construction of *Lulu*[607]

Strictly speaking, that statement applies to the musical treatment only of Dr. Schön and Alwa. Let us take a closer look at these two figures.

Berg chose the sonata form for the violent altercations between Lulu and Dr. Schön. It is divided into two parts – the exposition and a first recapitulation, on the one hand, and the development and second recapitulation, on the other – parts that are far apart: the first is located in the second scene of Act I (mm. 533-668), while the second concludes the third scene (mm. 1209-1361).

In the scene accompanied by the first part of the sonata, Lulu, at the instigation of Dr. Schön, has married the painter Schwarz while remaining Schön's mistress. Schön, who now wants to break off relations with her, comes to see her and asks her to stop her visits: he longs for a well-ordered life and plans to become shortly engaged.

The exposition of the sonata is composed of several sections, which are expressly entitled "main theme," "transitional group," "secondary theme," and "coda," and which differ in character, tempo and meter. Thus the main theme is in 4/4 time, the transitional group in 6/8 time, the side theme in 2/4 time, and the coda again in 4/4 time. The division into four sections of a different character corresponds to the four topics of the exchange between Dr. Schön and Lulu. The *main theme* is linked to Dr. Schön's basic relationship with Lulu. The music of the transitional group expresses the Lulu's relation to the painter, who oddly enough is not on to the extramarital escapades of his wife. The gavotte-like secondary theme symbolizes Dr. Schön's longing for orderly bourgeois circumstances, his urgent wish, to lead his bride under a pure roof. The coda, finally, gives expression to the profound human bond between Lulu and Dr. Schön.

As this first dramatic confrontation between Lulu and Dr. Schön is interrupted by the entrance of the painter, Berg lets the exposition of the sonata be followed immediately by the recapitulation. Dr. Schön enlightens the clueless painter about Lulu's past, whereupon the latter commits suicide.

At the beginning of the third scene, Lulu appears as a dancer in a theater, forms a closer contact with Alwa, flirts with the prince, her latest beau, and pretends to faint when she spots Dr. Schön with his fiancée in the parquet. Dr. Schön's renewed extended conversation with Lulu is the scenic background of the second part of the sonata and ends with his capitulation, as Lulu forces him to dissolve his engagement. The gavotte-like secondary theme of the sonata now assumes the form of the famous letter duet, as Lulu triumphantly dictates a farewell letter to his bride to Dr. Schön.

The construction of the rondo form is similar to that of the sonata. Berg chose it as an appropriate frame for the relationship between Alwa and Lulu. This famous andante of Alwa's, too, is not developed through to the end but is interrupted twice before it is completed. The exposition of the Andante accompanies the dressing-room scene in Act I (mm. 1020-1040). Here the music gives expression to Alwa's romantic adoration of Lulu. A symptomatic stage direction reads: "Alwa, almost painfully dazzled by her sight, puts his hand over his heart." The rondo is continued and powerfully developed in the first scene of Act II (mm. 243-337). Alwa and Lulu get nearer to each other – the music has an erotic aura in places. Of the three themes that are presented and at times even contrapuntally intertwined, the third has the semantics of Alwa's kissing Lulu's hand. The rondo is not completed, however, until the second scene of the second act (mm. 1059-1096), after the death of Dr. Schön, when it is already obvious that Lulu has chosen Alwa to be her father's successor. A climactic moment of this section occurs when Lulu kisses Alwa "deliberately" to the sounds of the kiss theme (m. 1075).

To analyze the use of musical forms in *Lulu*, one obviously has to keep their treatment in *Wozzeck* in mind. Berg in the latter was not content to give to each of its 15 scenes an individualized musical form but structured the scenes of the three acts according to a superior formal principle. Thus the five scenes of Act I are formed as "character pieces": as suite, as rhapsody on a sequence of three chords, as military march and cradle song, as passacaglia and as *Andante affettuoso*.

By contrast, the second act exhibits the form of a spaciously designed symphony in five movements. The first scene (between Marie, the child and Wozzeck) is shaped as a sonata movement. The second (between the captain, the doctor and Wozzeck) is a fantasia and fugue on three themes. The third scene (between Marie and Wozzeck) is the famous Largo for chamber orchestra (15 instruments). The great scene in the pub is composed as a scherzo for large orchestra and for a *heurigen* (wine bar) band on stage. The fifth scene, finally, is a *Rondo con Introduzione*.

Especially ingenious are the six *Inventions* of the third act: inventions on a theme (Bible scene), on a note (the ominous B in the murder scene), on a rhythm (bar scene), on a hexachord (Wozzeck's death scene), on a key (orchestra interlude after Wozzeck's death), and on a uniform series of eighths (song of the children).

One can demonstrate on countless examples that the choice of the individual musical forms is motivated by the dramatic events, and that there is thus a striking congruence between musical form and stage action.

Turning from there to the formal realm of *Lulu*, one discovers that Berg continued on the path chosen for *Wozzeck* and came up with many new results and solutions. What is to be emphasized especially is the much greater wealth and much larger diversity of forms in *Lulu*. We can distinguish five categories.

A first category consists of contrapuntal forms and some of the types of the baroque suite. In contrast to *Wozzeck*, there are no fugues in *Lulu*; but there is a notable predilection for canons and canonic formations. Thus the coquettish scene between Lulu and the painter in the very first scene of the opera is composed as a strict two-voiced canon (I, mm. 156-185). The same canon, expanded to include a third voice, recurs later in the orchestral interlude between scenes 1 and 2 (I, mm. 367-395). There is a canon each also in Acts II (mm. 173-194) and III (mm. 192-199).

We may note secondly that each of the three acts adapts chorale forms. In the first act, a chorale followed by a concertante chorale adaptation is reserved for the Prince (mm. 1113-1149). A shorter chorale episode in the second act (mm. 250-261) alludes, of all people, to the Valet, who, like so many others, has succumbed to Lulu's charms. The third act contains no fewer than twelve chorale variations, which, no doubt ironically, are assigned to the pimp Casti Piani: 1st var. mm. 83-66, 2nd var. mm. 99-102, 3rd var. mm. 146-153, 4th var. mm. 154-157; 5th var. mm. 182-187, 6th var. 188-191, 7th var. (canon) mm. 192-199, 8th var. mm. 200-207, 9th var. mm. 208-215, 10th var. 216-223, 11th mm. 224-227, 12th var. (stretto) mm. 228a-230.

Finally, one might mention the gavotte- and musette-like passages in the sonata (mm. 586-614 and 649-665). They suggest an orientation on Schönberg's *Piano Suite* op. 25 of 1921.

In a second category, we can include larger forms of the classic-romantic music, which Berg partly used in *Wozzeck*. As we have shown, the sonata form serves him for the dramatic altercations between Lulu and Dr. Schön, whereas the rondo form is chosen as a frame for the depiction of the Alwa-Lulu relationship.

Something that is new in *Lulu* are two pieces of chamber music, of which the first (an ingenious nonet for woodwinds) applies to Schigolch and Lulu in the first act (I, mm. 463-532), whereas the second, strictly in 9/8 time, is meant for the prep-school student, Alwa and the athlete (II, mm. 834-952).

Oddly enough, there are hardly any typical vocal forms in *Wozzeck* –apart from Marie's cradle song and the Bible scene. One gets the impression that Berg had an ambition to furnish his opera solely with instrumental forms. *Lulu* constitutes a reorientation in that respect, as it surprises the listener by its plethora of typically operatic musical forms.

These include the *recitative* (I, mm. 86 ff., 284-304, 1100 ff., II, mm. 3 ff., 195 ff., 287 ff., 722 ff., 774 ff., etc.), the *melodrama* (I, mm. 196-257, II, mm. 953-1000), the *arioso* (II, mm. 329-350), the *aria* (II, mm. 387 ff.), the *arietta* (II, mm. 620-644), the *canzonetta* (I, mm. 258-283), the *cavatina* (II, mm. 61-87), the *lied* (II, mm. 491-538), the *duet* (I, mm. 305-328), the *duettino* (I, mm. 416-462), the s*extet* (I, mm. 1177-1208), the *hymn* (II, mm. 1097-1150) and others.

Jazz dance music makes up a fourth category. In the dressing-room scene in the first act, Berg has a jazz band play a ragtime (mm. 992-1020 and 1155-1168) and an English waltz (mm. 1040a-1094) behind the scene. Jazz here is clearly meant to evoke the ambience.

On-stage popular music plays an important role also in *Wozzeck*, specifically in the pub scene of the second act (landler, waltz) and in the bar scene of the third (polka on a honky-tonk piano).

A final group comprises the original forms Berg constructed for this opera, including primarily the *monoritmica* in the first act, the *tumultuoso* in the second, and the *allegretto* in the third act – three highly imaginative inventions on the leit-rhythm of the opera.

The palindromic forms likewise belong in this group, that is, structures whose second half is a retrograde of the first, such as the prologue, the sextet in the second act and the previously discussed ostinato.

In sum, it can be said that *Lulu*, like almost no other opera, presents an instructive compendium of old and new, traditional and futuristic forms, all of which are treated in an especially inventive way.

3.10.5 Parallel Situations and their Musical Treatment

> "The two-part tragedy was designed as a dance of death. The action constitutes a recurrence of the same. Each act leads to a catastrophe." Peter Unger and Hartmut Vinçon[608]

Wedekind's *Lulu* tragedy differs from classical drama in that the latter converges on a single catastrophe, whereas in the former catastrophes are the dramaturgical motor throughout. That explains the proximity of Wedekind's tragedy to the street ballad. There is an astonishing frequency of parallel situations in Wedekind's two dramas, which was bound to be especially enticing to Berg and prompted a corresponding musical treatment.

Parallel situations are composed analogously in the opera, in such a way that the viewer-listener is made aware of the parallelism. Berg creates musical relationships between different scenes of the opera: the leitmotif technique has a field day in *Lulu*, as the following examples will show.

Lulu brings disaster upon the three men with whom she has an intimate relationship: the painter commits suicide, Dr. Schön is killed, and Alwa is slain by the black. The parallelism in dramatic situation dictates an analogous musical construction.

While one cannot speak of repetition, there are highly significant, previously overlooked musical relations between the *Monoritmica* of the first act, the *Tumultuoso* of the second and the *Allegretto* of the third. All three forms can be called inventions on the rhythm

$$\tfrac{5}{4} \; \; \text{𝅗𝅥.} \; \; \text{𝅗𝅥.} \; \; \text{♪ 𝅗𝅥} $$

a rhythm that functions as a fate or death symbol in the opera.

In the *Monoritmica*, a long composition of 174 bars, there is not a single measure that does not contain the characteristic leit-rhythm. But the originality of the *Monoritmica* is also owing to the principle of progressive and regressive nuancing of the tempo used systematically here.

Of the two halves of the mirror-symmetric composition, one is an *accelerando*, the other a *ritardando*. Both halves undergo 18 different tempi, with the difference that while in the accelerando the increase in tempo occurs in stages, the tempo decrease in the ritardando is to take place "altogether uniformly."

Monoritmica

Diagram of Structure:

Accelerando			Ritardando		
T. 666	♪ =	76	T. 957	♩ =	38
T. 699 – 671	♪ =	84	T. 955	♩ =	42
T. 672 – 674	♪ =	92	T. 953	♩ =	46
T. 675 – 678	♪ =	100	T. 952	♩ =	50
T. 679 – 686	♪ =	108	T. 951	♩ =	54
T. 687 – 693	♪ =	120	T. 950a	♩ =	60
T. 694 – 701	♪ =	132	T. 949 – 950	♩ =	66
T. 702 – 709	♩ =	76	T. 945 – 948	♩ =	76
T. 710 – 716	♩ =	86	T. 938 – 944	♩ =	86
T. 717 – 723	♩ =	96	T. 928 – 937	♩ =	96
T. 724 – 731	♩ =	106	T. 922 – 927	♩ =	106
T. 732 – 738	♩ =	118	T. 920 – 921	♩ =	118
T. 739 – 746	♩ =	132	T. 915 – 919	♩ =	132
T. 747 – 765	𝅗𝅥 =	76	T. 910 – 914	𝅗𝅥 =	76
T. 766 – 786	♩ =	172	T. 885 – 909	𝅗𝅥 =	86
	(𝅗𝅥 =	86)			
T. 787 – 811	♩ =	192	T. 873 – 884	♩ =	192
	(𝅗𝅥 =	96)		(𝅗𝅥 =	96)
T. 812 – 832	𝅗𝅥 =	112	T. 853 – 872	𝅗𝅥 =	112
T. 833 – 842	𝅗𝅥 =	132	T. 843 – 852	𝅗𝅥 = 𝅗𝅥	

The peculiar musical structure is, of course, intended as a mirror of the dramatic situation. Whereas the accelerando expresses the growing excitement of the characters – the painter, learning from Dr. Schön about Lulu's past, loses his mind and commits suicide – the ritardando illustrates the gradual restoration of calm. The midpoint of the composition marks the moment when Lulu discovers the body of the painter and cries out abruptly. Another important moment is when Dr. Schön, having informed the police of the painter's suicide and cited "persecution mania" as the motive, regains his composure (stage direction in m. 944).

The *Tumultuoso* (mm. 553-604), the music of the scene that begins with the shooting of Dr. Schön, is a wholly independent composition, which, however, exhibits multiple textual and musical analogies with the *Monoritmica*. These result not only from the use of the leit-rhythm but also from the significant presence of the "*ur*-row" in both sections. In line with the new dramatic situation, the row of Dr. Schön plays an important role, but it gradually recedes in favor of the *ur*-series – in the same degree as Dr. Schön's life ebbs away.

Dr. Schön-Reihe II, T. 587–590

Urreihe II, T. 603/604

Three additional features are worth noting:

1. At several points during the *Tumultuoso*, the motif of persecution mania comes portentously to the fore, suggesting that the same paranoia that Dr. Schön previously ascribed to the painter now takes possession of him.
2. In the *Monoritmica*, the painter reacted to Dr. Schön's disclosures with a grievous "Oh God! Oh God!" (m. 679) – an exclamation to which Dr. Schön coolly replies: "No 'Oh God!', what's done is done!" Now, in the *Tumultuoso* (mm. 603/4), it is Dr. Schön who utters a groaning "Oh God, oh God!."
3. After the painter's suicide, toward the end of the *Monoritmica*, Dr. Schön quickly regained his cool. At the end of the *Tumultuoso*, after Schön's death, it is Lulu who rapidly recaptures her lost composure (stage direction in mm. 602/603).

The *Allegretto* in the third act (mm. 1058-1100), the music of the scene in which the black appears and kills Alwa, presents itself like an altogether new version of the *Monoritmica*." Like the latter, the *Allegretto*, too, constitutes an invention on the leit-rhythm, which is present in every bar and is also treated in *stretto*. And as in the *Monoritmica* with regard to the percussion group as a whole, so here, too, the jazz drum is given a prominent role.

Parallels in situation occur at every step in *Lulu*: a careful study will yield added insight into the personalities of the characters involved. A telling aspect is the way in which Lulu reacts to the deaths of her victims. Each time she suffers a kind of shock but quickly regains her composure and returns to business as usual. After the death of the public health officer Dr. Goll, she sings a *canzonetta* (mm. 258-283) significantly marked *Andantino grazioso* and indeed *grazioso* in character. Her reaction after the death of Dr. Schön is similar. She bends down to him and strokes his forehead, singing "Er hat es überstanden" (He is at rest). Immediately thereafter, the music shifts into a *quasi grazioso*, as Lulu implores Alwa in her arietta not to hand her over to the law. Her reaction to Alwa's death is similar. For a moment she is motionless. Then she hurries to the door, briefly checks her step at the sight of Alwa's body, and then quickly exits. At that point (III, mm. 1107/1108), the orchestra intones her fleet-footed "scale-like song theme."[609]

3.10.6 Lulu's Bond with Dr. Schön

> "In everything I have written until now I lack that *great love* to which [Gerhart] Hauptmann owes his powerful appeal." Wedekind in 1904[610]

Upon close study of Berg's music for *Lulu*, one can clearly distinguish several idioms in it: lyrical, dramatic, expressive, jazz – diverse stylistic levels take turns governing. Expressive traits are found especially in the coda to the sonata, a measured music that recurs with little change in all three acts. Most notable besides its polyphonic structure is its tendency toward forming tonal and pseudotonal harmonies.

Berg himself noted on a sketch sheet that the opera's fatalistic leit-rhythm in 5/4 time dictates the rhythmic division of the theme:[611]

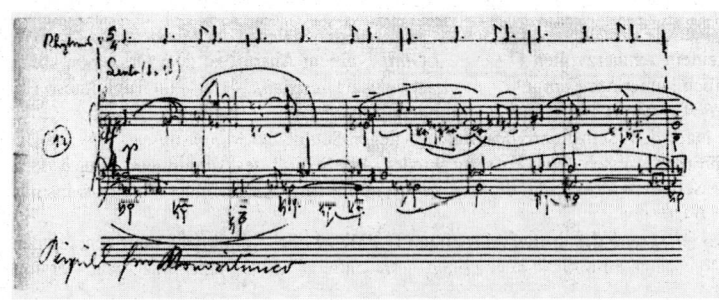

What is the semantics of this *Lento*? Willi Reich[612] was the first to point out that it accompanies words of Lulu's that "express her profound bond with Schön."[613] Hans Ferdinand Redlich spoke of a "fatalistic love melody," which "returns at every emotional turning-point in Lulu's love life."[614] More precise interpretive statements are possible if one assembles and compares all the places where the expressive music of this "coda" crops up.

I, mm. 615-624

(music excerpt: Lento ♩(♩ = 58), "Mei-nes Man-nes"... "Wenn ich einem Menschen auf dieser Welt angehöre, gehöre")

Lulu "My husband's" ...If I belong to any human being in this world, it is to you without you I would be – I won't say where. — You have taken me by the hand, have given me to eat, had me clothed, when I tried to steal your watch. Do you think something like that can be forgotten? Who in the whole world besides you has ever cared for me?

I, mm. 666-668

Twice as slow ♪ = 76

Painter *What's going on?*

Lulu *Speak up, why don't you!*

Painter *What's with you then?*

Lulu *None of your concern.*

Dr. Schön *Quiet!*

Lulu *He's sick of me.*

Dr. Schön *It had to be said finally ... I have to have my hands free at long last...*

Painter *Is that your idea of a joke?*

I, mm. 957-992

Grave ♩ = 38

Orchestral interlude

I, mm. 1356-1360

Lento (coda) ♩ = 46

Dr Schön   *Now ... comes ... the execution*
           (collapsing)

Jetzt... kommt... die Hin - - rich - tung.

II, mm. 82/83

Lulu (always on his neck)

Dei - ne Lie - be zu mir.

II, mm. 472-481

p cantabile e legatiss.

Ich mich schei - den las-sen!

Dr. Schön   How can there be divorce, if two people have grown one into the other, and
(continues):   half of the person is taken along.

III, mm. 1235-1247

($\quarternote$ = 58)

Jack	turns to Lulu again and gazes at her searchingly
Lulu	*Why do you suddenly stare at me so?*
Jack	*I judge you by the way in which you walk. I told myself she must be well-built, that one.*
Lulu	*How can one see something like that?*
Jack	*I even saw that you have a pretty mouth.*

From this survey one can see that the music of the coda and its theme appear wherever the emotional relationship between Lulu and Dr. Schön is being sounded. By Lulu's own confession, Dr. Schön is the only man with whom she really feels a close bond. But Dr. Schön, too, feels deeply attached to her. She, who should know, speaks of his "love" for her. He is aware that he is enslaved to Lulu and unable to escape her spell. "Now ... comes ... the execution," he calls, collapsing, at the end of the first act, after Lulu had elicited a promise of marriage from him. But he later also professes his inability to get divorced from her: "How can there be divorce, if two people have grown one into the other, and half of the person is taken along?"

The bond between Lulu and Dr. Schön is thus mutual, and Berg's repeated reiteration of the expressive music of the coda endowed it with a depth dimension it doesn't really have in Wedekind. What Wedekind said he missed in his plays, the "great love," Berg did insert in his opera.

3.10.7 The Catastrophe Rhythm and the Fatal Five

> "The very thing that is the death of us renews her strength and health." Countess Geschwitz (*Lulu* II/2)

The bar scene in *Wozzeck* is composed as an invention on a rhythm – a "main rhythm" that, as Berg explained in his Oldenburg lecture (Schr. 286), underlies the scene and, "detectable in every measure," guarantees its unity. It is first heard in the previous scene-change music (mm. 109-121), the music around the ominous b, the note symbolizing the death of Marie. It is clear that the main rhythm here functions semantically as a symbol of catastrophe.

A main rhythm (marked RH) plays a revealing role also in *Lulu*. Here, however, it is not confined to a single scene but counts among the structural principles governing the entire opera. Its structure is syncopated, evinces four beats, and is fitted into a latent 5/4 or 5/8 meter.

With regard to the uses of the main rhythm in the opera, three main categories can be distinguished. It functions, to begin with, as an invariable clamp connecting the ends and beginnings of the three acts with each other. It opens both the second and the third act, and is also heard at the beginning of the circus music in the Prologue to the first act, after the animal tamer has exhorted the audience to visit the menagerie.

I, mm. 9/10

Ponderous chords in the characteristic leit-rhythm conclude all three acts, thus appearing to seal the dramatic action.

I, mm 1360/1361

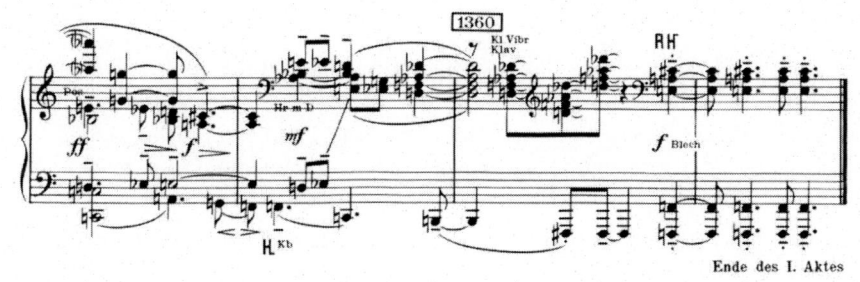

[musical notation: Ende des I. Aktes]

The main rhythm secondly serves as a principal element in the construction of the dramatic forms we have discussed: the *monoritmica*, the *tumultuoso* and the *allegretto*. In addition, it appears as a leitmotif at numerous critical moments. Thus it is intoned after the death of the public health officer Dr. Goll in the arioso of the first act, when the painter addresses the body: "Would I could trade places with you, dead one" (m. 331) and when somewhat later he calls out to it to "Awake!" (mm. 336/337 and 338). It is likewise present when Alwa broods about Lulu's eventful life in the dressing-room scene and recalls the "first scene" of the tragedy, the public health officer (mm. 1100-1103).

If one takes every passage in which the main rhythm can be ascertained into account, it clearly has the semantic function of a symbol of catastrophe. Significantly, it underlines the words of the Countess Geschwitz quoted as a motto above: "The very thing that is the death of us renews her strength and health" (II, mm. 740-744).

One should also note in this connection the latent tie of the main rhythm to a quintuple meter. Oddly, it was not discovered until 1978 that the number five has an ominous meaning in *Lulu*.[615] It appears wherever doom is about to strike. To cite some examples: the main rhythm is frequently notated in 5/4 time. The *Monoritmica*, at the climax of which the painter commits suicide, is based "on a 5/4 rhythm" according to Berg. At the conclusion of the first scene of Act II (*Tumultuoso*), Lulu fires five shots at Dr Schön as a "response" to his urging her to shoot herself. Berg composed Dr. Schön's challenge as a five-strophe aria and based the "Song of Lulu," which contains the title-figure's self-defense, on a text comprised of five sentences:

> If people have killed themselves on account of me, that does not diminish my own worth.
>
> You knew fully as well why you took me to wife as I knew why I took you for a husband.

You have cheated on your best friends with me; you could not well cheat also on yourself with me.

If you sacrifice your old age to me, you have had my entire youth in return. –

I never wanted to seem anything else in the world except what people took me for; and people have never in the world taken me for anything other than what I am.

In Wedekind, this text comprises seven sentences; Berg symptomatically reduced it to five!

Two additional examples: the *Funèbre* played in Act III after Alwa's death is again in 5/4 time; and five, finally, is also the number of Lulu's victims – the public health officer, the painter Schwarz, Dr. Schön, Alwa, and the Countess Geschwitz.

3.10.8 Persecution Mania

After his marriage to Lulu, Dr. Schön, like the painter Schwarz before him, acquires a persecution complex. His fears of being betrayed are well-founded, as Lulu is maintaining several liaisons while married to Dr. Schön – with the athlete, with Schigolch, with the prep-school student, with the valet and with the Countess Geschwitz – and is about to start an affair with Schön's own son Alwa.

The motif of persecution mania recurs in leitmotif manner in the first scene of Act II. It is composed of the five (!) notes e-a-b-c-f but also occurs in transpositions and repeatedly also appears as a chord. It is first heard in mm. 203/204. When asked by the athlete, "Is he [Dr. Schön] not at the Exchange?" Lulu replies: "He is, but he is also quite paranoid –":

Somewhat later (mm. 419/420), Lulu tries to get Dr. Schön to believe that he suffers from persecution mania. The *Tumultuoso* that introduces this passage is derived from the notes of the persecution motif.

The motif occurs at several points in the score when Dr. Schön's suspicion becomes certainty that another admirer of Lulu's has made himself at home in his house. It is sounded in the *Tumultuoso* (mm. 338-343), when Dr. Schön becomes aware of the athlete and takes aim at him with his revolver. Later, after Lulu's five gun shots, the motif plunges over several octaves from high to low (mm. 555-557), while the student, "leaping with a loud din out from under the table," catches the falling Dr. Schön, whereupon the latter stammers: "And …there … is …yet another." The motif is also intoned in m.

606 when the dying Dr. Schön stiffly rears up at the sight of the Countess Geschwitz and whispers: "The Devil …."

The persecution motif refers primarily to Dr. Schön, but does not do exclusively so. In mm. 371-377 it undergirds the fear of the athlete of being killed by Dr. Schön, and it also sounds at the beginning of the ostinato (mm. 650-655) as a signal that the police are in pursuit of the murderess Lulu.

3.10.9 Alwa = Alban?

"One could certainly write an interesting opera about that one [Lulu]." Alwa (*Lulu* I/3)[616]

"What sort of work are you doing? You have written a horror opera, in which the calves of my bride are the two main figures, and which no court theater will perform." Rodrigo to Alwa (*Lulu* II/2)[617]

"We can be certain that a man who lived as much in cipher symbolism as Berg did might well have been profoundly shaken by the consonance of the names Alwa and Alban." Ernst Krenek[618]

In Wedekind's *Lulu* tragedy, Alwa, Dr. Schön's son, is a sensitive writer who succumbs to Lulu's irresistible charm. His father's death so cuts him to the quick that he is unable to write another line thereafter. Even so, he falls for his father's murderess. Tilly Wedekind, the writer's wife and the first actress to portray Lulu, testifies that in Alwa her husband had partly drawn an ironic portrait of himself.[619]

Berg transformed Alwa into a composer and gave him autobiographic traits, surely not without self-irony. As the sketches reveal (28/III fol. 33), the Rondo was initially to do justice to the three sides of Alwa's personality: the editor, the artist, and the lover. Later on, Berg decided on the sequence a) lover, b) editor and c) artist, adding "Wozzeck composer."[620] In the dressing-room scene of the first act, Alwa meditates about the adored Lulu and recites to the notes of his tone row the words: "One could certainly write an interesting opera about that one." This is accompanied by a witty self-quotation in the orchestra – the opening chords of *Wozzeck* (I, mm. 1095-1098):

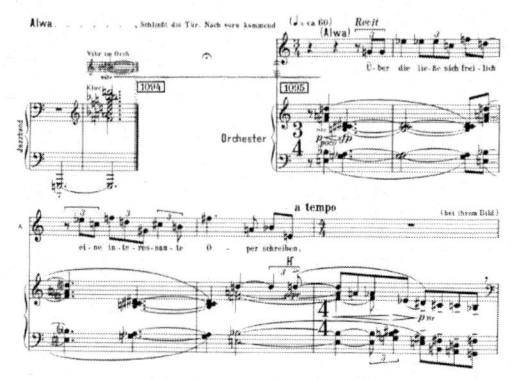

Is Berg's ironic identification with Alwa a mere gesture, or does it conceal a deeper meaning? To be able to answer this question would require a careful study of the Alwa music. What is striking is its throughout soft, lyrical effect. In his musical portrait, Alwa seems like a soft counter-image to the "brute" Dr. Schön. It is quite possible that Berg discovered traits of his own personality in Alwa. It is in any case no coincidence that Alwa's music in the first scene of the second act has the tempo marking *Andante* and bears the metronome notation ♩ = 69, the triple of Berg's fatal number of 23. This *Andante*, culminating in Alwa's declaration of love to Lulu, the wife of his father, is conceived as a great colloquy, which is time and again interrupted – by the repeated entrances of the valet, by the appearance of Dr. Schön on the gallery, and by that of Rodrigo. The five dialogues into which the colloquy is thus divided are arranged according to the principle of climactic *steigerung*, as Berg's sketches indicate.[621] The andante is composed of three clearly defined themes (x y z), which in the cantabile are intertwined contrapuntally. The first of these themes, the actual Alwa theme, is developed from his row. The second theme prefers close intervals, whereas the third, the theme of the fervent hand kiss, is distinguished by wide intervals:

Willi Reich called the Rondo the "lyrical center piece" of the opera and saw in it "the profession of the special bond" between Berg and Lulu, "his last operatic figure, whose reflected gleam still lit up his final fever fantasies."[622]

In a sketch for the *Symphonic Pieces*, Berg himself characterized the Rondo by the motto "How Alwa, the artist, sees [Lulu], and how one must see her in order to comprehend that she is loved so much."[623]

From this note, too, we can conclude that Berg identified with Alwa the artist. In Lulu, however, he evidently saw, on the one hand, a female Don Juan, who destroys whomever she comes in contact with, and, on the other hand, an immensely charming, lovable woman, who casts her spell over one and all.

3.10.10 Music in Slow Motion

Berg, as we know, was a fan of film and took a lively interest in the details of cinematic technique. Already in the sketches for *Lulu*, he had planned a "sizable film with film music" for the "scene change" between the two scenes of the second act (28/III fol. 23 verso). The sketches also contain the striking phrase "Music in slow motion" (28/III fol. 25). What could have been meant by that?

To answer that question, we might start with the directions for the stage set in the printed libretto. The action in both scenes of the second act takes place in a "magnificent hall" in the house of Dr. Schön. But there is a large temporal gap between the two scenes. The silent film accompanied by the ostinato shows, quasi in time-lapse motion, the dramatic events from Lulu's arrest to her eventual liberation. After the latter, she returns to her previous place of residence. But as the directions about the set also indicate, the situation has changed radically. "The gallery," the libretto states, "is completely draped, likewise the balcony window stage-right (heavy curtains) and the portière stage-left." There is to be, "in contrast to the earlier scene, a general lifelessness, dustiness, unoccupied quality to the room, which is artificially sealed off from the daylight outside."[624]

This "lifelessness" is also reflected in the music. Although there are multiple links, scenic as well as musical, between the two scenes, the formerly vivid and resplendent is bathed in a dim, dull light. A more detailed juxtaposition of the two scenes might look like this:

1st scene	2nd scene
mm. 94-120	~ mm. 788-814
Slow ♩ (= 56)	*Largo* ♩ = 56-66

(Schigolch, Athlete, Student)   (Schigolch, Countess Geschwitz, Athlete)
Quasi slow motion of the corresponding part in the 1st scene of this act, mm. 94-120

mm. 145-172   ~ mm. 953-1000
L'istesso tempo (but triple time)   *quadruple time* (8/4) *melodrama*
(Lulu, Student, Schigolch, Athlete)   (Lulu, Schigolch, Athlete)

mm. 243-337   → mm. 1001 ff.
Dialogue Rondo Alwa-Lulu   *a tempo* (♩ = 69)
with insertions   continuation of the Rondo (Lulu, Alwa)

Of primary importance is Berg's note on the *Largo* of the second scene (mm. 788-814) to the effect that it is to be understood as a "quasi slow motion of the corresponding part in the first scene" (mm. 94-120. The two passages largely coincide without being identical. But the tempo is twice as slow, which gives the music an unreal quality. Berg's proximity to surrealism is especially marked here.

The two sections correspond very closely. Both feature Lulu's satellites: Schigolch, the Athlete, and the Student or else the Countess Geschwitz. The second scene, however, seems like a matte mirror image of the first: all the clan is gone. Schigolch, who even in the first scene appeared "always short-winded (asthmatic)," now drags along laboriously, repeatedly stops and yawns. The athlete, who in the first scene came tromping down the stairs carrying the student on his arm, now lounges idly on the sofa. The student, with his fidgety legs, is replaced by the Countess, who sits, deeply bedded in pillows, in an armchair and has trouble rising from it.

Similar observations can be made in comparing Lulu's appearances in the two scenes (mm. 145-172 and 953-1000). Willi Reich justly said that the melodrama accompanying Lulu's entrance in the second scene corresponded in "slow motion" to the music of her appearance in the first.[625] The music of the first scene is indeed picked up again in the second, though the correspondence is a far cry from being one of identity. The harmonies of the first section of the second scene are transposed downward by a whole tone.

Melodic figures from the first section now reappear in rhythmic augmentation. The scale-like theme of Lulu, for example (mm. 153-156)

[Musical notation: Lulu — "Sie sind in ei-ne net-te Ge-sell-schaft ge-ra-ten"]

now appears in the following form (mm. 961-965):

[Musical notation: Fl.]

Here, too, the thoroughgoing change of the musical character is dictated by a change in dramatic-scenic situation. In the first scene of the second act Lulu enters quasi in full bloom: in a ball dress, "in wide décolletage, with flowers at her breast." In the second scene, she gives the impression of being ill. Propped on Schigolch's arm, she slowly drags herself down the stairs, pretending an infirmity in order to fool and get rid of Rodrigo. Only after he has left does she stop play-acting and "in the most cheerful tone" extols her regained freedom. At this point she turns altogether to Alwa. The Rondo of the first scene is now continued and ends in the concluding hymn that seals the lovers' union.

3.10.11 From the Spoken to the Sung Word

When Berg was working on the composition of *Wozzeck*, he took care to treat the human voice in his opera in as nuanced a manner as possible. Every kind of utterance – ordinary speech, pure song, and the typically Schönbergian *sprechgesang* (speech song) – is utilized. Peter Petersen, in his definitive study of *Wozzeck*, has distinguished no fewer than 65 different gradations between singing and speaking.[626] The sphere of song extends from the cantabile to virtuoso coloratura. In his article "Die Stimme in der Oper" (Voice in Opera), first published in 1928, Berg, who gave much thought to the question whether bel canto was reconcilable with the principles of modernist opera, remarked that he had "by no means foregone" any "opportunity to deploy *bel canto*" in *Wozzeck*.[627]

The polar opposite of pure song is "ordinary speech," which Berg, in the preface to both the score and the piano score of *Wozzeck*, defined as "conversation conducted quite naturally/realistically to the music underneath it." He noted that he had used it in four scenes of his work: the 3rd scene of Act I and the 4th and fifth scene of Act III.

A third area between pure song and regular speech is the melodramatic treatment of the voice, the so-called "rhythmic declamation" that Schönberg introduced in the choral speeches in the *Glückliche Hand* (1910-1913) and the *Pierrot Lunaire* melodramas (1912). Berg was downright proud to have been the one to use it "for the first time, and for a long time as the only one in an opera" (in *Wozzeck*), and to have "given so much room" to it. He regarded this "melodically, rhythmically and dynamically fixed way of speaking" as "a perfect complement and an attractive contrast to the "sung word."

When Berg wrote the essay "The Voice in Opera" in 1928, his mind was already occupied with *Lulu*. He reflected on his experiences with vocal treatment in *Wozzeck* and took stock with a view to further increasing the expressive possibilities already gained. It is against this background that we should understand the following statement: "It may be that not all the possibilities of voice are equally exploited in my opera (I just realized that it contains in fact only a dozen bars of recitative), but the opportunity to deploy *bel canto* is by no means foregone." In the score of *Lulu*, at any rate, much more space is given to the recitative and the arioso than in *Wozzeck*.

The most important result of a close study of the vocal treatment in *Lulu*, however, is the realization that the system of vocal potential here is even more subtly gradated than in *Wozzeck*. No shade is omitted, and Berg is strikingly fond of transitions from one gradation to the next. Some passages are designed according to the principle of intensification (*steigerung*) in terms of their vocal treatment. An instructive example of this is presented by the already cited sequence of five dialogues between Alwa and Lulu in the first scene of Act II, in which the recitation of the singers strikingly rises from ordinary speech to *molto cantabile*. To sketch that development in more detail:

In the first dialogue, Alwa and Lulu speak without any orchestral accompaniment (II, mm. 241/242). Normal speech is also the mode of the second dialogue, except that the speakers are now accompanied by the orchestra, which intones the first Rondo theme (mm. 243-249). There follows, quasi as a parenthesis, a chorale episode with recitative interjections by Alwa, Lulu and the valet (mm. 250-261). The third dialogue between Lulu and Alwa is governed by Schönberg's melodramatic chanting (mm. 262-274). In the first half of the fourth dialogue, the expression marks *sung parlando* (mm. 275-280) and *poco cantabile* (mm. 281 ff.) are specified. The fifth and last dialogue, finally, reaches the highest rung of the ladder, the *molto cantabile* (mm. 319 ff.).

A similarly but even more subtly gradated manner of recitation is given to the animal tamer in the Prologue. In several stages, it describes an arc from spoken word to cantabile and then returns, likewise in stages, to the starting point – yet another striking example of mirror-symmetric structuring in Berg. The individual recitative nuances in the first part of the tripartite piece are as follows: spoken word (mm. 6-8), rhythmic declamation (melodrama) (9-16), *half-sung* (16-20), *sung parlando* (21-41). For the middle part of the Prologue (mm. 44-62), in which a pot-bellied stagehand is to carry the singer of the role of Lulu in her Pierrrot costume to the front of the curtain, is prescribed as *cantabile* throughout. The gradation in the third part of the Prologue is palindromic: *parlando* (mm. 63-67), *semi-spoken* (68-72), melodrama (73-79) and spoken word (80-82).

3.11 The Violin Concerto:
Requiem for Manon and Berg's "Farewell" to the World

> "The Violin Concerto is, after all, Alban Berg's farewell to this world, a dolorous-wistful-resigned language (the last), on everything that was dear to him, a purely personal confession of his relation to the world – to death – to God." Helene Berg on August 12, 1958[628]

3.11.1 The Biographical Background:
Manon Gropius and Alma Mahler

Berg composed most of his works on his own accord. Only the concert aria *Der Wein* and the Violin Concerto were commissioned. In February of 1935, the American violinist Louis Krasner turned to him requesting that he compose a violin concerto for him. The request was inopportune for Berg, as he was then fully occupied with the orchestration of the third act of *Lulu*. But after lengthy hesitation, he accepted the offer for pecuniary reasons.[629] His financial situation was precarious at the time: he had no income, had to incur debts and even entertained the idea of selling his forest house, to which he was deeply attached. The honorarium offered (roughly 1500 dollars) was thus something he could well use. He was unhappy at the thought of having to interrupt the orchestration of *Lulu* for five, six months. Even so, he did all kinds of "preliminary work" for the Violin Concerto, as he told his American client on March 28, 1935.[630] On the other hand, according to Willi Reich,[631] he took his time with the execution, and was undecided about the form the work should have.

It took a tragic event in the house of Alma Mahler-Werfel – the Mahler Villa on the Hohe Warte – to set off the decisive creative impulse in him. Manon

Gropius, called Mutzi, Alma's daughter from her marriage with Walter Gropius, had been stricken with poliomyelitis and was confined to a wheelchair. On Holy Saturday, April 20, 1935, she fell gravely ill and died two days later on Easter Monday.[632] The event deeply affected Berg. On April 24, he wrote to Erich Kleiber: "Your 'Happy Easter' wishes found me at the ghastliest of Easters. On Holy Saturday, around noon, Manon, Alma's daughter, fell violently ill: unending vomiting, followed soon by cardiac insufficiency. On Easter Monday, a death-struggle commenced, and in the afternoon she expired. She will be buried today in the Heiligenstadt cemetery..."[633]

Manon was interred in the cemetery, not of Heiligenstadt, but of Grinzing. The funeral scene has been immortalized literarily by Elias Canetti, who had a great many resentments against Alma. Canetti had taken it amiss that Alma had affianced her already paralyzed daughter to a young man, in order to give her the illusion of a possible recovery. He was also offended by Alma's parading her grief over the loss of her beloved daughter so theatrically at the funeral: "She wept, it struck me that her tears, too, were of an unusual format."[634]

To fully understand the situation, one needs to know that Berg and his wife knew and loved Manon, who impressed many as a girl of angelic beauty. In a letter of condolence addressed to Alma probably on April 23, Helene wrote:

> Mutzi was not only your child – she also was mine. We should not lament that God has called her to Him, for she was an angel. We must be thankful that she gave us 18 years of happiness by her lovely earthly sojourn, and we can still have that, for the bright spirit that descended to us with her can never be lost to us."[635]

(Manon Gropius, born on October 16, 1916, lived to the age of eighteen and a half.)

Berg himself seems to have decided soon after Manon's death to dedicate the Violin Concerto to her memory, in order to provide consolation to the grief-stricken mother and to give expression to his sympathy with her. In an undated condolence letter, he wrote to Alma that he would not try in a letter "to find words where language fails." "However: one day, before yet this dreadful year is over, may to you and Franz resound from a score that will be dedicated

To the memory of an angel

what I feel and for which today I cannot find expression."[636]

For many years, Berg and his wife had been close friends with Alma and Franz Werfel. In her diary for July 14, 1926, Alma referred to them as their "closest friends – as "difficult people, but capable of sacrifice to the utmost."637 In his letters to his wife, Berg, too, again and again speaks of Alma. He tells her about frequent visits to Alma and about lively conversations with her and with Werfel.638 He was not only bound in friendship to Alma but also felt obligated to her. He could naturally not forget that she had made possible the printing of the piano score of *Wozzeck*, in thanks for which he had dedicated the opera to her. After Manon Gropius's tragic death, he is said to have remarked to his wife: "I shall dedicate this already begun violin concerto to Manon's memory and thus have an opportunity for once to return a favor to Alma."639

Photograph 11: Manon Gropius

(with kind permission of the Alban Berg Foundation Vienna)

3.11.2 A "Birthday Homage" for Alma: Willi Reich's Hermeneutic "Paraphrase"

In previous discussions and analyses of the Violin Concerto, a decisive factor has remained unheeded: the fact that Berg actually composed the concerto for Alma Mahler-Werfel. Although the official dedicatee is Louis Krasner, the work is secretly dedicated to Alma, who was to observe her 56th birthday on August 31, 1935 – her first birthday after Manon's death. On August 30, Helene sent her a letter imploring her not to mourn any longer.

> We humans [she wrote], who live in darkness here, cannot judge why we have just this or that fate. The spiritual background of everything that happens here we will be able to grasp only at a much later time. Our beloved angel of light may have important things to accomplish for herself in the beyond.

Helene closed her letter with the important words:

> Perhaps Alban succeeded after all with what he has been preparing for this day for weeks, and what will certainly reach you indirectly, and what represents at least an outward sign of months of his thinking (and feeling) about Mutzi and you.[640]

Helene Berg and Willi Reich concur in reporting that Berg conceived and completed the Violin Concerto in a "feverish tempo." And indeed, no larger work of his was written in so short a time. He probably started to sketch the work in earnest after April 22 of 1935, the day on which Manon died. On Juli 15, he reported the completion of the composition to Webern.[641] That is to say, the particello was finished on that day.[642] The orchestration probably took a little less than four weeks. According to Berg's own statement in a letter to Rudolf Kolisch, he completed the full score on August 12.

However many reasons for this hurry might be cited, one of the weightiest was in all likelihood the wish to present Alma Mahler-Werfel with the completed concerto on the thirty-first of August – a goal Berg achieved. He not only co-signed Helene's letter to Alma, but he saw to it that an analysis of the Violin Concerto written by Willi Reich appeared in the *Neue Wiener Journal* of August 31 as a "birthday homage" to Alma. The analysis reads as follows:

> To the extent that a paraphrase in words is at all possible, the "tone" – a favorite expression of Berg's – of the work in its entirety can be roughly rendered as follows. From the up-and-down hovering, preluding of the Introduction, tender andante melodies begin to dawn, which condense into a grazioso middle portion and then dissolve again into the undulations of the opening. Above the same background rises the beginning of the Allegro-Scherzo that fixates the vision of the lovely girl in the form of a graceful round dance, which assumes now a tender, *dreamy* character, now the earthy one of a Carinthian folk tune. – A wild *shriek* of the orchestra introduces the second main part, which commences as a free, stormy cadence. Irresistibly, the demonic fury rushes toward catastrophe, interrupted only by a brief moment of bated repose. *Groans* and piercing *cries for help* become audible in the orchestra, choked off by the doom approaching in suffocating rhythm. At length, over a long pedal point,

> a gradual breaking down. – Then, at the moment of intensest anxiety, the chorale rises gravely and solemnly in the solo violin, each strophe answered in organ-like registration by the woodwinds with the original harmonies of the classic model. Artful variations follow, but they always remain based on the *cantus firmus* of the original chorale melody, which rises *misterioso* from the bass, while the solo violin intones a slowly upward-struggling "song of lamentation." Ever louder grows the dirge, the soloist, with a visible gesture, making himself the leader of the entire violin and viola section, which, in a mighty crescendo, chimes in bit by bit with his melody and then gradually separates from it again. – An indescribably sad recapitulation of the Carinthian folk tune, fading in *as if from far away (but much slower than the first time)* reminds once more of the image of the winsome girl, and then the chorale, harshly harmonized and overarched by ever-renewed traces of the dirge in the solo violin, concludes the mournful farewell.[643]

Reich stated in 1963 that his text had been prompted and authorized by Berg himself. A study of the sketches confirms this statement. They contain several programmatic catchwords that also play a key role in Reich's text – the terms *verträumt*, *Aufschrei*, *Stöhnen*, and *Rufe* (dreamy, shriek, groans, cries [for help]). That suggests that Reich wrote his "paraphrase" after detailed oral programmatic explications given by Berg.[644] A semantic analysis of the music likewise leads to the conclusion that Reich's text explicated the course of the musico-programmatic contents correctly and fittingly.

Berg's wish that the composition of the Violin Concerto would give pleasure to Alma was fulfilled. On September 1, 1935, he wrote to Reich:

> Before I had even read the article, I received a telegram with the following text: "Only beloved people! With your immeasurable act of love you have given me the only birthday present that could still give me joy. My longing for you is unbearably intense. I kiss Alban's blessed hand and Helene's dear mouth. Forever and always yours, Alma." - I was of course very, very happy. We have once again hit upon the right thing. My thanks to you, too, dear friend![645]

The secret dedication to Alma, however, is of particular significance for a deeper understanding of the work: the Violin Concerto is, along with the *Three Pieces for Orchestra* op. 6, the chief document of Berg's creative reception of Mahler. It contains a number of momentous allusions to Mahler symphonies – especially to the head movement of the Ninth – that Alma was bound to catch.

3.11.3 In Berg's Workshop

> "I have actually been as industrious as never before in my life. Add to that that the work gave me more and more pleasure." Berg to Louis Krasner, July 16, 1935[646]

> "Yesterday I finished the Violin Concerto; the whole work (incl. score) thus took me only three months." Berg to Rudolf Kolisch, August 13, 1935[647]

The chief sources of information about the genesis of the Violin Concerto are Berg's calendar of 1935 (signature: F 21 Berg 432/XV) and two bundles of sketch sheets (F 21 Berg 85/I and II).[648] Berg's calendar for 1935 (*Hesses Musiker-Kalender 1935*, 57th annual ed.) contains on pp. 159-162 the earliest notes about the work. They concern above all the overall plan of the concerto and the shaping of the solo part.

These notes indicate, to begin with, that from the start Berg had remarkably precise ideas about the shape and structure of the work. Although a comparison with the final version shows that in working out the composition he deviated from his early ideas in countless details, the basic features of the original conception remained intact. Thus it was certain from the start that the work would be divided into two parts and each part would have two movements. The tempo markings and in part also the time signatures and the character of the movements coincide with those of the final version. The first movement was planned as an *Andante*, it was to exhibit "mixed measures" and to be a "freely rhapsodic" kind of introduction; the final version begins the Andante in 4/4 time but switches to 2/4 time at m. 11, and its beginning has the character of a prelude. The second movement, *Allegretto*, was to be based on a "dreamy landler melody" – Berg even had a vague notion of writing variations on a "Carinthian folk song"; there are no variations in the finished composition of the Allegretto, but the "Carinthian folk tune" is built into it. The second part of the concerto was to consist of an *Adagio* designed as a chorale and a chorale adaptation and an *Allegro* shaped as a cadenza; in the end, Berg reversed the two movements, without, however, greatly changing their character.

For the Allegretto and the Andante, Berg had originally planned an a-b-a form. He dropped those plans – the movements of the final version exhibit far more complex structures. In a number of cases, however, Berg realized the dynamics design originally envisioned. Thus the Allegretto closes piano, while the Adagio is composed as a gigantic crescendo-decrescendo arc.

The sketches reveal, secondly, that Berg planned from the start to base the Allegretto on a Carinthian folksong and to structure the Adagio as a chorale arrangement. There can be no doubt that the "landler melody" originally chosen is the one Berg then actually used – the Carinthian folksong, as Herwig Knause has shown,[649] "Ein Vogel auf'm Zwetschgenbaum" (A Bird in the Plum Tree). The chorale melody originally envisioned, however, was not the Ahle-Bach chorale "Es ist genug" (It is Enough), as Berg, on p. 159 of the calendar, had jotted down a chorale melody of his own invention,

and had also considered treating it as a canon. A second chorale melody of his own is found on fol. 35 verso of the second bundle of sketches (see below). This finding and additional observations prove that Berg decided only at a late stage of the composition to adapt the Bach chorale.

The notes in the sketches also prompt the conclusion that Berg approached the composition of the Violin Concerto with some definite extra-musical (programmatic) intentions. The Allegretto was from the start to have a "merry" character; the "landler melody" at its base was to be "dreamy." The Adagio then was conceived as a "dream": Berg must from the start have had some religious vision in mind.

Additional notations in the calendar (on pp. 159 and 160) make it evident that Berg thought from the beginning about the virtuoso development of the solo part. For the cadenza, for example, he jotted down a small-scale figure of four sixteenths (a^1-g^1-a^1-b^1), from which a wide-ranging figure on all four strings of the violin was to be developed. He had, moreover, planned to furnish the solo part with chains of trills, mordents, syncopations and echoes ("Question and answer (echo) by shifts of position").

The famous twelve-tone series is not noted down in the calendar (which supports the surmise that these notations are older than the sketches). But on p. 160, there is an eleven-note series constructed from the C major and the G^b-major scale.

And on the next staff there are unhappily faded notes, which at least make it evident that Berg had planned to construct thematic characters from this "row."

The next question is: at what point did Berg decide to build the Bach chorale "Es ist genug" into the concerto?

Willi Reich, who was the first to provide detailed information about the genesis of the Violin Concerto, and who belonged to Berg's inner circle, maintained that the idea of including Bach's chorale had not been there from the beginning. Already in 1937, he wrote: "In its general outline, Berg must have had the form of the piece in mind from the start; decisions about details he then made in the course of working on it, such as the incorporation of the chorale and the structuring of the beginning of the second part, which was originally planned as a sonata movement, as a fully composed cadenza."[650]

Hans Ferdinand Redlich, on the other hand, proposed the contrary thesis that all of the concerto's themes evolved from the melodic-harmonic givens of the chorale's melody.[651]

The matter is a complicated one because there is a close connection between the twelve-tone row on which the work is based and the initium of the chorale. Reich already pointed out that the row consists of a chain of overlapping minor and major triads and a whole-tone sequence, and drew attention to the fact that the last four notes of the row coincide with the initium of the chorale.

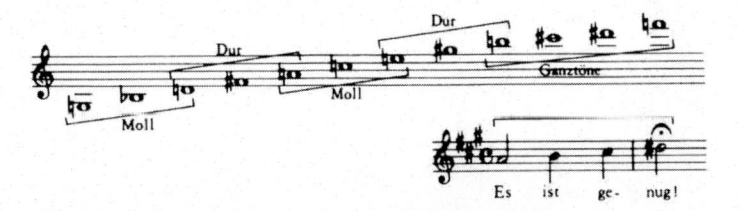

A reader who takes Reich's statement seriously that Berg only later decided to incorporate the chorale would have to regard this conformity as fortuitous.

In 1963, Reich made additional statements regarding this complex of questions. Letters and personal communications of Berg's cited by Reich supposedly indicate that "the idea to include the chorale took concrete form in Berg only when the composition had already progressed quite far." Reich reports the following:

After having told me about the quick progression of his work on June 7 (1935), he wrote the following day: "Please send me (by way of a loan) the *St. Matthew Passion* (score or piano score) and, if you have it, a chorale collection (I need a chorale melody for my work: please keep it confidential!)." When I visited him a week later in the Forest House, he showed me in the collection I had sent him, *Sechzig Choralgesänge von Johann Sebastian Bach* (selected and introduced by Hermann Roth, Drei Masken Verlag, Munich, 1920; the chorale selected by Berg bears the number 55) the chorale *Es ist genug!...*, saying: "Isn't this remarkable: the first four notes of the chorale (a whole-tone sequence) correspond exactly to the last four notes of the twelve-tone row with which I am constructing the entire concerto?" – And on July 1, he wrote me: "I hope to finish the composition by mid-July, and the score before the Carlsbad Music Festival. I *hope*, and please knock on wood three times! – And please, please, copy the *text* of the chorale *Es ist genug! So nimm, Herr, meinen Geist* from your chorale booklet. I forgot to do that (Only the text!) I did copy the music for myself."[652]

The sketches now completely prove Reich's statements and enable us to give them even greater precision. Berg had originally conceived the plan of basing the second part of the concerto on a chorale melody of his own invention and only much later had the idea of adapting the Bach chorale. As we have seen, he sketched such a four-bar melody already in the calendar. On fol. 35 verso of the second bundle of sketches, he then notated a thirteen-bar, four-line chorale melody (derived from the twelve-tone row and expressly marked *chorale*) but eventually rejected it, evidently because it did not appear suitable to him:

On fol. 34 verso of the second bundle, the Ahle-Bach chorale melody "Es ist genug" is then noted down, in A major, which is also the key in which Bach wrote the chorale. Berg did not write the melody out completely but divided it into three sections, supplying each section with a repeat sign. He dispensed with inserting the complete text but merely jotted down several words and phrases, such as the incipit "Es ist genug," the word "gefällt" (pleases), and the verses "Ich fahr ins Himmelhaus" (I go to my heavenly home) and "mein großer Jammer bleibt darnieden" (my great affliction stays below). Some numbers above or under several of the notes suggest that he tried to construe some connections between the chorale melody and segments of the underlying twelve-tone row. Thus the four last notes of the chorale melody accord with the inversion of the row from the eighth to the eleventh note:

On fol. 6 verso of the second bundle the complete text of the chorale then appears in typescript on a pasted-on slip of paper, together with the name of Johann Rudolf Ahle and the bracketed date 1662. Conceivably the sticker is the very piece of paper on which Willi Reich had written and sent the chorale text Berg had asked for. Theses findings show clearly that Reich's statements are correct, that is to say, that Berg decided at a fairly advanced stage of the work to base the second part of the concerto on the Bach chorale, and that the connection between the chorale's initium and the whole-tone sequence of the dodecaphonic row is a happy coincidence. An entry on fol. 3 verso of the first bundle of sketches can also be made to harmonize with such an interpretation of the situation. At the very top of this page, the row is notated in retrograde inversion beginning with g. Berg numbered the notes g-a-b-c#, which form a whole-tone sequence, with the numbers 12, 11, 10 and 9 and added a bracket. Two staves down, he then notated the beginning of the Bach chorale, beginning with b♭, and labeled it *Adagio-Melodie*. The first four notes of the chorale correspond to the first four notes of the row in its retrograde inversion.

Of importance, finally, is another entry in the first bundle. Folio 6 recto contains a most interesting table of "Chords and Cadences," which Berg, trying out every possible combination, extracted from the row (see Sketches 6). At the beginning of the sixth staff, he noted down a sequence of three chords, the B major triad, the second chord (third-inversion seventh chord) of A major and the ninth chord of B♭ major and, following the last of these chords, the final notes of the chorale f-d-c-b♭ with the text "Es ist genug." This "chorale quotation" seems to permit the conclusion that the table of the "chords and cadences" came about only after Berg had decided to use the Bach chorale as a basis for his work.

303

Sketches 6: Sketches for the Violin Concerto

Austrian National Library, Music Collection, Fonds 21 Berg 85/1 fol. 6 Table of the "Chords and Cadences"

To recapitulate: the facts cited indicate that the plan to base the Adagio on the Bach chorale was definitely adopted only on June 15, 1935. On June 7, Berg was still rather irresolute how to shape the final movement, as is clear from his note to Webern: "I'm at a standstill at the moment: a difficult cliff must be circumnavigated." At this point the first three movements of the concerto were completely sketched.

3.11.4 Reconciliation of Opposites: Dodecaphony and Tonal Thinking

The assertion that, despite occasional pseudo-tonal formations, the Violin Concerto is a composition constructed rigorously according to the rules of twelve-tone technique is as old as Berg scholarship itself. Willi Reich stressed already in 1937 that the appearance of such seemingly tonal chord formations must not be taken as the product of an intention of Berg's "by their means to want to establish a reference to certain key notes, that is, tonality in the old sense." The chords were brought into play "within the framework of the twelve-tone structure dictated by the given row" and in general had "no cadential functions" to fulfill.[653] For Hans Ferdinand Redlich, too, the Violin Concerto is "the first soloist-concertante orchestral concerto in strict dodecaphony."[654] Herwig Knaus was the first, in the 'seventies and 'eighties, to state things in a more differentiated fashion. He pointed out certain serial techniques of Berg's, referred to the "strong anchorage" of large stretches in the concerto in ever-recurring tonal regions, and in interpreting such portions harmonically also made use of the term *Reihentonalität*, "serial tonality."[655]

The sketches now teach us that in conceiving the Violin Concerto Berg thought more strongly along pseudo-tonal lines than previously assumed. One telling aspect is the structure of the twelve-tone row adopted by Berg, which Joseph Rufer already cited as a paradigm of a "tonally colored" series.[656] The sketches prove that it was indeed tonally conceived. In two places in the second bundle (fols. 4 and 10), Berg notated it as a sequence of the triads G minor, D major, A minor and E major plus the attached whole-tone phrase, which significantly is both times harmonized with a ninth chord on E flat:

No less instructive is the already cited table of "chords and cadences" (85/I fol. 6), which Berg developed by trying out the diverse possibilities of the row (see Sketches 6). This table is divided into two halves. The chord formations of the upper half are based on the row in its original form on c-sharp, those of the lower half on the row in its inversion on f-sharp. The upper half of the table exhibits eight chord sequences, the lower one seven. Berg forms chords of two, three, four, five and six notes. The chord sequences that he arranges in groups are for the most part modulating progressions. Thus some groups in the upper half of the table begin on C♯ minor or D♭ minor and close with the ninth chord on g. Tellingly, Berg furnishes the chords of many of the progressions with designations from the degree theory (*Stufentheorie*) with which he was familiar from his studies under Schönberg. Thus the penultimate group in the upper half of the table reads:

[musical example: I — V₉   Mod. in den Triton]

In one instance there is a kind of cadence to A♭ major, where Berg considers the possibility of a modulation to C minor.

[musical example: IV   I   I/7   II   10 11 VII₇♮   I]

The table also shows that Berg took a special interest in grouping notes of the row in such a way that sequences of pure triads and an incomplete ninth chord result:[657]

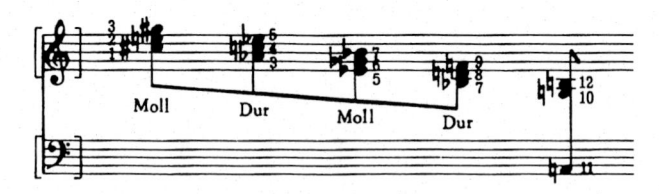

[musical example: Moll   Dur   Moll   Dur]

The draft of a thematic-rhythmic figure for the Allegretto in the second bundle (fol. 21 verso) exhibits the same interest in sequences of pure triads. Berg here forms the following chord sequence from the inversion of the row on b:

[musical example: U VIII ... $\frac{6}{8}$ = I♭]

The sequence was used in modified form in the *Quasi Trio I* and in the *quasi stretta* of the *Allegretto*. In the *Quasi Trio I*, mm. 147-151, Berg lines up four such chord sequences. They may evoke pseudo-tonal associations in the listener, but they are so deeply embedded in the rather dense musical happening that the atonal structure of the passage is not impaired. In the *quasi stretta*, mm. 240-245, the chord sequences play a dominating role in the brasses for several bars.

Here they are structured, through ingenious superimposition and pseudo-canonical rhythmic shifts, in such a way that associations with seemingly bitonal sounds may well arise. Tonal "centers" in the horn passage are A^b major and E^b major; in the pseudo-canonical trumpet and trombone passage, they are B major and $F^\#$ major. The passage is undoubtedly worked strictly dodecaphoniclly, yet it reminds one distantly of scores by Richard Strauss, such as *Salome* or *Electra*.

The tonal (or bitonal) character is even more unequivocal in those places where the chorale is adapted or the Carinthian folk tune is slotted in. Redlich,[658] and especially Knaus, have tried to interpret these passages in terms of *reihentonalität*, serial – or row – tonality, that is, to cite one example, they conceive, say, the Carinthian folk tune as a melodic figure whose individual notes represent a selection from a (fictive) twelve-tone series. In my view, however, the term does not really capture the state of affairs.

One of my own theses is that that there are portions of the Violin Concerto that are not dodecaphonically handled, but are treated tonally, bitonally or in free atonality. The Carinthian tune, for example, is in my judgment clearly bitonally harmonized; the passage *come una pastorale* (1st part, mm. 214-228) can be interpreted as a combination of the keys G^b major and C major, and similarly E^b major and A^b major are superimposed at the return of the landler melody in the Adagio (part two, mm. 200-214). One should note further that Berg's adaptation of the chorale is at times altogether free of any dodecaphonic traits – for instance the formation of the solo part in mm. 219-221 of the Adagio.[659]

3.11.5 Andante and Allegretto: Visions of a Winsome Girl

Soon after the completion of the Violin Concerto, Willi Reich published a short article about the work, under the title "Requiem for Manon," in the *Musikblätter des Anbruch*, in which he wanted to present the latest composition of his revered mentor to the musical world. He emphasized that a profoundly shocking experience, the sudden death of Manon Gropius, had become the "spiritual content" of the work for Berg, a work that, "far removed from any program music clinging slavishly to biographical details," wished to shape "the tragedy of that wondrous being," the young girl, "as a purely musical vision." The work, he said, appertained in equal measures to the realm of *absolute music* and to that of an ideal *symphonic poem*. And Reich did not omit to summarize the content of his recent *paraphrase*, published in the *Neue Wiener Journal*, for a better understanding of the work and of its idea of a *program*.[660]

Bruno Walter has recorded in his memoirs how Manon Gropius had made the impression on him of an unearthly apparition, a girl of angelic beauty, and had evoked in him the mystical feeling of the far away. When, at the age of eighteen, she had been stricken by polio in Venice and been brought to Vienna, Walter remembered her as lying in bed, "pale and of a heavenly serenity."[661]

Berg told Willi Reich that in composing the first part of the concerto he had sought to translate traits of the girl into musical characters. The remark seems plausible, not least when one recalls that, as we have seen, he had designed variations in the first movement of the Chamber Concerto as portraits of Erwin Stein, Rudolf Kolisch and Joseph Polnauer, and had composed a portrait of Lulu in the famous *Bildharmonien*.

It appears therefore that the diverse musical characters of the first part emblematize different sides of Manon's personality. The Andante, stamped by the characters *espressivo*, *delicato* and *grazioso*, depicts Manon more from the serious side. The more differentiated Allegretto, on the other hand – barring the exceptionally delicate music of the second Trio and the dream-like Carinthian tune – seems more like a playfully cheerful "scene," in which the characters *scherzando*, *Viennese*, and *rustico* dominate – a scene, to be sure, to which somber accents, too, are by no means alien.

All this needs to be concretized. Let us begin with some indispensable numerological considerations. There is, for one thing, the peculiar fact that the Andante and the Allegretto, as much as they differ in character – Berg initially wanted to call them *Prelude* and *Scherzo*[662] – have he same pulse. The notation ♩ = 56 in the Andante is equivalent to the prescription ♪ = 112 in the Allegretto – a metronome specification that, as Adorno rightly remarked,[663] is oddly slow for an allegretto.

In terms of the number of measures, too, there is an astonishing symmetry between the two movements. Although nominally the Andante has 103 bars and the Allegretto 154, the actual ratio is 112 1/2 : 113, because the Andante, whose basic time is 2/4, contains ten "double" (i.e. 4/4) and two 3/8 measures.

Conversely, the allegretto, whose basic meter is 6/8, includes 82 "half," i.e., 3/8 measures. Calculations Berg made on a sketch sheet (85/II fol. 20) prove that in constructing the first part of the concerto he accorded a fundamental significance to the number 112. He there reckoned the extent of the Andante as 113 bars, that of the Allegretto as 112 bars, specifically 33 + 36 (= 18 + 12+ 6) + 43 (see Sketches 7). It is only after one has realized that he regarded the 3/8 bars of the Allegretto as "half" measures that his seemingly enigmatic calculation on fol. 17 verso of the same bundle of sketches makes sense. Here he noted: 232-175 = 57 = 28. That means: the section mm. 176-232 comprises 57 "half" measures, or (nearly) 28 "whole" ones.

Based on the metronomic notations, but lacking the knowledge of the tectonic data we have just cited, Douglas Jarman proposed the thesis that, following the theories of Wilhelm Fließ, Berg based the first part of the concerto on the 28 as being a "feminine" number.[664]

That assumption is plausible as such, but one needs to keep in mind that Berg composed the Violin Concerto also as an homage to Alma Mahler-Werfel on her 56th birthday!

The Andante is much more artfully constructed than it might seem. Several commentators interpret it as a tripartite ABA form with a ten-bar introduction. Upon closer inspection, however, the tectonics of the movement appears mirror-symmetric in design, albeit not strictly speaking retrograde:

↓mm. 1-10	mm. 92-103 ↑
Introduction ("preluding")	("preluding")
mm. 11-27	mm. 84-91
espressivo	*espressivo*
mm. 28-37	mm. 77-83
delicato	*delicato*
mm. 38-46	
un poco grazioso	
mm. 47-53	mm. 63-76
↓*un poco più animato*	*un poco più mosso* ↑
→	→ mm. 54-63 →
	grazioso

Sketches 7: Violin Concerto

Austrian National Library, Music Collection Fonds 21 Berg 85/II fol. 20 Piano sketch of the end of the Allegretto (mm. 240-257). The calculations on the left margin prove that Berg attached fundamental importance to the number 112 in constructing part one of the concerto. First published by permission of the Austrian National Library

This mirror-symmetric design, moreover, should be understood not merely schematically but also as dictating the sequence of characters and the entire course of the movement. The music, which begins very calmly and *pianissimo*, increases bit by bit, essentially in stages, reaches an agogic and dynamic climax (*ff* in the solo part) in m. 74, and then returns to its original state, the undulating of the start. In looking at the solo part, one can translate the gradual acceleration and rhythmic agitation, and the subsequent `subsidence, into the following rhythmic values: mm. 15-34 eighths and quarter notes, mm. 35-46 triplets, mm. 47-62 sixteenths, mm. 63-74 sextuplets, mm. 75-83 deceleration (sixteenths and triplets, tremolo, eights), mm. 84-103 half-notes, quarter-notes and eighths.

The more closely one studies the characters, the more one has to marvel at Berg's inventiveness and rich imagination. His ability to derive the most diverse characters from the basic twelve-tone row is phenomenal, In the case of some characters, one can recognize their derivation from the twelve-tone row at once, as for example the four-bar phrase of the solo violin mm. 47-50, which recites the notes 4-12 of the series first in inverted sequence and then in the original one:

In numerous other instances, laborious analyses and operations would be required to make the connection of figures with the row at all recognizable. To cite two examples: the thematic character that the solo violin intones in m. 15-18 is merely a rhythmicized version of the original form:

The appended half-tone "sigh", however, seems at first an alien element because the row does not contain a singe half-tone or chromatic step. Yet Berg succeeded in inventing the following *delicato* character (mm. 28-32):

(The second and fourth bar are inversions of the first and third.)

As the outline makes plain, there are correspondences between individual sections of the Andante. One must not think of note-for-note repetitions: both the substance and the instrumentation are altered with every recurrence. Thus the just-quoted *delicato* character appears in inversion at its recurrence (mm. 77-80) and is now initially intoned by a muted trombone (!)"

311

The Allegretto not only adopts an altogether different tone from that of the Andante but also exhibits a far greater wealth of thematic characters. Constructed on the pattern of an arc (ABCB'A'), it is clearly divided into five sections (Main Movement – Trio I – Trio II – Trio I – Main Movement), though here, too, one should not think in terms of simple relations or literal repetitions. Here, to begin with, is a structural outline of the movement:

A Section

mm. 104-117   a   *scherzando – Viennese – rustico*
       118-125   b   *tranquillo*
       126-136   a^1 *Viennese – rustico – scherzando*

B Section
Subito un poco energico (Quasi Trio I)

mm. 137-154 at the start, sixths-leap motifs; mm. 140/141 and 147-151 ominous *ritmico* sounds in the brasses

C Section

Meno mosso (Trio II)
mm. 155-166

B' Section
di nuovo un poco energico (Trio I)

mm. 167-172

A' Section
Quasi Tempo I

mm. 173-199   a^2 *scherzando – Viennese – rustico*
       200-207   b^2 *tranquillo*
       208-239   a^3 *scherzando – Carinthian folk tune – scherzando*

Coda

A tempo, ma quasi stretta
mm. 240-257 initially the *ritmico* sounds in the brasses, then the *scherzando* motif from the second Trio

Whereas the music of the Andante continuously evolves to a climax and then returns to its original situation, the Allegretto is assembled on the principle of contrast. Thus the energetic, even robust B sections stand in stark contrast to the framing A parts, in which the *scherzando* character predominates, and a similar contrast obtains between the very delicate music of the second trio and the robust B sections. If one thinks of the structure of the movement as of a set of concentric circles, the second trio (C section) represents the nucleus, and it is surely no coincidence that the second part of the concerto (Allegro) has recourse mainly to the tender music of this trio.

Let us now scrutinize the individual parts. Berg based the first section on four clearly defined characters, which he labeled *scherzando*, *Viennese*, *rustico* and *tranquillo*.[665] With some training in dodecaphonic analysis, one can see immediately that the characters *rustico* and *tranquillo* constitute different rhythmic arrangements of the serial tones. Similarly, one can without much difficulty determine that the thirds of the exuberant *Viennese* motif, so reminiscent of waltzing ecstasies, result from the combination of row notes in groups of two. In the sketches (85/II fol. 21), Berg analyzed the motif dodecaphonically thus:

Determining the dodecaphonic structure of the *scherzando* character is more difficult. Berg analyzed it in the sketches (85/II fol. 12 verso) as follows:

What is the semantics of these characters? Their difference points to different facets of Manon's personality, different elements of her being, a playfully serene disposition and moments of stillness, as well as to the contrast between city and country life. Alma Mahler-Werfel, Franz Werfel and Manon generally spent their summer vacations on the Semmering Pass in Styria.

The physiognomy of the B section is largely determined by the energetic main theme, first intoned by the first violins (mm. 137-141). It consists of four major sixths, two ascending and two descending, plus the rhythmicized original row on c sharp. It is instructive to observe how, in mm. 141 ff., the solo violin picks up the theme and transforms it according to the procedure of the "developing variation," with the effect that the interval of the major sixth is progressively widened:

Important in this section are the massive brass strains – trumpets, trombones and horns – sounding in mm. 141/2 and 147-51 and to be recited *ritmico*. As we discover only much later, in the Allegro, when the *molto-ritmico* section begins, they portend the eventual catastrophe.

The impression of sweetness made on the listener by the C section (the second trio) is owing to several attributes: for one thing, to the style of the swaying theme, which implies several chromatic steps;[666] then to the mode of recital, *espressivo* and *dolcissimo flautando*; to the dynamics confined to the *piano* and *pianissimo* range; the inclusion of triangle and harp, which add a new, especially delicate timbre; and others. A teasing effect in this context is produced by the *scherzando* interpolation of the solo violin (mm. 161/162), which Berg expressly marked to be played *liberamente*.

Compared with the B section, the B' section is shortened by two thirds. Whereas the former comprises 18 bars, the latter has only six. It goes without saying that the substance and instrumentation, too, have been altogether altered. The characteristic intervals of sixths, originally performed by the first violins, are now given to the leading bass tuba; and instead of the ascending thirds of the theme (m. 139), we now hear fourths (m. 169). Berg, however, saved the portentous *ritmico* strains for the end of the Allegretto.

The A' section is a varied and at the same time intensified recapitulation of the first section. It is not confined to the latter's musical substance, however, but also includes the Carinthian folksong and, besides, has recourse to elements from the two trios. The most conspicuous difference to the first section is the abandonment of the 6/8 meter in favor of a 3/8 time (from m. 176 on). The music is now to sound "like a waltz," "always in four or two measures." The characters of the first section, *scherzando*, *Viennese*, *rustico* and *tranquillo*, return, albeit radically varied in part. The character *Viennese*, for example, is greatly altered (mm. 180-189) and is no longer called that, evidently because the music has waltz-like features anyway. The strongest alterations vis-à-vis the first section appear in mm. 208-239: following the *scherzando* character, the Carinthian folk tune here comes in "imperceptibly," intoned at first by the horn and then by the trumpet, while the solo violin plays the so-called *überschlag*, a harmonizing upper voice, to it. After this dreamlike interpolation (the tune is to sound *come una pastorale*), the solo violin picks up the *scherzando* motif from the second trio and develops and intensifies it further (mm. 231-239).

Diverse speculations have been advanced about the semantics of the *Carinthian folksong*.[667] Several recent observations permit the conclusion that it symbolizes the realm of "earthly reverie," in contrast to the Bach chorale, which stands for the beyond. In the earliest notations for the Violin Concerto (432/XV p. 161), Berg described the landler melody as "verträumt" or dreamy.

If we ask why Berg chose this *particular* tune to insert into the first part of the Violin Concerto, we might simply answer: because he liked it. We might also keep in mind, however, that he first met Manon Gropius in Carinthia and that, with his penchant for encryptions, he may also have seen a deeper symbolic meaning in the song.

The text of the song is as follows:

A Vegale af'n Zweschpm-bam	A birdie in the plum tree
håt me aufgweckt,	sang me awake,
tri-di-e, tri-di-e, i-ri tu-li-e!	tri-di-ay, tri-di-ay, i-ri tu-li-ay!
sist hiatt i verschlåfn	else I would have overslept
in der Miazale ihrn Bett,	In Molly her bed,
tri-di-e, ri tu-li-e!	tri-di-ay, ri tu-li-ay!
Wenn an iader a Reiche,	If each wants a rich and
a Scheane will håbm,	a beautiful mate,
tri-di-e, tri-di-e, i-ri tu-li-e!	tri-di-ay, tri-di-ay, i-ri tu-li-ay!
wo soll denn derTeixl	where then shall the Devil
de Schiachn hinträgn?	the ugly ones take?
tri-di-e, ri tu-li-e!	tri-di-ay, ri tu-li-ay!
's Diandle is katholisch	Tho' my gal she is Cath'lic
und I bin verschriebm;	and a Luth'ran am I,
tri-di-e, tri-di-e, i-ri tu-li-e!	tri-di-ay, tri-di-ay, i-ri tu-li-ay!
sie werd jå die Betschnur	she'll surely put the rosary

wohl wegtoan ban Liegn. away when we lie.
tri-di-e, ri tu-li-e! tri-di-ay, ri tu-li-ay!

I suggest that the song may allude not only directly to Manon but also indirectly to Alma, to whom the Violin Concerto, we recall, was secretly dedicated. The text evokes an erotic episode between a young woman and a young man: the woman is Catholic, the man Lutheran (the term *verschriebm* refers to the tolerance patent of Emperor Josef II). That constellation fits Manon's parents, the Catholic Alma and the Lutheran Gropius. The song thus may have been intended to secretly allude to the love relationship, from which Manon had sprung.[668]

At the start of the coda (mm. 240-245), first the horns, then the trumpets and the trombones enter with those fanfare-like strains, to be played *ritmico*, from the first Trio, which are arranged in such a way that bitonal combinations result. The horn fanfares aim at the A♭ major and the E♭ major chords, while

40. A Vögele af'n Zwefchpm-bam

Sehr heiter (1 Takt ~ 2")   1890

1. A Begale af'n Zwefch-pm-bam / hat me auf-gwedt,
2. Wenn an ia - der a Rei - che, a Schea-ne will habm,
3. 's Diandle if la - tho-lifch und i bin ver-fchriebm,

tri - di - e, tri - di - e i - ri tu-li - e! /

fift¹ hiatt² i ber-fchlä-fn/in der Miaza-le ihrn Bett,
wo foll denn der Tei - zl de Schia - chn hin - trägn?
fie werd jä de Betfchnur⁴ wohl weg-toan ban Liegn.

tri - di - e, ri tul-li - e_____!

the trumpets and first trombone aim at the fourth-sixth chords of B major and F♯ major. In mm. 245-253, the solo violin intones once more the *scherzando* motif from the second Trio. At the conclusion of the Allegretto, there is an unmistakable gravitation toward G minor. The four-note chord on which the first part of the concerto closes consists of g-b♭-d-f♯, the first four notes of the twelve-tone row.

The Allegretto as a whole seems ambivalent, double-bottomed. On the one hand it strikes one as playfully cheerful and charming. At the same time, as in the second trio and the stretta, it includes uncanny accents. Willi Reich justly referred to a "connection to the world of Mahler in the dance characters of the piece,"[669] and Adorno aptly called the Allegretto "perhaps the most Mahleresque movement of the deeply Mahler-bound Berg."[670] The double-bottomed quality that marks a number of Mahler's scherzos is indeed present also in this allegretto, which at times seems to assume the character of a dance of death and has a special affinity with the Scherzo of Mahler's Fourth Symphony (*Goodman Death fiddles for the dance*). The (heretofore missed) similarity between a landler tune of Mahler's in that scherzo and the *überschlag*, the harmonizing, yodeling upper part, of the Carinthian folksong is especially striking:

Mahler, Fourth Symphony, Scherzo, mm. 84-94

Carinthian folksong "A Vögele af'n Zweschpm-bam," *Überschlag* (transposed)

We cannot conclude this discussion of the Allegretto without noting that in the first part of the concerto the low tamtam sounds five times, in mm. 79, 118, 147, 200 and 256, the penultimate bar. In Mahler, the tamtam functions as an idiophonic sound symbol of death,[671] while in Berg's *Wozzeck* it connotes eternity.[672] In view of these precedents, it is fairly certain that the five tamtam strokes confer upon the first part of the Violin Concerto the semantics of an epitaph.

3.11.6 Allegro and Adagio: Death and Transcendence

> This entire movement rests on the intimation of death. Time and again it announces itself. All terrestrial dreaming culminates in it (hence the repeated crescendos, always like new bursts of passion, after the gentlest of passages), most powerfully, of course, at that tremendous moment when the intimation of death becomes *certainty*, when in the midst of the deepest, most agonizing zest for life, death announces itself *with supreme force*. Along with it, that hair-raising viola and violin solo, and those chivalric sounds: death in armor! All rebellion is vain here! – What still happens thereafter seems like resignation to me. Always with the thought of the 'Beyond,' which at the *misterioso* (pp. 44/45) seems to appear as if in very thin air – still higher than the mountains – as if in the most rarefied, ethereal space." Berg to Helene, about the first movement of Mahler's Ninth Symphony (ABB 238).

> "There is no death, after all, only a higher mode of being."

> "But I hope very much that you can take death as what it is: the end of an earthly mission and the birth into higher worlds." Helene Berg[673]

In 1923, Alma Mahler-Werfel presented Berg with a precious gift: the draft score of the first three movements of Mahler's Ninth Symphony. In an undated letter to Helene, Berg spoke with the greatest enthusiasm of the work ("the most glorious thing Mahler ever wrote") and attempted a subtle hermeneutic interpretation of the first movement, which centers on the contrast between the terrestrial and the transcendent. Of special moment to him are the following perceptions: that the music is "the expression of an unheard-of love of this earth"; that the entire first movement "rests on the intimation of death"; that this intimation becomes certainty *with supreme force* "at the tremendous moment" of mm. 314-320; and, finally, that the *misterioso* passage (m. 376) is a vision of the Beyond (ABB 238 f.). The contrast between the earthly and the transcendent was a subject Berg thought much about. Thus in a letter to Helene of May 27, 1913, he spoke, on the one hand, of the "dear earth" and, on the other, of the yearning for a state where there was no longer any distance, any separation, any time or space – the "Beyond" (ABB 240).

A close study of the Violin Concerto makes clear that the work's programmatic conception has much in common with Berg's interpretation of the head movement of Mahler's Ninth. If the Allegretto can be read as an expression of the "love of this earth," the second part of the Concerto, consisting of an

Allegro and an Adagio, surely treats of Death and Transcendence. Let us focus, to begin with, on the structure of the Allegro.

Redlich has described it as a "sonata movement with recapitulation"[674] – probably relying on a questionable statement made by Reich.[675] I myself cannot detect anything sonata-like in the tectonics of the Allegro. Rather, the movement exhibits a clear ABA' design: two similar massive outside sections bracketing a thematically *independent* middle part of a delicate character.

The first part of the movement (mm. 1-43) divides unmistakably into two sections, a rhapsodic *rubato* one (mm. 1-22) and a rigidly structured *molto ritmico* one (mm. 23-43). The *rubato* section, which is to be played "freely like a cadenza," is opened and closed by a gradually evolving shrill dissonance. The *molto ritmico* commencing in m. 23 is based on a one-measure main rhythm, which is literally present in each and every bar.

The considerably longer middle portion (mm. 43-95) contrasts strongly with the outer sections and is linked thematically with the Allegretto. One could call it a development-like fantasia with a canon on the thematic substance of Trio II. All of its ideas recur, but everything is now much more broadly executed and regularly developed. Whereas the Trio II comprises only twelve measures, the middle potion of the Allegro has no fewer than 52 bars. A comparative outline can illustrate the relationship of the two sections better than any lengthy explanations:

Allegretto		*Allegro*
mm. 155-160: Theme of Trio II	~	mm. 44-53: Theme of Trio II
mm. 161/162: *Scherzando insertion*	~	mm. 54-57: *poco scherzando*
		mm. 58-63: free
		mm. 64-77 fantasia-like (working in the head motif of the theme of Trio II)
mm. 163-166: theme of Trio II now played by the solo violin	~	mm. 78-89: theme of Trio II, now in the form of a four-part canon for the solo violin
		m. 90: preluding figure from the Andante

mm. 245-250: scherzando idea (not designated as such)	~ mm. 91-93: *poco scherzando*
mm. 111/112: *Viennese*	~ mm. 93-95: *scherzando* in the two clarinets

In keeping with the design of the first section of the movement, the totally varied recapitulation (mm. 96-135) is conceived at first as more strongly rhapsodic and then as more strongly rhythmic. Its foundation is the famous pedal point on f, which, with a brief interruption (m. 121) is held for 38 bars.[676] After several crescendos, the recapitulation at the *più fortissimo* (m. 125) reaches its *climax*, designated as such by the composer.

Much about the semantics of the Allegro can be gathered from a study of the sketches. They enable us to realize that Berg formed the movement as a highly dramatic scene *sub specie mortis*. To no fewer than three elements of the Allegro he assigned a programmatic meaning.

The dissonant sound of the beginning, which recurs in modified form at the end, he wanted to be understood as an *Aufschrei*, a shriek or outcry (85/II fol. 35 verso):

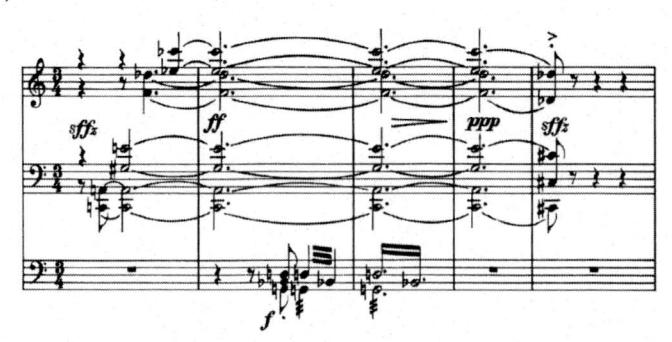

Berg seems to have had great trouble finding the definitive form of this sound, as he sketched the spot time and again[677] – though he had a firm idea early on that the sound was to include the small or the big drum – the sound symbols of catastrophe.

Another revealing aspect is that the *molto ritmico* section repeatedly bears the title *A la Marcia* or simply *Marcia* in the sketches. A plausible explanation as to why a section in 3/4 time, of all things, should be so entitled can be found on fol. 3 of the second bundle of sketches, where the main rhythm (with the marking *Alla Marcia*) is still sketched in 4/4 time. Berg must have realized that the rhythm notated thus lacked saliency and was not suited for an ostinato treatment and promptly modified it into the pithier 3/4 rhythm, the main rhythm of the Allegro.

That rhythm is now consistently accompanied by a "secondary rhythm," which in the sketch is furnished with the significant remark *Stöhnen immer nach*, "groaning always after" (see Sketches 8). Obviously the designation *Alla Marcia*, which was suppressed in the published edition of the score, here has the semantics of a march to death.

Sketches 8: Sketches for the Violin Concerto

Austrian National Library, Music Collection, Fonds 21 Berg 85/II fol.3 Drafts for the Allegro (programmatic key phrase: "Groaning always after")

An important entry on fol. 4 of the first bundle of sketches is likewise of programmatic import. Berg there notated a sequence of four incomplete ninth chords with the third and fifth omitted, and marked it *Rufe* or "calls."[678] An arrow signals that the chords are to follow upon the main rhythm of the Allegro. An analysis of the matter led to the realization that from these ninth chords Berg formed those characteristic three-note unison motifs that sound with dwindling intensity at the "climax" of the Allegro and contrast to the catastrophe-like main rhythm:

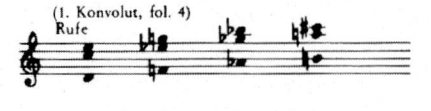

(1. Konvolut, fol. 4)
Rufe

Allegro T. 126–130

Viewing the Allegro as a whole, one can clearly see that the middle portion serves a retarding function. The recourse to the Allegretto at this point has the character of a reminiscence – appears, in the face of death, like a vision of the past life. Richard Strauss' symphonic poem *Death hand Transfiguration*,[679] composed in 1888, came about in a similar way: as the vision of an artist who in the hour of his death thinks of his past life.[680] Some of the sentences with which Berg interpreted the head movement of Mahler's Ninth Symphony also present a kind of secret program for the Allegro of the Violin Concerto, so that we might quote them here again:

> This entire movement rests on the intimation of death. Time and again it announces itself. All terrestrial dreaming culminates in it (hence the repeated crescendos, always like new bursts of passion, after the gentlest of passages), most powerfully, of course, at that tremendous moment where the intimation of death becomes *certainty*, where in the midst of the deepest, most agonizing zest for life, death announces itself *with supreme force*.

To this passage, marked *mit höchster Gewalt*, "with supreme force" or "violence," in Mahler, where the trombones and the bass tubas intone the leit-rhythm in triple *forte*, corresponds the "climax" of the Allegro (m. 125) in Berg, a passage in which the leit-rhythm is likewise powerfully intoned, in triple *forte* – by individual woodwinds, the brass and the strings. It is obvious that this climax marks the onset of the death throes. Thereafter, the intensity of the music diminishes continuously. The step-by-step reduction of the volume (*fff, ff, f, mf, mp, p, pp, ppp*) is paralleled by a concurrent shrinking of the thickness of sound: the number of the notes from which characteristic sounds in the dotted main rhythm are formed lessens more and more: 8, 7, 6, 5, 4, 3, 2, 1. Cries for help alternate several times with the initium of the *Es ist genug*, which the solo violin intones. The death scene, signaled not least by the addition of the low tamtam,[681] gradually yields to a religious vision. Berg's mastery of the art of transition is truly incomparable.

Es ist genug! so nimm, Herr, meinen Geist

Joh. Rud. Ahle. 1662

Aus der Kantate N° 60: O Ewigkeit, du Donnerwort (Zweite Komposition)

Berg, as mentioned before, selected the chorale *Es ist genug* (It is enough) from the collection *Sechzig Choralgesänge von Johann Sebastian Bach* as a basis for the Adagio of his Concerto. That chorale forms the conclusion of the Cantata for the 24th Sunday after Trinity, *O Ewigkeit, du Donnerwort* (*Eternity, thou Word of Thunder*) BWV 60 – a cantata that is constructed as a "dialogue between fear and hope" and has the soul's wavering between despondency and confidence as its theme.[682] Berg will have been not a little astonished when he came upon this chorale. Not only did he find in the verses of Franz Burmeister and the melody of Johann Rudolf Ahle a deeply stirring expression of the religious vision he had in mind, but the first four notes of the chorale, a sequence of whole tones, corresponded exactly, as we have noted, to the last four notes of the twelve-tone row on which he had erected the Concerto. Significantly, in this context, the whole-tone phrase of the chorale's initium corresponds to the figure of *parrhesia* (speaking freely or frankly) and, as Alfred Dürr observes, depicts the passing over from life to death.[683] Ahle's melody to the ten-line chorale is clearly divided into three sections, which are repeated according to the schema abc + abc + dd + ee. In Berg's adaptation, each sections is recited at first by the solo violin and is then repeated organ-like by four woodwinds (two clarinets, a third clarinet or a saxophone, and a bass clarinet) – all in Bach's original harmonization, but intertwined with dodecaphonically invented counter-voices in the solo violin: another instance of the symbiosis of tonality and dodecaphony so characteristic of Berg. Interestingly, Berg supplied individual lines of the chorale with expression marks, which he also retained for later intonations of the chorale melody:

Deciso	Es ist genug!	It is enough!
doloroso	Herr, wenn es Dir gefällt,	Lord, if it pleases thee,
	so spanne mich doch aus!	Take off my harness now!
religioso	Mein Jesus kommt:	My Jesus comes:
	nun gute Nacht, o Welt!	o world, good night to thee!
	Ich fahr in's Himmelhaus.	To heaven's home I go.
risoluto	Ich fahre sicher hin in Frieden,	In peace from here I surely go,
	mein großer Jammer	All my great sorrows
	bleibt darnieden.	stay below.
Molto espr.	Es ist genug.	It is enough.
amoroso	Es ist genug.	It is enough.

Something else, too, must be emphasized here: Bach's chorale extends to 20 bars in the original. Berg now arranges it in such a way that during its first intonation in the Adagio it takes up 22 bars (mm. 136-157). The expansion serves a numerological purpose: Manon Gropius died on April 22, 1935. (The double bar after m. 157 is thus meant as a mourning-border.) Several marginalia in the particello (PhA 2176) likewise suggest that Berg accorded a special meaning to the number 22 in the conception of the second part's Allegro. P. 7 contains an enumeration of exactly 22 instruments, and it is surely no coincidence that mm .32 ff. and m. 100 are orchestrated for exactly 22 instruments!

The two very artful variations the chorale melody undergoes (mm. 158-177 and 178-197) complement each other and form a single block. Both are distinguished by their logic and density of structure and maximal expressivity. Functioning as *cantus firmus*, the chorale melody is worked in its original form in the first variation and in its inversion in the second. In both cases, Berg exploits the sinister tritonic relation: in both variations the individual sections of the chorale melody are imitated in tritone intervals. Berg also manages to shape the first chorale section as a canon in the pure fifth. If the chorale melody worked thus forms a firm scaffolding, the density of the structure results from superadded contrapuntal counter-voices.

The beginning of the first variation bears the heading *Misterioso*. On the foundation of the canonically worked first chorale section – a canon between the cellos and the harp – we hear four muted horns playing a four-part passage *pianissimo*. The portentous term *misterioso* is to be taken as an allusion to the linearly conceived passage with the same heading in Mahler's Ninth Symphony – the passage that Berg interpreted as a vision of the Beyond. After the first six bars of the first variation, the muted solo violin enters with a highly expressive chant rich in sighing figures, which Willi Reich rightly interpreted as a "dirge."[684]

This "dirge," the voice of a deeply stirred subjectivity in this epitaph, is arranged as a great crescendo-diminuendo arc. Beginning in *pianissimo*, it gradually rises all the way to *fortissimo* ("Ever louder grows the lament for the dead," Willi Reich wrote) and thus brings about the "climax" (marked as such) of the Adagio. Then the intensity gradually shrinks (*mf, mp, più p, p, pp*). Importantly, the soloist, according to a direction on p. 85 of the printed score, is supposed to assume the lead, with a visible gesture to that effect, of the violins and violas, which gradually join him/her and later split off again.

The second chorale variation is followed by the Carinthian folk tune (mm 198-213), which is again harmonized bitonally, but which is now to sound "*as if from far away, and hence much slower than the first time.*" With this performance direction, Berg unmistakably refers to Mahler again, who had a special predilection for the type of "music from farthest distances."685 Like so many passages in Mahler, the penultimate section of the Violin Concerto, too, appears like an unreal, dreamlike sound image. This "indescribably wistful recapitulation of the Carinthian tune," Willi Reich wrote, is to recall once more "the image of the winsome girl."

The concluding coda (mm. 214-230) represents yet another adaptation of Ahle/Bach's chorale melody. The glossing "dirge" of the soloist, too, is heard again, albeit in a different shape. Surprisingly, the melody of the first two chorale sections is no longer repeated. In its place, the final section, the concluding *Es ist genug*, is recited altogether three times, at first by the solo violin, then by the first trumpet, and finally by two horns. We should also note the different scoring of the three choral sections: if the woodwind color dominates at first (the particello notes that the passage is to sound like an organ), the second section is characterized by a kind of mixed sound composed of the high woodwinds, the first horn, and pizzicato violins and violas. In the last section, however, the brasses come strongly to the fore. The chorale is concluded by quasi tonally cadencing trombones and horns, whose low register and overall timbre make for a rather somber effect. In the penultimate measure, however, the sound lightens. An unclouded B-flat major triad with added sixth defines the "celestial" character of the final notes, while the hollow-fifth sequences from the Andante float up "as if from a distance" in the violins and then the double basses.686

Willi Reich opined quite incidentally in 1963 that Berg shaped the Violin Concerto not only as a memorial for Manon, but in a "vague presentiment" also as his own "requiem."687 Five years earlier, Helene Berg had spoken far more pointedly of the work as "Alban Berg's farewell to this world" and as "a purely personal confession of his relation to the world – to death – to God." Numerous fresh observations, which I presented in an article published in April of 1985,688 in fact support this interpretation. When Berg began with the composition of the Violin Concerto, he was in a rather depressive frame of mind. Since his opera *Wozzeck*, on whose royalties he had been living, was no longer performed in Germany and Austria after 1932, he had serious financial worries. In a letter to Webern of June 7, 1935, he also complained about his state of health: all this time, he said, he had not felt well ("asthmatic, nervous heart and deathly tired").

A major symptom of this personal dimension is the fact that the number 23, Berg's fatal number, plays an important role in the structure of the second part of the Concerto. That part comprises exactly 230 measures; the metronome notation for the Allegro is ♩ = 69 (= 3 x 23); the *Marcia* (the "march to death") begins in m. 23;[689] and the twenty-two-bar section in which the Bach chorale is first intoned (mm. 136-157) is in fact expanded to twenty-three measures by the anticipation of the chorale's initium in the viola (m. 135 with upbeat). The 23 also forms a ghostly presence in the sketches.[690]

There is much to suggest that after Manon's passing Berg wrestled intensively with the problem of death and found in the Bach chorale a quietist answer to the questions that agitated him. One would not go wrong in interpreting the inclusion and adaptation of the chorale as a personal religious confession.[691]

Photograph 12: the last photo of Alban Berg

(with kind permission of the Alban Berg Foundation Vienna)

Afterword: Berg – a Janus Face

> "Alban Berg was certainly the most gifted of the entire crop of Schönberg pupils, probably altogether the most significant of the time." Mahler[692]

> "With faithful insistence, Berg, one of the boldest musical inaugurators of the twentieth century, yet preserved the postulates of the nineteenth, conserved the unbroken even after the break." Adorno[693]

> "For everything reassuring that these worthy musicians discover in Berg is precisely what we value the least: his Romanticism and – one regrets to have to say it – his dependence on tradition."

> "In truth, Berg is merely a final supreme flowering of the Wagner succession, one in which additionally the amiability of the Viennese waltz – in all its ghastly literal sense – and the emphatic nature of Italian verismo fuse in equal measure." Pierre Boulez[694]

In historical perspective, Alban Berg presents the twofold countenance of an artist who looks to the past as well as to the future. He was, to speak with Theodor W. Adorno, one of the boldest musical inaugurators of the twentieth century. His work contains germs that came to fruition only after his death. At the same time he was not prepared to dispense with certain aesthetic postulates of the nineteenth century. Adorno's dialectically balanced aperçu conforms much more closely to the facts of the matter than the rather undifferentiated judgments of Pierre Boulez.

The broad appeal of Berg's work is in large measure due to this twofold character of his art. His affinity with the nineteenth century is most patently manifest in his special relation to tonality, which he, in contrast to Webern, nowhere negated altogether. It further reveals itself in the immense expressive power of his music, which is at times akin to the musical idiom of Wagner, Mahler and Schönberg. His intense interest in the semantic content of music, and the autobiographic dimension of many of his works, are aspects that likewise demonstrate his close connection with the nineteenth century. In 1925, a time when many prominent composers sought to distance themselves at all cost from the "Romantic" spirit of that age, Berg flatly confessed to having "Romantic propensities."[695] Ten years later, on September 16, 1935, he wrote to his friend Hermann Watznauer: "We are just incorrigible Romantics! My new violin concerto, too, confirms it again."[696]

One outcome of this study, however, is also the realization that Berg in the 'twenties developed a number of pre-serial compositional procedures.

Mathematical calculations fascinated him in the conception of nearly all of his major works. Numbers and number operations play an eminently important role in his oeuvre. Decisive factors are not only that in his "mature" compositions he works with twelve-tone series and, by means of certain permutations, develops secondary rows from them, but, beyond that, that certain specific numbers determine the formal design, the dimensions of the parts, the agogics, the metric division and frequently also the rhythm. The *Presto delirando* of the *Lyric Suite* is especially instructive in this respect. The formal articulation in the two *Tenebroso* trios there follows, as we have demonstrated, the arithmetic series 1 2 3 4 5 (also retrograde). No less telling is the fact that, in conceiving the movement, Berg at first thought of organizing a number of durational sequences according to the same arithmetic row.

Oddly enough, Berg's pre-serial compositional discoveries were not recognized by the composers who embraced Serialism in the 'fifties and 'sixties.

4 Appendix

4.1 Unpublished Aphorisms of the Young Berg

About the "Consequences of Weakness"

Hours of weakness are often followed by days of weakness.

(Quotation Collection no. 50)

The Eternal Feminine strips us down.

(Quotation Collection no. 213; take-off on the end of Goethe's *Faust*)

About *"Greatness"*

We spoke of the stars – of the great longing – of weltschmerz –. How did that come about?: She felt elevated by the prospect of distant worlds – I felt humbled – insignificantly small! – And she said: "Because he who feels greatness is great himself –" July 1903

(Quotation Collection no. 215)

About *"Nature"*

The happy man can only be made happier by Nature –.But the unhappy one should "avoid the meads" (Rückert) –! Certainly it is lovely to feel the wind wafting through your hair – lying in the grass –! Then the soul echoes –; yet all this wafting is wailing – and woe!!

June 1903

(Quotation Collection no. 216)

About *"Music"*

It is so good to be able to cry out – to free one's heart from all adversity – – that is my "Nature" – – that's what I call "lying in the sun, – giving no more thought to all the disgusting to-do of the great, the middling and the small mixed together – forgetting and slowly fading, drowsing off and thus slipping away" (H. Barr) - – – "Music – " From the "summer letters" 1903

(Quotation Collection no. 217)

About "Spiritual Marriage"

I don't think I would be capable of a purely spiritual marriage, because I am too weak – too corrupt! It would be so beautiful – eternally beautiful – – ! But soon that shameful desire would rise up in me – and everything would collapse in a heap of garbage – –! You see, that is what I am like!!!! And this feeling is so oppressive – like a crime!!–

(Quotation Collection no. 235)

About *"Predestination"*

Well, yes, during unexpected events, people suddenly get far-sighted – and truckle to their impotence. Then the word is: "It's all predetermined, after all," or "Oh how helpless man is!" – Oh, you lucky nearsighted ones, who need such events for your enlightenment! – Certainly, in a few days you will be making plans for the future again and will think you have acknowledged your impotence sufficiently by humbly beating your breast and mumbling: "If I'm still alive" …..! As if that was the only predetermination – the only "If" !!!

From a letter to Hermann Watznauer, Fall 1903

(Quotation Collection no. 236)

About the *"Female Mind"*

There are two kinds of women: those who are stupid, and those who think they are smart.

(Quotation Collection no. 964)

With most people, music goes into their legs, with not so many, into their hands and arms; the number is even smaller of those with whom it goes into their mouth, but the fewest are those with whom it goes into their head – and yet it goes into the heart of all men.

(Quotation Collection no. 1000)

4.2 Abbreviations

ABB	Alban Berg, *Briefe an seine Frau*. Munich, Vienna, 1965
GS	Arnold Schönberg, *Stil und Gedanke*. *Aufsätze zur Musik*. Ed. Ivan Vojtech (Gesammelte Schriften 1). S. Fischer Verlag, 1976.
m./mm.	measure/s
Schr.	Alban Berg, *Glaube, Hoffnung und Liebe. Schriften zur Musik*. Ed. Frank Schneider (Reclams Universal-Bibliothek). Leipzig, 1981.
S&I	Arnold Schönberg, *Style and Idea. Collected Writings*. Ed. Leonard Stein, transl. Leo Black. London: Faber & Faber, 1975.
Mahler 1	*Die geistige Welt Gustav Mahlers in systematischer Darstellung*. Breitkopf & Härtel, 1st ed. Wiesbaden 1977, 2nd ed. 1987
Mahler 2	*Gustav Mahler and the Symphony of the 19th Century*, Peter Lang, New York, 2014
Mahler 3	*Gustav Mahler. The Symphonies*. Amadeus Press, 1993, paperback edition 1977, 2000

4.3 Notes

Part One: Personality Aspects
Principles

[1] Theodor W. Adorno, "Alban Berg," in *Klangfiguren . Musikalische Schriften I* (Berlin and Frankfurt a. M., 1959), 121-137; p. 133.

[2] Theodor W. Adorno, *Mahler. Eine musikalische Physiognomik* (Frankfurt a. M., 1960), 37, 169. On this see my paper „Eine musikalische Physiognomik. Über Adornos *Mahler-Interpretation,* in: Dan Diner (Ed.): Simon-Dubnow-Institut. *Jahrbuch.*Yearbook XI 2012, 235-243.

[3] Ibid., 37.

[4] Theodor W. Adorno, *Berg. Der Meister des kleinsten Übergangs* (Österreichische Komponisten des XX. Jahrhunderts, vol. 15) (Vienna, 1968), 41, 22 ff., 26.

[5] Hektor Rottweiler (pseudonym for Theodor W. Adorno) "Erinnerung an den Lebenden," 23. *Eine Wiener Musikzeitschrift*, nos. 24/25 (February 1, 1936), 129-29. This double issue of the journal is dedicated to Berg's memory.

[6] See Gordon W. Allport, *Pattern and Growth in Personality* (New York, 1961) and Hans Thomae, *Persönlichkeit. Eine dynamische Interpretation* (Bonn, 1971; 5th ed. Bonn, 1973).

Creativity

[7] Hans W. Heinsheimer, "Begegnung mit einem Riesen – Alban Berg," in *Schönste Grüße an Aïda. Ein Leben nach Noten* (Munich, 1969), 55-73; p. 57.

[8] Alban Berg, *Glaube, Hoffnung, Liebe. Schriften zur Musik*, ed. Frank Schneider (Reclam Universal-Bibliothek) (Leipzig, 1981); hereafter Schr.

[9] The piano scores are of Schreker's opera *Der ferne Klang* and Schönberg's *Gurrelieder*, as well as of the final two movements (*Litanei* and *Entrückung*) of Schönberg's second String Quartet op. 10. A probably four-handed piano score of Schönberg's Chamber Symphony op. 9 is presumed lost; a four-handed piano score of Schönberg's *Pelleas und Melisande* op. 5 remained a fragment.

[10] A list of his lieder is to be found in the *Katalog der Musikhandschriften, Schriften und Studien Alban Bergs* (Alban Berg Studien vol. 1) (Vienna, 1980), 43 f.

[11] As evident from Berg's letters to Schönberg of June 8, 1914, November 20, 1914 and November 1915.

[12] See Rosemary Hilmar, *Alban Berg. Leben und Wirken in Wien bis zu seinen ersten Erfolgen als Komponist* (Vienna, Cologne, Graz, 1978), 152-161.

[13] Berg to Schönberg, February 12, 1921

[14] Ibid.

[15] Webern to Berg, September 26, 1926 and June 5, 1929.

[16] Webern to Berg, July 13, 1928.

[17] Erich Alban Berg, *Der unverbesserliche Romantiker. Alban Berg, 1885-1935* (Vienna, 1985), 154-156.

[18] Schönberg to Berg, April 10, 1930.

[19] Berg to Schönberg on Easter Monday (April 21, 1930).

Asthma

[20] Ibid.

[21] To all appearances, this first attack was causally related to his father's death (Conrad Berg died on March 30, 1900) and to the traumatic consequences the mournful event had for the entire family.

[22] Quoted from R. Hilmar, *Berg* (1978), 119.

[23] Berg to Webern, September 20, 1929.

[24] Berg to Schönberg, July, 25, 1912.

[25] Berg to Schönberg, July 5, 1923.

[26] Jan Meyerowitz, *Arnold Schönberg* (Köpfe des XX. Jahrhunderts, vol. 47) (Berlin, 1967), 13. See also Schönberg's letter to Hans Rosbaud, February 13, 1932, in Arnold Schönberg, *Ausgewählte Briefe*, ed. Erwin Stein (Mainz, 1958), 175.

[27] Berg to Schönberg in an undated letter of the summer of 1911 ("Samstag nachts").

[28] Webern to Berg, August 7, 1913.

[29] Webern to Schönberg, August 5, 1913.

[30] On Adler's life and psychology of the individual, see Dieter Eicke, ed., *Tiefenpsychologie* (Kindlers *Psychologie des 20. Jahrhunderts*, vol 4: *Individualpsychologie und Analytische Psychologie* (Weinheim and Basel, 1982).

[31] Alfred Adler's best-known works include *Über den nervösen Charakter* of 1912, *Menschenkenntnis* (a series of lectures given in Vienna in 1926) and *Der Sinn des Lebens* of 1933.
[32] Webern to Schönberg, August 5, 1913.
[33] Webern to Schönberg, August, 1913.
[34] Webern to Berg, August 7, 1913.
[35] Arthur Jores and Margit von Kerékjártó, *Der Astmathiker. Ätiologie und Therapie des Asthma bronchiale in psychologischer Sicht* (Bern and Stuttgart, 1967), 47 f., 175 f.

The "Godforsaken" City

[36] Quoted in E. A. Berg, *Der unverbesserliche Romantiker*, 120.
[37] Ibid., 127.
[38] Egon Friedell, *Ecce Poeta* (Berlin, 1912), 258-262.
[39] Paul Stefan, "Frühling," *Der Ruf*, no. 2 (March, 1912), 4 f.
[40] Heinrich Jalowetz, "Abschied von Alban Berg," in *23. Alban Berg zum Gedenken* (1936), 12-15.
[41] Berg to Schönberg, September 19, 1931.
[42] Berg to Schönberg, October 20, 1931.
[43] Hektor Rottweiler (Th. W. Adorno), "Erinnerung an den Lebenden, *23* (1936*),* 28.
[44] Karl Ludwig Schneider, *Zerbrochene Formen. Wort und Bild im Expressionismus* (Darmstadt, 1967), 116-118.
[45] Berg to Schönberg, September 19, 1931.
[46] David Josef Bach, "Arnold Schönberg und Wien," *Musikblätter des Anbruch, 3 (1921),* 216-218
[47] Emil Petschnig in the *Allgemeine Zeitung*, quoted in Frank Schneider , *Berg-Schriften*, 354.
[48] H. H. Stuckenschmidt, *Schönberg - Leben – Umwelt* (Munich, 1989), 493.
[49] Alban Berg, "Aufruf für Schönberg" (1911), in Ernst Hilmar, ed., *Schönberg. Gedenkausstellung 1974* (Vienna, 1974), 228.
[50] Undated letter to Webern (dateable 1911 or 1912). Published in *Katalog der Schriftstücke und Dokumente Alban Bergs* (Alban Berg Studies, vol. 1/2) (Vienna, 1985),136 f.
[51] Ibid.
[52] *Schönberg-Gedenkausstellung 1974*, 227.
[53] A. Schönberg, *Ausgewählte Briefe* (1958), 27.
[54] See H. H. Stuckenschmidt, *Schönberg*, (1989), 141, 169.
[55] R. Hilmar, *Berg*, 75.
[56] Adolf Opel, *Konfrontationen. Schriften von und über Adolf Loos* (Vienna, 1988), 122.
[57] *Schönberg-Gedenkausstellung 1974*, 195 f.
[58] Facsimile of the program in Stuckenschmidt, *Schönberg*, 171.
[59] See Stefan Zweig, *Die Welt von Gestern. Erinnerungen eines Europäers* (Fischer Taschenbuch) (Frankfurt a. M., !970), 62.
[60] Walter Szmolyan, "SchönbergsWiener Verein für musikalische Privataufführungen," in *Schönberg Gedenkausstellung 1974*, 71-82; p. 71.
[61] Ibid., 73.
[62] Walter Szmolyan, "Die Konzerte des Wiener Schönberg-Vereins," in *Schönbergs Verein für musikalische Privataufführungen* (Musik-Konzepte 36) (Munich, 1984), 101-114; p. 111.

[63] Konrad Vogelsang, *Dokumentation zur Oper "Wozzeck" von Alban Berg. Die Jahre des Durchbruchs, 1925-1932* (Lauber, 1977), 44, 48.
[64] Ibid., 44.
[65] See Jochen Schürmann, ed., *Die Korngolds in Wien. Der Musikkritiker und das Wunderkind. Aufzeichungen von Julius Korngold* (Zurich/St. Gallen, 1991).
[66] R. Hilmar, *Alban Berg 1885-1935. Ausstellung der Österreichischen Nationalbibliothek, Prunksaal. 23. Mai bis 20. Oktober 1985* (Vienna, 1985), 77.
[67] Vogelsang, *Dokumentation*, 77.
[68] *Berg-Ausstellungskatalog 1985*, 123.
[69] R. Hilmar, *Berg*, 156.
[70] Elias Canetti, "Alban Berg," in *Das Augenspiel. Lebensgeschichte 1901-1937* (Fischer Taschenbuch) (Frankfurt a. M., 1988), 218-223; p. 219.

Composing in the Country

[71] *Jugendbriefe von Robert Schumann*, ed. Clara Schumann, 4th ed, (Leipzig, 1910), 278.
[72] Berg to Schönberg, May 18, 1930.
[73] Hans and Rosaleen Moldenhauer, *Anton von Webern. Chronik seines Lebens und Werkes* (Zurich, 1980), 201.
[74] *Berg-Ausstellungskatalog 1985*, 21. See the picture of the "Berghof" in ABB, illustration no. 8.
[75] R. Hilmar, *Berg*, 20.

The Insidiousness of Success

[76] Schönberg, *Ausgewählte Briefe*, 261.
[77] Adolf Loos, "Die kranken Ohren Beethovens" (1913), in *Loos, Trotzdem 1900-1930* (Innsbruck, 1931; reprinted Vienna, 1982), 118.
[78] Schönberg, "Kriterien für die Bewertung von Musik," GS I, 123-133; p. 130.
[79] Willi Reich, *Alban Berg* (Vienna, Leipzig, Zurich, n.d. [1937]), 9.
[80] Erich Alban Berg, ed., *Alban Berg. Leben und Werk in Daten und Bildern* (Insel Taschenbuch 194) (Frankfurt a. M., 1976), 21
[81] Austrian National Library, Music Collection, PhA 2340, p. 49.
[82] Austrian National Library, Music Collecton, F 21 Berg 610.
[83] E. A. Berg, *Der unverbesserliche Romantiker*, 99.
[84] Adorno, *Berg*, 18.
[85] Ibid., 36.

Humanity

[86] Hans W. Heinsheimer, *Menagerie in Fis-dur*, transl. Willi Reich (Zurich, 1953), 280.
[87] Elias Canetti, *Das Augenspiel*, 221.
[88] Willi Reich, "Alban Berg," *Die Musik*, 22:5 (February 1930), 347-3353; p. 353.
[89] Facsimile of the article under the title "Der Komponist als Lebensretter" in Volker Scherliess, *Alban Berg in Selbstzeugnissen und Bilddokumenten* (rowohlts monographien 225) (Reinbek, 1975), 75.
[90] R. Hilmar, *Berg*, 119-123.
[91] Berg to Schönberg, December 14, 1914.

[92] Cf. Paul Schick, *Karl Kraus mit Selbstzeugnissen und Bilddokumenten* (rowohlts monographien 980), Reinbek, 1965), 85.
[93] Adorno, *Berg*, 11 f.
[94] Ernst Bloch, *Erbschaft der Zeit* (1935); quoted from Attila Csampai and Dietmar Holland, eds., *Alban Berg. Wozzeck. Texte, Materialien, Kommentare* (rororo opernbuch 7929) (Reinbek, 1985), 6.

Longing for Happiness or Deliverance through Art

[95] Joan Allen Smith: "The Berg-Hohenberg Correspondence," in Rudolf Klein, ed., *Alban Berg Symposion Wien 1980. Tagungsbericht* (Alban Berg Studien, vol. 2) (Vienna, 1981), 189-197; p. 191.
[96] Austrian National Library, Music Collection F 21 Berg 100, I-XII.
[97] E. A. Berg, *Der unverbesserliche Romantiker*, 66.
[98] "Erinnerung an den Lebenden," in *23. Eine Wiener Musikzeitschrift*, no. 24/25 (February 1936), 27.
[99] Adorno, *Berg*, 23.
[100] Quotation Collection no. 391 (Peter Altenberg).
[101] Berg wrote her on June 18, 1921: "I already wrote to you about alcohol. Have no fear my goldie, alcohol means something altogether different to me than it does to my various family members, it is a holy matter to me, like music" (ABB 464).
[102] Reproduced in Scherliess, *Berg*, 17.
[103] *Berg-Ausstellungskatalog 1985*, 98 f.
[104] Quoted from Attila Csampai and Dietmar Holland, eds. , *Alban Berg. Lulu. Texte, Materialien, Kommentare* (rororo opernbuch 7340) (Reinbek, 1985), 207. On the friendship between Frida Semler and Alban Berg, see Donald Harris, "Berg and Miss Frida," in *Alban Berg Studien*, vol. 2, 198-208.
[105] Sigmund Freud, *Abriss der Psychoanalyse. Das Unbehagen in der Kultur* (Fischer Bücher 47) (Frankfurt a. M. and Hamburg, 1953), 79 ff.
[106] Adorno, *Berg*, 26.
[107] Among the apothegms from Eduard Hanslick's *Vom musikalisch Schönen* that Berg excerpted for his Quotation Collection (527-532) we find the sentence: "Every art sets out from the sensuous and moves within it" (no. 527).

Fidelity

[108] On Berg's affair with Hanna Fuchs-Robettin, see Part III below and Constantin Floros, *Alban Berg and Hanna Fuchs. The Story of a Love in Letters*, transl. Ernest Bernhardt-Kabisch (Bloomington and Indianapolis, 2008; original German edition Zurich-Hamburg, 2001).
[109] The essay was published by Hans Ferdinand Redlich in *Alban Berg. Versuch einer Würdigung* (Vienna, Zurich, London, 1957), 328 f.
[110] "Erinnerung an den Lebenden," *23*, nos. 24/25 (1936), 28.
[111] Adorno, *Berg*, 60 f.
[112] Ibid., 25.

From Goethe to Wedekind

[113] Berg's voluminous library remains to this day in his Hietzing apartment (the seat of the Alban Berg Foundation) in Trauttmansdorffgasse 27.

[114] Soma Morgenstern "Im Trauerhaus," *23. Eine Wiener Musikzeitscrift*, nos 24/25, 16.

[115] Susanne Rode, *Alban Berg und Karl Kraus. Zur geistigen Biographie des Komponisten der "Lulu"* (Europäische Hochschulschriften, series XXXVI, vol. 36) (Frankfurt a. M., 1988).

[116] Elias Canetti, *Die Fackel im Ohr. Lebensgeschichte 1921-1931* (Munich, Vienna, 1980).

[117] Allan Janik & Stephen Toulmin, *Wittgensteins Wien*, 2nd ed. (Munich 1989), 107.

[118] A pagination error occurred in the last volume of the Quotation Collection (100/XII fol. 10'/11 and 11'/12): Berg accidentally let the number 1099 be followed by the number 2000. Unaware of the mistake, he continued to paginate wrongly to the end, so that the collection closes with the number 2061 instead of the number 1161.

[119] Cf. Maurizio Calvesi, "Von der Secession zum Expressionismus," in *Wien um 1900. Kunst und Kultur* (Vienna and Munich, 1985), i-iii.

[120] Hermann Bahr, "Die Überwindung des Naturalismus," in Gotthart Wunberg, ed., *Die Wiener Moderne. Kunst und Musik zwischen 1890 und 1910* (Reclam Universal-Bibliothek no. 7742[9]) (Stuttgart, 1982), 199-205.

[121] Hermann Bahr, "Die Décadence," in *Die Wiener Moderne*, 225-232.

[122] Quoted from Janik/Toulmin, *Wittgensteins Wien*, 102.

[123] Karl Kraus, "Hermann Bahr und Emanuel Reicher," in *Die Wiener Moderne*, 313-315.

[124] Cf. Constantin Floros, *Gustav Mahler*, vol. 1: *Die geistige Welt Gustav Mahlers in systematischer Darstellung*, 1st ed. (Wiesbaden, 1977), 68.

[125] R. Hilmar, *Berg*, 27.

[126] Berg to Webern, July 18, 1914.

[127] E. A. Berg, *Der unverbesserliche Romantiker*, 64.

[128] Berg's personal copy of Strindberg's *Nach Damaskus* contains, next to the list of characters (the Unknown, The Lady and the Beggar) the pencil entry "Ich" (I).

[129] Webern to Berg, December 27, 1921.

[130] Undated letter to Webern, written probably in August of 1911.

[131] Berg to Webern, July, 1912.

[132] Ibid.

[133] Webern to Schönberg, May 24, 1912, February 22, 1914 and May 10, 1914.

[134] Webern to Schönberg, September 12, 1912.

[135] Webern to Schönberg, September 17, 1912.

[136] Webern to Berg, May 23, 1913.

[137] Webern to Schönberg, August, 1913.

[138] Webern to Schönberg, June 18, 1913.

[139] Webern to Schönberg, May 23, 1914.

[140] Paul Stefan, *Gustav Mahler*, 3rd ed. (Munich, 1912).

[141] Richard Specht, *Gustav Mahler* (Berlin and Leipzig, 1913), 21 f. n.1

[142] Dostoevksy, *Die Brüder Karamasoff*, vol. 1 (Munich and Leipzig, 1908), 636-656.

[143] Hugo Friedrich, *Die Struktur der modernen Lyrik von Baudelaire bis zur Gegenwart* (rowohlts deutsche enzyklopädie, vol. 25) (Hamburg, 1956), 27.

[144] Bertha Zuckerkandl,, "Modernes Kunstgewerbe," in *Die Wiener Moderne*, 177-182; p. 181.
[145] Hermann Bahr, "Die Décadence," in *Die Wiener Moderne*, 225-232; p. 227.
[146] Munich, 1920.
[147] 3rd ed. (Berlin, 1914).
[148] Webern to Berg, December 28, 1911
[149] Cf. Floros, *Alban Berg and Hanna Fuchs. The Story of a Love in Letters*, 21, 87 f., 114-116.
[150] Janik/Toulmin, *Wittgensteins Wien*, 103.
[151] Peter Altenberg, "Selbstbiographie," in *Was der Tag mir zuträgt. 55 neue Studien* (Berlin, 1901; 9th – 11th enlarged and modified ed. 1921). Reprinted in J. Schweiger, ed., *Das große Peter Altenberg-Buch* (Vienna, Hamburg, 1977), 9-14; p. 10.
[152] See Mark DeVoto, "Alban Berg's Picture-Postcard Songs," diss., Princeton, 1967.
[153] Cf. Rode, *Alban Berg und Karl Kraus*, 204-206.
[154] Csampai/Holland, *Alban Berg. Lulu*, 207.
[155] Jan Maegaard, "Die Komponisten der Wiener Schule und ihre Textdichter sowie das Komponisten-Dichter-Verhältnis heute," in Otto Kolleritsch, ed., *Zum Verhältnis von zeitgenössischer Musik und Dichtung* (Studien zur Wertungsforschung, vol. 20) (Vienna, Graz, 1988), 168-183.
[156] Quoted from E. A. Berg, *Der unverbesserliche Romantiker*, 118.
[157] Adorno, *Berg*, 19.
[158] Ibid., 17.
[159] Reich, *Berg*, 18.
[160] Marie Herzfeld, "Fin-de-siècle," in *Die Wiener Moderne*, 260-265; pp. 260 f.
[161] Karl Kraus, "Nestroy und die Nachwelt," in *Auswahl aus dem Werk* (Fischer Bücherie 377) (Frankfurt a. M. And Hamburg, 1961), 122-137.
[162] Adorno, *Berg*, 134.
[163] See Aldo Keel, ed., *Erläuterungen und Dokumente. Henrik Ibsen. Nora (Ein Puppenheim)* (Reclam Universal-Bibliothek no. 8185) (Stuttgart, 1900).
[164] Annegret Stopczyk, comment on Otto Weininger, *Geschlecht und Charakter. Eine prinzipielle Untersuchung*, 1st ed. (Vienna, 1903), reprint (Munich, 1980), 654 f.
[165] Ibid., 447.
[166] Ernst Bloch, *Das Prinzip Hoffnung*, 3 vols. (Wissenschaftliche Sonderausgabe, Suhrkamp) (Frankfurt a. M., 1959), 2:692.
[167] Countess Geschwitz in the final scene of the opera (III.2): "This is the last evening I will spend with this crowd. I am returning to Germany. I'll enroll in a university. I must fight for women's rights, study law."

Love of Nature

[168] Cf. Rainer Bischof, "Versuch über die philosophischen Grundlagen von Alban Berg," in *Alban Berg Studien*, 2:209-215; pp. 213-215.
[169] Cf. Rode, *Alban Berg und Karl Kraus*, 120 ff.
[170] Weininger, *Geschlecht und Charakter*, 326.
[171] Berg in an undated letter to Webern from the year 1914.
[172] Quoted from E. A. Berg, *Der unverbesserliche Romantiker*, 135.

[173] Webern to Berg, October 8, 1925.
Religiosity
[174] Redlich, *Berg*, 293.
[175] Adorno, *Berg*, 23.
[176] E. A. Berg, *Der unverbesserliche Romantiker*, 186.
[177] Sigmund Freud, *Das Unbehagen in der Kultur*, 65.
[178] Webern to Berg, May 23, 1913; to Schönberg, September 12, 1912 and August 9, 1913.
[179] Webern to Berg, April 18, 193.
[180] Cf. Constantin Floros, *Gustav Mahler*, vol. 2: *Gustav Mahler and the Symphony of the 19th Century* (New ytork:Peter Lang, 2014), 249-251
[181] ABB 238 f. Cf. Floros, *Gustav Mahler*, vol. 3: *The Symphonies* (Portland, 1993), 341 n. 15.
[182] Berg to Helene, January 28, 1914 (ABB 245).
Faith, Love and Hope
[183] Reproduced in E. A. Berg, *Der unverbesserliche Romantiker*, 77.
[184] Richard Wagner, *Religion und Kunst*, in *Sämtliche Schriften und Dichtungen (Volksausgabe*, 16 vols., 6th ed. (Leipzig, n.d.), 10:211-253. See also Floros, "Wagners Idee der Kunstreligion," in *Musik als Botschaft* (Wiesbaden, 1989), 39-53.
[185] Richard Wagner, "Programmatische Erläuterung des Vorspiels zum ersten Aufzug des Parsifal," in *Sämtliche Schriften und Dichtungen*, 12:349.
[186] *Arnold Schönberg zum 60. Geburtstag, 13. September 1934*, Universal-Edition Vienna.
Commitment to Radical Modernism and German Music
[187] Webern to Schönberg, July 15, 1926.
[188] The letters stand for "Internationale Gesellschaft für Neue Musik (im Arsch [up the ass])."
[189] Alban Berg, "Verbindliche Antwort auf eine unverbindliche Rundfrage," Schr, 221-226; pp. 225 f.
[190] Berg to Hermann Watznauer, July 16, 1903. Quoted from R. Hilmar, *Berg*, 27.
[191] Webern to Berg, September 23, 1925
[192] On May 13, 1949, Schönberg told Amadeo de Philippi that he wrote the *Satiren* when he had become greatly upset about the attacks from some of his younger colleagues and wanted to warn them that it was not a good idea to "tangle" with him. See Josef Rufer, *Das Werk Arnold Schönbergs* (Kassel, Basel, London, New York, 1959), 31.
[193] Anton Webern, *Briefe an Hildegard Jone und Josef Humplik*, ed. Josef Polnauer (Vienna, 1959), 10.
[194] Theodor W. Adorno, *Philosophie der neuen Musik* (Frankfurt a. M., 1958), 127-199.
Part Two: Theoretical Presuppositions
Questions Regarding the Psychology of Creation
[195] Quoted from Max Kalbeck, *Johannes Brahms*, vol. 2, 3rd ed. (Berlin, 1921) 181 f. See also Constantin Floros, *Brahms und Bruckner. Studien zur musikalischen Exegetik* (Wiesbaden, 1980), 30-34.
[196] *Gustav Mahler in den Erinnerungen von Natalie Bauer-Lechner*, ed. from the diaries by Herbert Killian (Hamburg, 1984), 161.
[197] Arnold Schönberg, *Harmonielehre*, 1st ed. (Leipzig, Vienna, 1911), 464.

[198] Adorno, *Berg*, 41.
[199] Ibid. 23.
[200] Adorno, *Mahler*, 37.
[201] Ibid., 169.
[202] Bruno Stäblein, *Schriftbild der einstimmigen Musik* (Musikgeschichte in Bildern, vol. 3: *Musik des Mittelalters und der Renaissance*, no. 4) (Leipzig, 1975), 194 f.
[203] Louise Duchesneau, *The Voice of the Muse: A Study of the Role of Inspiration in Musical Composition* (European University Studies, series XXXVI. Musicology, vol. 19) (Frankfurt a. M., 1986).
[204] Arthur M. Abell, *Talks with Great Composers* (New York, 1955).
[205] Hans Pfitzner, *Über musikaliche Inspiration* (Berlin, 1940), 30.
[206] Duchesneau, *The Voice of the Muse*, 66
[207] *Richard Wagner an Mathilde Wesendonck. Tagebuchblätter und Briefe, 1853-1871*, ed. Wolfgang Golther, 54th ed, (Volksausgabe) (Leipzig, 1916), 221.
[208] Arnold Schönberg, "Mahler," GS I, 7-24; p. 23
[209] H. H. Stuckenschmidt, *Schönberg*, 473.
[210] *Gustav Mahler in den Erinnerungen von Natalie Bauer-Lechner*, 33.
[211] Gustav Mahler, *Briefe,* new ed. enlarged and revised, ed. Herta Blaukopf (Vienna, Hamburg, 1982), 122.
[212] Arnold Schönberg "Aphorismen," *Die Musik*, 9 (1921), 159-163; p. 162.
[213] Cf. Floros, *Mahler*, 1:136-142.
[214] *Documenta Bartókiana*, ed. Denis Dille (Budapest, 1970), 78 f.
[215] Schönberg, "Mahler," GS, 1:11.
[216] GS, 1:165-168.

Inward and Outward Nature
[217] Schönberg, *Harmonielehre*, 15.
[218] Wassily Kandinsky, "Die Bilder," in *Arnold Schönberg* (Munich, 1912), 59-64; p. 60.
[219] Schönberg, *Ausgewählte Briefe*, 154.
[220] Adorno, *Berg*, 23.
[221] Gutav René Hocke, *Die Welt als Labyrinth, Manier und Manie in der europäischen Kunst* (rowohlts Deutsche Enzyklopädie, vol. 50/51) (Hamburg, 1957), 44.
[222] Schönberg, *Harmonielehre*, 15.
[223] Wassily Kandinsky, *Das Geistige in der Kunst*, 6th ed. with an introduction by Max Bill (Berne-Bümpliz, 1959; 1st ed. 1912; 4th ed. 1952), 54, 55 f., 49.
[224] Jelena Hahl-Koch, ed., *Arnold Schönberg, Wassily Kandinsky: Briefe, Bilder und Dokumente einer außergewöhnlichen Begegnung* (Deutscher Taschenbuch-Verlag 2883) (Munich, 1983), 35.
[225] *Arnold Schönberg in höchster Verehrung* (Munich, 1912), 59-64.
[226] Quoted from E. A. Berg, *Der unverbesserliche Romantiker*, 65 f.

From Overt to Covert Program Music
[227] Quoted from J. Rufer, *Das Werk Arnold Schönbergs*, 13.
[228] Autograph marginal note in Schönberg's personal copy of Ferruccio Busoni's *Entwurf einer neuen Ästhetik der Tonkunst* (Leipzig, 1916); quoted from the Insel-Verlag edition (Frankfurt a. M., 1974), 63.

[229] David Josef Bach, "Arnold Schönberg und Wien," *Musikblätter des Anbruch*, 3 (1921), 216-218; p. 217.
[230] Walter B. Bailey, *Programmatic Elements in the Works of Schoenberg* (Studies in Musicology, no. 74) (Ann Arbor, 1984).
[231] See the fundamental study by Peter Petersen, "'A grave situation was created': Schönbergs Klavierkonzert von 1942," in Otto Kolleritsch, ed., *Die Wiener Schule und das Hakenkreuz. Das Schicksal der Moderne im gesellschaftspolitischen Kontext des 20. Jahrhunderts* (Studien zur Wertforschung, vol. 22 (Vienna, Graz, 1990), 65-91.
[232] Christian Martin Schmidt, "Schönbergs 'very definite – but private' Programm zum Streichquartett Opus 7," in Rudolf Stephan und Sigrid Wiesmann, eds., *Bericht über den 2. Kongress der Internationalen Schönberg-Gesellschaft "Die Wiener Schule in der Musikgeschichte des 20. Jahrhunderts"* (Vienna, 1986), 230-234.
[233] Frank Schneider, "Autobiographische Symptome in Schönbergs Musik. Modell: Streichquartett II op. 10," in Goldschmidt, Kepler & Niemann, eds., *Komponisten auf Werk und Leben befragt*, 83-98.
[234] Bailey, *Programmatic Elements*, 130.
[235] Walter Rubsamen, "Schönberg in America," *The Musical Quarterly* 37:4 (Oct. 1951), 469-489.
[236] Thomas Mann, "Die Entstehung des Doktor Faustus," in *Doktor Faustus. Roman. Die Entstehung des Doktor Faustus* (Frankfurt a. M., 1967), 826.
[237] Schönberg, *Die glückliche Hand* (1928), in GS, 1:235-239; p. 237. Reprinted in Jelena Hahl-Koch, *Schönberg, Kandinsky*, 129-135.
[238] Theodor W. Adorno, *Philosophie der Neuen Musik*, 42 f.
[239] Schönberg, "Franz Liszts Werk und Wesen" (October 1911), in GS, 1:169-173.
[240] See Michael Mäckelmann, *Schönberg. Fünf Orchesterstücke op. 16* (Meisterwerke der Musik, n. 45) (Munich, 1987), 49ff.
[241] See my "Verschwiegene Programmusik," in *Musik als Botschaft*, 140-154.
[242] Schönberg, *Die glückliche Hand*, in GS, 1:237.
[243] Carl Dahlhaus, "Schönberg und die Programmusik," in *Schönberg und andere. Gesammelte Aufsätze zur Neuen Musik* (Mainz, 1978), 125-133; p. 126.
[244] Ibid., 132.
[245] See Floros, "Psychodramen, tönende Autobiographie und illustrierende Programmusik. Zu Richard Strauss' Tondichtungen," in *Kongressbericht zum VI. Internationalen Symposium RICHARD STRAUSS (1989)* (Frankfurt, Leipzig, 1991), 36-40. See also my book, *Hören und verstehen. Die Sprache der Musik und ihre Deutung*, Mainz 2008, 164-172.
[246] Richard Strauss, *Betrachtungen und Erinnerungen*, ed. Willi Schuh (Munich, 1989), 14-41
[247] "Alban Bergs Kammerkonzert für Geige und Klavier mit Begleitung von dreizehn Bläsern," *Pult und Taktstock: Fachzeitschrift für Dirigenten*, 2 (1925), 23-28. Reprinted in *Schriften zur Musik* (1981), 228-235.
[248] Arnold Schönberg, *Texte* (Universal Edition no. 7731) (Vienna, New York, 1926), 56.
[249] Goethe to Friedrich Wilhelm Riemer, December 12, 1806.

[250] Sigmund Freud, *Zur Psychopathologie des Alltagslebens. Über Vergessen, Versprechen, Vergreifen, Aberglaube und Irrtum* (Fischer Bücher des Wissens, vol. 68) (Frankfurt a. M. und Hamburg, 1954), 218.
[251] Adorno, *Philosophie der Neuen Musik*, 66 f.
[252] Rosemarie Puschmann, *Magisches Quadrat und Melancholie in Thomas Manns Doktor Faustus. Von der musikalischen Struktur zum semantsichen Beziehungsnetz* (Bielefeld, 1983), 61.
[253] See my review of Puschmann's book in the *Neue Zeitschrift für Musik*, no. 3 (1985), 57.
[254] *Musik-Konzepte* no 9: *Alban Berg / Kammermusik II* (July 1979), 9 f.
[255] Berg to Webern, October 12, 1925.
[256] Schönberg, "Prager Rede auf Mahler"(1912), GS, 1:14.
[257] Erwin Stein, "Alban Berg – Anton Webern," *Musikblätter des Anbruch*, 5 (1923), 13-16; p. 14.
[258] Helmut Schmidt-Garre, "Berg als Lehrer, " *Melos*, 22 (1955), 40 f.
[259] Ursula von Rauchhaupt, *Schönberg / Berg / Webern. Die Streichquartette. Eine Dokumentation* (Hamburg, 1971), 105-116.
[260] Berg, "Wiener Musikkritik," in Schr, 182-190; p. 185. The review by Julius Korngold that Berg quotes appeared on July 17, 1920 in the *Neue Freie Presse*.
[261] E. A. Berg, *der unverbesserliche Romantiker*, 91 f.
[262] Ernst Hilmar, "Alban Bergs Selbstzeugnisse zu Entstehung und Auffführbarkeit der Oper 'Lulu'," in *Alban Berg. Lied der Lulu. Faksimile Ausgabe der Anton v. Webern gewidmeten autographen Partitur*, ed. Wiener Stadt- und Landesbibliothek (Vienna, n.d.), 12.
[263] Berg to Schönberg, September 1, 1928.
[264] Hans W. Heinsheimer, *Menagerie in Fis-dur*, transl. Willi Reich (Zurich, 1953), 280 f.
[265] *Berg-Ausstellungskatalog 1985*, 83.
[266] Alma Mahler, *Gustav Mahler. Erinnerungen und Briefe*, 2nd ed. (Amsterdam, 1949; 1st ed., 1940), 145 f.
[267] August Göllerich und Max Auer, *Anton Bruckner. Ein Lebens- und Schaffensbild*, vol. 4, pt. 3 (Regensburg, 1936), 457.
[268] Schönberg, "Prager Rede auf Mahler," GS, 1:23.
[269] Jan Meyerowitz, *Arnold Schönberg*, 37.
[270] H.H. Stuckenschmidt, *Schönberg*, 370.
[271] The 13 played a role also in the life of Richard Wagner, who was born in 1813 and died on February 13, 1883. His name consists of 13 letters, and his consecrational stage festival play *Parsifal* was completed on January 13, 1882.
[272] Austrian National Library, Music Collection, PhA 2340p, p. 11.
[273] See Gertrud Schönberg's account in Stuckenschmidt, *Schönberg*, 473 f.
[274] Josef Rufer, *Das Werk Arnold Schönbergs*, 42.
[275] Hans W. Heinsheimer, *Menagerie in Fis-dur* 281 f.
[276] Wilhelm Fließ, *Vom Leben und vom Tod. Biologische Vorträge*, 2nd ed., expanded (Jena, 1914; 1st ed. 1909).
[277] Willi Reich, *Alban Berg. Leben und Werk* (Zurich, 1963), 24.
[278] Berg to Schönberg, June 20, 1915.
[279] According to Redlich, *Berg*, 335.

[280] Willi Reich, *Berg*, 18.
[281] E. A. Berg, *Der unverbesserliche Romantiker*, 115-117.
[282] Berg's double-acrostich distichs first appeared in the festschrift for Loos's 60th birthday on December 10, 1937. Willi Reich reprinted them in his *Berg* (202). See also Schr, 311.
[283] Berg to Schönberg, June 20, 1915.
[284] George Perle, "Das geheime Programm der Lyrischen Suite," in *Musikkonzepte*, no. 4: *Alban Berg / Kammermusik I* (Munich, April 1978), 49-74; p. 57. Cf. also Floros, *Alban Berg and Hanna Fuchs*, 99.
[285] See especially Jürg Stenzl, "Lulus 'Welt'," in *Alban Berg Symposion Wien 1980* (Vienna, 1981), 31-39, and Peter Stadlen, "Berg's Cryptography," ibid., 171-180.
[286] In the Open Letter to Schönberg, Schr, 231.

Tone Ciphers
[287] *Musik-Konzepte*, no. 9 (1979), 9.
[288] See Albert Schweitzer, *Johann Sebastian Bach*, 7. ed. (Leipzig, 1929), 394 f.
[289] Karl H. Wörner, *Robert Schumann* (Zurich, 1949; licensed ed. Munich, 1987), 103.
[290] See Constantin Floros, *Johannes Brahms. "Free but Alone": A Life for a Poetic Music*, transl. Ernest Bernhardt-Kabisch (Frankfurt a. M., Berlin, New York, Oxford, Vienna, et al., 2010; German ed., 1997), 35-40.
[291] Robert Schumann, *Gesammelte Schriften über Musik und Musiker*, 5th ed., ed. Martin Kreisig, 2 vols. (Leipzig, 1914), 1:116-122; 2:279-283.
[292] Alban Berg, "Die musikalische Impotenz der 'neuen Ästhetik' Hans Pfitzners," in Schr, 191-204.
[293] According to Redlich (*Berg*, 333) the Four Lieder op. 2 were begun in early 1909 and completed in the spring of 1910.
[294] According to Walter B. Bailey (*Programmatic Elements in the Works of Schoenberg* 133), all of the movements of the Suite op 29 begin and end with the notes g-es (g-e^b), the initials of Gertrud Schönberg, to whom the work is dedicated.
[295] *Musik-Konzepte*, no. 9, 10. Can it be a mere coincidence that Adrian Leverkühn, like Alban Berg, was born in 1885, and that he died on May 23 (!), 1941?
[296] See Rosemarie Puschmann, *Magisches Quadrat*, 21 ff.

Magic Music
[297] Thomas Mann, *Ausgewählte Essays in drei Bänden*, vol. 2: *Politische Reden und Schriften* selected, introduced and elucidated by Hermann Kurzke (Fischer Taschenbuch 1907) (Frankfurt a. M., 1977), 285.
[298] Cf. Karlheinz Hasselbach, *Thomas Mann. Doktor Faustus* (Munich, 1977); Frank Baron, *Faustus. Geschichte, Sage, Dichtung* (Munich, 1982).
[299] See Puschmann, *Magisches Quadrat*, 88.
[300] Jules Combarieu, *La musique et la magie. Etude sur les origines populaires de l'art musical, son influence et sa fonction dans les societés* (Paris, 1909; reprint Geneva, 1978).
[301] Thomas Mann, *Doktor Faustus*, 330.
[302] Puschmann, *Magisches Quadrat*, 17-19.
[303] Thomas Mann, *Doktor Faustus*, 66.

[304] Puschmann, *Magisches Quadrat*, 76

[305] Josef Rufer, *Die Komposition mit zwölf Tönen* (Stimmen des XX. Jahrhunderts, vol. 2) (Berlin and Wunsiedel, 1952), 50.

[306] Erwin Stein, "Neue Formprinzipien," in *Arnold Schönberg zum fünfzigsten Geburtstage 13. September, 1924*, *Musikblätter des Anbruch*, 6 (August-September special issue, 1924), 286-303.

[307] Gustav René Hocke, *Die Welt als Labyrinth*, 7 f.

[308] See Rufer, *Die Komposition mit 12 Tönen*, 92 f.

[309] Ibid., 96.

[310] Anton Webern, *Der Weg zur Neuen Musik*, ed. Willi Reich (Vienna, 1960), 60.

[311] Ursula Rauchhaupt, *Schönberg / Berg / Webern*, 93.

[312] Puschmann, *Magisches Quadrat*, 265.

[313] Rufer, *Die Komposition mit 12 Tönen*, 49.

[314] Anton Webern, *Briefe an Hildegard Jone und Josef Humplik*, ed. Josef Polnauer (Vienna, 1959), 18.

[315] Webern's reading seems to be the correct one. If, however, one reads the lines of the square from left to right (thus: *sator arepo tenet opera rotas*), one reads to all appearances wrongly, as Puschmann (p. 67) noted. One should add that Gustav René Hocke (*Manierismus in der Literatur. Sprach-Alchemie und esoterische Kombinationskunst* [Hamburg, 1959], 24) translates the formula as follows: "The farmer (sower) Arepo (proper name) guides the plough (wheels) with his hand (work)."

[316] Jan Maegaard, *Studien zur Entwicklung des dodekaphonen Satzes bei Arnold Schönberg*, vol. 1 (Copenhagen, 1972), 118 f.

Symmetry and Palindrome

[317] Adorno, *Berg*, 21.

[318] Fritz Paul, *August Strindberg* (Sammlung Metzler) (Stuttgart, 1979), 55.

[319] Quoted from Fritz Paul, ibid.

[320] John C. Crawford, "The Relationship of Text and Music in the Works of Schoenberg, 1908-24," diss., Harvard Univ. (Cambridge, Mass, 1963), 168 ff.

[321] Michael Mäckelmann, "'Die glückliche Hand'. Eine Studie zu Musik und Inhalt von Arnold Schönbergs 'Drama mit Musik'," in *Musiktheater im 20. Jahrhundert* (Hamburger Jahrbuch für Musikwissenschaft, vol. 10) (Laaber, 1988), 7-36; p. 27.

[322] Schönberg, *Texte*, 37-65.

[323] For a much simpler construction, see the palindromic theme of the variations in the *Serenade op. 24*.

[324] Theodor W. Adorno, "Zur Vorgeschichte der Reihenkomposition," in *Klangfiguren. Musikalische Schriften I* (Frankfurt a. M., 1959), 95-120; p. 117.

[325] Berg, Schr, 227, 347.

[326] Josef Rufer, "Hommage a Schönberg," in *Arnold Schönberg: Berliner Tagebuch*, ed. Josef Rufer (Frankfurt a. M., Berlin, Vienna, 1974), 55.

[327] See above all Michael Mäckelmann, *Arnold Schönberg und das Judentum. Der Komponist und sein religiöses, nationales und politisches Selbstverständnis nach 1921* (Hamburger Beiträge zur Musikwissenschaft, vol 28) (Hamburg, 1984).

[328] Berg, Oldenburg *Wozzeck* lecture of 1929, in Schr 267-289; pp. 269 f.
[329] Otto F. Best, *Handbuch literarischer Fachbegriffe. Definitionen und Beispiele* (Fischer Handbücher 6092) (Frankfurt a. M., 1972), 187.
[330] Mauricio Kagel's *Anagrama* of 1957/58 is based on the Latin palindrome *In girum imus nocte et consumimur igni* (We walk in a circle in the night and are consumed by fire).
[331] For details, see the *Lulu* chapter below.
[332] Redlich, *Berg*, 156 f.
[333] Ernst Krenek, "Music und Mathematik," in *Über neue Musik. Sechs Vorlesungen zur Einführung in die theoretischen Grundlagen* (Vienna, 1937; reprinted Darmstadt, 1977), 71-89; p. 88.

Tonality, Atonality and Dodecaphony: Transvaluation of All Values

[334] Anton Webern, lecture given February 12, 1932, in *Wege zur neuen Musik*, 55.
[335] Paul Hindemith, *Unterweisung im Tonsatz. I: Theoretischer Teil*, new, expanded ed. (Mainz, 1940), 185.
[336] Ibid., 137.
[337] Ibid., 183.
[338] Arnold Schönberg, *Harmonielehre*, 1st ed. (Leipzig, Vienna, 1911), 145.
[339] Ibid., 145.
[340] Ibid., 169.
[341] Ibid., 440.
[342] Ibid., 466.
[343] See Constantin Floros, "Kompositionstechnische Probleme der atonalen Musik," in *Bericht über den Internationalen Musikwissenschaftlichen Kongress in Kassel 1962* (Kassel, 1963), 257-260; Reinhold Brinkmann, *Arnold Schönberg: Drei Klavierstücke op. 11. Studien zur frühen Atonalität bei Schönberg* (Wiesbaden, 1969); Elmar Budde, *Anton Weberns Lieder op. 3. Untersuchungen zur frühen Atonalität bei Webern* (Wiesbaden, 1971); Albrecht Dümling, *Die fremden Klänge der hängenden Gärten. Die öffentliche Einsamkeit der Neuen Musik am Beispiel von Arnold Schönberg und Stefan George* (Munich, 1981).
[344] Hanns Eisler, "Schönberg-Anekdoten," in *Musikblätter des Anbruch*, special issue (August-September, 1924), 327 f.
[345] The essay first appeared in the festschrift for Schönberg's 50th birthday, *Musikblätter des Anbruch* (1924), 329-341. Reprinted in Berg, Schr, 205-220.
[346] Berg, Schr, 306.
[347] Willi Reich, *Arnold Schönberg oder der konservative Revolutionär* (Deutscher Taschenbuch Verlag 1041) (Munich, 1974), 254.
[348] Quoted from A. Csampai and D. Holland, *Alban Berg. Lulu*, 244 f.
[349] Thus he writes in *Composition with Twelve Tones* (GS, 1:76): "Doubling means giving special emphasis, and a note so emphasized could be taken as a foundation or even a tonic." Already in the *Harmonielehre*, Schönberg recommended avoiding octave doublings.
[350] Schönberg, "On revient toujours" (1949), GS, 1:146 f.
[351] Adorno, *Philosophie der neuen Musik*, 115.
[352] Cf. Floros, *Gustav Mahler 2*, 177-190

[353] Marie Louise Göllner, "Der Tritonus in der Komposition des 20. Jahrhunderts," in Detlef Gojowy, ed., *Quo vadis musica? Bericht über das Symposium der Alexander von Humboldt-Stiftung Bonn-Bad Godesberg 1988* (Kassel, 1990), 77-81; p. 81.

[354] Wolfgang Rogge, *Das Klavierwerk Arnold Schönbergs* (Forschungsbeiträge zur Musikwissenschaft, vol. 15) (Regensburg, 1964), 41.

[355] Schönberg, *Komposition mit zwölf Tönen*, GS, 1:87.

[356] Chr. Fr. D. Schubart, *Ideen zu einer Ästhetik der Tonkunst* (Vienna, 1806; reprint Leipzig, 1924), 261.

[357] Berg, *Wozzeck* lecture of 1929, Schr, 280.

Part III: Life and Work
Helene and Alban: "The Story of a Great Love"

[358] That Helene Nahowski was a natural daughter of the Emperor Francis Joseph I., with whom her mother, Anna Nahowski, had a liaison of many years, is quite probable and was regarded as an open secret in Viennese society. However, the recently published diaries of Anna Nahowski contain no hint that the emperor might have been Helene's father. See Friedrich Saathen, *Anna Nahowski und Kaiser Franz Joseph. Aufzeichnungen* (Vienna, Cologne, Graz, 1986), 12.

[359] E. A. Berg, *Der unverbesserliche Romantiker*, 68.

[360] Ibid., 72.

[361] A poem written for Helene by Peter Altenberg, especially the line "You only beget longing, God's noble torment, in me," suggests that she evidently evoked *sehnsucht* in a number of sensitive men. See Werner J. Schweiger, *Das große Peter Altenberg Buch* (Vienna, Hamburg, 1977), 254.

[362] Redlich, *Berg*, 316; Berg, Schr, 277.

[363] Austrian National Library, Music Collection, F 21 Berg 67. *Handschriftenkatalog* (1980) 47.

[364] According to Hermann Watznauer. See E. A. Berg, *Der unverbesserliche Romantiker*, 74.

[365] F 21, Berg 10. *Handschriftenkatalog*, 47 f.

[366] E. A. Berg, *Der unverbesserliche Romantiker*, 179.

[367] The term *Schwarzalben*, derived, like the opposite *Lichtalben*, from Wagner's *Ring of the Nibelung*, appears to have been current in Austrian literature of the time. Thus Peter Altenberg, in his brief essay "Pilsner," speaks of a "Schwarzalbe," a "Hunding [!] of life." See P. Altenberg, *Vita ipsa* (Berlin, 1918), 56 f.

[368] E. A. Berg, *der unverbesserliche* Romantiker, 173.

[369] Adorno to Helene Berg, April 16, 1936. This important letter appears in translation in Floros, *Alban Berg and Hanna Fuchs: The Story of a Love in Letters*, 125-129; p. 128. The original is reprinted in the German edition. [2001] of the book, 125-129; p.127).

[370] ABB 559. Cf. also ABB 599 and 623 f.

[371] Willi Reich, "Alban Berg," *Die Musik*, 22:5 (February 1930), 347-353; p. 348.

[372] Floros, *Alban Berg and Hanna Fuchs. The Story of a Love in Letters*, 58 f.

[373] Adorno to Helene Berg, April 16, 1936, in Floros, *Alban Berg and Hanna Fuchs*, 127.

[374] According to the housekeeper Annerl Lenz, as reported in E. A. Berg, *Der unverbesserliche Romantiker*, 170.

³⁷⁵ Unpublished letter of Helene to Alma Mahler, November 28, 1936, in the possession of the Berg Foundation.

³⁷⁶ Excerpts from the letters to Anny Askenase were published in 1988 in the auction catalogues of J. A. Stargardt; see the catalogues no. 641 (1988), 259, and no. 642, 216. See also Herwig Knaus and Thomas Leibnitz, eds., *Altenberg bis Zuckerkandl. Briefe an Alban Berg. Liebesbriefe von Alban Berg* (Vienna, 2009).

³⁷⁷ *Musik-Konzepte*, 9 (1979), 9.

The string Quartet for Helene

³⁷⁸ E. A. Berg, *Der unverbesserliche Romantiker*, 76.

³⁷⁹ R. Hilmar, *Berg* (1978), 32 f., 47.

³⁸⁰ E. A. Berg, *Der unverbesserliche Romantiker*, 78.

³⁸¹ R. Hilmar, *Berg*, 48 f.

³⁸² Tonal centers, however, are at times detectable. Thus in the second movement, mm. 154-172, the note $c^\#$ is dominant – the "black" c-sharp that plays a large part in Berg's music.

³⁸³ Webern to Berg, October 13, 1910. Quoted from Rauchhaupt, *Die Streichquartette*, 121.

³⁸⁴ Rudolf Kolisch, "Webern – Opus 5 and Opus 7" (1959). Quoted from Rauchhaupt, ibid., 122.

³⁸⁵ E. A. Berg, *Der unverbesserliche Romantiker*, 140

³⁸⁶ Adorno, *Philosohie der Neuen Musik*, 56-61.

³⁸⁷ Adorno, *Berg*, 64.

³⁸⁸ Ibid., 69.

³⁸⁹ Compare, e.g., the motif to be played "freely" of the cello in I, mm. 45/46, with the motif of the first violin in II, mm. 190/191.

³⁹⁰ See my "Bruckners Symphonik und die Musik Wagners," in Othmar Wessely, ed. , *Bruckner Symposion 1984: Bruckner, Wagner und die Neudeutschen in Österreich* (Linz, 1986), 177-189; pp. 179 f.

³⁹¹ According to Ernst Morwitz, *Kommentar zu dem Werk Stefan Georges* (Düsseldorf, 1960*)*, 97, the first 9 of the altogether 15 poems precede the fulfillment of love, "whose consummation is hinted at by the large space before the tenth poem" (as told to Morwitz by George).

³⁹² Berg to Schönberg in 1912.

³⁹³ © 1914 by Universal Edition no. 5338 (F 21 Berg 165).

³⁹⁴ Description of the ms and facsimile of the first page in the auction catalogue J. A. Stargardt no. 641 (1988), 214 f.

³⁹⁵ Not the least telling utterance here is a remark made about Schönberg's symphonic poem *Pelleas und Melisande* op. 5: of its middle movement (the "love scene that ends so terribly") Berg thought, in a letter to Helene of February 26, 1912, that it had only *one* thing comparable to it: "the second act Tristan" (ABB 225).

March of an Asthmatic

³⁹⁶ R. Hilmar, *Berg*, 112.

³⁹⁷ Berg to Schönberg, April 10, 1914.

³⁹⁸ Berg to Schönberg, August 2, 1914.

[399] Berg to Webern, July 13, 1915.
[400] Among friends, Helene was called "Pfersch" (peach), "Pferschi" or sometimes "Pfeschima," on account of her peculiar complexion. See E. A. Berg, *Der unverbesserliche Romantiker*, 180.
[401] Berg to Helene, August 31, 1910 (ABB 193): "Until I have read tomorrow's mail, I can't think of anything to write myself, it is like a great, anxious expectation, like a daylong asthma attack that must be followed either by death – or by the happy liberation from all affliction."
[402] Adorno, *Berg*, 90.
[403] Redlich, *Berg*, 93-101.
[404] Mark De Voto, "Alban Bergs Drei Orchesterstücke op. 6: Struktur, Thematik und ihr Verhältnis zu *Wozzeck*," in *Alban Berg Symposion* (Vienna, 1980), 97-106.
[405] To all appearances, this fanfare is the first thing that Berg jotted down in the aforementioned sketches (p. 30) for the "March" (Finale of the Pieces for Orchestra).
[406] See my *Mahler*, vol. 2, table LXVII.
[407] Paul Stefan, *Gustav Mahler*, 3rd ed. (Munich, 1912), and Stefan, *Das Grab in Wien. Eine Chronik 1903-1911* (Berlin, 1913).
[408] Berg also owned the piano score for four hands of the Sixth Symphony, made by Alexander von Zemlinsky and published in 1906 by C. F. Kahnt in Leipzig. In it we find occasional hermeneutic entries in Berg's or Helene's hand, such as the name "Alma" to mark the "spirited" side-theme in the first movement (p. 7) and the significant note "children Putzi and Gucki" in the *Grazioso* (p. 43).
[409] Richard Specht, *Gustav Mahler* (Berlin, Leipzig, 1914), 293, 298.
[410] Cf. my *Gustav Mahler*, 2:109f.
[411] See my *Mahler*, 1:105-107.
[412] Paul Stefan, *Gustav Mahler. Eine Studie über Persönlichkeit und Werk*, new, expanded and modified ed. (Munich, 1920), 147 (1st ed., 1910).

Wozzeck as a Message for Humanity
[413] Quoted from Konrad Vogelsang, *Dokumentation zur Oper "Wozzeck" von Alban Berg. Die Jahre des Durchbruchs 1925 1932* (Laaber-Verlag, 1977) 62 f.
[414] Facsimile of the program sheet in Ernst Hilmar, *Wozzeck von Alban Berg. Entstehung – erste Erfolge – Repressionen (1914-1955)* (Vienna, 1975), 71.
[415] Letter to Anton Webern, August 19, 1918. Quoted by Hilmar, ibid., 21.
[416] Arnold Schönber about Berg in 1949. Quoted from Redlich, *Berg*, 329.
[417] According to Karl Rankl, *Arnold Schönberg* (The Ambassador Publishing Co., issue 6) (London, 1952), 40 ff., Schönberg supposedly remarked that music should rather deal with angels than with officers' servants. Quoted from Redlich, *Alban* Berg, 105.
[418] According to Ernst Hilmar, *Wozzeck von Alban Berg*, 28.
[419] See the register of performances in Vogelsang, *Dokumentation zur Oper "Wozzeck,"* 120-124.
[420] Hans Mayer, *Georg Büchner und seine Zeit*, 2nd ed. enlarged (Wiesbaden 1960), 442 (1st ed. 1946).
[421] Quoted fromVogelsang, *Dokumentation*, 36.

[422] Wolfgang Rihm, "Als ob Berg Geburtstag hätte," in Imre Fabian and Gerhard Persche, eds., *Oper 1985. Jahrbuch der Zeitschrift "Opernwelt"* (Zurich, 1985), 48.

[423] See Aloyse Michaely, "Toccata – Ciacona – Nocturno. Zu Bernd Alois Zimmermanns Oper *Die Soldaten*," In *Musiktheater im 20. Jahrhundert* (Hamburger Jahrbuch für Musikwissenschaft, vol. 10) (Laaber, 1988), 127-204.

[424] Redlich, *Alban Berg*, 104.

[425] Bo Ullman, "Produktive Rezeption ohne Mißverständnis. Zur Büchner–Deutung Alban Bergs im 'Wozzeck'," in Attila Csampai and Dietmar Holland, eds., *Alban Berg. Wozzeck. Texte, Materialien, Kommentare* (rororo opernbuch 7929) (Reinbek, 1985), 221-246; pp. 233, 235.

[426] Rudolf Schäfke, "Alban Bergs Oper *Wozzeck*," *Melos*, 5 (1926), 267-283.

[427] Georg Büchner *Werke und Briefe. Gesamtausgabe*, ed Fritz Bergemann (Wiesbaden, 1958), 152; Alban Berg, *Wozzeck*, I.1, piano score, 23-25.

[428] Büchner, *Werke und Briefe*, 158; Berg, *Wozzeck*, II.1, piano sore, 92.

[429] Rainer Maria Rilke wonderfully captured the essence of the Fragment when he wrote to Maria von Thurn und Taxis on July 9, 1915: "Nothing but the fate of a common soldier, who stabs his unfaithful mistress to death, but showing powerfully how all the grandeur of Being surrounds even the least existence, for which even the uniform of a common infantryman seems too large and too emphatic, surrounds even the recruit Wozzek showing how he cannot prevent that, now here, now there, in front of, behind, alongside his dim soul the horizons open into the vast, the immense, the infinite; a spectacle without compare, how this abused being stands in the cosmos in his stable-jacket, malgré lui, in the infinite frame of reference of the stars. That is theater, that's how theater could be."

[430] Alban Berg, *Wozzeck*, II.3, piano score 132 f.

[431] Georg Büchner, *Werke und Briefe*, 12-19.

[432] See Ernst Hilmar, *Wozzeck von Alban Berg*, 12-19.

[433] Peter Petersen, *Wozzeck. Eine semantische Analyse unter Einbeziehung der Skizzen und Dokumente aus dem Nachlass Bergs* (Musikkonzepte, special issue) (Munich, 1985), 76-88.

[434] Berg, *Wozzeck*, score, 233; piano score, 108.

[435] Georg Büchner, *Werke und Briefe*, 161.

[436] In this letter, Berg conveyed to Schönberg his impressions of Maurice Maeterlinck's *Vom Tode*. Evidently he was influenced at the time by Webern's opinion, who had written to him on May 4, 1913: "I am currently reading Maeterlinck's *Vom Tode*. I don't much like it. I'll soon write you in detail about it. It is written against Christianity, atheistic, materialist, almost feuilletonistic. Full of respect for science (black magician). There are practically only black magicians now." Quoted from the still unpublished typescript of the correspondence between Webern and Berg.

[437] Berg, *Wozzeck*, I.4; piano score, 65 f.

[438] Willi Reich , *Alban Berg* (Vienna, Leipzig, Zurich, 1937), 75, n. 2 = *Alban Berg. Leben und Werk* (Zurich, 1963), 121, n. 2.

[439] See the table of leitmotifs in Petersen, *Alban Berg. Wozzeck*, 83-87.

[440] Redlich, *Berg*, 326.

[441] *Pult und Taktstock*, 2 (1925), 23-28.

[442] Redlich, *Berg*, 139-144.
[443] Petersen , *Wozzeck*, 102-106.
[444] Erich Forneberg, *Wozzeck von Alban Berg*, 3rd ed. (Berlin-Lichterfelde, 1963), 69.
[445] Willi Reich, *Berg* (1937), 68; (1963), 113.
[446] Fritz Mahler, *Zu Alban Bergs Oper "Wozzeck." Szenische und musikalische Übersicht* (Vienna, 1957), 7.
[447] Quoted from Redlich, *Berg*, 326.
[448] Quoted from Ernst Hilmar, *Wozzeck von Alban Berg*, 21.
[449] Alban Berg, "Das 'Opernproblem'," *Neue Musik-Zeitung*, 49:9 (1928); reprinted in Willi Reich, *Berg* (1937), 174-177.
[450] Ernst Viebig, "Alban Bergs 'Wozzeck'. Ein Beitrag zum Opernproblem," *Die Musik*, 25:7 (April, 1923), 506-510.
[451] Richard M. Meyer, *Die deutsche Literatur des neunzehnten Jahrhunderts* (Berlin, 1900); quoted in Viebig, ibid., 508.
[452] *Berg-Ausstellungskatalog 1985*, 60.
[453] On the vicissitudes in Berg's life during the war years 1914-1918, see R. Hilmar, *Berg*, 113-129.
[454] Rosemary Hilmar, *Katalog der Schriftstücke von der Hand Alban Bergs, der fremdschriftlichen und gedruckten Dokumente zur Lebensgeschichte und zu seinem Werk* (Alban Berg Studien, Vol. 1/2) (Vienna, 1985), 110 f. – See also E. A. Berg, *Der unverbesserliche Romantiker*, 92.
[455] Kurt Blaukopf, "Autobiographische Elemente in Alban Bergs 'Wozzeck'," *Österreichische Musikzeitschrift*, 9 (1954), 155-158; p. 156.
[456] Iwan Martynow, *Dmitri Schostakowitsch* (Berlin, 1947). Quoted in H. H. Stuckenschmidt, *Neue Musik*, vol. 2, *Zwischen den beiden Kriegen* (Berlin, 1951), 329-332.
[457] According to Adorno, *Philosophie der Neuen Musik* (1958), 45.
[458] Ferruccio Busoni, *Von der Einheit der Musik. Verstreute Aufzeichnungen* (Berlin, 1922), 275-279.

Berg, Schönberg and Webern
[459] A detailed account of it is given by R. Hilmar, *Berg*, 32-107.
[460] Thus Schönberg offered Helene financial assistance on November 3, 1920, after Berg had fallen ill.
[461] This guide (Universal-Edition no. 3695) appeared on the occasion of the premiere of the *Gurrelieder* on February 23, 1913, in Vienna, under the direction of Franz Schreker.
[462] Berg to Schönberg, February 12, 1921.
[463] On June 9, 1921, Berg wrote to Helene that his work in *Wozzeck* was slowly progressing but asked her not to tell Mathilde Schönberg, so as to leave her husband in the firm belief that he was working on the book (ABB 457).
[464] Schönberg to Berg, November 28, 1913.
[465] Berg to Schönberg, November 1915.
[466] Adorno, *Berg* 36.
[467] Berg to Schönberg, May 11, 1927.
[468] Berg to Schönberg, April 4, 1929.
[469] Berg to Schönberg, December 13, 1932.

[470] "Vincent" was planned as Part Two of a trilogy – the thee W's – to consist of "Wozzeck" op. 7, "Vincent" op. 9 and "Wolfgang" op. 11. In a draft (Fonds 21 Berg 70/1 fol. 2), Wozzeck, Vincent and Wolfgang are expressly labeled "servant," "friend" and "master," respectively. "Vincent" was to comprise two acts, the second to be constructed as the "crab" of the first. An orchestral interlude was to link the two acts.

[471] Elisabeth Du Quesne-Van Gogh, *Persönliche Erinnerungen an Vincent van Gogh*, 2nd ed. (Munich, 1911); Vincent van Gogh, *Briefe*, 4th ed. (Verlag Bruno Cassirer, 1911); Paul Gauguin, *Noa Noa*, 3rd ed. (Verlag Bruno Cassirer, Berlin W.); all three books have underlinings.

[472] *Berg-Ausstellungskatalog 1985*, 76.

[473] The volume is in the Berg library. Nothing came of the project.

[474] In letters to Helene of September 22 to 24, 1918 (ABB 396-400), Berg writes about a grave case of ill feelings between Webern and Schönberg.

[475] Adorno, *Berg*, 97.

The Chamber Concerto: Homage to Schönberg, Mathilde and the Schönberg Circle

[476] On March 19, 1923, Berg wrote to his wife (ABB 493): "Awake at seven o'clock this morning. Breakfast at a quarter past seven and worked on the Chamber Concerto in my head, happily resolving a crucial passage about which I had been racking my brain for weeks."

[477] Redlich, *Berg*, 157 f.

[478] Berg to Webern, July 18, 1923.

[479] Redlich, *Berg*, 159.

[480] Emil Petschnig, "Atonales Opernschaffen," *Die Musik*, 16 (1923/24), 340-345.

[481] Alban Berg, "Die musikalischen Formen in meiner Oper "Wozzeck," *Die Musik*, 16 (1924), 587-589.

[482] R. Hilmar, *Berg*, 160.

[483] F 21 Berg 74/II fol. 2, 74/III fol. 5 and 74/X fol. 7.

[484] A. Pernye, "Alban Berg und die Zahlen," *Studia Musicologica Academiae Scientiarum Hungaricae*, 9 (1967), 141-161; p. 150.

[485] Adorno (*Berg*, 108) pointed out that the dynamic structure of this passage obeys the principle of the "minutest transition" (*des kleinsten Übergangs*). The volume degrees are $pp - p - mp - mf - ff$.

[486] F 21 Berg 74/IV fol. 20 verso and fol. 21 verso.

[487] Constantin Floros, "Das Kammerkonzert von Alban Berg. Hommage à Schönberg und Webern," in *Alban Berg. Kammermusik II* (Musik-Konzepte 9) (Munich, 1979), 63-90.

[488] I noted the numerous allusions to Schönberg's Serenade op. 24 already in my 1979 essay (ibid., 82-88). The study of the sketches fully confirms my observations then.

[489] The music of the third scene of Act Two of *Wozzeck* – the famous *Largo* – is likewise set for 15 players, with the chamber-musical instrumentation exactly corresponding to that of the Chamber Symphony op. 9 of Schönberg. As he declared in his Oldenburg lecture, Berg wanted to present an homage to his teacher and master at this prominent spot in the opera. See Redlich, *Berg*, 321.

[490] Needless to say, Berg knew Schönberg's Chamber Symphony inside out, as he had composed a thematic analysis of the work.

[491] Berg made the following annotation in the score, p. 18: "This violin passage only if the entire chamber concerto is played, and even then as unobtrusively as possible in the execution, without coming forward soloistically."

[492] See Berthold Türcke, "Rudolf Kolisch. Eine biographische Skizze," in *Rudolf Kolisch. Zur Theorie der Aufführung* (Musik-Konzepte 29/30) (Munich, 1983), 122-127.

[493] Redlich, *Berg*, 168.

[494] See the photograph reproduced in H.H. Stuckenschmidt, *Schönberg*, 137.

[495] Heinsheimer, *Menagerie in Fis-dur*, 21-24.

[496] In the sketchbook 74/V fol. 20 verso, Berg noted these ideas quasi stenographically with the key word coun*terpoint* and the dynamic marking *ppp > fff*.

[497] See, e.g., the contrapuntal combination of the *Meno Allegro* theme (piano) with an idea from the "spirited" theme in the flute (mm. 220-228).

[498] Thus the wind passage (mm. 199-210) forms a strict canon in the octave.

[499] Stuckenschmidt, *Schönberg*, 38.

[500] Eberhard Freitag, *Arnold Schönberg in Selbstzeugnissen und Bilddokumenten* (rowohlts monographien) (Reinbek, 1973), 17.

[501] See Otto Kallir, "Richard Gerstl (1883-1908). Beiträge zur Dokumentation seines Lebens und Werkes," in *Mitteilungen der Österreichischen Galerie* (1974), 125-193; Patrick Werkner, *Physis und Psyche. Der österreichische Frühexpressionismus* (Vienna, Munich, 1986), 60-62.

[502] Meyerowitz, *Schönberg*, 16.

[503] Freitag, *Schönberg*, 115.

[504] On September 11, 1923, Helene Berg wished Schönberg on his upcoming 49th birthday "that the new year in your life may bring you the complete recovery of your dear, good Mathilde." Webern wrote to Schönberg on September 12, 1923: "How much it pains us, too, that your wife has become so ill." To Berg, Webern wrote on the same day: "The appearance and condition of Frau Schönberg worry me greatly." Berg replied on September 16: "Dear friend, your news concerning Frau Schönberg has caused us the greatest consternation."

[505] *Musik-Konzepte*, 9 (1979), 69 f.

[506] Entries in the sketches show that Berg had planned from the start to conclude the Variations movement with a crescendo to fortissimo and to begin the second movement pianissimo (F 21 Berg 74/III fo. L).

[507] Berg to Helene on February 26, 1912: "So, 10 in the morning to 1:30 rehearsal of *Pelleas und Melisande*. Let me not speak of my first impression: it was magnificent beyond all measure and expectations! The gigantic middle part (the love scene that ends so terribly) can be compared to only *one* thing: the second act *Tristan*. One cannot say more, and yet it is still too little." On the following day, he expressed himself to Helene with equal exuberance about Schönberg' symphonic poem: "Can you imagine with what ears I listened to those new tones. And what then came was possibly the high point of the work: the conclusion of *Pelleas*, Melisande's death. The mood, as the servants approach the bed of the dying Melisande, and how then the ghastly suspicion begins to choke Golo again

whether he is the father of the child (in one last of the hundred gigantic crescendos in this work!), and how the work concludes in this agonizing and desperate state of mind – and not blissfully fading away – one cannot speak of it – but for that very reason I could have cried that you cannot hear it. It is too magnificently beautiful, of unimaginable agonizing voluptuousness – that you did not hear that!!!!" See ABB 225-227.

[508] Berg's "Concise Thematic Analysis" of Schönberg's *Pelleas und Melisande* appeared in the Universal Edition (no. 6368) in June of 1920.

[509] F 21 Berg 74/IV fol. 7 verso and 74/X fol 6.

[510] Freitag, *Schönberg*, 115.

[511] Schönberg to Zemlinsky, November 16, 1923. Alexander Zemlinsky, *Briefwechsel mit Arnold Schönberg, Anton Webern, Alban Berg und Franz Schreker*, ed. Horst Weber (Darmstadt, 1995), 256.

[512] Ibid., 265 (August 21, 1924).

[513] Cf. the outline in *Musik-Konzepte*, 9 (1979), 72.

[514] See, e.g., mm. 505/506.

[515] Berg's term in 74/X fol. 1 verso.

[516] See my *Mahler*, 2:41-56.

[517] Cf. Redlich, *Berg*, 246-249.

[518] Berg had initially thought of letting the Schönberg anagram be played by all the winds unisono (74/X fol. 6).

[519] Berg to Schönberg, July 12, 1923; cf. Redlich, *Berg*, 159.

[520] F 21 Berg 74/IX fol. 6 and fol. 9.

[521] *Berg-Ausstellungskatalog*, 163 f.

[522] The present chapter is based largely on the findings published in my 1979 and 1987 studies of the Chamber Concerto . My essay on the work's secret program was composed in 1986 and appeared in November 1987 in the *Neue Zeitschrift für Musik*. Immediately therafter it was translated into Japanese and published in the Yearbook of the Japanese Berg Society (1986/1987). Barbara Dalen presented very similar arguments without referring to my work in her essay "'Freundschaft Liebe und Welt': The Secret Programme of the Chamber Concerto," in *The Berg Companion*, ed. Douglas Jarman (London, 1989), 141-180.

From Helene to Hanna: The Two Versions of the Storm Lied *Schließe mir die Augen...*

[523] *Die Musik*, 22:5 (February 1930).

[524] W. Reich, *Berg* (1937), 15.

[525] Hans Ferdinand Redlich, afterword to the new edition of the *Zwei Lieder* (Universal Edition, no. 12241).

[526] E. A. Berg, *Der unverbesserliche Romantiker*, 69.

[527] See Christian Baier, "Fritz Heinrich Klein. Der ‚Mutterakkord' im Werk Alban Bergs," *Österreichische Musikzeitschrift*, 44:12 (December, 1989), 585-600.

[528] *Berg-Ausstellungskatalog*, 162.

[529] Ibid. ,165.

[530] Rauchhaupt, *Schönberg/Berg/Webern. Die Streichquartette,* 92-95.

[531] Cf. *Musik-Konzepte*, 9 (1979), 86 f.

String Quartet for Hanna: the *Lyric Suite*

532 *Briefwechsel zwischen Wagner und Liszt*, vol. 2: *Vom Jahre 1854 bis 1861* (Leipzig, 1887), 46.

533 Theodor W. Adorno, contribution about the *Lyric Suite* in Willi Reich, *Alban Berg* (1937), 92.

534 Klaus Schweizer, *Die Sonatensatzform im Schaffen Alban Bergs* (Freiburger Schriften zur Musikwissenschaft, vol 1) (Stuttgart, 1970), 86.

535 F 21 Berg 1535/66. See *Berg-Ausstellungskatalog*, 175.

536 Constantin Floros, "Das esoterische Program der L yrischen Suite von Alban Berg," *Hamburger Jahrbuch für Musikwissenschaft*, 1 (1975), 101-145. Expanded version in *Alban Berg/Kammermusik I* (Musik-Konzepte, 4) 5-48. See also Floros, *Alban Berg und Hanna Fuchs. The Story of a Love in Letters*, 65-72, 83-105 and passim.

537 Reginald Smith Brindle, "The Symbolism in Berg's 'Lyric Suite'," *The Score*, 21 (October 1957), 60-63.

538 A Pernye, "Alban Berg und die Zahlen," 148-150.

539 Klaus Schweizer, *Die Sonatensatzform im Schaffen Alban Bergs*, 88 f.

540 George Perle, "Das geheime Programm der Lyrischen Suite," in *Musik-Konzepte* 4 (1978) 49-74. For the definitive version of these letters, see Floros, *Alban Berg und Hanna Fuchs. Die Geschichte einer Liebe in Briefen* (Zurich, Hamburg, 2001), 19-90, and *Alban Berg and Hanna Fuchs. The History of a Love in Letters*, transl. Ernest Bernhardt-Kabisch (Bloomington, 2008), 13-64.

541 Some biographic data about Hanna Werfel can be found in Peter Stephan Jungk, *Franz Werfel. Eine Lebensgeschichte*, 3rd ed. (Frankfurt a. M., 1987). See also *Alban Berg and Hanna Fuchs*, 65-82.

542 Frantisek Edvin Fuchs-Robettin, pet name Munzo, was born late in June of 1918 in Prague. See Peter Stephan Jungk, *Franz Werfel*, 98.

543 Douglas M. Green, "Berg's De Profundis: The Finale of the Lyric Suite," *The International Alban Berg Society Newsletter*, no. 5 (1977).

544 Berg to Hermann Watznauer, July 14, 1926. See E. A. Berg, *Der unverbesserliche Romantiker*, 127.

545 Don McLean, "Schloss und sein Schlüssel: New Documents on Berg's Lyric Suite; the Schloss Collection
  at McGill University," paper read at the meeting of the American Musicological Society in April of 1988 (typescript).

546 *Musik-Konzepte*, 9 (1979), 9 f.

547 Rauchhaupt, *Schoenberg/Berg/Webern. Die Streichquartette*, 91.

548 Ibid., 101.

549 Willi Reich, *Alban Berg. Bildnis im Wort. Selbstzeugnisse und Aussagen der Freunde* (Zurich, 1959), 45-54.

550 Rauchhaupt, *Die Streichquartette*, 91-117.

551 By some calculations, there are altogether 3856 all-interval rows. See Hanns Jelinek, *Anleitung zur Zwölftonkomposition* (Vienna, 1952), 14 f, 19-23; and above all Herbert Eimert, *Grundlagen der musikalischen Reihentechnik* (Vienna, 1964), 39-86.

[552] The term *Urreihe* (ur-row) das not occur in Berg's analysis of the *Lyric Suite*. We can nonetheless employ it here because Berg did use it in the sketch sheets for *Lulu* that Willi Reich first published in "An die Seite von Berg," *Melos* (1960), 36-42.

[553] This designation (properly spelled *gioioso*) is used in the autograph. The clean copy of the score, however, has the marking *Allegretto gioviale*. For copies of the pages in question, see Rauchhaupt, *Die Streichquartette*, 97, 99.

[554] Cf. Wolfgang Budday, *Bergs Lyrische Suite. Satztechnische Analyse ihrer zwölftönigen Partien*) Tübinger Beiträge zur Musikwissenschaft, vol. 8) (Neuhausen-Stuttgart, 1979).

[555] In the autograph (23/I fol. 12 verso), Berg himself marked the theme at its later recurrence (m. 81) with the term *zärtlich* (tender).

[556] Adorno, *Berg*, 115.

[557] Redlich, *Berg*, 198.

[558] Pernye, "Alban Berg und die Zahlen," 149.

[559] Fritz Bouquet, "Alban Bergs 'Lyrische Suite'. Eine Studie über Gestalt, Klang und Ausdruck," *Melos*, 15 1948), 227-231; p. 229.

[560] The four series forms are set down already in 76/V fol. 9, with the note "8 + 4." Berg wrote them down here thinking he would use them "for the third to the fifth" movement. As elsewhere, the letter note h in German signifies our our b, b our b-flat.

[561] Rauchhaupt, *Die Streichquartette*, 92-95.

[562] The earliest notations of these double motifs with the characteristic 7/5 "partition" occur in 76/V fol. 9.

[563] Cf .Berg's note in 76/V fol. 2 verso.

[564] Berg noted this refrain – or, more exactly, the vocal part (without text) and the piano score (no. 43/44) – down in 76/IX fol. 2.

[565] Of the seven Tagore poems on which Alexander von Zemlinsky based his *Lyric Symphony*, "Du bist die Abendwolke" is one of the most expressive. The poems were taken from the collection *Der Gärtner* (The Gardener). Zemlinsky presumably selected them from the first volume of the eight-volume collected edition of Tagore's works, published in 1921 in Munich (Verlag Kurt Wolff).

[566] See alo the draft written down in 76/IX fol. 3 recto and verso.

[567] Don McLean, "Schloss und sein Schlüssel" (cf. n. 188, above).

[568] A second, shorter list is preserved in 76/I fol 10.

[569] On the nomenclature of the Wagnerian leitmotifs, see Alfred Lorenz, *Der musikalische Aufbau von Richard Wagners "Tristan und Isolde"* (vol. 2 of *Das Geheimnis der Form bei Richard Wagner*) (Berlin, 1926), 15.

[570] Cf. the analysis in Ernst Kurth, *Romantische Harmonik und ihre Krise in Wagners "Tristan,"* 2nd ed. (Berlin, 1923), 343.

[571] The first third of m. 231was added on later in the autograph (Berg 23/I fol. 53 verso).

[572] Ernst Kurth, *Romantische Harmonik*, 125, 502-510. In contrast to other commentators, who ascribe the motif to the person of Tristan, Kurth identifies it as motif of *Verhängnis* (doom), arguing at length that the fate of death is the key idea of the drama.

[573] Notes to that effect are found already in the sketches (76/XII fol. 3 and fol. 4).

[574] Redlich, *Berg*, 323 f., and Berg, Schr, 285.

[575] See Pierre Jean Jouve and Michel Fano, *Wozzeck ou le nouvel opéra* Paris, 1953), passim ; Erich Forneberg, *Wozzeck von Alban Berg*, 70 f.; Gerd Ploebsch, *Alban Bergs "Wozzeck". Dramaturgie und musikalischer Aufbau* (Straßburg/Baden-Baden, 1968), 70, 82.
[576] For particulars about the "half-row," see Wolfgang Budday, *Alban Bergs Lyrische Suite*, 72 f., 77 f.

Aspects of *Lulu*

[577] Csampai/Holland, *Alban Berg, Lulu*, 214.
[578] Wilhelm Emrich, "Wedekind. Die Lulu Tragödie," in Benno von Wiese, ed., *Das deutshe Drama vom Barock bis zur Gegenwart. Interpretationen*, vol. 2 (Düsseldorf, 1958), 207-228; pp. 226 f.
[579] See Günter Sehaus, *Frank Wedekind in Selbstzeugnissen und Bilddokumenten* (rowohlts monographien 213) (Reinbek, 1974), 61 f.
[580] A facsimile of the program sheet from this performance is reproduced in Csampai/Holland, *Alban Berg. Lulu*, 157.
[581] Kraus's introductory address is reprinted ibid., 158-169.
[582] W. Reich, *Berg* (1937), 106 f.
[583] Adorno, *Berg*, 32-34.
[584] *Berg-Ausstellungskatalog*, 93.
[585] Karl Kraus, *Sittlichkeit und Kriminalität*, special edition, ed. Heinrich Fischer (Munich, 1970; 1st ed. 1908, 2nd ed. 1924; 3rd ed. 1963). The volume contains essays written by Kraus for *Die Fackel* between 1902 and 1907.
[586] Artur Kutscher, "Frank Wedekinds Lulu-Tragödie," in *Wedekind. Leben und Werk*, ed. Karl Ude (Munich, 1964; reprinted in Csampai/Holland, *Alban Berg. Lulu*, 132-148.
[587] Frank Wedekind, *Ausgewählte Werke in 5 Bänden*, ed. Fritz Strich, vol 2 (Berlin 1923), 111-118.
[588] Csampai/Holland, *Alban Gerg. Lulu*, 216.
[589] Munich: George Müller Verlag, 1921 (F 21 Berg 132/I-III).
[590] Csampai/Holland, 214.
[591] W. Reich, *Berg* (1937), 110 f.
[592] Berg to Adorno, November 30, 1927. Facsimile in Adorno, *Berg*, 33 f.
[593] Csampai/Holland, 208.
[594] H. F. Redlich, *Berg*, 208.
[595] Csampai/Holland, 208.
[596] Ibid., 214.
[597] Alban Berg, *Lulu* (Univeral Edition 10746), 77.
[598] See Friedrich Cerha, *Arbeitsbericht zur Herstellung des 3. Aktes der Oper LULU von Alban Berg* (Universal Edition, 26233) (Vienna, 1979).
[599] Peter Petersen, "Lulus Untergang aus Gründen der Symmetrie? Gedanken zum III. Akt von Bergs Oper 'Lulu'," in Program 9 of the BremenTheater (1982/83), 37-45.
[600] Csampai/Holland, 226.
[601] The detailed sketches for the "ur-row" and the secondary rows derived from it are found in Fonds 21 Berg 28/X-XI, XVII-XXII and 80/VIII. See *Berg Studien*, I/1, no. 40, 42-44, 46-50 and 72. Some sketch pages, on which Berg drew up the twelve-tone rows

and the chief themes of the opera for his pupil Willi Reich, have become famous. Good facsimiles of these leaves can be found in Rudolf Stephans essay, "Drei Autographe von Alban Berg," in *Komponisten des 20. Jahrhunderts in der Paul Sacher Stiftung* (Basel, 1986), 149-156.

[602] W. Reich, *Berg*, 112 f.

[603] Redlich, *Berg*, 227-231. Manfred Reiter, *Die Zwölftontechnik in Alban Bergs Oper LULU* (Kölner Beiträge Zur Musikforschung, vol. 71) (Regensburg, 1973); George Perle, *The Operas of Alban Berg*, vol. 2: *Lulu* (Berkeley, Los Angeles, London, 1985).

[604] Berg to Helene, March 9, 1934 (ABB 641).

[605] Csampai/Holland, 213.

[606] Ernst Hilmar, *Wozzeck von Alban Berg*, 21.

[607] W. Reich, *Berg* (1937), 112.

[608] Peter Unger and Hartmut Vinçon, "Nachwort," in Frank Wedekind. *Erdgeist. Die Büchse der Pandora. Tragödien* (Goldmann Klassiker No. 7534) (Munich, 1980), 177.

[609] In Reich's formulation; *Berg* (1937), 114.

[610] Quoted from Günter Seehaus, *Frank Wedekind*, 45.

[611] See the facsimile in the essay by Rudolf Stephan (cf. note 244), 154.

[612] Reich, *Berg* (1937), 115.

[613] Berg's personal copy of *Erdgeist* (Munich, 1920; F 21 Berg 130, p. 58) has the marginal note "Adagio. Verbundenheit" (bond).

[614] Redlich, *Berg*, 231.

[615] See *Musik-Konzepte*, 4 (1978), 21.

[616] Alban Berg, *Lulu*. Text, 43.

[617] Ibid., 84.

[618] Ernst Krenek, "Alban Bergs 'Lulu'," in *Zur Sprache gebracht. Essays über Musik* (Berlin, Darmstdt, Vienna, 1958), 249.

[619] Tilly Wedekind, *Lulu – die Rolle meines Lebens* (Munich, Berne, Vienna, 1969), 100.

[620] It is worth mentioning that in the type-written libretto of the opera (F 21 Berg 133), Alwa, Dr. Schön's son, is called a writer. Berg crossed the word out and added a question mark.

[621] F 21, Berg 28/XXXVI fo; 36. Facsimile in Rode, *Alban Berg und Karl Kraus*, 382 f.

[622] Reich, *Berg* (1937), 117.

[623] F 21 Berg 28/VIII fol. 2. Facsimile in Rode, 380.

[624] Alban Berg, *Lulu*. Text, 79.

[625] Reich, *Berg* (1937), 120.

[626] Peter Petersen, *Alban Berg. Wozzeck*, 251-255.

[627] W. Reich, *Berg* (1937), 164; Berg, Schr, 260-262. The article first appeared in 1928 in the November/December issue of *Musikblätter des Anbruch*.

Violin Concerto

[628] From an unpublished letter draft of Helene Berg (in the possession of the Alban Berg Foundation).

[629] Berg to Smaragda Eger, March 31, 1935, and to Erich Kleiber, April 24, 1935. See Ernst Hilmar, *Alban Bergs Selbstzeugnisse zu Entstehung und Aufführbarkeit der Oper "Lulu"*, 21; E. A. Berg, *Der unverbesserliche Romantiker*, 141 f.
[630] E. A. Berg, *Der unverbesserliche Romantiker*, 141.
[631] Reich, *Berg* (1937), 126 f. = *Berg* (1963), 91 f.
[632] On April 22, 1935, Alma Mahler-Werfel wrote in her diary: "Today my most beautiful, most gracious child was taken from me, after Franz Werfel and I had fought for her recovery for a whole year." See Alma Mahler-Werfel, *Mein Leben* (Fischer Bücherei 545) (Frankfurt a. M. and Hamburg, 1963), 211.
[633] E. A. Berg, *Der unverbesserliche Romantiker*, 91 f.
[634] Elias Canetti, *Das Augenspiel* (1988), 190-195.
[635] George Perle, "'Mein geliebes Almschi ...'. Briefe von Alban und Helene Berg an Alma Mahler," *Österreichische Musikzeitschrift*, 35 (1980), 2-15; p. 7.
[636] *Katalog der Schriftstücke und Dokumente Alban Bergs*, 126. Facsimile on p. 46.
[637] Alma Mahler-Werfel, *Mein Leben*, 145.
[638] ABB 269, 482-485, 528, 626.
[639] E. A. Berg, *Der unverbesserliche Romantiker*, 114.
[640] Perle, see note 635, above, 7.
[641] See Redlich, *Berg*, 269. On July 16, 1935, Berg reported the completion of the composition also to Louis Krasner. See the facsimile of the letter in E. A. Berg, *Alban Berg. Leben und Werk in Daten und Bildern* (insel taschenbuch 194) (Frankfurt a. M., 1976), 238.
[642] Reich's (1937, p. 17) July 23, 1935, dating of the completion of the particello is incorrect.
[643] Reich, *Berg* (1937), 127 f. = *Berg* (1963), 169 f.
[644] Reich also knew the particello of the Violin Concerto and possibly the sketches. In his book of 1963 (93), he relates that on August 10 and 11, 1935, he and Berg played the entire concerto fourhanded on the piano from the particello.
[645] Reich, *Berg* (1963), 94.
[646] E. A. Berg, *Der unverbesserliche Romantiker*, 142.
[647] Ibid., 142.
[648] For a description of the sources, see my article, "Die Skizzen zum Violinkonzert von Alban Berg," in *Alban Berg Symposion* (Vienna, 1980), 118-135.
[649] Herwig Knaus, "Die Kärntner Volksweise aus Alban Bergs Violinkonzert," in *Musikerziehung* (Vienna, 1969/1970), 117 f.
[650] Reich, *Berg* (1937), 128.
[651] Redlich, *Berg*, 271.
[652] Reich, *Berg* (1963), 93.
[653] Reich, *Berg* (1937), 131 f.
[654] Redlich, *Berg*, 269.
[655] Herwig Knaus, "Studien zu Alban Bergs Violinkozert," in Theophil Antonicek, Rudolf Flotzinger and Othmar Wessely, eds., *De ratione in musica. Festschrift Erich Schenk zum 5. Mai 1972* (Kassel, etc. 1975), 255-274; Knaus, "Die Reihenskizzen zu Alban Bergs Violinkonzert," *Österreichische Musikzeitschrift*, 37 (1982), 105-108.

[656] Josef Rufer, *Der Komponist mit zwölf Tönen*, 97.

[657] In this connection, we should refer to another table headed "Scales etc." (85/I fol. 8). Berg there forms chromatic sequences by selecting from the row in certain ways, and tries out how far these can be combined contrapuntally with whole-tone sequences.

[658] Redlich, *Berg*, 272.

[659] See the musical specimen in Knaus, "Studien zu Bergs Violinkonzert," 266.

[660] Willi Reich, "Requiem for Manon," *Musikblätter des Anbruch*, 17 (September/October, 1935), 250-252.

[661] Bruno Walter, *Thema und Variationen. Erinnerungen und Gedanken* (Frankfurt a. M., 1960), 411.

[662] As Berg had told Webern, who refers to it in a letter to Berg of June 18, 1935.

[663] Theodor W. Adorno, "Alban Berg; Violinkonzert," in *Der getreue Korrepetitor. Lehrschriften zur musikalischen Praxis* (Frankfurt a. M., 1963), 187-216; p. 193.

[664] Douglas Jarman, "Alban Berg, Wilhelm Fließ und das geheime Programm des Violinkonzertes," *Österreichische Musikzeitschrift*, 40/1 (January 1985), 12-21.

[665] The characteristic expression marks, which are absent fron the sketches, first appear in the particello.

[666] Berg explains the derivation of the theme from the twelve-tone row in 85/II fol. 21 verso.

[667] Berg very likely took the melody of the Carinthian folksong "A Vögele af'n Zweschpm-bam" from the collection *Wulfenia-Blüten. Einige fünfzig Lieder und Jodler aus Kärnten* (Vienna and Leipzig: Univeral Edition, 1932), 35. Reprinted in Rudolf Stephan, *Alban Berg. Violinkonzert(1935)* (Meisterwerke der Musik, no. 49) (Munich, 1988), 42.

[668] Professor Bernhardt-Kabisch has poined out to me that Carinthia has a sizable Protestant tradition. He also notes that the song, with its tri-di-e and ri-tu-li-e refrains, is in fact a yodel song, whose text also reminds of the four-line *schnadahüpfel* or *gstanzln* popular in Austria and Bavaria, metrically as well as in type of content.

[669] Reich, *Berg* (1937), 133.

[670] Adorno, *Der getreue Korrepetitor*, 312.

[671] See my *Mahler*, 2:311-317.

[672] Petersen, *Alban Berg. Wozzeck*, 271 f.

[673] From hitherto unpublished letter drafts of Helene Berg's (in the possession of the Alban Berg Foundation).

[674] Redlich, *Berg*, 275.

[675] Reich, *Berg* (1937), 128.

[676] The pedal point comes in at m. 97.

[677] What is probably the earliest draft is found in fol. 8 (3rd and 4th staff) of the second bundle of sketches. Another "version" is notated on fol. 4 (1st and 2nd staff) of the second bundle. Berg, moreover, sketched this "outcry" no fewer than four times on fol. 29 of the second bundle. There the passage finally found its definitive shape.

[678] The chords are also notated, without the programmatic "key word," in fol. 26.

[679] We learn from E. A. Berg (*Der unverbesserliche Romantiker*,161) that of all of Strauss' compositions, Berg in the end approved, and loved, only *Death and Transfiguration*.

[680] Strauss to Friedrich von Hausegger; quoted from Erich H. Mueller von Asow, *Richard Strauss. Thematisches Verzeichnis*, vol. I (Vienna/Wiesbaden, 1959), 116 f.

[681] Mm. 19, 57, 69, 97, 125-136 (nine times).

[682] Bach's cantata prompted Oskar Kokoschka in 1914 to create 11 remarkable lithographs that appeared in 1916-1919 in three editions: as a portfolio, in book form and as a "popular edition." Berg must have known these lithographs, since they were included in his estate. See Rosemary Hilmar, *Ausstellungskatalog* (1985), 109. Lothar Lang edited the 11 lithographs together with supplementary material in 1984 in Leipzig (licensed edition at Drei-Lilien-Verlag, Wiesbaden).

[683] Alfred Dürr, *Die Kantaten von Johann Sebastian Bach*, vol. 2 (Kassel, etc., 1971), 519. See also Arnold Schmitz, *Die Bildlichkeit der wortgebundenen Musik Johann Sebastian Bachs* (Mainz, 1950), 51-55.

[684] In two places (mm. 180, 183), the part of the solo violin is accordingly headed by the term *dolente*. In the particello, m. 183 is explicitly marked *klagend* (plaintive).

[685] See my *Mahler*, 2:118-123.

[686] The conclusion of the Violin Concerto reminds distantly of the "celestial" ending of the slow movement of Mahler's Fourth Symphony.

[687] W. Reich, *Berg* (1963), 92.

[688] Constantin Floros, "Alban Bergs 'Requiem'. Das verschwiegene Programm des Violinkonzerts," *Neue Zeitschrift für Musik*, April 1985, 4-8. This essay was also translated into Japanese, Bulgarian and Greek.

[689] I first pointed to the semantics of the *Marcia* (a funeral march), and to the significance of the number 23 for the *molto ritmico* section, in my essay in *Alban Berg Studien*, vol. 2 (1981), 129 f.

[690] 85/II fol. 17 and fol. 34.

[691] In 1985 – a few weeks before the appearance of my second study of the Violin Concerto – Douglas Jarman published the article already cited (see note 664), in which he argued that the program of the work refers not only to Manon Gropius and Berg himself but also to Hanna Fuchs-Robettin and even to Marie Scheuchl, the mother of Berg's illegitimate daughter. Jarman cited numbers symbols and other considerations to support his thesis. I regret to say that this study is wholly speculative and that many of the arguments adduced are entirely baseless. To cite only two examples: Jarman interprets the fact that the *Introduction* of the Violin Concerto comprises exactly ten measures as an "additional allusion" to Hanna Fuchs, although the number 10, as we have seen, can refer also to other people, such as Alma Mahler. Moreover, he boldly asserts that "every structurally significant point, every mark and every section in the last Adagio begins and ends in a unit of 23, 28 or 10 (or a multiple of ten) bars." He overlooks an elementary fact, namely that the Bach chorale comprises exactl 20 measures and that therefore the two variations it undergoes exend of necessity to 20 bars each!

A second example of a total misreading: as we have noted, Berg gives to the last two lines of the chorale the expression mark *espressivo e amoroso* – a "strange" and "seemingly inappropriate direction, " according to Jarman, that can be explained only as an allusion to Hanna. Every person who knows the material will confirm, however, that the term in this context can mean only spiritual love, the rapture of the dying.

Afterword: Berg – a Janus Face
[692] Alma Mahler-Werfel, *Mein Leben*, 148.
[693] Adorno, *Berg*, 25.
[694] Pierre Boulez, "Missverständnisse um Berg," in *Anhaltspunkte. Essays*. German transl. Josef Häusler (Kassel etc., Munich, 1979), 318 f.
[695] Open Letter to Schönberg of February 9, 1925. Schr., 232.
[696] Quoted from Ernst Hilmar, "Alban Bergs Selbstzeugnisse zu Entstehung und Aufführbarkeit der Oper 'Lulu'," in *Lied der Lulu*. Facsimile edition of the autograph score (Vienna, n.d.) 22.

4.4 Selected Bibliography

Literature and philosophical Texts

ADORNO, Theodor W.

Philosophie der Neuen Musik. Frankfurt am Main 1958; Engl. translation: *Philosophy of Modern Music.* New York 1974

ALTENBERG, Peter

Vita ipsa. Berlin 1918

AVNI, Abraham

"A Revaluation of Baudelaire's ‚Le Vin': Its Originality and Significance for Les Fleurs du Mal, in: *The French Review* 44, no. 2 (December 1970), 310-321

BARON, Frank

Faustus. Geschichte, Sage, Dichtung. Munich 1982

BAUDELAIRE, Charles

Gesammelte Schriften, translated Max Bruns, 5 vols., Minden in Westfalen

BRANDSTÄTTER, Christian (Publishing House)

Wien um 1900. Kunst und Kultur. Vienna/ Munich 1985

BÜCHNER, Georg

Werke und Briefe. Gesamtausgabe. Ed. Fritz Bergemann. Wiesbaden 1958

CANETTI, Elias

Das Augenspiel. Lebensgeschichte 1901-1937 (Fischer Taschenbuch Verlag 9140). Frankfurt am Main 1988

Die Fackel im Ohr. Lebensgeschichte 1921-1931 (Fischer Taschenbuch Verlag 5404). Frankfurt am Main 1982

DOSTOJEWSKI, Fjodor M.

Schriften, 14 vols. Piper 1914

DUCHESNEAU, Louise

The Voice of the Muse: A Study of the Role of Inspiration in Musical Composition (European University Studies, Series XXXVI. Musicology, Vol. 19). Frankfurt am Main 1986

EMRICH, Wilhelm

„Wedekind. Die Lulu-Tragödie," in: Benno von Wiese (ed.), *Das deutsche Drama. Vom Barock bis zur Gegenwart. Interpretationen*, vol. II. Düsseldorf 1958, 207-228

FAES, Urs

Als hätte die Stille Türen. Suhrkamp Frankfurt am Main 2005

FRIEDRICH, Hugo

Die Struktur der modernen Lyrik. Von Baudelaire bis zur Gegenwart (Rowohlts deutsche Enzyklopädie, Vol. 25). Hamburg 1956

HASSELBACH, Karlheinz

Thomas Mann. Doktor Faustus. Munich 1977

HOCKE, Gustav René

Die Welt als Labyrinth. Manier und Manie in der europäischen Kunst (Rowohlts deutsche Enzyklopädie, Vol. 50/51). Hamburg 1957

IBSEN, Henrik

Sämtliche Werke in deutscher Sprache. Ed. Georg Brandes, Julius Elias, Paul Schlenther, 10 vols, Berlin 1892-1904

JANIK, Allan - ROULMIN, Stephen

Wittgensteins Wien (Serie Piper, Band 519), 2. ed. Munich 1989

JUNGK, Peter Stephan

Franz Werfel. Eine Lebensgeschichte, 3. ed. Frankfurt am Main 1987

KANDINSKY, Wassily

Das Geistige in der Kunst, 1st ed. 1912, 4th. ed. 1952, 6th ed. (Introduction Max Bill). Bern-Bümpliz 1959

KEEL, Aldo (Ed.)

Erläuterungen und Dokumente. Henrik Ibsen. Nora (Ein Puppenheim) (Reclam Universal-Bibliothek No. 8185). Stuttgart 1990

KRAUS, Karl

Auswahl aus dem Werk (Fischer Bücherei 377). Frankfurt am Main and Hamburg 1961

Sittlichkeit und Kriminalität, 1st ed. 1908, 2nd ed. 1924, 3rd ed. 1963; Sonderausgabe, ed. Heinrich Fischer. Munich 1970

KUTSCHER, Artur

Wedekind. Leben und Werk. Ed. Karl Ude. Munich 1964

LAGERCRANTZ, Olaf

Strindberg. German translation Angelika Gundlach, Frankfurt am Main 1980

LOOS, Adolf

Trotzdem 1900-1930, lst ed. Innsbruck 1931, Reprint Vienna 1982

MANN, Thomas

Doktor Faustus. Roman. Die Entstehung des Doktor Faustus. Frankfurt am Main 1967

Ausgewählte Essays in drei Bänden, Vol. 2: *Politische Reden und Schriften*, selected and ed. Hermann Kurzke (Fischer Taschenbuch Verlag 1907). Frankfurt am Main 1977

MAYER, Hans

Georg Büchner und seine Zeit, lst ed. Wiesbaden 1946, expanded version 1960

OPEL, Adolf

Konfrontationen. Schriften von und über Adolf Loos. Vienna 1988

PAUL, Fritz

August Strindberg (Sammlung Metzler; M 178: / Sect. D: Literaturgeschichte), Stuttgart 1979

PUSCHMANN, Rosemarie

Magisches Quadrat und Melancholie in Thomas Manns Doktor Faustus. Von der musikalischen Struktur zum semantischen Beziehungsnetz. Bielefeld 1983

RIECKMANN, Jens

Aufbruch in die Moderne. Die Anfänge des Jungen Wien. Österreichische Literatur und Kritik im Fin de Siecle, 2nd ed. Frankfurt am Main 1986

SCHICK, Paul

Karl Kraus in Selbstzeugnissen und Bilddokumenten (Rowohlts Monographien 980). Reinbek 1965

SCHNEIDER, Karl Ludwig

Zerbrochene Formen. Wort und Bild im Expressionis.us, Darmstadt 1967

SCHORSKE, Carl E.

Wien. Geist und Gesellschaft im Fin de siecle. Transl. Horst Gunther, 2nd ed. Frankfurt am Main 1982

SCHUTZE, Peter

August Strindberg in Selbstzeugnissen und Bilddokumenten (Rowohlts Monographien 383). Reinbek 1990

SCHWEIGER, Werner J. (Ed.)

Das große Peter Altenberg Buch. Vienna/Hamburg 1977

SEEHAUS, Gunter

Frank Wedekind in Selbstzeugnissen und Bilddokumenten (Rowohlts Monographien 213). Reinbek 1974

STRINDBERG, August

Werke (deutsche Gesamtausgabe). Ed. Emil Schering, 46 vols., Munich 1902-1930

THOMPSON, William (ed.)

Understanding Les Fleurs du Mal: Critical Readings. Vanderbilt University Press 1997

TIMMS, Edward

Karl Kraus, *Apocalyptic Satirist: Culture and Catastrophe in Habsburg Vienna.* Yale University Press 1989

WEDEKIND, Frank

Ausgewählte Werke in 5 vols. Ed. Fritz Strich, Vol. II. Berlin 1923

WUNBERG, Gotthart (Ed.)

Die Wiener Moderne. Literatur, Kunst und Musik zwischen 1890 und 1910 (Reclam Universal-Bibliothek No. 7742 [9]). Stuttgart 1982

WYSOCKI, Gisela van

Peter Altenberg. Bilder und Geschichten des befreiten Lebens (Fischer Taschenbuch Verlag 6457). Frankfurt am Main 1986

ZOHN, Harry

Karl Kraus. Transl. Ilse Goesmann. Frankfurt am Main 1990

ZWEIG, Stefan

Die Welt von Gestern. Erinnerungen eines Europäers (Fischer Taschenbuch Verlag 1152). Frankfurt am Main 1970

Psychological Studies

ADLER, Alfred

Menschenkenntnis (Fischer Taschenbuch Verlag 6080). Frankfurt am Main 1966

Der Sinn des Lebens (Fischer Taschenbuch Verlag 6179). Frankfurt am Main 1973

ALLPORT, Gordon W.

Gestalt und Wachstum in der Persönlichkeit. Ed. Helmut van Bracken. Meisenheim am Glan 1970; English edition: *Pattern and Growth in Personality.* New York 1961

EICKE, Dieter (Hrsg.)

Tiefenpsychologie (Kindlers „Psychologie des 20. Jahrhunderts"), 4 vols. Weinheim and Basel 1982

FLIESS, Wilhelm

Vom Leben und vom Tod. Biologische Vorträge, 1st ed. 1909, expanded ed. Jena 1914

FREUD, Sigmund

Abriss der Psychoanalyse. Das Unbehagen in der Kultur (Fischer Bücherei. Bücher des Wissens 47). Frankfurt am Main and Hamburg 1953

Zur Psychopathologie des Alltagslebens. Über Vergessen, Versprechen, Vergreifen. Aberglaube und Irrtum (Bücher des Wissens 68). Frankfurt am Main and Hamburg 1954

Die Traumdeutung (Fischer Bücherei. Bücher des Wissens 428/429). Frankfurt am Main and Hamburg 1961

THOMAE, Hans

Persönlichkeit. Eine dynamische Interpretation, 1st ed. Bonn 1971, 5th ed. Bonn 1973

WEININGER, Otto

Geschlecht und Charakter. Eine prinzipielle Untersuchung, 1st ed. Vienna 1903, reprint Munich 1980

Writings about Arnold Schonberg, Anton Webern and the Second Viennese School

ADORNO, Theodor W.

"Zur Vorgeschichte der Reihenkomposition," in: *Klangfiguren. Musikalische Schriften I.* Frankfurt am Main 1959

BACH, David Josef

"Arnold Schönberg und Wien," in: *Musikblätter des Anbruch*, 3 (1921), 216-218

BAILEY, Walter B.

Programmatic Elements in the Works of Schoenberg (Studies in Musicology, No. 74). Ann Arbor, Michigan 1984

BRINKMANN, Reinhold

Arnold Schönberg: Drei Klavierstücke op. 11. Studien zur frühen Atonalität bei Schönberg. Wiesbaden 1969

BUDDE, Elmar

Anton Weberns Lieder op. 3. Untersuchungen zur frühen Atonalität bei Webern. Wiesbaden 1971

CHOLOPOWA, Valentina und CHOLOPOW, Juri

Anton Webern. Leben und Werk. Transl. From Russian Christoph Hellmundt, Berlin 1989

CRAWFORD, John C.

"The Relationship of Text and Music in the Works of Schoenberg, 1908-24." Diss. Harvard University, Cambridge/Mass. 1963

DAHLHAUS, Carl

Schönberg und andere. Gesammelte Aufsätze zur Neuen Musik. Mainz 1978

DÖHL, Friedhelm

Webern. Weberns Beitrag zur Stilwende der Neuen Musik. Studien über Voraussetzungen, Technik und Ästhetik der "Komposition mit 12 nur aufeinander bezogenen Tönen" (Berliner musikwissenschaftliche Arbeiten, Band 12). München/Salzburg 1976

DÜMLING, Albrecht

Die fremden Klänge der hängenden Gärten. Die öffentliche Einsamkeit der Neuen Musik am Beispiel von Arnold Schönberg und Stefan George. Munich 1981

FLOROS, Constantin

"Kompositionstechnische Probleme der atonalen Musik," in: *Bericht über den Internationalen Musikwissenschaftlichen Kongress in Kassel 1962*. Kassel 1963, 257-260

"Probleme der Amalgamierung von Dichtung und Musik in der Kunst des 20. Jahrhunderts," in: Otto Kolleritsch, ed., *Zum Verhältnis von zeitgenössischer Musik und zeitgenössischer Dichtung* (Studien zur Wertungsforschung, Vol. 20). Vienna/Graz 1988, 35-50

"Die Wiener Schule und das Problem der deutschen Musik", in: Otto Kolleritsch, ed., *Die Wiener Schule und das Hakenkreuz: Das Schicksal der Moderne im gesellschaftspolitischen Kontext des 20. Jahrhunderts* (Studien zur Wertungsforschung, Vol. 22). Vienna/Graz 1990, 35-50

"Zum Beethoven-Bild Schönbergs, Bergs und Weberns," in: Otto Kolleritsch, ed., *Beethoven und die Zweite Wiener Schule* (Studien zur Wertungsforschung, Vol. 25). Vienna/Graz 1992, 8-24

New Ears for New Music. New York: Peter Lang 2013

Humanism, Love and Music. New York: Peter Lang 2012

"Die Zweite Wiener Schule in den zwanziger Jahren," in: *Hamburger Jahrbuch für Musikwissenschaft*, vol. 26 (Frankfurt am Main 2009), 143-148

FREITAG, Eberhard

Arnold Schönberg in Selbstzeugnissen und Bilddokumenten (Rowohlts Monographien 202). Reinbek 1973

FRISCH, Walter

Schoenberg and His World. Princeton 1999

HAHL-KOCH, Helena (Ed.)

Arnold Schönberg, Wassily Kandinsky: Briefe, Bilder und Dokumente einer außergewöhnlichen Begegnung (Deutscher Taschenbuch Verlag 2883). Munich 1983

HILMAR, Ernst (Ed.)

Arnold Schönberg. Gedenkausstellung 1974. Vienna 1974

KOLNEDER, Walter

Anton Webern. Genesis und Metamorphose eines Stils (Österreichische Komponisten des XX. Jahrhunderts, Vol. 19).Vienna 1974

KRONES, Hartmut

"'Wiener' Symbolik? Zu musiksemantischen Traditionen in den beiden Wiener Schulen," in: *Studien zur Wertungsforschung* 25 (Vienna/Graz 1992), 51-79

LEIBOWITZ, René

Schoenberg and His School. The Contemporary Stage of the Language of Music. New York 1970

MÄCKELMANN, Michael

Arnold Schönberg und das Judentum. Der Komponist und sein religiöses, nationales und politisches Selbstverständnis nach 1921 (Hamburger Beitrage zur Musikwissenschaft, Vol. 28). Hamburg 1984

Schönberg. Fünf Orchesterstücke op. 16 (Meisterwerke der Musik, Issue 45). Munich 1987

"'Die glückliche Hand'. Eine Studie zu Musik und Inhalt von Arnold Schönbergs 'Drama mit Musik'", in: *Musiktheater im 20. Jahrhundert* (Hamburger Jahrbuch für Musikwissenschaft, Vol 10) (Laaber 1988), 7-36

"Auf der Suche nach dem Gottesgedanken. Arnold Schönbergs unvollendetes Oratorium 'Die Jacobsleiter'," in: Peter Petersen, ed., *Musikkulturgeschichte. Festschrift für Constantin Floros zum 60. Geburtstag* (Wiesbaden 1990), 399-413

MAEGAARD, Jan

Studien zur Entwicklung des dodekaphonen Satzes bei Arnold Schönberg, 3 vols. Copenhagen 1972

"Schönbergs Zwölftontechnik," in: *Die Musikforschung*, 29 (1976), 385-425

"Die Komponisten der Wiener Schule und ihre Textdichter sowie das Komponisten-Dichter- Verhältnis heute," in: Otto Kolleritsch, ed., *Zum Verhältnis von zeitgenössischer Musik und zeitgenössischer Dichtung* (Studien zur Wertungsforschung, Vol. 20) (Vienna/Graz 1988), 168-183

METZGER, Heinz-Klaus, and RIEHN, Rainer (Eds.)

Musik-Konzepte. Sonderband. Arnold Schönberg. Munich 1980

Musik-Konzepte. Sonderband Anton Webern I Munich 1983

Rudolf Kolisch. Zur Theorie der Aufführung (Musik-Konzepte 29/30). Munich 1983

Schönbergs Verein für musikalische Privataufführungen (Musik-Konzepte 36). Munich 1984

Musik-Konzepte. Sonderband Anton Webern II. Munich 1984

MEYEROWITZ, Jan

Arnold Schönberg (Kopfe des XX. Jahrhunderts, Vol. 47). Berlin 1967

MOLDENHAUER, Hans und Rosaleen

Anton von Webern. Chronik seines Lebens und Werkes. Zurich 1980

ÖSTERREICHISCHE MUSIKZEITSCHRIFT (Publishing House)

Die Wiener Schule und ihre Bedeutung für die Musikentwicklung im 20. Jahrhundert, Vienna 1961

PETERSEN, Peter

"'A grave situation was created'. Schönbergs Klavierkonzert von 1942," in: Otto Kolleritsch, ed.) *Die Wiener Schule und das Hakenkreuz. Das Schicksal der Moderne im gesellschaftspolitischen Kontext des 20. Jahrhunderts* (Studien zur Wertungsforschung, Vol. 22) (Vienna/Graz 1990), 65-91

RAUCHHAUPT, Ursula von

Schoenberg/Berg/Webern. Die Streichquartette. Eine Dokumentation. Hamburg 1971

REICH, Willi

Arnold Schönberg oder Der konservative Revolutionär (Deutscher Taschenbuch Verlag 1041). Munich 1974

REXROTH, Dieter (ed.)

Opus Anton Webern. Berlin 1983

ROGGE, Wolfgang

Das Klavierwerk Arnold Schönbergs (Forschungsbeitrage zur Musikwissenschaft, Vol. XV). Regensburg 1964

RUBSAMEN, Walter

"Schoenberg in America," in: *The Musical Quarterly,* 37/4 (October 1951), 469-489

RUFER, Josef

Die Komposition mit zwölf Tönen (Stimmen des xx. Jahrhunderts, Vol. 2). Berlin and Wunsiedel 1952

Das Werk Arnold Schönbergs. Kassel etc. 1959

SCHMIDT, Christian Martin

"Schönbergs 'very definite - but private' Programm zum Streichquartett Opus 7," in: Rudolf Stephan and Sigrid Wiesmann, eds., *Bericht über den 2. Kongress der Internationalen Schönberg-Gesellschaft "Die Wiener Schule in der Musikgeschichte des 20. Jahrhunderts"* (Vienna 1986), 230-234

SCHNEIDER, Frank

"Autobiographische Symptome in Schönbergs Musik. Modell: Streichquartett 1, op. 10," in: Harry Goldschmidt, Georg Knepler und Konrad Niemann, eds., *Komponisten auf Werk und Leben befragt,* Leipzig 1985, 83-98

SCHÖNBERG, Arnold

Harmonielehre, 1st ed. Leipzig/Vienna 1911; Engl. translation Roy E. Carter. Berkeley and Los Angeles 1978

"Aphorismen," in: *Die Musik,* 9. (1921), 159-163

Texte (Universal-Edition Nr. 7731). Vienna/New York 1926

Ausgewählte Briefe, ed. Erwin Stein, Mainz 1958; engl. translation Eithne Willkins and Ernst Kaiser. London 1964

Stil und Gedanke. Aufsätze zur Musik, ed. Ivan Vojtech (Gesammelte Schriften 1). S. Fischer Verlag 1976 (abbrev.: GS): engl. edition: *Style and Idea.* Collected Writings, ed. Leonard Stein, trans. Leo Black. London 1975 (abbrev.: S&I)

SCHÖNBERG-Festschriften

Arnold Schönberg. R. Piper, Munich 1912

Arnold Schönberg zum fünfzigsten Geburtstage 13. September 1924, Sonderheft der *Musikblätter des Anbruch,* 6 (August-September 1924)

Arnold Schönberg zum 60. Geburtstag 13. September 1934. Universal Edition Vienna

SICHARDT, Martina

Die Entstehung der Zwölftonmethode Arnold Schönbergs. Mainz 1990

STEIN, Erwin

"Neue Formprinzipien," in: *Arnold Schönberg zum fünfzigsten Geburtstage 13. September 1924, Musikblätter des Anbruch* (1924), 286-303

STEIN, Leonard (Ed.)

Journal of the Arnold Schoenberg Institute, 8 vols. 1976-1984

STEPHAN, Rudolf

Vom musikalischen Denken. Gesammelte Vorträge. Ed. Rainer Damm and Andreas Taub. Mainz 1985

STEPHAN, Rudolf (Ed.)

Die Wiener Schule (Wege der Forschung, Vol. 643). Darmstadt 1989

STUCKENSCHMIDT, H. H.

Schönberg - Leben - Umwelt – Werk. Munich 1989

VOGEL, Martin

Schönberg und die Folgen. Die Irrwege der Neuen Musik, Teil 1: Schönberg (Vol. 35 der ORPHEUS-Schriftenreihe zu Grundfragen der Musik). Bonn 1984

WEBERN, Anton

Briefe an Hildegard Jone und Josef Humplik. Ed. Josef Polnauer. Vienna 1959

Der Weg zur Neuen Musik. Ed. Willi Reich. Vienna 1960

Writings about Alban Berg

ADORNO, Theodor W.

"Alban Berg," in: *Klangfiguren. Musikalische Schriften.* Berlin und Frankfurt am Main 1959), 121-137

"Die Instrumentation von Bergs frühen Liedern," in: *Klangfiguren* (1959), 138-156

"Bergs kompositionstechnische Funde," in: *Quasi una fantasia. Musikalische Schriften II* (Frankfurt am Main 1963), 245-273

"Alban Berg: Violin Concerto," in *Der getreue Korrepetitor. Lehrschriften zur musikalischen Praxis.* Frankfurt am Main 1963, 187-216

Berg. Der Meister des kleinsten Übergangs (Österreichische Komponisten des XX. Jahrhunderts, vol. 15), Vienna 1968; *Berg. Master of the Smallest Link.* Transl. Juliane Brand and Christopher Hailey, Cambridge UP 1991

BEAUMONT, Antony

Zemlinsky. London: Faber and Faber, 2000

BERG, Alban

Briefe an seine Frau. Munich/Vienna 1965 (Abbr.: ABB): *Letters to his Wife.* Transl. Bernard Grun. London: Faber and Faber 1971

Glaube, Hoffnung und Liebe. Schriften zur Musik. Ed. Frank Schneider (Reclams Universal-Bibliothek). Leipzig 1981 (Abbr.: Schr.)

BERG, Erich Alban

Alban Berg. Leben und Werk in Daten und Bildern (Insel Taschenbuch 194). Frankfurt am Main 1976

Der unverbesserliche Romantiker. Alban Berg 1885-1935. Vienna 1985

BISCHOF, Rainer

"Versuch über die philosophischen Grundlagen von Alban Berg," in: *Alban Berg Studien*, vol. II, 209-215

BLAUKOPF, Kurt

"Autobiographische Elemente in Alban Bergs 'Wozzeck'", in: *Österreichische Musikzeitschrift* 9 (1954), 155-158

BORCHMAYER, Dieter

"Adorno als Postillon d'amour," in: *Frankfurter Allegemine Zeitung*, March 27, 2002

BOULEZ, Pierre

Anhaltspunkte. Essays. Transl. Josef Hausler Kassel etc., Munich 1979

BOUQUET, Fritz

"Alban Bergs '.Lyrische Suite'. Eine Studie über Gestalt, Klang und Ausdruck," in: *Melos* 15 (1948), 227-231

BRAND, Juliane, HAILEY, Christopher, und HARRIS, Donald

The Berg-Schoenberg Correspondence. Selected Letters. New York/London 1987

BRINDLE, Reginald Smith

"The Symbolism in Berg's 'Lyric Suite'," in: *The Score*, October 21, 1957, 60-63

BRUHN, Siglind

Encrypted Messsages in Alban Berg's Music.London 1998

BUDDAY, Wolfgang

Alban Bergs Lyrische Suite. Satztechnische Analyse ihrer zwölftönigen Partien (Tübinger Beitrage zur Musikwissenschaft, Vol. 8).Neuhausen-Stuttgart 1979

CARNER, Mosco

Alban Berg. The Man and the Work.London 1975

CERHA, Friedrich

Arbeitsbericht zur Herstellung des 3. Akts der Oper LULU von Alban Berg (Universal Edition No. 26233).Vienna 1979

CSAMPAI, Attila, und HOLLAND, Dietmar, eds.

Alban Berg. Wozzeck. Texte, Materialien, Kommentare (rororo opernbuch 7929). Reinbek 1985

Alban Berg. Lulu. Texte, Materialien, Kommentare (rororo opernbuch 7340). Reinbek 1985

DEUTSCH, Max

"Le Concerto de chambre d' Alban Berg," in: *Schweizerische Musikzeitung*, 89 (1949), 328-333

DEVOTO, Mark

Alban Berg's Picture-Postcard Songs, Phil. Diss. Princeton 1967 (typoscript)

Alban Bergs Drei Orchesterstücke op. 6: Struktur, Thematik und ihr Verhältnis zu Wozzeck, in: Alban Berg Symposion Vienna 1980, 97-106

FLOROS, Constantin

"Das esoterische Programm der Lyrischen Suite. Eine semantische Analyse," in: *Hamburger Jahrbuch für Musikwissenschaft*, Vol. I (Hamburg 1975), 101-145. Expanded version in: *Alban Berg. Kammermusik I* (Musik-Konzepte 4). Munich 1978, 5-48. Italian translation in: Carlo de Incontrera, ed., "Com' era dolce il profumo del tiglio. *La musica a Vienna nell' eta di Freud* (Monfalcone 1988), 233-277. Japanese translation in: *Jahrbuch der Alban Berg Gesellschaft* (Japan, 1988/89), 1-38

"Das Kammerkonzert von Alban Berg. Hommage a Schönberg und Webern," in: *Alban Berg. Kammermusik I* (Musik-Konzepte 9). Munich 1979, 63-90

"Die Skizzen zum Violinkonzert von Alban Berg," in: *Alban Berg Studien*, vol. II (Vienna 1981,(118-135

"Alban Bergs 'Requiem'. Das verschwiegene Programm des Violinkonzerts," in: *Neue Zeitschrift für Musik*, 146 (April 1985), 4-8; Translations in Japanese, Greek and Bulgarian

"Das verschwiegene Programm des Kammerkonzerts von Alban Berg. Eine semantische Analyse," in: *Neue Zeitschrift für Musik*, 148 (November 1987), 11-22; Japanese translation in: *Jahrbuch der Alban Berg Gesellschaft*, 1986/87, 64-84

"Alban Bergs 'Wozzeck' als Botschaft an die Menschheit," in: Ute Jung-Kaiser, ed., *Der kulturpädagogische Auftrag der Musik im 20. Jahrhundert* (Musik im Diskurs, Vol. 9), Regensburg 1991, 25-42

"Alban Berg und die Wiener Moderne," in: *Bericht über das Symposion "Die Wiener Moderne"*. Kassel 1991

Alban Berg and Hanna Fuchs. The Story of a Love in Letters, transl. Ernest Bernhardt-Kabisch. Indiana University Press 2008: Spanish transl. Susana Zapke. Madrid 2005; French transl. Sylvain Fort. Actes Sud Janvier 2014

"Alban Berg, Anton Webern und die Neue Musik," in: J. Bungardt, M. Helfgott, E. Rathgeber, N. Urbanek, eds., *Wiener Musikgeschichte. Festschrift für Hartmut Krones* (Vienna/Cologne/Weimar 2009), 487-501

"Zum Mozart-Bild von Alban Berg," in: Hartmut Krones and Christian Meyer, eds., *Mozart und Schönberg. Wiener Klassik und Wiener Schule* (Vienna/Cologne/Weimar 2012), 301-307

Mahler 1: Die geistige Welt Gustav Mahlers in systematischer Darstellung. Breitkopf & Härtel, 1st ed. Wiesbaden 1977, 2nd ed. 1987

Mahler 2: Gustav Mahler and the Symphony of the 19th Century. New York: Peter Lang, 2014

Mahler 3: Gustav Mahler. The Symphonies. Amadeus Press 1993; paperback edition 1977, 2000

FORNEBERG, Erich

Wozzeck von Alban Berg, 3rd ed. Berlin-Lichterfelde 1963

FUSS, Hans-Ulrich

Musikalisch-dramatische Prozesse in den Opern Alban Bergs (Hamburger Beiträge zur Musikwissenschaft, Vol. 40), Hamburg/Eisenach 1991

GRASBERGER, Franz, and STEPHAN, Rudolf, eds.

Katalog der Musikhandschriften, Schriften und Studien Alban Bergs im Fond Alban Berg und der weiteren handschriftlichen Quellen im Besitz; der Österreichischen Nationalbibliothek (ed. Rosemary Hilmar) (*Alban Berg Studien*, vol. 1/1). Vienna 1980

Katalog der Schriftstücke von der Hand Alban Bergs, der fremdschriftlichen und gedruckten Dokumente zur Lebensgeschichte und zu seinem Werk, ed. Rosemary Hilmar (*Alban Berg Studien*, Vol. 1/2). Vienna 1985

Alban Berg Symposion Wien 1980. Tagungsbericht. Ed. Rudolf Klein (*Alban Berg Studien*, Vol. II), Wien 1981

GREEN, Douglas M.

"Berg's De Profundis: The Finale of the Lyric Suite," in: The *International Alban Berg Society Newsletter*, No. 5, June 1977; German transl: "Das Largo desolato der Lyrischen Suite von Alban Berg," in: *Österreichische Musikzeitschrift*, February 1978

HAILEY, Christopher

Alban Berg and His World. New York 2010

HEADLAM, David John

The Music of Alban Berg. Yale University Press 1996

HEINSHEIMER, Hans W.

"Begegnung mit einem Riesen - Alban Berg," in: *Schönste Grüße an Aida. Ein Leben nach Noten*. Munich 1969, 55-73

Menagerie in Fis-dur. Transl. Willi Reich. Zurich 1953

HILMAR, Ernst

Wozzeck von Alban Berg. Entstehung - erste Erfolge - Repressionen (1914-1935). Vienna 1975

"Alban Bergs Selbstzeugnisse zu Entstehung und Aufführbarkeit der Oper 'Lulu',"in: *Alban Berg. Lied der Lulu. Faksimile-Ausgabe der Anton v. Webern gewidmeten autographen Partitur*, ed. Wiener Stadt- und Landesbibliothek. Vienna n. d.

HILMAR, Rosemary

Alban Berg. Leben und Wirken in Wien bis zu seinen ersten Erfolgen als Komponist. Vienna/Cologne/Graz 1978

Alban Berg 1885-1935. Ausstellung der Österreichischen Nationalbibliothek. Prunksaal. 23. Mai bis 20. Oktober 1985. Vienna 1985

JAMEUX, Dominique

Berg. Paris 1980

JARMAN, Douglas

The Music of Alban Berg. London/Boston 1979

"Alban Berg, Wilhelm Fliess und das geheime Programm des Violinkonzerts," in: *Österreichische Musikzeitschrift*, vol. 40/1, (Jan 1985, 12-21

Ed. *The Berg Companion*. London 1989

JOUVE, Pierre Jean und FANO, Michel

Wozzeck ou le nouvel opera. Paris 1953

KATSCHTHALER, Karl

Latente Theatralität und Offenheit. Zum Verhältnis von Text, Musik und Szene in Werken von Alban Berg, Franz Schubert und György Kurtág. Frankfurt am Main: Peter Lang 2012

KNAUS, Herwig

"Studien zu Alban Bergs Violinkonzert," in: Theophil Antonicek, Rudolf Flotzinger and Othmar Wessely, eds., *De ratione in musica. Festschrift Erich Schenk zum 5. Mai 1972.* Kassel etc. 1975, 255-274

"Die Reihenskizzen zu Alban Bergs Violinkonzert," in: *Österreichische Musikzeitschrift,* 37 (1982), 105-108

"Alban Bergs Skizzen und Vorarbeiten zur Konzertarie 'Der Wein'," in: Manfred Angerer et al., eds., *Festschrift Othmar Wessely zum 60. Geburtstag.*Tutzing 1982, 355-379

KNAUS, Herwig/LEIBNITZ, Thomas /Eds.)

Altenberg bis Zuckenkandl: Briefe an Alban Berg. Löcker 2007

KNAUS, Herwig/SINKOVICZ, Wilhelm

Alban Berg. Zeitumstände - Lebenslinien, Residenz Verlag, St. Pölten/Salzburg 20

KRENEK, Ernst

"Alban Bergs 'Lulu'," in: *Zur Sprache gebracht. Essays über Musik.* Berlin/ Darmstadt/Vienna 1958

LORKOVIC, Radovan

Das Violinkonzert von Alban Berg. Analysen - Textkorrekturen - Interpretationen (Musikreflektionen, Vol. III). Winterthur 1991

MAGGART, Alison

"The Labyrinth in Berg's Der Wein," in: *Resonance. Interdisciplinary Music Journal,* Spring 2013

MCLEAN, Don

"Schloss und sein Schlüssel: new documents on Berg's Lyric Suite; the Schlofi collection at McGill University." Paper presented at the Meeting of the American Musicological Society in April of 1988 (typescript)

METZGER, Heinz-Klaus, and RIEHN, Rainer, eds.

Alban Berg. Kammermusik I (Musik-Konzepte 4). Munich 1978

Alban Berg. Kammermusik II (Musik-Konzepte 9). Munich 1979

MONSON, Karen

Alban Berg. A Biography. London 1979; German edition: *Musikalischer Rebell im kaiserlichen Wien.* Frankfurt am Main/Berlin 1989

MORGENSTERN, Soma

Alban Berg und seine Idole: Erinnerungen und Briefe, ed. Ingolf Schulte. Lüneburg 1995

MÜLLER, Thomas

Die Musiksoziologie Theodor W. Adornos. Ein Modell ihrer Interpretation am Beispiel Alban Bergs (Campus Forschung, vol. 642). Frankfurt am Main/New York 1990

PALMER, Peter

"Burning numbers." Review of Constantin Floros: *Alban Berg and Hanna Fuchs*, in: *The musical Times*, Autumn 2009, 114 f.

PERLE, George

"Das geheime Programm der Lyrischen Suite," in: *Musik-Konzepte* 4 (Munich 1978), 49-74

"Mein geliebtes Almschi ... ", Briefe von Alban und Helene Berg an Alma Mahler-Werfel, in: *Österreichische Musikzeitschrift*, 35. (1980), 2-15

The Operas of Alban Berg. Vol. one: *Wozzeck,* Berkeley/Los Angeles/ London 1980; vol. two: *Lulu.* Berkeley/Los Angeles/London 1985

PERNYE, A.

"Alban Berg und die Zahlen," in: *Studia Musicologica Academiae Scientiarum Hungaricae*, IX (1967), 141-161

PETERSEN, Peter

Alban Berg. Wozzeck. Eine semantische Analyse unter Einbeziehung der Skizzen und Dokumente aus dem Nachlass Bergs (Musik-Konzepte. Sonderband). Munich 1985

"Lulus Untergang aus Gründen der Symmetrie? Gedanken zum III. Akt von Bergs Oper 'Lulu'," in: Programmheft 9 des Bremer Theaters (1982/83), 37-45

"Zu einigen Spezifika der Dodekaphonie im Schaffen Alban Bergs," in: *Bericht über den 2. Kongress der Internationalen Schönberg-Gesellschaft*, ed. Rudolf Stephan and Sigrid Wiesmann. Vienna 1986; 168-179

PETSCHNIG, Emil

"Atonales Opernschaffen," in: *Die Musik*, XVI (1923/24), 340-345

POPLE, Antony, ed.

The Cambridge Companion to BERG. Cambridge University Press 1997

PLOEBSCH, Gerd

Alban Bergs "Wozzeck". Dramaturgie und musikalischer Aufbau. Straßburg/Baden-Baden 1968

REDLICH, Hans Ferdinand

Alban Berg. Versuch einer Würdigung. Vienna/Zürich/London 1957; Engl. edition: *Alban Berg, the Man and his Music*. London 1957

REICH, Willi

"Alban Berg," in: *Die Musik*, XXIII:5 (February 1930), 347-353

"Requiem for Manon," in: *Musikblätter des Anbruch*, 17 (Sept./ Oct. 1935), 250-252

Alban Berg. Mit Bergs eigenen Schriften und Beiträgen von Theodor Wiesengrund-Adorno und Ernst Krenek. Vienna/Leipzig/Zurich 1937

"An die Seite von Alban Berg," in: *Melos*, 27 (1960), 36-42

Alban Berg. Leben und Werk. Zurich 1963; *Life and Works of Alban Berg*, transl. Cornelius Cardew, London 1965

Ed. *23. Eine Wiener Musikzeitschrift*, Nr. 24/25 (1. February 1936), Alban Berg zum Gedenken

Alban Berg. Bildnis im Wort. Selbstzeugnisse und Aussagen der Freunde. Zurich 1959

REITER, Manfred

Die Zwölftontechnik in Alban Bergs Oper LULU (Kölner Beitrage zur Musikforschung, vol. LXXI). Regensburg 1973

RODE, Susanne

Alban Berg und Karl Kraus. Zur geistigen Biographie des Komponisten der "Lulu" (Europäische Hochschulschriften, Reihe XXXVI, Vol. 36). Frankfurt am Main 1988

SCHERLIESS, Volker

Alban Berg in Selbstzeugnissen und Bilddokumenten (Rowohlts Monographien 225). Reinbek 1975

SCHMIDT-GARRE, Helmut

"Berg als Lehrer," in: *Melos*, 22 (1955), 40 f.

SCHWEIZER, Klaus

Die Sonatenform im Schaffen Alban Bergs (Freiburger Schriften zur Musikwissenschaft, vol. I), Stuttgart 1970

SIMMS, Bryan R.

Alban Berg: A Research and Information Guide (Routledge Music Bibliographies, 2). Edition Routledge Chapman & Hall 2009

Review of Constantin Floros: *Alban Berg and Hanna Fuchs*, in: *Notes*, vol. 65, no.3 (March 2009), 507-510

SIMMS, Bryan R. (Ed.)

Pro Mundo – pro Domo. The Writings of Alban Berg. 2013

STADLEN, Peter

"Berg's Cryptography," in: Alban Berg Studien, II (1981), 171-180

STEIGER, Martina (Ed.)

*"Immer wieder werden mich thätige Geister verlocken". Alma Mahler-Werfels Briefe an Alban Berg und seine Frau.*Seifert-Verlag 2008

Briefe der Freundschaft. Alban Berg – Erich Kleiber. Seifert-Verlag 2013

STEIN, Erwin

"Alban Berg - Anton von Webern," in: *Musikblätter des Anbruch*, V (1923), 13-16

STENZL, Jurg

"ulus 'Welt'," in: *Alban Berg Studien*, II (1981), 31-39

"Alban Berg und Marie Scheuchl," in: *Österreichische Musikzeitschrift*, 40 (1985), 22-30

STEPHAN, Rudolf

"Alban Bergs LULU," in: *Neue Zeitschrift für Musik*, 122 (1961), 269- 276

"Zur Sprachmelodie in Alban Bergs LULU-Musik," in: Günter Schnitzler, ed., *Dichtung und Musik. Kaleidoskop ihrer Beziehungen.*Stutttgart 1979, 246-264

"Alban Berg als Schüler Arnold Schönbergs. Auf dem Weg zur Sonate op. 1," in: *Bericht über den 2. Kongress der Internationalen Schönberg-Gesellschaft*, ed. Rudolf Stephan and Sigrid Wiesmann. Vienna 1986, 22-30

"Drei Autographe von Alban Berg," in: *Komponisten des 20. Jahrhunderts in der Paul Sacher Stiftung*. Basel 1986, 149-156

Alban Berg. Violinkonzert (1935) (Meisterwerke der Musik, Issue 49), Munich 1988

VIEBIG, Ernst

"Alban Bergs 'Wozzeck'. Ein Beitrag zum Opernproblem," in: *Die Musik*, XV/7 (April 1923), 506-510

VOGELSANG, Konrad

Dokumentation zur Oper "Wozzeck" von Alban Berg. Die Jahre des Durchbruchs 1925-1932. Laaber-Verlag 1977

WECHSLER, Julia

The Scientific Reception of Alban Berg in the West: Paradigms, Tendencies, Methods (russ.) in: musXXI, gnesin-academy ru/wcontent

ZEMLINSKY, Alexander

Briefwechsel mit Arnold Schönberg, Anton Webern, Alban Berg and Franz Schreker. Ed. Horst Weber. Darmstadt 1995

4.5 Index of names

A

Adler, Alfred 14, 15, 81, 83, 124, 334, 335
Adorno, Theodor W. 3, 4, 28, 29, 32, 34, 36, 45, 46, 48, 55, 64, 65, 66, 67, 69, 74, 78, 79, 88, 92, 93, 100, 102, 112, 125, 126, 134, 135, 136, 145, 146, 165, 167, 204, 205, 208, 215, 228, 262, 264, 308, 317, 329, 333, 335, 336, 337, 339, 340, 341, 342, 343, 345, 346, 347, 348, 349, 351, 352, 355, 356, 357, 360, 362, 374, 380
Albert, Victor 20, 344
Altenberg, Peter 6, 20, 37, 38, 39, 42, 44, 77, 117, 120, 337, 339, 347, 348, 366, 378

B

Bach, David Josef 19, 72, 335, 342
Bach, Johann Sebastian 63, 89, 103, 110, 113, 300, 301, 302, 303, 304, 315, 323, 324, 326, 327, 344, 361
Bahr, Hermann 37, 39, 43, 338, 339
Baier, Christian 354
Bailey, Walter B. 72, 342, 344
Bartók, Béla 62, 67, 68, 162
Baudelaire, Charles 37, 39, 42, 43, 198, 207, 244, 251, 252, 257, 261, 338, 363, 364
Bauer-Lechner, Natalie 67
Beethoven, Ludwig van 27, 32, 34, 61, 110, 189, 198, 369
Bekker, Paul 161
Berg, Erich Alban 28, 56, 80, 86, 123, 124, 334, 336, 374
Berg, Helene 340, 347, 348, 349, 351, 352, 353, 354, 358, 359, 360
Berg, Helene (née Nahowski) 4, 5, 11, 12, 17, 18, 23, 26, 33, 35, 37, 38, 40, 42, 43, 44, 51, 53, 55, 57, 58, 59, 60, 78, 79, 85, 88, 89, 92, 93, 103, 116, 117, 118, 119, 120, 121, 122, 123, 124, 125, 126, 127, 128, 129, 131, 138, 141, 142, 143, 144, 159, 163, 165, 166, 186, 195, 196, 197, 205, 222, 223, 242, 294, 295, 296, 297, 298, 318, 326, 379
Bernhardt-Kabisch, Ernest 2, 337, 344, 355, 360
Bie, Oskar 67
Bienenfeld, Elsa 22
Bloch, Ernst 32, 49, 337, 339
Brahms, Johannes 24, 26, 65, 66, 108, 109, 110, 192, 340, 344
Brosche, Günter 2
Bruckner, Anton 82, 138, 264, 340, 343, 348
Büchner, Georg 45, 151, 152, 153, 154, 159, 160, 273, 349, 350, 365
Buschbeck, Erhard 20
Busoni, Ferrucio 62, 161, 162, 341, 351

C

Canetti, Elias 4, 23, 29, 38, 295, 336, 338, 359
Casella, Alfredo 62
Cerha, Friedrich 268, 357, 375

D

Da Vinci, Leonardo 94
Dehmel, Richard 72, 73, 75
Dent, Edward 63
DeVoto, Mark 146, 339
Dostoevsky, Fyodor 42
Duchesneau, Louise 66, 341
Dumas, Alexandre 50
Dürer, Albrecht 94

E

Einem, Gottfried von 2
El Greco 53
Emerson, Ralph Waldo 195

F

Falke, Gustav 73, 122
Finckh, Ludwig 122
Fliess, Wilhelm 85, 87, 377
Freitag, Eberhard 186
Freud, Sigmund 14, 15, 32, 34, 56, 78, 79, 81, 124, 163, 195, 337, 340, 343, 375
Friedell, Egon 17, 262, 335
Friedrich, Hugo 42, 338, 364
Fuchs-Robettin, Edvin Frantisek 355
Fuchs-Robettin, Hanna (née Werfel) 2, 35, 43, 88, 89, 92, 105, 123, 124, 125, 126, 197, 201, 203, 204, 206, 207, 208, 209, 212, 222, 228, 237, 242, 337, 339, 344, 347, 355, 361, 376, 379, 381
Fuchs-Robettin, Herbert von 35, 81, 124, 206

G

Gauguin, Paul 167, 352
George, Stefan 43, 70, 106, 130, 138, 139, 140, 165, 206, 207, 251, 344, 346, 348, 355, 357, 358, 359, 368, 379
Georges, Stefan 348
Gerstl, Richard 74, 178, 179, 353
Goethe, Wolfgang von 3, 7, 15, 35, 37, 38, 39, 45, 47, 50, 55, 67, 75, 78, 151, 331, 338, 342
Gorky, Maxim 46, 49
Göttel, August 161

Grillparzer, Franz 46
Gropius, Manon 294, 295, 296, 307, 308, 315, 324, 361
Gropius, Walter 295, 316

H

Hart, Julius 18
Hartleben, Otto Erich 123
Hauptmann, Carl 123
Hauptmann, Gerhart 9, 37, 49, 262, 281
Hausegger, Friedrich von 361
Hebbel, Friedrich 129
Hegel, Georg Wilhelm Friedrich 3
Heine, Heinrich 47
Heinsheimer, Hans W. 4, 5, 29, 81, 84, 85, 177, 334, 336, 343, 353
Herodotus 3
Hertzka, Emil 23, 165, 195, 196, 197, 198
Herzfeld, Maria 46, 339
Hesse, Hermann 55, 56
Heyking, Elisabeth von 29
Heym, Georg 18
Hilmar, Ernst 2, 334, 335, 336, 338, 340, 343, 348, 349, 350, 351, 352, 358, 359, 361, 362, 376
Hindemith, Paul 106, 162, 346
Hinrichsen, Henri 75
Hohenberg, Paul 32, 123, 337
Hohenheim, Paul 45, 129
Hollaender, Friedrich 23
Honegger, Arthur 62

I

Ibsen, Henrik 32, 38, 39, 40, 42, 48, 49, 50, 51, 117, 339, 364

J

Jalowetz, Heinrich 17, 335
Jókai, Mór 49
Jone, Hildegard 45, 64, 98, 340, 345, 373
Jores, Arthur 16, 335
Joseph, Franz 347

K

Kandinsky, Wassily 69, 70, 71, 341, 342, 369
Kasack, Hermann 167
Kassowitz, Gottfried 1, 17, 28, 161
Kempis, Thomas à 55
Kerékjártó, Margrit von 16, 335
Kiepenheuer, Gustav 167
Kleiber, Erich 81, 151, 261, 264, 265, 295, 359, 381

Klein, Fritz Heinrich 97, 160, 194, 196, 198, 199, 200, 201, 202, 213, 214, 216, 354, 376
Klein, Rudolf 337
Kleist, Heinrich von 48
Klimt, Gustav 27, 32, 34
Kodaly, Zoltán 62
Kokoschka, Oskar 179, 361
Kolisch, Gertrud 74, 186
Kolisch, Rudolf 133, 174, 176, 214, 228, 233, 244, 245, 253, 297, 299, 308, 348, 353, 370
Korngold, Julius 21, 22, 80, 336, 343
Korngold, Wolfgang Erich 22
Krasner, Louis 26, 294, 296, 299, 359
Kraus, Karl 7, 13, 15, 17, 29, 30, 37, 38, 39, 44, 46, 48, 50, 52, 59, 102, 165, 262, 263, 264, 272, 337, 338, 339, 357, 358, 365, 366, 380
Krauss, Clemens 21
Krenek, Ernst 62, 106, 162, 288, 346, 358, 380

L

Lenau, Nikolaus 45, 73, 123
Lessing, Gotthold Ephraim 55
Liliencron, Detlev von 18
Liszt, Franz 51, 75, 89, 192, 204, 355
Loos, Adolf 20, 27, 38, 44, 86, 88, 335, 336, 344

M

Mäckelmann, Michael 101
Maeterlinck, Maurice 20, 42, 72, 350
Mahler, Fritz 159
Mahler, Gustav 3, 4, 20, 22, 24, 27, 38, 40, 42, 57, 65, 66, 67, 69, 73, 75, 80, 81, 82, 145, 149, 150, 151, 192, 264, 294, 298, 317, 318, 322, 325, 326, 329, 333, 338, 340, 341, 343, 346, 349, 351, 354, 360, 361, 376
Mahler-Werfel, Alma 28, 124, 126, 294, 295, 296, 297, 298, 309, 313, 316, 318, 343, 348, 349, 359, 361, 362, 381
Mann, Thomas 74, 79, 93, 94, 342, 344, 364
Martynov, Ivan 161
Miethke-Juttenegg, Elke 58
Milhaud, Darius 62
Morgenstern, Soma 38, 54, 61, 262, 338
Mueller, Erich H. 361

N

Nahowski, Anna 347
Nahowski, Franz 118, 127
Nahowski, Helene *see* Berg, Helene (née Nahowski)
Nausen, Peter 33
Nestroy, Johann 46, 339

Newlin, Dika 74
Nietzsche, Friedrich 33, 38, 39, 47, 50, 263

P

Papsdorf, Thomas 2
Paul, Fritz 100, 345, 365
Paul, Jean 55, 349
Paul, Julius Elias 364
Paul, Schick 365
Paul, Stefan 338
Perle, George 206, 344, 355, 358, 359
Pernye, A. 172, 205, 228, 352, 355, 356
Petersen, Peter 153, 158, 268, 292, 342, 350, 351, 357, 358, 360, 370
Petschnig, Emil 19, 169, 335, 352
Pfitzner, Hans Erich 6, 34, 66, 117, 341, 344
Poldauer, Joseph 177
Polnauer, Joseph 103, 174, 308, 340, 345, 373
Pythagoras, von Samos 86

R

Rauchhaupt, Ursula von 215, 343, 345, 348, 354, 355, 356
Ravel, Maurice 62
Redlich, Ferdinand 55, 105, 145, 152, 158, 160, 176, 196, 228, 264, 281, 301, 305, 307, 319, 337, 340, 343, 344, 346, 347, 349, 350, 351, 352, 353, 354, 356, 357, 358, 359, 360
Reich, Willi 4, 30, 45, 46, 84, 85, 86, 110, 125, 154, 196, 215, 262, 264, 270, 273, 281, 290, 291, 294, 296, 297, 298, 301, 302, 303, 304, 307, 308, 317, 319, 325, 326, 336, 339, 343, 344, 345, 346, 347, 350, 351, 354, 355, 356, 357, 358, 359, 360, 361, 373, 377
Reinhardt, Max 20
Reuter, Gabriele 47
Riemer, Friedrich Wilhelm 342
Rottweiler, Hector 32, 333, 335
Rücker, Michael 2
Rufer, Josef 95, 98, 305, 340, 341, 343, 345, 360

S

Saathen, Friedrich 347
Sartre, Jean Paul 262
Schalk, Franz 22
Scherber, Ferdinand 21
Scherchen, Hermann 21, 28
Scheuchl, Marie 361, 381
Schick, Paul 337
Schiller, Friedrich 7, 27, 382
Schmidt-Garres, Helmut 80
Schnitzler, Arthur 38, 50

Scholz, Wilhelm von 47
Schönberg, Arnold 1, 4, 5, 6, 7, 8, 9, 10, 12, 13, 14, 15, 16, 17, 18, 19, 20, 21, 22, 23, 24, 25, 26, 27, 28, 29, 30, 31, 35, 36, 37, 38, 41, 42, 45, 52, 53, 57, 58, 59, 60, 61, 62, 63, 64, 65, 67, 68, 69, 70, 71, 72, 73, 74, 75, 76, 77, 78, 79, 80, 81, 82, 83, 84, 85, 87, 89, 91, 93, 94, 95, 96, 97, 98, 99, 100, 101, 102, 103, 104, 105, 106, 107, 108, 109, 110, 111, 112, 113, 129, 130, 131, 138, 139, 142, 143, 144, 149, 151, 154, 158, 161, 163, 164, 165, 166, 167, 168, 169, 170, 172, 174, 175, 176, 177, 178, 179, 180, 184, 185, 186, 187, 192, 193, 194, 198, 201, 202, 205, 212, 214, 215, 217, 218, 230, 236, 248, 265, 269, 273, 276, 293, 306, 329, 333, 334, 335, 336, 338, 340, 341, 342, 343, 344, 345, 346, 347, 348, 349, 350, 351, 352, 353, 354, 362, 368, 371, 376, 382
Schönberg, Gertrude 74
Schönberg, Mathilde 89, 169, 178, 179, 180
Schopenhauer, Arthur 48, 189
Schreker, Franz 5, 9, 334, 351, 354, 382
Schubert, Franz 5, 109, 378
Schumann, Clara (née Wieck) 24, 90, 336
Schumann, Robert 24, 89, 90, 91, 336, 344
Schweizer, Klaus 204, 205, 259, 355
Semler, Frida 33, 44, 45, 50, 337
Seneca 46
Shakespeare, William 33
Smith, Joan Allen 337
Smith, Reginald Brindle 205, 355, 374
Specht, Richard 27, 42, 150, 338, 349
Stefan, Paul 17, 42, 150, 151, 335, 349
Stein, Erwin 80, 111, 174, 177, 215, 259, 308, 333, 334, 343, 345, 372
Steuermann, Eduard 174, 176
Stockhausen, Karlheinz 66
Storm, Theodor 9, 122, 123, 125, 194, 195, 196, 197, 201, 202, 209, 354
Strauss, Richard 72, 76, 77, 117, 307, 322, 342, 360, 361
Stravinsky, Igor 63, 64
Strindberg, August 14, 33, 34, 37, 38, 39, 40, 41, 42, 44, 47, 48, 49, 100, 101, 123, 338, 345, 365, 366
Stuck, Franz 33
Stuckenschmidt, Hans Heinz 82, 335, 341, 343, 351, 353
Sudermann, Hermann 51
Swarowsky, Hans 1

T

Thackeray, William 55

U

Ullman, Bo 152, 350
Unger, Josef 47, 278, 358
Ünlü, Altug 2

V

Van Gogh, Vincent Willem 167, 352
Viebig, Ernst 160, 351

W

Wagner, Richard 28, 36, 37, 43, 49, 58, 66, 67, 68, 109, 110, 118, 121, 122, 138, 140, 141, 204, 231, 251, 252, 255, 256, 261, 329, 340, 341, 343, 347, 348, 355, 356
Watznauer, Hermann 17, 32, 39, 49, 51, 118, 129, 196, 208, 329, 332, 340, 347, 355
Webern, Anton 1, 4, 5, 7, 8, 9, 10, 12, 13, 14, 15, 16, 17, 18, 19, 20, 22, 24, 25, 26, 27, 28, 29, 34, 36, 37, 40, 41, 42, 43, 45, 51, 53, 54, 55, 56, 57, 61, 62, 63, 64, 67, 68, 71, 78, 80, 82, 83, 89, 94, 97, 98, 99, 100, 101, 102, 104, 106, 108, 110, 129, 133, 143, 145, 160, 161, 163, 165, 166, 167, 169, 170, 174, 175, 176, 177, 180, 186, 197, 198, 209, 214, 215, 273, 297, 304, 326, 329, 334, 335, 336, 338, 339, 340, 343, 345, 346, 348, 349, 350, 351, 352, 353, 354, 355, 360, 368, 369, 370, 371, 375, 376, 377, 381, 382
Wedekind, Frank 33, 37, 38, 39, 42, 44, 45, 47, 48, 49, 117, 261, 262, 263, 264, 265, 266, 268, 271, 272, 273, 278, 281, 284, 286, 288, 338, 357, 358, 364, 365, 366
Weininger, Otto 37, 39, 40, 48, 49, 52, 53, 339
Wellesz, Egon 6, 164
Wesendonck, Mathilde 66, 341
Wilde, Oscar 27, 29, 37, 38, 39, 46, 48, 50, 61

Z

Zemlinsky, Alexander von 6, 7, 20, 124, 166, 179, 186, 205, 207, 208, 209, 212, 223, 224, 225, 226, 233, 234, 235, 236, 237, 238, 239, 241, 271, 349, 354, 356, 373
Zimmermann, Bernd Alois 152
Zweig, Stefan 335, 367